NOURISHED WITH PEACE

Scholars Press
Homage Series

No Famine in the Land: Studies in Honor of John L. McKenzie
James W. Flanagan and Anita W. Robinson, editors

Israelite Wisdom: Theological and Literary Essays in Honor of Samuel Terrien
John G. Gammie, editor

Selected Papers of Lionel Pearson
Donald Lateiner and Susan A. Stephens, editors

Mnemai: Classical Studies in Memory of Karl K. Hulley
Harold D. Evjen, editor

Classical Texts and Their Traditions: Studies in Honor of C. R. Trahman
David F. Bright, and Edwin S. Ramage, editors

Hearing and Speaking the Word: Selections from the Works of James Muilenburg
Thomas F. Best, editor

Greek Poetry and Philosophy: Studies in Honour of Leonard Woodbury
Douglas E. Gerber, editor

Nourished with Peace: Studies in Hellenistic Judaism in Memory of Samuel Sandmel
Frederick E. Greenspahn, Earle Hilgert, and Burton L. Mack, editors

ספר זכרון לשמואל סנדמעהל

NOURISHED WITH PEACE

Studies in Hellenistic Judaism in Memory
of Samuel Sandmel

edited by

Frederick E. Greenspahn, Earle Hilgert,
and Burton L. Mack

Scholars Press
Chico, California

NOURISHED WITH PEACE

Studies in Hellenistic Judaism
in Memory of Samuel Sandmel

edited by
Frederick E. Greenspahn, Earle Hilgert,
and Burton L. Mack

Library of Congress Cataloging in Publication Data
Main entry under title:

Nourished with peace.

(Homage series ; no. 9)
Bibliography: p.
1. Philo, of Alexandria—Addresses, essays, lectures.
2. Judaism—Relations—Greek—Addresses, essays,
lectures. 3. Greece-Religion—Addresses, essays, lectures.
4. Sandmel, Samuel—Addresses, essays, lectures.
I. Sandmel, Samuel. II. Greenspahn, Frederick E., 1946–
. III. Hilgert, Earle. IV. Mack, Burton L. V. Series:
Scholars Press homage series ; no. 9.
B689.Z7N68   1984   296.3'092'4   84–1417
ISBN 0–89130–740–0

Printed in the United States of America
on acid-free paper

Publication of this volume made possible
through the cooperation of

Center for Judaic Studies, University of Denver
Divinity School, University of Chicago
Hebrew Union College–Jewish Institute of Religion
The Philo Institute

CONTENTS

Forewords   xi
   Alfred Gottschalk
   Stanley M. Wagner

Preface   xv
   Earle Hilgert

Samuel Sandmel
   On Christian Origins: Common Sense, Uncommon Grace,
     Michael J. Cook   1
   Ecumenist Scholar, *Gerard S. Sloyan*   5
   Man of Largess, *Jonathan Z. Smith*   9
   A Friend and His Philo-Connection, *Krister Stendahl*   13

Studies in Hellenistic Judaism
   The Transference of Greek Allegories to Biblical
     Motifs in Philo, *Yehoshua Amir*   15
   The "One Who Sees God" in Philo, *Gerhard Delling*   27
   Abraham the General in Josephus, *Louis H. Feldman*   43
   The Exegetical Contexts of Philo's Interpretation
     of Circumcision, *Richard D. Hecht*   51
   Decoding the Scripture: Philo and the Rules
     of Rhetoric, *Burton L. Mack*   81
   "*Moyses palpans vel liniens*": On Some Explanations
     of the Name of Moses in Philo of Alexandria,
     Valentin Nikiprowetzky   117
   Further Greek Fragments of Philo's *Quaestiones*,
     James R. Royse   143
   Philo's Priestly Descent, *Daniel R. Schwartz*   155
   A Philonic Fragment on the Decad, *Abraham Terian*   173
   The Beginning of the Seleucid Era and the Chronology
     of the Diadochoi, *Ben Zion Wacholder*   183

Samuel Sandmel's Correspondence with Valentin Nikiprowetzky   213

The Writings of Samuel Sandmel: A Bibliography
   Frederick E. Greenspahn   221

Abbreviations used in this volume are listed in *Studia Philonica* 1 (1972) 92–96 and the *Journal of Biblical Literature* 95 (1976) 331–46.

FOREWORD

The blessed memory of Samuel Sandmel, alumnus, former professor and provost of the Hebrew Union College–Jewish Institute of Religion, will forever remain in the hearts of those who were privileged to know him as mentor and friend. I take great personal pleasure in submitting these sentiments to be included in the Memorial Volume to his life and work.

Ordained in 1937, at the Cincinnati School, Rabbi Sandmel pursued further graduate studies at Duke University, and received the Doctor of Philosophy degree at Yale University. After a period of serving as Jewish Chaplain in the Navy, he occupied the Hillel Chair in Judaic Studies at Vanderbilt University until he was called to the College–Institute to become a member of the faculty. In addition to teaching, he held the administrative position as Provost and later Director of the School of Graduate Studies. Dr. Sandmel was Distinguished Service Professor of Bible and Hellenistic Literature from 1952 until his retirement, at which time he became Helen A. Regenstein Professor of Religion at the University of Chicago.

As a scholar, Dr. Sandmel earned the respect and admiration of colleagues as well as his students. He authored many books and articles and delivered scholarly lectures which reflected deep understanding and appreciation of Hellenistic and Christian literature. His academic contributions enhanced the spirit of brotherhood between Jews and Christians, encouraging the honest study of our different yet similar traditions. His clear and forceful expositions of Pauline Christianity in light of its mother religion Rabbinic Judaism brought to light open and fresh discussions of new ideas. His research uncovered cultural and historical ties linking the adherents of both religions in a context of intellectual honesty and cooperation unseen before Dr. Sandmel's time. His work promoted growth and improvement in the attitudes Jews and Christians held toward each other.

In his books, *A Jewish Understanding of the New Testament* (1957) and *We Jews and Jesus* (1965), Dr. Sandmel provided a general background for an understanding of the New Testament as a whole and of Jesus in particular. His concern was to achieve a thoughtful and balanced view of Jewish perspectives on these issues. He concluded that Jews and Christians share a common point of departure—the Bible.

Pirke Avot teaches us, "Find yourself a good teacher and acquire a fellow student." Dr. Sandmel inspired many disciples in his years as devoted teacher, colleague and friend. His students, Christian as well as Jewish, continue to revere his legacy.

Alfred Gottschalk, President
Hebrew Union College–Jewish
Institute of Religion
Cincinnati, Ohio

FOREWORD

Samuel Sandmel, of blessed memory, established a relationship with the Center for Judaic Studies, University of Denver, during the first year of its existence, in 1975, when he appeared as a guest lecturer speaking on "Hellenism and Judaism" as part of a series dealing with "Great Confrontations in Jewish History." His thought provoking and stimulating paper was subsequently incorporated in a volume we published in 1977.

Having been inspired by his efforts to build bridges of understanding between the Christian and Jewish communities while he was in Denver, I discussed with him our Center's intention of establishing a department of ecumenic activities which would provide course offerings in Judaic Studies at the major Christian theological seminaries in our community, among other endeavors. His enthusiasm for our plan played no small role in the launching of our program in 1976 and, hence, his spirit continues to live in our achievements and attainments.

It is for this reason that our Center welcomes the opportunity to honor the memory of this great scholar and visionary by cosponsoring this volume of outstanding articles penned by some of the most eminent scholars, Dr. Sandmel's colleagues and co-workers, in the field of Hellenistic Studies. No more fitting tribute could be paid to one who gave his life to the understanding of this fascinating period in Jewish history.

The words of ben Sirah apply with special poignancy to the life of Samuel Sandmel:

> "Some of them there are who have left a name,
>   That men might tell of it in their inheritance . . .
> Their memory abideth forever,
>   And their righteousness shall not be forgiven . . .
> The assembly recounteth their wisdom,
>   And the congregation declareth their praise."
>
> (ben Sirah 44:8,13,15)

Stanley M. Wagner, Director
Center for Judaic Studies
University of Denver

PREFACE

"μετ' εἰρήνης οὖν τραφεὶς" γαληνὸν καὶ εὔδιον κτησάμενος βίον, εὐδαίμον' ὡς ἀληθῶς καὶ μακάριον. . . .

"Nourished with peace," having gained a calm and unclouded life, truly fortunate and blessed. . . . (Philo of Alexandria, *Who is the Heir of Divine Things*, 285).

יפיותו של יפת יהא באהלי שם

Let the beauty of Japheth be in the tents of Shem
(*b. Megillah 9b*).

"Nourished with peace"—such was the life and work of Samuel Sandmel, whose memory these pages honor. These words from his beloved Philo, together with a rabbinical dictum affirming the appropriateness of Hellenistic Judaism—the beauty of Japheth in the tents of Shem—reflect much of Sandmel's concern and contribution. Philo, an unswervingly loyal Jew of the first century, devoted his scholarship to expounding the traditions of his faith in terms drawn from his Hellenistic environment. In so doing he was to achieve an impact on early Christianity more significant than that of any other Jewish writer outside the Bible itself. In the twentieth century, Philo was modeled in striking ways by Samuel Sandmel, who perhaps as no other Jew in America succeeded in building bridges of understanding with the second historic faith. Through his scholarship, his more popular writings and his personal contacts as teacher, speaker and friend, his life was indeed "nourished with peace" as he strove for deeper appreciation between the children of Japheth and Shem. Therefore, while his writings covered a wide spectrum of interests—from technical scholarship to short stories—it is altogether appropriate that a volume of essays in his honor should focus on Hellenistic Judaism and in particular on Philo of Alexandria, to whom his first and last books, as well as numerous articles, were devoted.

Many persons have been involved in planning and bringing this *sefer zikkaron* into being. The project was conceived initially by the editors of *Studia Philonica* and the Board of Directors of the Philo Institute. Two members of the Board, Jonathan Z. Smith of the University of Chicago and Richard D. Hecht of the University of

California at Santa Barbara, were particularly helpful in laying plans
and seeking support. Mrs. Frances Fox Sandmel gave gracious en-
couragement throughout and provided the portrait reproduced in this
volume. Gratitude for generous institutional support is due Stanley M.
Wagner, Director of the Center for Judaic Studies at the University of
Denver, Franklin I. Gamwell, Dean of the Divinity School of the
University of Chicago, and Alfred Gottschalk, President of Hebrew
Union College—Jewish Institute of Religion and Michael A. Meyer,
chairman of its Publications Committee. Appreciation is also extended to
Conrad Cherry, Director; and Davis Perkins, former Editor; and John
Crowell, Production Manager, of Scholars Press for their interest in this
volume and for undertaking its production. The responsibilities of
editorship have been divided among Burton L. Mack of the Claremont
Graduate School, who solicited the articles, Frederick E. Greenspahn of
the University of Denver's Center for Judaic Studies, who served as
managing editor, and the writer, who was responsible for the preparation of materials for the press.

Many private contributions helped make this memorial volume possible. We acknowledge with particular gratitude the generous support of:

> The Dosick Family
> Dr. Walter Jacob
> Rabbi Philip N. Kranz
> Rabbi Charles Kroloff
> Rabbis Bernard H. Mehlman and Ronne Friedman
> Rabbi Ely E. Pilchik
> Congregation Rodeph Shalom (Philadelphia)

Thus as a cooperative project of Jews and Christians, in authorship,
editorship and support, this volume reflects the spirit of brother- and
sisterhood that animated the life of Samuel Sandmel.

Earle Hilgert
McCormick Theological Seminary

SAMUEL SANDMEL ON CHRISTIAN ORIGINS: COMMON SENSE, UNCOMMON GRACE

MICHAEL J. COOK

Hebrew Union College–Jewish Institute of Religion

The writings of Philo were Samuel Sandmel's particular love. Yet he was also a specialist in New Testament and internationally renowned for his studies on the relationship between Judaism and Christianity in both the Hellenistic and modern worlds. Most of his publications focused on Christian origins and the subsequent history of Christian-Jewish relations. In these areas he was my special mentor. Years after his passing, I remain in his debt, devoted to memories of his abiding friendship and imposing presence.

He spoke as lovingly of his own mentors, B. Harvie Branscomb and Erwin Goodenough. In 1939, when Sam applied to the Old Testament doctoral program at Duke University, Branscomb was chairman of the Biblical Studies department. He prevailed upon Sam to venture instead into *New* Testament, thereby launching Sam on a career which was to bring him acclaim as the outstanding Jewish New Testament scholar in America and possibly the world. Following chaplaincy service (1942–1946), Sam completed his Ph.D. studies at Yale. There he encountered Goodenough, who opened to him the vistas of Greek religion in general and Hellenistic Judaism in particular.

While at Yale, Sam became convinced that many treatments of Philo, Paul and early Christianity were deficient because scholars underestimated the degree of *dis*similarity between Diaspora and Palestinian Judaism. Despite repeated assaults on this position throughout his career, Sam remained resolute, considering his stance fundamental for a correct understanding of intertestamental literature.[1]

The effect of many twentieth century studies of intertestamental times had been the virtual homogenization of Diaspora and Palestinian Judaism. This was achieved through obliterating the earlier commonly

---

[1] See especially the posthumously published essay, "Palestinian and Hellenistic Judaism and Christianity: the Question of the Comfortable Theory," *Hebrew Union College Annual* 50 (1979) 137–48.

recognized lines of distinction. Scholars in increasing number began to argue that Palestinian Judaism was itself a product of the Hellenism characteristic of the general Mediterranean world. Facets of ancient Judaism customarily associated with the Hellenistic Diaspora were now declared to have been indigenous to Palestine as well. Often, presentations of these findings were accompanied by strident derogations of any scholar resisting the new trend.

Sam was open to this endeavor, but urged reservation! In analyzing the question of Hellenism's incursions into Palestine, he preferred to resolve Hellenistic influence into three categories of penetration: Hellenization through adoption of language; Hellenization through adoption of Greek ways of living; and Hellenization through adoption of Greek modes of thought and the content of Greek philosophy and religion. He concluded that, while Hellenistic overtones were undeniably evident in Palestine, Hellenism nevertheless did not permeate Palestinian Jewish life in as thoroughgoing a manner or degree as was now commonly being alleged. With Diaspora Judaism, however, the case was significantly different. Sam's studies of Philo revealed to him a Diaspora Judaism thoroughly penetrated by Greek philosophy and religion. The degree of integration was so extensive as to have produced in Hellenistic Judaism a religious flavor markedly distinct from all varieties of Palestinian Judaism.

Sam suspected, moreover, that underlying the new trend of research was an unconscious *need* by some to view ancient Judaism as monolithic. Subtly influencing their scholarship, he believed, was a value system which regarded a Diaspora Judaism, *detached* from Palestine, as of diminished worth. Accordingly, a Christianity substantially derived from such a non-Palestinian Hellenistic milieu would likewise emerge as inauthentic and in some sense contaminated in addition. The obvious Hellenistic flavor of developing Christianity would prove less disturbing, however, if such Hellenism could be demonstrated indigenous as well to the Palestine of Jesus' day! Such was the powerful inducement to blur the genuinely substantive distinctions between Diaspora and Palestinian Judaism. Since Sam shared an abiding respect for the Greeks as a people and a culture, he decried as unwarranted and distortive attempts to shield Christianity from such supposed contamination.

From this characteristic stance flowed many themes of Sam's studies in early Christianity and the New Testament, especially his concern with proper methodology in the analysis of intertestamental literature. Sam was intensely critical, for example, of scholars utilizing Palestinian and Babylonian rabbinic literature as a primary tool in understanding Hellenistic figures such as Philo or Paul. Thus, despite the seeming parallels which were commonly adduced, Sam denied any significant relationship between Philo and Pharisaism. As for Paul, Sam asserted that affinities between Paul and the later rabbis were limited only to some minor and elusive strands. Further, the mis-characterization of Paul as a good rabbinic Jew issued not only from uncritical reliance on the Book of Acts but from two additional misjudgments: that there was no marked difference between Hellenistic and Palestinian Judaism, and that the recognition of Hellenistic influence on Paul somehow reduced his authenticity.[2]

In comparing different bodies of ancient literature, Sam by no means opposed the quest to find parallel texts, provided that the corpora of literature compared were fundamentally related. At the same time, he believed that scholars often heaped up parallels indiscriminately, the resulting excesses generating unrealistic and untenable theories of sources and derivation. While particularly skeptical of attempts to interrelate rabbinic literature with writings of Philo or Paul, he was open to the search for parallels between rabbinic literature and gospel teachings, or between the Dead Sea Scrolls and the New Testament. Yet in these instances as well he cited numerous excesses. He highlighted his views in his celebrated Presidential Address, "Parallelomania," at the annual meeting of the Society of Biblical Literature, in 1961.[3]

Though Sam was not the first Jewish scholar to enter the field of New Testament studies, he was a pioneer in major respects. More so than any of his predecessors, he successfully persuaded fellow Jews that New Testament study was a legitimate and vital field of endeavor for Jewish scholars. At the same time, he viewed himself in *dis*continuity with most of his Jewish predecessors because he insisted on mastering Christian scholarship on the New Testament before daring to contribute studies of his own:

> All too often Jewish scholars have by-passed the Christian scholarship on the Gospels and have trespassed directly into the Gospels themselves. . . . There is a difference between an amateur understanding of Christian literature, and a professional one, and I am sometimes aghast at the amateurishness of Jewish scholars in Christian literature.[4]

Sam was gifted with the ability to speak harsh truths without harshness. While he loved the study of the New Testament, he did not shrink from communicating to Christian audiences the depths of woe he felt because of the New Testament's anti-Jewishness and the attendant consequences for millions of Jews throughout history. Yet what his listeners discerned was not polemic but simple honesty forthrightly conveyed.

---

[2] See especially *The Genius of Paul*, 2nd ed., rev. (New York: Schocken, 1970), perhaps Sam's finest work.

[3] See *Journal of Biblical Literature* 81 (1962) 1–13.

[4] "The Jewish Scholar and Early Christianity," *The Seventy-fifth Anniversary Volume of the Jewish Quarterly Review* (Philadelphia: JQR, 1967) 473–81; repr. *Two Living Traditions* (Detroit: Wayne State, 1972) 16.

It was, of course, his involvement in early Christian studies which opened for him and for those he addressed the avenues and opportunities for interfaith communication. But it was his personal depth of integrity which allowed him to penetrate the hearts of those who flocked to hear him. For what Jews and Christians, academicians, clergy, and laity alike all saw in Samuel Sandmel was a combination of common sense and uncommon grace. This explains why he was so influential and effective in so many circles, and why, in the particular arena of Jewish-Christian relations, Samuel Sandmel achieved more durable results than possibly any other contemporary figure.

SAMUEL SANDMEL, ECUMENIST SCHOLAR

GERARD S. SLOYAN

Temple University

My friendship with Samuel Sandmel was of fairly long standing before I learned of his interest in Philo. His 1956 publication *Philo's Place in Judaism* had not come to my attention when I first began to encounter him at academic gatherings of Jews and Christians. These were few enough at the start, and a distinct relief from an early interfaith dialogue in which discussion of religion was outlawed. Only popular sociology, peoplehood, and "prejudice" were thought safe topics in those valiant days of N.C.C.J. and A.D.L. and A.J.C. sponsorship. John Oesterreicher tried to break the mold at Seton Hall in the late 1950s, but his yearbook *The Bridge* was suspect for its lack of Jewish voices. He later rectified this through symposia. My problem was that in the '50s and '60s I was coming to know something in depth about the first centuries B.C.E. and C.E. and did not find myself in the company of any learned Jews of religious interest. The only Jews I encountered were those who had decided that discussing religion with Christians could get them nowhere in achieving their quite specific social goals.

An early meeting with Samuel Sandmel at close range was a three-day meeting sponsored by the publisher Sheed and Ward, through its enteprising editor Philip Scharper, in January 1965. It was an invitational affair held at St. Vincent Archabbey (Benedictine) in Latrobe, Pennsylvania. Roland Murphy and I were the two representatives of The Catholic University of America faculty who gave papers. I knew the other Catholics: Bishop John Wright and Fathers John Sheerin, Aidan Kavanagh and John Cronin. But that conference was where I met Professors Sandmel, Bamberger, Grayzel, and Gilbert for the first time. (Rabbis Freehof and Tanenbaum had been partners on numerous platforms before then.) Archabbot Rembert Weakland and Bishop William Connare of Greensburg were our hosts.

It was an exhilarating week. Papers had been prepared beforehand and the exchanges were recorded. A volume appeared at perhaps too high speed entitled *Torah and Gospel, Jewish and Catholic Theology in Dialogue*. This post-Council era (1966) was a time when symposia on all matters touching Vatican II were still assured a sale. The three days of common living were a new experience for most of us. Religious dialogue that was non-defensive, with no hidden agenda, was not so readily come by in those days. I well remember a Jewish colleague, who had attended the daily conventual Mass of the monks, marveling at the morning's gospel reading which contained the phrase, "I have come, not to abolish [the Law and the prophets], but to fulfill them" (Mt. 5:17). He thought it was a "plant" because of the presence of Jewish visitors and was surprised to be told that it had simply come up in the daily lectionary readings. He had thought that total replacement of Israel by a gentile church was the only Christian theory and was pleased to learn that another tradition was kept alive by so thin a thread as constant verbal reminder.

Professor Sandmel would not have been surprised. I was the one surprised by him at that gathering, hearing the stock of learning that came from him in his soft, southern Ohio cadences. There was no Flusser or Winter of my acquaintance at the time, only Montefiore and Klausner and Schoeps. But here was an American who could trade blows with the New Testament fraternity to which I belonged. His historical agnosticism concerning New Testament materials distressed me then as it did later, when I came to know his *The First Christian Century in Judaism and Christianity* and *We Jews and Jesus*. Still, he had learned it from Christian form critics even if not from his *Doktorvater* at Yale, Erwin R. Goodenough. The latter, not professedly in New Testament studies, was remarkably conservative in some of his historical positions. But Professor Sandmel had done his work in a period when the Bultmann school was regnant. He liked to maintain that you could only state what you had hard evidence for, and it was lacking for much that intervened between the lifetime of Jesus and the composition of the gospels. I came to respect him as someone who was never picky, never captious in matters of Christian scholarship, but always respectfully skeptical about what could be maintained with certainty.

The one matter I could have been most informed by him on at the Latrobe symposium I was not ready for. His statement of Philo's principle of allegorical interpretation, which he described in his paper there as "completely alien" to rabbinic interpretation, might have put me on the path of distinguishing ways to be Jewish in the first century. As it was, I had to do much more work in the distinct hermeneutical approaches of the Dead Sea Scrolls, 4 Ezra and 2 Baruch, and the Mishnah of the Tannaim to learn how the New Testament authors were part of a larger company in their interpretation of the Bible. In 1965, however, the bulk of Professor Neusner's material had not yet been produced nor the Charlesworth-led body of work on the pseudepigrapha. Neither, for that matter, had Nikiprowetzky on Philonic commentary (1974) appeared, in light of which Sandmel completed his *Philo of Alexandria: An Introduction*, long in incubation but published only in the last year of his life.

In 1971 the journal *Judaism* which was edited by Professor Robert Gordis—another Latrobe symposiast and by this time my Temple University colleague—ran an issue on the trial of Jesus to which Professor Sandmel and I contributed. I made use of his essay on the trial, subtitled "Reservations," in a small book I wrote on the gospel narratives of the Jewish and Roman trials two years later. His point had been that Jewish life was likely to go its course even if, by some marvel, the truth of how and why Jesus was sentenced were at last to become known. The impact would be minimal, since "historical scholarship is almost powerless against the persistence of motifs in a religious tradition, whether it be Christianity or Judaism." He must have thought I had caught his meaning in *Jesus on Trial*, for he repaid me in the way that scholars can, namely by mention in footnotes in his two penultimate works: *Judaism and Christian Beginnings* and *Is the New Testament Anti-Semitic?* The mentions were kindly. There is always the other possibility.

The second book disappointed me, not because the Sandmel answer to his own question was a fairly resounding "Yes," but because his argument lacked nuance. A cardinal rule of ecumenical exchange is that it be honest. He was, so there was no problem there. The assumption underlying the book, however, is that the Christian community was severed from its parent Israel in *all* respects by the time the New Testament was written. Its authors and the communities they belonged to were presumed totally gentile ethnically, for obviously no born Jew could write or think about the people Israel in the manner of these books. There seemed to be no room in his theorizing for a gradual separation which would include some Christian polemic that pitted ethnic Jew against Jew. I tried to say this in a review of *Is the New Testament Anti-Semitic?* in nuanced fashion—not because I knew he was dying, for I did not—but because I so respected the man that the only way to lodge my objections was to employ the historical discriminations he had failed to. He did not live to read my well-intended observations. I am sure I would have had a courteous response.

This was a man of large stature in every way. He was a pioneer in interfaith dialogue, new style, because he took the pains to explore in depth the founding documents of the Christians. If Jews suffer from Christian ignorance of postbiblical Judaism, so do Christians at Jewish hands for comparable reasons.

Coupled with an armory of New Testament knowledge in Samuel Sandmel was an absolute integrity in thought and speech. He was a truth seeker and a truth speaker.

One of my last exchanges with him will illustrate an important life goal he cherished. As a department chairman, I had been unable to forward the candidacy of a Christian graduate of Hebrew Union College for a post in Judaica because the man was not Jewish. Professor Sandmel did not take the discriminatory mentality kindly. "I hear this all the time," he said, "and it angers me. Our Hebrew Union graduates are well prepared. A man like that knows the Judaism of the early Christian period well. He can be trusted in it. To refuse him a job on religious grounds is to defeat the serious study of religion."

SAMUEL SANDMEL, MAN OF LARGESS*

JONATHAN Z. SMITH
University of Chicago

Sam was a large man, in his bodily frame, in his deep, resonant voice, in his contagious and frequent laughter, in his gusto. I recall occasions when he seemed so large that a volume of the Loeb Library edition of his beloved Philo seemed dwarfed and out of place in his hands, hands more evenly matched by the thick cigars which he used to punctuate his conversation.

Sam was a large man. He was also a man who enlarged, a man of largess. And because of this he left an indelible mark on two learned professions in this country: that of scholarship and that of clergy. It may well be that it was more a matter of Sam's character, a character that was generous, a character that was expansive, a character that he had honed into a precise tool, than any particular act of learning—although he had an uncommon share of that—which was responsible for this influence.

Sam was a man who enlarged, fundamentally altering the contours and boundaries of his chosen area of activity, and the fact that this enlargement seems so commonplace today is a tribute to his success which ought not to obscure the surprising daring of his enterprise.

For a scholar who was a deeply committed Jew, for a scholar who devoted a major portion of his life to the training of young men (and, more recently, young women) for the rabbinate to have begun his academic career by earning a doctorate in New Testament and Early Christian Literature from a department closely associated with a Christian Divinity School, and to have begun his career by a major study of Philo; for this same scholar to have come to the close of his life as a named professor in another Divinity School and as the chief editor of an international team of scholars who prepared the Oxford Study Edition of the *New English Bible*—Old Testament, and Apocrypha, and New Testament—only begins to hint at this capacity for enlarging, a capacity he took very much for granted. For, by his labor, he reclaimed for Jewish

* This tribute is reprinted by permission from *Criterion: a Publication of the Divinity School of the University of Chicago* 19:1 (Winter 1980) 28–29.

scholarship two neglected resources, one largely reflecting Palestinian modes, the other, Alexandrian modes of Judaism from which it had largely barred itself. He gave, in this country, a legitimacy by example to Jewish scholarship on Early Christianity that allowed the possibility of parity with the superb Christian scholarship on Early Judaism.

At the level of his primary academic activities, this should not be confused with interreligious dialogue. What Sam proposed was not a conversation between faiths, but a seminar of scholars. Scholars who would enlarge their world to more closely conform to *the* world, a world in which Jewish and Christian and Greek and Roman sources mutually illuminate one another, a mutual illumination from which no one who was a scholar might in conscience abstain.

At other levels, this had the not at all unintended consequence of setting Jewish and Christian relations within a responsible context. No longer an exercise in sheer good will or historical regrets, but a capacity to understand that to which one will not assent, a capacity to set the focus on issues that are central, and, hence, most difficult. There was nothing in Sam of the popular cant of the "common Judaeo-Christian heritage" where so much is concealed by the slim hyphen; a cant that refuses the stubborn particularity of the several traditions; a cant that makes unnecessary the labor of interpretation and understanding that was his life-long occupation.

His books, *A Jewish Understanding of the New Testament*, *We Jews and Jesus*, *The Genius of Paul*, his studies on the first centuries, are all remarkable for their capacity to confront the *skandalon*, but to do so with an irenic confidence that can only have been won by constant labor in his study, the classroom, the conference hall, the pulpit. He enlarged the possibility for conversation by constricting the discourse to that which was fundamental. He eliminated the temptation to mutual congratulations or lamentation by requiring a mutual respect that both validates and is made valid by scholarly work.

Sam was often impatient with some forms of scholarship, not always fairly so. He used to quote, with deep chuckles of appreciation, the complaint of our common teacher, Erwin Goodenough, against those works that were always right in their footnotes but always wrong in their text. For what he brought to the usual tools of a scholar in such matters were two qualities rare in our circles: an uncommon degree of common sense, and an uncommon capacity for delight. The old tag goes, "nonsense is nonsense even in Latin" (Sam would have said, "German") and he used common sense as a means of evaluating both what a text might mean and the scholars' arguments. In so doing he contributed new elements to our critical arsenal, such as his oft-quoted pejorative, "parallelomania." As to delight, only Sam could have entitled a work, *The Enjoyment of Scripture*, and have meant it with such utter gusto.

Sam enlarged the audience for scholarship with a host of books that were original contributions designed for the general reader, books like his recent *Philo of Alexandria: An Introduction* that were devilishly, unobtrusively learned, except to the connoisseur. His books were characteristically filled with considered judgments on controversial matters which reflected a wide reading, unrecorded at the bottom of the page, but which could be readily supplied. His books were usually not written for those of us who are specialists, but for an intelligent lay audience. They were preeminently teaching books, and yet, many of us must confess ourselves to having frequently been taught.

For those of us who work in Sam's areas, he taught in other modes, the full extent of which I had not realized until he shared my office in Swift Hall and I could not escape cognizance of the volume of his mail. Manuscript upon manuscript, each annotated by him for the author, each carefully criticized, each the beneficiary of Sam's largess.

For me, Sam's most enduring contribution to scholarship, his most significant enlargement was in quite another, though not unrelated, area. For Sam made possible, perhaps for the first time, the notion of the study of Judaism within a secular university. Not that he provided the curriculum, the method, the theories; that would be left to a younger generation; but rather, by being *there*. In the often all too parochial world of Jewish learning, a world that still finds it surprising when a non-Jew with other than marriage in mind is attracted to the study of Judaism; a world that, with its nepotisms, its passionate quarrels and quibbles, often does not seem to know how to behave itself within a university—Sam was the striking exception. All the more striking because he seemed so comfortable, so effortlessly at home. A Philo as citizen of Alexandria, a Sandmel as citizen of the university, these are examples of an earned integrity to be emulated.

I identify Sam more with Philo than with a figure by which he was equally intrigued, than with Paul. For it is the scholar of "mature faith," the unbounded curiosity for other modes of meaning, the cosmopolitanism (a word Philo appears to have coined) that marked Sam's life, rather than the skilled practitioner of the brilliant diatribe. And I identify Sam as well with the quieter figure of the grandson of Jesus ben Sira, who translated his grandfather's work from Hebrew into Greek in order that "all who love learning" might "acquire understanding." It surely was the contemporary equivalents of rare men like Sam, as well as the ancestors, that the old man had in mind when he penned his well known encomium:

> Let us now praise famous men,
>   and our fathers in their generations. . . .
> There were those who were leaders of the
>   people . . .

in understanding of learning *for* the
people,
wise in words of instruction . . .
these were honored in their generation,
and were the glory of their times. . . .
Their bodies were buried in peace,
and their name lives to all generations.

Or, to render what is undoubtedly the *Urtext*, adding only, for this occasion, Sam's name:

Let us now praise Samuel Sandmel,
for he was a *Mensch* among the people.

A FRIEND AND HIS PHILO-CONNECTION

KRISTER STENDAHL

Harvard University

Samuel Sandmel was a gift of God to both Jews and Christians. It was given to him to help change the climate and sometimes even the agenda of Jewish-Christian conversations. His genteel spirit, his sojourns in the gentle South, his years as a theologian among gentiles at a Christian divinity school — it all added up to a freedom from that defensiveness which often mars the image of others and of self.

When the Second Vatican Council and its Declaration concerning the Jews gave focus, visibility, and new impetus to Christian rethinking of Jewish-Christian relations, Sandmel responded by writing "A Proposed Declaration: The Synagogue and the Christian People."[1] I think it is proper to lift up this item from his many writings, for it exemplifies for me so much of his spirit and of his understanding of the two communities which parted ways 1900 years ago. I read that declaration as a sign of his great sensitivity, his recognition that dialogue is a two-way street. As a Jew, he could not just let Christians do their repenting while Jews stood by judging how well and how much, how badly or insufficiently the Christians did. He knew that there was a reciprocal need also for Jews to express afresh their understanding of Judaism, taking steps toward correcting false Jewish stereotypes of Christianity. And so he wrote his Proposed Declaration:

> The Synagogue views the Christian people as among its offspring. It acknowledges that Christian people have laudably spread the message of the Synagogue among people and in areas of the world beyond where the Synagogue had penetrated. The Christian people have adapted that message to their own character and their own ways of thinking and speaking, and they have both preserved much which is familiar to the Synagogue and also created much which is not. Man, in his weakness, has been incapable of maintaining unbroken unity. Neither the Synagogue nor the church has been free from division, and a by-product of such division has been irreligious hatred, bitter recrimination, and persecution, both within and without. Since

[1] Published in S. Sandmel, *We Jews and You Christians, An Inquiry Into Attitudes* (Philadelphia: Lippincot, 1967) 144–46.

> hatred, recrimination, and persecution are irreligious, the Synagogue
> laments all such manifestations within its past, and respecting the
> present and the future repudiates them as inauthentic manifestations
> of the spirit of Judaism. The Synagogue holds that its message must
> spread not by power or by might, but only by the Spirit of God and in
> the love of mankind.

> The Synagogue is aware that Christian assemblies, lamenting and
> disavowing the Christian persecution of the Jews, have spoken in
> recent times in the same vein. The Synagogue welcomes these pio-
> neer utterances . . .

Sandmel's scholarship centers around his understanding of Hellenistic Judaism. As a student of Erwin Goodenough's at Yale, he wrote his
dissertation on Philo. In obvious and subtle ways that gave him the key
to his understanding of Christianity and perhaps especially of the Apostle Paul, whose genius he discerned in Hellenistic ways. I sometimes feel
that Sandmel made it a little too easy for himself—and for his readers—
to come to grips with early Christianity by reading Paul so consistently
in a Hellenistic key. To be sure, both Paul, and early Christianity by and
large, are Hellenistic phenomena— as is early Rabbinic Judaism in its
own way. Both the gathering of tradition and teaching by commentary
on and interpretation of the greats is part of the Hellenistic ethos. But
when I read Sandmel on Paul—and especially those parts of the picture
where Sandmel is most appreciative of *The Genius of Paul*—I cannot
free myself from the impression that the true Paul was far more rooted
in a world closer to Palestinian Judaism with stark eschatology and far
less spiritualized, ethicized, and philosophized than the Philonic world.
The very issues which were central to Paul's apostleship are miles apart
from Philo's elegant discourses about reality. Paul's arguments about the
status of his Gentile converts spring from a Judaism which sounds more
Jewish than that of Philo—if by "Jewish" we mean Judaism as it came
down through the centuries of the Common Era. The enigma is stark
and puzzling: In style and conceptuality the Christian Paul is more "Jewish" than the faithfully Jewish Philo.

But Sandmel chose the other line—maximizing the Hellenistic Paul—
toward an understanding of Christianity which continued as an evermore
acute Hellenization of its biblical base. To me this is a fateful choice, for it
deprives the historian and the theologian of the option to let Paul call
Christians back to their deep roots in the common ground in and with the
God of Abraham and the God of Isaac and the God of Jacob . . .

From time to time I loved to argue such points with Samuel Sandmel.
It may strike some people odd to recall such criticisms in a note of appreciation. But I believe that Sam and I both agreed that an honest argument is
the authentic homage one scholar gives to another whose work he deems
important. And Samuel Sandmel's was and will remain just that.

THE TRANSFERENCE OF GREEK ALLEGORIES
TO BIBLICAL MOTIFS IN PHILO*

YEHOSHUA AMIR

University of Tel-Aviv

John Dillon, at the beginning of his article on the allegorization of Ganymede,[1] presents certain Greek mythical allegories with which Philo can be shown to have been acquainted. Among these there is one for which a knowledge on Philo's part can, surprisingly, be definitively demonstrated even though he does not mention the name in question. He never speaks specifically of the suitors who seek the hand of Penelope and who, when they cannot win it, in the meantime dally with her maidens. That he was familiar with the explication of this story may only be inferred from the fact that he, as Dillon notes, "makes use" of it. This use consists in the fact that he carries it over into a biblical motif, namely the relationship of Abraham to Sarah and Hagar. This transference is no isolated phenomenon. It constitutes a technique of Philo's, and likely also of pre-Philonic biblical allegory, of which I have noted several examples. This collection makes no claim to completeness, and I present a provisional list with a request to fellow scholars to add to it from their knowledge. With this as a starting point, it should be possible to achieve significant perspectives on the history of Jewish-Hellenistic biblical allegory and its relation to its Greek environment, and to make instructive observations concerning the way in which transfer to Jewish soil took place, as well as to raise serious reservations against too hurried an equation with midrash that flourished in Palestine in the same period. But all this must be preceded by a correct understanding of the pertinent material, with which we can make only a beginning here.

I.

Penelope: Maidens; Sarah: Hagar

The sarcasm was current among a number of Greek philosophers[2]

---

* This article was translated by Earle Hilgert.

[1] *SP* 6 (1979–80) 37–40.

[2] Bion Borysthenites in Plutarch, *De Liberis Educandis* 10 = *Moralia* 7D; Aristippus in *SVF* 1.349; Aristo Chius in *SVF* 1.350.

that those students who devoted themselves to general studies and did
not proceed from there to philosophy are to be likened to the suitors in
the *Odyssey* who, unable to win Penelope, entertained themselves the
while with her maidens. Unmistakably Philo is dependent on the schema
inherent in this philosophical dictum when he sketches the education of
the "learner" (Abraham), which must first lead to general education
(Hagar), in order to proceed from there to philosophy (Sarah). If we ask
why the transfer of this Greek motif leads him specifically to Sarah and
Hagar, the answer must be that we have to do here with an antagonism
between mistress and maid, and that such is presented in the Bible
paradigmatically in the relationship between Sarah and Hagar. With this
as a point of departure, his exegetical ingenuity immediately carries him
further. He finds his most important confirmation—in accord with the
kanones tēs allēgorias derived from Greek allegorical technique—in the
etymology of the two names, of which the one means "mistress" and the
other "a sojourner." The recognized rules of his craft oblige him to
enquire as to the etymologies, and since the names are Hebrew, in case
he understands no Hebrew, he must seek his information concerning the
etymological meaning from those who have knowledge of the language.
The etymologies confirm for him that Sarah is "the" mistress and Hagar
"the" maid, which nevertheless do not restrain him from introducing
experimentally other mistress-maid relationships.[3] In carrying over the
Greek prototype, the appearance of the one Hagar in place of the
numerous maidens in the house of Odysseus is awkward. For the philosophers, the many maidens stand for the multiplicity of the individual
subjects of study. In Philo these had now to be brought together, in as
far as possible, into a singular image.[4] Generally speaking he was successful in this;[5] but where Philo divides collective "general education"
into the various subjects of instruction, he slips then[6] into the plural, and
here his prototype shines through and betrays him. This is particularly
the case in Congr 77, which sounds almost like a citation of the philosophers' dictum:[7] "For many, bewitched by the love lures of the *handmaidens*, have neglected the mistress, philosophy." In one passage[8] Philo
patches over the difficulty scantily by having the mistress, philosophy,
characterize the subjects of study as *tēs emēs therapainidos ta ekgona*

---

[3] Congr 24.

[4] Cf. *SVF* 1.350: *ta egkyklia paideumata* (the general subjects) with Congr 9: *hē dia tōn propaideumatōn egkyklios mousikē* (the culture [gained] through the general prepara-
tory subjects).

[5] Identified as *mesē paideia* (intermediate education; Gongr 20) or as *hē egkyklios paideia* (general education; Congr 72).

[6] Congr 74, 77, 80.

[7] *SVF* 1.350.

[8] Congr 152.

(the offspring of my handmaidens), with which however little is gained, as the Bible knows only one son of Hagar.

In retrospect it may be possible now also to make progress in the question of the Greek *Vorlage*. This is known to us from similar sayings of Bion, Aristippus and Aristo Chius. Strictly speaking, these are not allegories, but *homoiōmata*;[9] while they compare the attitude of students with that of the suitors in the *Odyssey*, they do not assert that the story in the *Odyssey* really means a ranking of philosophy as the mistress or queen and of the individual studies as the handmaidens.[10] But the relationship between these sayings and the Philonic Sarah-Hagar allegory is indisputable. Although a direct transfer even orally of an obiter dictum of Greek education into a biblical allegory is intrinsically unlikely and finds no parallels, in what follows we will come to recognize examples of the transfer of mythological into biblical allegories. With confidence, therefore, we may insert a no longer extant middle term between the philosophical dicta we have cited and the allegory present in Philo, i.e. the consolidation of the philosophers' association of ideas into an allegory on Homer which, through an ingenious application of the Homeric story, transplants the reference to the relationship between philosophy and the studies into the content intended by the poet himself. In this way the Philonic text provides us with information as to the history of the interpretation of Homer.[11]

When we return to Philo himself, we must first consider how he comes to terms with the new situation which arises through the transplanting of his motif into biblical soil. Since an exhaustive answer to this question would amount almost to a reinterpretation of the entire tractate *De Congressu*,[12] I must limit myself here to a few brief cues.

1. In place of the wanton suitors, in Philo the righteous Abraham appears, who is identified as being an ideal. Thus he cannot seek his

---

[9] *SVF* 1.350 testifies to this as the title of Aristo's work.

[10] My friend Refael Freundlich of the University of Tel-Aviv made me aware of this difference.

[11] After completing this article, I found in Félix Buffière, *Les mythes d'Homère et la pensée grecque* (Paris: Les Belles Lettres, 1956) 389, evidences for an interpretation of Homer which expounds Penelope allegorically as *tēn methodikēn kai kanonikēn philosophian* (systematic and regular philosophy). Here the transference of the Homeric *homoiōma* into an allegory on Homer is clearly accomplished. Since these evidences are found in Eustathius, *Ad Odysseam* (pp. 1390, 1437), they offer us no leverage on dating the conversion of the association of ideas into an allegory. However, on the basis of the above line of thought, we can consider Philo as the *terminus ante quem* for it.

[12] As Burton L. Mack, from other points of view, had demonstrated in his important article, "Weisheit und Allegorie bei Philo von Alexandrien," *SP* 5 (1978) 57–105. However, it appears to me doubtful when he proceeds from a characterization of Sarah as mistress, without anchoring it in the background of the history of its exposition, i.e. the *relationship* of mistress and maid.

satisfaction with the handmaiden while basely forgetting the mistress.

2. Even more—in faithfulness to the biblical narrative[13]— it is the mistress herself who, in noble selflessness, directs him to her handmaiden because in his present stage he can procreate only with her.

3. Accordingly, throughout the time during which he lives with the handmaiden, he also remains faithful to the mistress[14] and presents the child who is begotten to her, his wife of noble birth.[15]

4. Since, in contrast with the suitors, he has not lost himself in his relationship with his handmaiden, at the end of the necessary intermediate stage he returns to the mistress and now begets with her their own true son.

By incorporating these alterations, made possible for him by the biblical text, Philo achieves a deepened conception of the dialectical relationship between philosophy and the individual studies. The fact that the individual studies constitute *propaideumata*, that is, indispensable prerequisites for the ascent to philosophy, had not been broached in the Homeric simile. In Philo, for the first time maiden and mistress do not stand in irreconcilable enmity to each other, but rather the maiden serves the mistress. And as on the human level of the literal meaning, so also on the scriptural level of the allegory, a dynamic fellowship emerges from rude antagonism. Out of an expression of professional jealousy on the part of the philosophers who felt themselves neglected, there was now made an outline of the way to human perfection, with all the obstacles to be overcome. Here I must forego a consideration of the additional development of the allegory which Philo undertakes in Congr 79 by means of a doubling of the maiden-mistress relationship.

II.

Charites—*ancestors*

The Sarah-Hagar allegory gains its legitimate meaning only through its orientation to Philo's conception of Abraham. Only in that Abraham means the "learner" is his progress from a Hagar-stage to a Sarah-stage meaningful, and only in this way do the two figures, in their interrelationship, achieve their status value. However, it seems not to have been noted before that the surrounding framework in which this conception of Abraham itself belongs also is drawn from an allegorical tradition rooted in the interpretation of myth. As is known, in Philo's allegorical work the three fathers of the race consistently represent the three *aretai* (virtues) which since Protagoras[16] were recognized as the three prerequisites to all

---

[13] Gen 16:2.

[14] Congr 73, 78.

[15] Congr 76.

[16] Protagoras, B3, DK⁶2, p. 264.

intellectual culture, i.e. *physis*, *didaskalia* and *askēsis* (nature, education and practice). What does it mean then that Philo, where he enumerates the three qualities, adds this relative clause to the list: ἃς ἑτέρῳ ὀνόματι Χάριτας ἰσαρίθμους ἄνθρωποι καλοῦσιν[17] (which by another name people call *Charites* [Graces], the same in number)? Those who call the three virtues which are requisite to human perfection by the name of *Charites* must of course be those who expound the myths allegorically. Now in Greek mythology the *Charites* are an element of much vagueness, fluctuating in their genealogy and their individual names; not even their number remained fixed: in Hellenistic times their number was generally accepted as three, and this is exclusively true of their presentation in art as well, although in local traditions other numbers were also possible. Accordingly they were allegorized in various ways. Seneca in *De Beneficiis* cites Chrysippus,[18] who makes them symbolize the demonstration of good deeds. In this connection the intertwining of the figures serves him as an indication of the mutual character of benefices.[19] This accords with the type predominant in pictorial art where three nude young women walk in a circle, each with her hand on the shoulder of the one ahead of her. Thus in another passage,[20] Philo can have the four qualities with which Moses, according to him, is endowed, step "in intimate intertwining while dancing together . . . an image of the virgin *Charites* which, according to the immutable law of nature, are not to be separated from one another." Here, obviously, Philo presents the *Charites* simply as a figure for human qualities interrelated with each other. But when in connection with the passage under consideration regarding the three basic prerequisites to human development which were normative for Greek pedagogy—natural gifts, learning and practice—he says that "people" call them by another name, *Charites*, then we have no longer to do with a personal product of florid Philonic style. Rather we must conclude from his words that one of the interpretations of the figures of the *Charites* presented by the allegorists is presupposed, that in fact they symbolize our three *aretai* (virtues). And Philo's statement shows us that the notion that the *Charites* were three is significant for this interpretation. According to the above parallels, we can presume that in this interpretation the union of the *Charites* with each other was not lacking. This presumption will now be confirmed.

In the place occupied by the three *Charites* in the mythical allegory, there appear in Philo's biblical allegory the three fathers of the race. The

---

17 Abr 54.
18 Seneca, *De Beneficiis* 1.3.
19 *Ibid.* 1.3, 4.
20 Vita Mos 2.7.

first announcement that Philo makes regarding these fathers is the assertion that all three of them are *mias oikias kai henos genous* (of one
household and one race); the last is the son of the middle one and the
grandson of the first.[21] This situation obviously is intended to legitimize
the fathers of the race as the biblical extension of the three intertwined
Charites.

While the interpretation of the *Charites* as the three presuppositions
of education is dropped in casually and we would not have known of it
were it not attested by Philo, his transference of it into biblical material
became the point of departure for his most pregnant and fruitful exegetical contribution. In spite of the different individual names given them,
the *Charites* remained figures scarcely distinguishable from each other,
and we do not know whether the allegorist of the myth took the trouble
to designate which of the three *Charites* should represent which of the
aretai (virtues). For Philo this was different. In character and destiny,
the three fathers of the race are perhaps the most sharply chiselled figures in the Hebrew Bible. Hence it is necessary to determine with the
greatest care which of the three basic virtues is to be matched with
which of the three fathers. For Philo the appropriate matching constituted henceforth the key for the allegorical understanding of the three
patriarchal figures and thus for the greatest part of Genesis, over which
exclusively his great Allegorical Commentary extends. Thus if Abraham
meant the way of learning, his life had to be conceived as a progressive
series of stages of which his departure from the Land of Chaldea for the
land of God and his passage through a Hagar-stage to a Sarah-stage were
parts. If Isaac meant fully developed natural ability, it was then understandable, for instance, why he was the only one of the fathers of the
race to have but one wife. If Jacob was the man of practice, then his
rolling the stone from the edge of the well and his struggle by night with
the angel find their meaningful place in his biography. Nowhere did
Philo's amazing exegetical ingenuity find a more responsive field of
endeavor than in the immeasurable realm of meanings that he opened
up here. The way in which he was able, in the Jewish sphere, to manipu-
late the key that he had won from Greek mythological allegory shows
him at the peak of his achievement.

                                    III.

Hemispheres

An area certainly predestined for allegorization was the interpretation of the equipment of the Temple. In view of the fact that according
to a primeval concept common throughout the whole ancient East, a

---

[21] Abr 50.

temple as the earthly residence of the deity was to be copied after his heavenly abode, it is understandable that the Temple building and its vessels were to be explained cosmologically. The "physical" school of Greek mythological allegory provided rich material for such interpretation. The question might indeed be raised whether the polytheistic character of the myths thus expounded did not preclude the Jewish author's making use of them, and Philo is rich in condemnation of mythological lie-spinning. Since, however, rationalistic interpretation had a tendency to render harmless the names of the gods as simply poetic terms for cosmic objects, he was not always consistent in maintaining this rejection. Thus in one instance[22] he finds that the ancients *appropriately* (*euthybolōs*) designated the earth as Hestia because this name meant "the one who stands," i.e. the Unmoved.

In individual cases it may be debatable in how far we should see carryover of the corresponding mythological allegories into the cosmological interpretations of the vessels of the Temple; but on closer inspection, certain elements should be expanded on. I should like here to limit myself to one instance in which such a relationship appears to me to be evident.

As early as Philolaus, the Dioscuri were seen as a representation of the two cosmic hemispheres.[23] According to this myth Zeus divided the gift of immortality between them in such a way that in shifts first the one and then the other of them could be in heaven, while the other had to spend the same period in hades. It may be that this formulation was indeed conceived as a mythological representation of the alternation of the hemispheres. In any case, for a cosmological allegorization it was an easy, in fact a compelling, thought that "sojourning in" the world above or the world below became in fact a representation of these worlds themselves. Thus it is no wonder that in late Hellenistic literature the Dioscuri are often spoken of as poetical representations of the hemispheres,[24] and this identity of both is occasionally apostrophized as the opinion "of the philosophers."[25] In this sense Philo[26] also cites this myth as one of the idolatrous fables of the poets of myths, who had divided heaven into hemispheres, the one above and the other under the earth, had named them Dioscuri and with this had invented the story of their every-other-day lives, while in truth in the heavenly spheres the ideas of above and below had no reality.

In spite of such criticism from the standpoint of natural philosophy, Philo nevertheless seeks equivalents in the arrangements of the Temple

---

22 Cher 26.
23 On this see F. Buffière, *Les mythes d'Homère*, 571.
24 Sextus Empiricus, *Adv. Mathematicos* 9.37; Julianus Imperator, *Orationes* 4.147a; cf. also R. Eisler, *Weltenmantel und Himmelszelt* (München: Beck, 1910) 417.
25 Joannes Lydus, *De Mensibus* 4.17, p. 78 (Wünsch).
26 Dec 56f.

for the myth which he elsewhere pillories as a sophistic invention. He could not expect, of course, to find such an articulate symbol as the myth of the Dioscuri. The rotation of the heavenly vault involves a dynamic momentum to which the alternating sojourn of the Dioscuri in heaven and hades could do justice in a way that the statically arranged vessels in the Temple could not. It was largely necessary therefore to forego this momentum in terms of a biblical equivalent. In this sense Philo first of all brings the two cherubim of the Holy of Holies into consideration,[27] which for him however merge without further ado with the cherubim posted at the entrance of Paradise (which, on the basis of this analogy, are likewise presumed to be two). In his conception the cherubim in the Holy of Holies stand to the right and the left of the Ark of the Covenant, which is thus an immovably fixed center, and as such is said to represent the earth, which stands unmoved. In contrast, the cherubim have wings which mark their mobility. For Philo this means movement about a fixed center, and thus the movement of the heavenly vault around the earth; and the duality of the cherubim then divides heaven into the two hemispheres. In another formulation, understood as a parallel, the fiery, circling sword, rather than the Ark of the Covenant, stands between the two cherubim, this, according to Philo, designating the circular movement of the cherubim, and thus of the hemispheres. In continuing his treatise *De Cherubim*,[28] Philo goes beyond his previous exposition of the cherubim as hemispheres by offering a deeper interpretation, which he presents with obvious inner emotion as having come by divine inspiration; concerning this we cannot go further here. It is possible, however, that this new insight came to him only after he had written down the previous one. In any case, nothing in his presentation of the cherubim as hemispheres offers any hint that he disavowed the concept in any way. The situation is different, however, in another passage,[29] apparently written at a later time, where he says: "In accord with their position facing each other, some (*tines men*) explain the cherubim as symbols of the two hemispheres. . . . But I (*egō de*) would like to think. . . . " Here one must consider the possibility that in this statement Philo is not completely honest and that he rejects an interpretation that earlier he had found acceptable, by thrusting it—in a completely unspecified way—on "some," and thus on others. Hay, in discussing other allegorists referred to by Philo,[30] did not write it off in this manner, as he places no question mark against the reference to "others" in our passage.[31] This appears to

27 Cher 25f.; Vita Mos 2.98.
28 Cher 27.
29 Vita Mos 2.98f.
30 David M. Hay, "Philo's References to Other Allegorists," *SP* 6 (1979–80) 41–76.
31 *Ibid.* 43, No. 37.

me to be correct. The allegory that leads to the interpretation of the cherubim as hemispheres is tied to the explanation of the Ark of the Covenant as a symbol of the earth's sphere. This is an expression of a flat rationalism, a levelling down of the divine into a purely mechanical-physical image of the world, whose author I cannot think Philo to have been. If it originated with a predecessor, Philo may have put up with it until such a time as he was accorded a more satisfying understanding by a higher inspiration. Thus I do not consider it legitimate to contest Philo's honesty in either of these two passages, although the possibility is not to be dismissed out of hand.

But if we accept Philo's testimony, we then have here a case of extra-Philonic, and thus presumably pre-Philonic, appropriation of a mythological allegory into the exposition of the Bible. As a base, this instance is too narrow for far-reaching conclusions. Should it however allow of broadening, it might provide insight into the development of biblical allegory, a process which could have led from some kind of simple dependence on the practices and the horizon of contemporary mythological allegory, gradually, especially throughout the work of Philo, to a breakthrough in the direction of specifically religious content in the allegorical study of the Bible. However, at this preliminary point, such a view cannot be confirmed.

Yet another allegory of the hemispheres is found in Philo. In the same treatise in which he rejects the interpretation of the cherubim as hemispheres, he argues on the other hand, in interpreting the two *shoham*-stones on the shoulder pieces of the high priest, that they are to be explained as symbols of the hemispheres, in contrast with others who refer the stones to the sun and moon.[32] We may perhaps suppose that, once he had freed himself from the unsatisfying allegory of the cherubim, Philo then sought another object in the cosmological symbolic world of the Temple which could take over the orphaned function of supporting an allegory of the hemispheres. He recommends his interpretation on the following grounds, to which he also later returns:[33] the two stones are identical, which speaks against their interpretation as sun and moon but fits well with the hemispheres; they lie upon each shoulder and thus flank the body on both sides (which was also true for the cherubim); they are circular, which corresponds with the hemispheres; their color is that of the sky; on each of these two jewels are engraved the names of six tribes, just as the twelve signs of the zodiac are divided equally between the two hemispheres. One can see that with the exception of movement, which the stones were unable to convey, Philo extracts from his symbol as many characteristic traits as he is able to

[32] Vita Mos 2.122f.
[33] Spec Leg 1.86; Quaes Ex 2.109.

find. Philo does not get as far as the methodical model of the Dioscuri, but the need to find a substitute for them gives him no relief.

IV.

Hydra—the serpent

As with "physical" allegory, we are also able to give an example of transference in the case of "ethical" allegory, as it has been identified in the study of myth. The main themes on which ethical allegory may be said to move are the interpretation of the *Odyssey* and the figure of Hercules; in the case of the latter the chief place is occupied by the interpretation of the "Twelve Labors." One of these is the battle with the Hydra. In a source designated specifically as Stoic this is identified as the embodiment of sensual pleasure, against which the wise man must struggle.[34] The heroic struggle of Hercules, identified as the wise man, is so difficult because the Hydra, i.e. pleasure, is a many-headed monster: as soon as one suppresses pleasure, it springs up anew. Hercules succeeds with her only through the use of firebrands; these symbolize the earnest exhortation, i.e. moral training, by which the wise man comes to master pleasure.[35] This myth, with this same Stoic interpretation, is repeated in Philo: Wisdom must wage a never-ending war with carnal pleasures. "When one enemy is subdued, there grows up another, in every respect stronger, as with the many-headed Hydra; for also in its case it is said, when one head is cut off another sprouts in its place."[36] Thus Philo is well acquainted with the Stoic interpretation of the Hydra as a symbol of pleasure. Therefore when he finds the serpent which leads men to sin in the Bible, its interpretation as pleasure is self-evident for him. In making this interpretation however, he cannot cite the polycephalism of the Hydra and the regrowth of two new heads in place of one lopped off. Instead, he gathers up other points of contact to confirm his allegorical definition of the meaning of the serpent: the serpent crawls on its belly (which therefore is its most important concern); it eats dust (is thus oriented toward the earthly); it carries its poison in its teeth (eating is for it of greatest importance); its movements are tortuous (which makes understandable its accessability to all sensual charms); it is capable of uttering human sounds (holds a view of the world that glorifies pleasure, that is, Epicurean philosophy).[37] Adam, of course, is no Hercules, no Stoic wise man who subdues pleasure through rigorous moral training, and so this time the serpent gains the upper hand. Philo's biblical scenario runs thus: the serpent (pleasure) with the help of the woman (sense perception)

---

[34] Heraclitus, *Quaestiones Homericae* 33.8; Stoic source: 33.1.
[35] This must be the sense of the slightly damaged text.
[36] Somn 2.14.
[37] Op 157–65; Leg All 2.74–78.

leads the man (the Logos, i.e. reason) astray, whereupon the man (the Logos) forsakes his father (God) and his mother (wisdom) and cleaves to his wife (sense perception) and becomes one flesh with her (is subdued by pleasure). This scenario was not provided Philo by the interpretation of the myth, although it was strongly influenced by Stoic ethics; but the instrument by which he was able to open up the biblical tradition for his meaning was, so to speak, slipped into his hand by the interpretation of the Hydra or serpent as pleasure, and thus by Greek mythical allegory.

Research on such relationships, their impact and the limits of their impact, appears to me to be one of the tasks of Philo research.

THE "ONE WHO SEES GOD" IN PHILO*

GERHARD DELLING

University of Halle

Philo prefaces his account of the embassy to Gaius with a perspective which gives his apology a particular accent. Here the author confesses emphatically "to behold the uncreated and divine, the primal good, the excellent, the happy, the blessed," (5) that is given the "suppliants' race"[1] "which the Father and King of the Universe and the Source of all things has taken for his portion," (3) and which "is called in the Hebrew tongue Israel, but, expressed in our tongue, the word is 'he that sees God'" (4; *PLCL* 10.5).[2]

Without question Philo is speaking here of the Jewry of his time whose fortunes under Caligula are the theme of *Ad Gaium*. With emphasis he calls them by their biblical name, Israel,[3] and by the use of this name he identifies their particular nature, the particular gift that God has given them. In this brief exposition of the name of their forefather, Philo has incorporated a biblically based confession of the faith of his people before the emperor and the empire.

I.

This point of view can be demonstrated first of all by a quotation from Conf 56 (*PLCL* 4.41): "For we are the 'race of the Chosen ones of

---

* This article was translated by Earle Hilgert.

[1] The phrase is found in Philo only here.

[2] Peder Borgen, *Bread from Heaven* (Leiden: Brill, 1965) 115–18, in recent years has discussed the theme of "the nation of vision"; he also gives particular attention to the earlier literature. Further, see Hans Windisch, *Die Frömmigkeit Philos und ihre Bedeutung für das Christentum* (Leipzig: Hinrichs, 1909) 42–46; Harald Hegermann, *Die Vorstellung vom Schöpfungsmittler im hellenistischen Judentum und Urchristentum* TU 82, 1961) 21f.; Esther Starobinski-Safran, *De Fuga et Inventione* (PM 17, 1970) 260f., n. 2; André Pelletier, *Legatio ad Gaium* (PM 32, 1972) 353f.

[3] It is found only here in *Ad Gaium*. The term "Jew(s)" is used by Philo in *De Vita Mosis, De Decalogo, De Specialibus Legibus, De Virtute, Quod Omnis Probus*, and *De Aeternitate Mundi* together only 26 times, while it appears in *In Flaccum* 28 times, in *Ad Gaium* 44 times. The corresponding adjective is used only in *In Flaccum* and *Ad Gaium*. Figures on the use of the name "Israel" are given below, p. 37.

that Israel' who sees God." With this joyous confession Philo cites Exod
24:11.[4] There the reference is to Moses, Aaron, Nadab, Abihu and the
seventy elders (v. 9), who are particularly noted in that they are allowed
to be nearer God than the rest of the people; for this reason they are
spoken of in Exod 24:11 LXX as the "chosen (epilektoi) of Israel." Philo
picks up on this title but he expands it: the chosen of Israel are not a part
of the people but the whole of the Jews—"we," and he calls these people
(as we must once more emphasize) "the 'race of the Chosen ones of that
Israel' who sees God." The text as we have it[5] gives no basis for Philo to
have inserted the translation of the name Israel, which was familiar to
him, into the biblical expression, "chosen of Israel", but he inserts this
interpretation, "those who see God," because it incorporates what for
him was an important statement concerning the Jews ("we are . . . ").[6]
"For we are the 'race of the Chosen ones of that Israel' who sees God,
'and there is none amongst us of discordant voice' (Conf 56 following
Exod 24:11),[7] so that the whole world, which is the instrument of the All,
may be filled with the sweet melody of its undiscording harmonies"
(PLCL 4.41).

The point that Philo makes here is developed theologically in his
running commentary on the Torah at Exod 24:16 (Quaes Ex 2.46; PLCL
Sup 2.90–92). The reference here to six days in connection with the
events at Sinai (the establishment of the covenant and the giving of the
Decalogue) refers back to the story of creation: "the even number, six
(i.e. days), He apportioned both to the creation of the world and to the
election of the contemplative (horatikos, 'able to see'[8]) nation"; therefore
he related each to the other[9] and accorded them both the same rank
(that the creator of the world is also he who chooses the people and vice
versa,[10] was for the Jews of Philo's time a meaningful concept). Thus the

---

[4] This is clear from the context in the LXX, which Philo uses in the same way (see
below).

[5] The LXX does not say that the elders saw God.

[6] The formulation "we are . . . " suggests moreover the language of worship; cf. 1 Pet
2:9: "You are a chosen race."

[7] The words, "and not one (of you) disagreed," are found in Num 31:49 (Conf 55) as
well as in Exod 24:11 (Conf 56). In accordance with the common practice in ancient Jewish exegesis, in Conf 55f., on the basis of a clause common to two biblical passages, Philo
expounds the one (Num 31:49) by the other (Exod 24:11). In this connection he applies to
the people of Israel, from the LXX, a use of the verb diaphōnein ("to sound discordantly"
in a musical sense), which derives from Plato, who uses the verb in connection with the
lyre (Gorgias 482b). Another exposition of Exod 24:11 is found in Quaes Ex 2.38. Philo
makes use of Num 31:49 also in Mut 109; on this passage see above, p. 31.

[8] On this attribute, see below, pp. 30–33.

[9] With the declared objective, "for virtue" (thus Marcus [PLCL Sup 2.91]; Aucher
understands otherwise). The Greek fragment apparently has abbreviated.

[10] "The Father and Maker of the world was in the truest sense also its Lawgiver," Vita
Mos 2.48 [PLCL 6.473].

number six, which occurs in both contexts, points out that according to the will of God the nation is "to be ordered and arrayed in the same manner as the whole world." The law according to which the world is created and the Torah are in agreement[11]: this also was a meaningful thought for Judaism.[12] Shortly before, in connection with Exod 24:12c Philo sets forth the ideal that God, in giving the law for the race that was capable of seeing,[13] has also set down the laws for the world (Quaes Ex 2.42).

In his commentary on Gen 17:12, among other things Philo makes clear that circumcision is a sign of election "according to the will and decision of the Father," for the race for whom it is commanded, "Israel, that is, seeing God" (Quaes Gen 3.49). The name of Israel as "He who sees God" recurs without further ado where Philo speaks of the election of the people of God, or where in Lev 15:31 he understandably puts "the sons of the one who sees" (Leg All 3.15) in place of "the sons of Israel," as he also does in connection with Exod 24:17 (Quaes Ex 2.47, both in the *quaestio*, where he cites the biblical text, and also in the *solutio*). These do not receive sight of the *essentia* of God, the glory of God (Exod 24:17), but the appearance of a flame (not a true flame), through which the glory of God manifests itself. Elsewhere Philo introduces his interpretation of the name of Israel where it has to do with the specific relationship of the people with God, particularly in connection with the revelation of God at Sinai.

Once Philo says specifically that "often indeed in the law-book" the identification, "sons of Israel," is found repeatedly and in the sense of "(sons) of him that sees" (Conf 148). Here we can see how firmly for him the continual connection of name and meaning is grounded formally in the Torah.

Thus it is understandable that Philo, without any particular basis[14] in the context, can add this interpretation to the name. Balaam sang numberless songs of praise to "him whose eyes were open (*ton horōnta*), even Israel" (Migr 1:13; *PLCL* 4.197; *ton horōnta* is applied here as a predicate of praise). Judah (Gen 38:18) is the "King of the nation that sees, even Israel" (Somn 2.44).[15] In neither passage, where the events of the

---

[11] The laws of Moses are "the most faithful picture of the world-polity," therefore the Torah begins with the creation (Vita Mos 2.51 [end; *PLCL* 6.475]); on this cf. *Aboth* 3.15: special love was shown the Israelites, "in that . . . to them was given the precious instrument by which the world was created," the Torah (*MD* 452).

[12] On this the rabbis appeal to Prov 8:30; see *SB* 2.356f.

[13] The translation "gens contemplativa" is inappropriate in view of the Greek text; in corresponding contexts, Aucher has *video* for this verb.

[14] Abraham employs the designation, "clear-sighted (*dioratikon*) race," quite without warning in Heres 36.

[15] In addition, see Migr 125, 224. In 224 there may lie behind the insertion the idea that no such evil may be found among the people to whom God has granted seeing.

history of the people are considered, is the interpretation of the name developed further in the context. For Philo the interpretation stands in harmony with the name. It is in fact so firmly bound up with the name that an abbreviation is sufficient to indicate it: "the one who sees God" is simply "the one who sees."[16]

In many texts of Philo it is not immediately recognizable that behind them stands this interpretation of the name of Israel. An example is Somn 2.271, where Philo moves from the name (Num 21:17, here a designation of the people) to a statement concerning those "who desire to see." The connection is understandable only to those who are familiar with the interpretation of the name from other texts. The adjective, used here in a substantival sense (*philotheamōn*), on the other hand appears in Her 79 in the context of a specific interpretation of the name (on the basis of Her 78; see below). The heavenly food of the soul which delights in seeing is the manna, the word of God (79), one may also compare Fuga 138: God causes the heavenly wisdom, the bread of heaven, to fall in drops upon the minds of those who delight in seeing[17] (137; Exod 16:4[18]); "this saying," is that "which the Lord ordained" (Exod 16:16, cited at Fuga 139)[19]. In Mut 88 reference is made to the Philonic exegesis of Gen 32:25–29[20] where the prizes are spoken of, which are "offered to a soul which rejoices to toil and seek the vision of truth" (*PLCL* 5.187). That behind this stands specifically the interpretation of Gen 32 is shown by the reference to the name Jacob,[21] as well as by the further context (see below in regard to Mut 81). Finally also Mut 209 alludes to Israel "which could see and which loved wisdom and the vision" (*PLCL* 5.251). The word *philotheamōn* ("loved . . . the vision") as such does not belong to the special vocabulary of the meaning of the name "Israel"; in my judgment two-thirds of the passages where it appears evince no reference to this meaning.

II.

In contrast, the use of the expression, "a race able to see" (*horatikon genos*),[22] is specific. Shem is an ancestor of "the race that is able to see" (Mut 189). Somn 2.276, 279 speaks of "the race able to see" in the context of

---

[16] Cf. Conf 146; see below, p. 33 on Mut 82; above, p. 29 on Quaes Ex 2.47.

[17] According to Fuga 195, souls who delight in seeing will be given to drink from the well (Gen 24:16) of divine wisdom.

[18] Cf. below, pp. 32–33 on Mut 258f.

[19] Philo understands these words not as the introduction to what follows, but as an independent statement.

[20] On this interpretation, see below, pp. 34–35.

[21] Along with the mention of the names of Abraham and Isaac; cf. Praem 27 in its context; on the passage see below, pp. 34–35.

[22] For this, see above on Quaes Ex 2.46,42.

the story of the Exodus, as does Conf 91 in connection with the wandering in the wilderness (Vita Mos 2.196; see below; also Quod Deus 144). In fact the epithet, "the race able to see," seems to have priority in those contexts which deal with the events of the time of Moses. In one instance it appears in a passage in which evident reference is made to the bestowal of the name Israel upon the patriarch according to Philo's understanding (Mut 109), which will be discussed later.

"The race[23] which is able to see[24] "[25] becomes for Philo simply a designation for the people of God. Accordingly he introduces it (as a participial expression) in interpreting texts of the Torah. Thus at Migr 18 in an exegesis of Gen 50:24, "God will take care of you ('will visit you,' *episkepsetai*)," Philo gives this as "God will take care of the race that is able to see." Even in his paraphrase of the words of Pharaoh in Exod 1:9, he substitutes "the race that is able to see the one who is" for "the race of the sons of Israel" (Migr 54). In Fuga 140 the use of this designation is suggested to him similarly by the expression "sons of Israel" in Ex 3:11 LXX.[26] In Vita Mos 2.196, in a retelling of Lev 24:10f., an individual Israelite is called "someone of the nation that is able to see and to know";[27] here the designation sets up a contrast between an Israelite and the son of (an Israelite woman and) a heathen (196, 193).[28]

---

[23] The word here translated (*genos*) has a relatively broad range of meanings. For Polybius alone, Arno Mauersberger (*Polybios-Lexikon* [Berlin: Akademie-Verlag, 1956] s.v.) gives among others, "Geschlecht," "Stamm," "Gattung," "Art," "Schlag"; cf. also Liddell-Scott-Jones (n. 24). At times Philo speaks more specifically of the people of God as "the kind (*tropos*) that is able to see" (Plant 69, see below p. 32). The German "Geschlecht" includes the relationship of the ones who are able to see with the ancestor of the race and with each other; cf. Alfred Götze, ed., *Trübners Deutsches Wörterbuch* (Berlin: de Gruyter, 1939) 3.126f., in regard to its use also in the sense of the German "Art." *Genus* would be preferable to Aucher's *gens*.

[24] On this translation, see in the first instance H. G. Liddell, R. Scott, H. S. Jones, *A Greek-English Lexicon* (Oxford: Clarendon Press, 1940/1953), who give "able to see" as the usual meaning for *horatikos*; accordingly Harry Austryn Wolfson, *Philo* II (Cambridge MA: Harvard, 1948) 84, 401 n. 25, translates, "endowed with vision." A similar rendering is given occasionally in *PCH*; thus A. Posner's translation at Migr 18, "zum Schauen . . . berufen." The correctness of the translation, "able to see," will be demonstrated in our subsequent discussion; see also n. 42. Wolfson further discusses the theme of the seeing of God, *op. cit.* 51f., 91f.

[25] As we will see later, Philo uses this word in regard to Israel, or the Jews, in other combinations as well. Here we may mention: "the race beloved of God," Migr 114, Heres 203 (on Exod 14:20); "the chosen race," Post 92 (on this passage see below, p. 38; cf. also above p. 28 on Conf 56).

[26] In Philo's conceptual world, the rendering of "sons" as "race" is thoroughly appropriate.

[27] Similarly Leg All 2.34: "Descendants of the one who sees, Israel" (without basis in the text cited, Exod 12:23).

[28] The status of the man, according to Lev 24:10ff., apparently is determined in terms of the heathen father. Philo takes the implications of this passage as a basis for broad exposition (without allegory).

A special term is connected with the expression in question finally at
Quod Deus 144. Here "those who are members of the race that is able to
see, which is called Israel," are referred to as wishing to travel "the royal
road." The latter expression is suggested by Num 20:17 (once more a
report from the time of wandering in the wilderness). According to Post
102, the royal road is "the utterance and word of God" (in Post 101f.[29]
Philo combines two texts of scripture, and on the basis of a particular
phrase[30] explains the one, Num 20:17, by the other, Deut 28:14; here
concern is with swerving from the word [hrēma] of divine guidance).
The royal road is the road that leads to God (Post 101; cf. Quod Deus
160); it is the road whose lord is God alone (Quod Deus 159), over which
he alone has authority (although in Quod Deus 160 it is stated that the
royal road is wisdom, this does not contradict Post 102; wisdom is given
in God's word[31]). Consequently one cannot travel the royal road except
God accords this possibility, a thought which is found elsewhere in Philo
in different form.[32]

In a corresponding use, Philo also combines the adjective with other
substantives or employs it as a substantive itself. According to Plant 60,
in Deut 32:9 "the character (tropos) that is able to see Him and accords
Him genuine devotion" is called "portion"[33] and "lot" of God. In Deut
32:8f. reference is made to the dividing up of the nations "according to
the number of the angels of God"; Israel was allotted to God himself.[34]
Here Philo replaces the name Israel as in the passages already discussed.
Later we encounter the reference to Deut 32:8f. once more (Post 91f.).
In Deut 32 we are dealing with one of the biblical texts which was also
basic for the Judaism of the Diaspora.[35] In a more abstract way Philo
speaks of "the mind (dianoia) which truly loves God, that is able to see
Him" (Congr 56); but also here in the immediate context he uses a biblical symbol for Israel, that of the noble vine which God plants (corresponding to Jer 2:21[36]). Israel is the vine and is the character that is able
to see.

In the usage under discussion we find the adjective as a substantive
in Mut 258: "only to the one who is able to see" does food come from
heaven. Philo bases this on Exod 16:4, "Behold I rain upon you bread

---

[29] As elsewhere, cf. above, n. 7.

[30] "Turn neither to the right nor to the left"; the Greek words are only partially the same.

[31] On this cf. below, pp. 33 and 36.

[32] Cf. below, pp. 33–35.

[33] "Over each nation he set a ruler, and (but) the portion of the Lord is Israel," Sir 17:17;
see Deut 32:9a.

[34] See below, p. 38.

[35] For Philo, cf. G. Delling, ὕμνος κτλ., TDNT 8.497.5.

[36] In addition, cf. Ps 80 (79):9, 16. Philo is particularly indebted to Jeremiah (Cher 49);
at Fuga 197 he cites Jer 2:13.

from heaven" (259). The manna is wisdom (Heres 191). These statements fit together (see above on Quod Deus 160; Post 102). Philo understands Exod 15:17 as a plea for the "in-planting" into the people of salvation of those who are able to see (Plant 46f.); he also relates this directly to the people of God in the present ("we," 49).

From a purely philological standpoint it certainly is possible to translate the verbal adjective, which we find here particularly in connection with the substantive "race" in statements concerning the people of God, by "seeing." At the same time there is little probability that Philo uses the adjective in addition to the participle without reason; for the adjective he has a precedent in the rendering of the name Israel as "seeing God"; obviously he also has a precedent for the verb used here (in the participle horōn). It is used as well in extra-philonic documents in the same context; see below.[37]

In any case Philo emphasizes strongly that man by himself is not capable of seeing God; God must give him eyes that are able to see. Several times Philo uses a particular verb (enommatoō) for this idea, a compound which appears to be first attested with him. It means "to provide with eyes."[38] He employs it first in statements concerning the giving of the name Israel to the ancestor of the people of God according to Gen 32:25–29. The wrestler Jacob carries off the crown of victory, which the new name designates: he becomes the one who sees God (Mut 81),[39] for this is the finest crown for the victorious soul, "which will enable him to behold the Existent with clear vision." The victor is "endowed with eyes to apprehend in bright light Him Who alone is worthy of our contemplation" (PLCL 5.183), i.e. God (82). In accordance with this, in Ebr 82 reference is made to the change of name from Jacob to Israel according to Gen 32:29: the God who rejoices in giving has provided the mind of the wrestler with eyes. For his own time Philo says in Somn 1.164: the spiritually blind will become keen sighted when they receive eyes from the most sacred oracles (of God).[40] Through them God gives seeing eyes for the recognition of himself; he gives them through his word[41] (cf. above on Post 102; Ques Ex 2.42). This saying

---

[37] Philo uses blepōn instead only occasionally, viz., Migr 224, Somn 1.114.

[38] Corresponding with the use of simpler terminology in, for instance, a contemporary of Philo: Daedalus was the first to provde statues with eyes (Diodorus Siculus 4.76.3).

[39] Concepts from athletics, only implied above, which are connected by Philo with the renaming of Jacob, recur similarly in Eusebius, Praeparatio Evangelica 7.8.26f., and again at 11.6.30f. (here in the context of the interpretation of biblical names in general). Since Eusebius repeatedly cites Philo—we are indebted to him alone for knowledge of parts of Philo's Hypothetica—it is quite possible that Eusebius was influenced by this passage from Philo.

[40] The context has to do with the knowledge of God as the Beneficent (in distinction from his lordliness), the love of God (164f.).

[41] It is forbidden to humanity to investigate anything "respecting the essence of Him

does not annul the thought that seeing God is entirely God's gift (as is also the gift of the name Israel).[42]

III.

The change of name in Gen 32:25–29 is clearly the basis of Philo's designation of the people of God as he (they) who sees God.[43] More briefly reference is made to the giving of the name and to its fixed exposition in Somn 1. 129[44]; 1.171. As in 129 the change of name is explained by the figure of the restamping of a coin, (see below Migr 39); Migr 201; Leg All 3.15.

The broad declarations in Praem 36–46 are launched on the basis of the brief report in Gen 32:25–29. The vision (*horasis*) of God is the choice gift of honor which the wrestler[45] Jacob receives (36; "the man of practice who by unwearied and unswerving labour has made the [morally] excellent his own has for his crown the vision of God," [PLCL 8.329][27]). "The Father and Savior" gave the power to see, to recognize him—to see, "not what He is," but "that He is" (39); "not how God is constituted . . . , but that He is" (44).[46] "This knowledge he has gained not

---

that is" (also to Moses, Exod 33:23); "the man that wishes to set his gaze upon the Supreme Essence, before he sees Him will be blinded by the rays that beam forth all around Him" (Fuga 165 [PLCL 5.99, 101]). On the first statement, cf. below.

[42] Cf. Conf 92 (PLCL 4.59; on 91 see above, p. 31: the sharp-sighted eye of the soul, "the eye which alone is permitted to look on God, the eye whose name is Israel." The statement relates to Exod 2:23 (cited at Conf 93), where reference is to the "sons of Israel." The passage cited from Conf 92 corresponds with a formulation in Mut 203 (PLCL 5.247); the eye of the soul, "which alone has been trained to see God . . . "; this statement also is placed in a context where an event in the history of Israel provides the point of departure.

[43] In connection with the interpretation of Gen 32:25–29, Philo appears never to draw on v. 31f.: the translation of the name Penuel in the LXX is inappropriate for his exegesis, and he evidently understands it differently than the translator. In Somn 1.79 he makes use of v. 32 in another way, taking the expression *eidos theou* in the sense of the "appearance of God," and as subject. In contrast, Clement of Alexandria, *Paedagogus* 1.57.2, connects Gen 32:31 with the explanation of the name; however he interprets the seeing of God christologically (as Melito of Sardis had already done, *Easter Sermon* 82). The translation of the name in Justin Martyr, *Dialogue* 125.3, corresponds rather with that preserved in Josephus, *Antiquities* 1.333, both relating the name directly with Jacob's struggle. In Jub (29:13) this is passed over completely.

[44] In 130 the wreath of victory is understood differently than elsewhere.

[45] On the athlete as a type of the correct way of life in the pagan world, cf. R. Merkelbach, "Der griechische Wortschatz und die Christen," *Zeitschrift für Papyrologie und Epigraphik* 18 (1975) 101–48, especially 110f.

[46] God is "knowable to us through his power, but unknowable/unknown as to how he is constituted in terms of his being," Josephus, *Contra Apionem* 2.167—one of the more frequently traditional statements in this work. For Josephus, however, this does not contradict his presentation in *Antiquities* 1.279, according to which at Bethel God appeared to Jacob, face to face (Gen 28:13). Cf. 1.191, 223 (Abraham); 6.38 (Samuel).

from any other source," from that which is present upon the earth or in the heavens, mortal or immortal, "but from Him alone . . . who has willed to reveal to him his existence at his supplication" (44). For God "is discerned through Himself alone, without anything co-operating or being able to co-operate in giving a perfect apprehension of His existence" (45; *PLCL* 8.339); "true born worshipers, those beloved of God," are able "to apprehend Him through Himself" without the need "of a reasoning process as a helper for seeing,"[47] without drawing a conclusion from the works in regard to the master workman (43).[48] Only those arrive at truth who "envision God through God, light through light."

On the basis of the renaming of the patriarch, Philo is able to make a number of similar statements in Migr 39f. Through the "reminting"[49] into "Israel," the one who sees, is achieved "seeing of the Divine light, identical with knowledge, which opens wide the soul's eye," wisdom (39; [*PLCL* 4.153] Quod Deus 160 is also concerned with this; Heres 191). "But he that shows each several object is God, who alone is possessed of perfect knowledge" (Migr 40; *PLCL* 4.155). In 41f. Philo adds a thought which amplifies similarly differentiating statements and helps us to understand: God "gives clear proof of His wisdom not only from His having been the Artificer of the universe, but also from His having made the knowledge of the things that had been brought into existence His sure possession" (41; *PLCL* 4.155; in 42 Philo bases this on Genesis 1:31: God knowingly apprehended all that He had made). This means: the knowledge of God derived from the creation is also a gift of divine revelation, of his wisdom, which he has revealed to Israel in his word.

The gift of seeing God is bound up with the particular relationship to God that God accords the Jews,[50] accords them as the company which worships him, the one God. A statement in Sacr 120 refers to this: "the fountain of that devout contemplation[51] of the only wise being, on which[52] Israel's [particular] rank is based, is the habit of [cultic] service to God" (*PLCL* 2.181);[53] its "identifying sign is Levi," the bearer of the cult

---

[47] When Philo emphasizes the sharp-sightedness of Israel (Sacr 134; Mut 82; on this passage see above, p. 33), he relates it to the difference between the limited knowledge of God from creation and his being known completely through divine revelation, as we find in Migr 41f.; Congr 51; see below.

[48] In 44 we find the common interpretation of the name Israel, see below, p. 37.

[49] The image of restriking a coin is found elsewhere in Philo; see Hans Leisegang, *Indices ad Philonis Alexandrini Opera* (Berlin: de Gruyter, 1930), vol. 2, s.v. *metacharattō*. On Somn 1.129, 171, see above, p. 34.

[50] Through conversion to Judaism, one becomes a member fully entitled to it, Spec Leg 1.51f.

[51] Wolfson, *Philo* 2.51 (see above, n. 2), on this passage: Israel's "capability of seeing God is based upon the habit of his service to God."

[52] I.e., seeing. In fact, his rank in the seeing accorded him becomes clear.

[53] It is simply "the race which honors him," Vita Mos 2.189.

(that for Philo the cult belongs to the worship of God is clear in his writings in many ways[54]). The full form of the statement in Sacr 120 does not contradict what is said elsewhere concerning the relation of the seeing of God and the word of God (or wisdom; Post 102; Somn 1.164; Heres 191; Migr 39); for Philo both belong together.

Twice Philo speaks of Jewry as a whole[55] as "the worshiping race," i.e. the one that is capable[56] of (right) worship[57] (Fuga 42; Vita Mos 2.189). How pregnant this designation is for him is shown especially in Fuga 42: "the worshiping race (in general) is a votive offering (anathēma) to God, consecrated for the great high priesthood to him alone." Clearly Philo alludes here to the notion that the Jews perform priestly service substitutionarily for all of humanity (Abr 98; Spec Leg 2.163; Vita Mos 1.149); he relates this particularly to the Jerusalem temple cult (Spec Leg 1.97, 168; 2.167). The will of God made known through Moses, as he says in Vita Mos 2.189, means helpful guidance toward that which is good for all men,[58] but in a particular way for "the nation of His worshippers, for whom He opens up the road which leads to happiness" (PLCL 6.543).

"Now to see the best, that is the truly existing,[59] is the lot of the best of races, Israel, for Israel means seeing God" (Congr 51; PLCL 4.483).[60] It is the Jewish people to whom the highest of all is given, that is "to see the Father and Maker of all" (Abr 58). Israel is the most meaningful name of the race which in the Bible is called "royal palace and

---

[54] E.g. Spec Leg 1.77f. (the required offerings have a cultic purpose); Migr 92 (polemic against depreciation of the cult); Flacc 48; Gai 191, (296), 347, and the passages mentioned below. On the thank-offerings brought to the temple, cf. Jean Laporte, La doctrine eucharistique chez Philon d'Alexandrie (Théologie historique 16; Paris: Beauchesne, 1972) 91–109.

[55] In Vita Cont 11 it is a designation for the group on Lake Mareotis (22). C. Daniel, "'Le voyant,' nom cryptique des Esséniens dans l'oeuvre de Philon d'Alexandrie," Studia et Acta Orientalia (Bucharest) 9 (1977) 25–47, has not convinced me that throughout Philo "those who see" are equivalent with the Essenes. The material we are considering contradicts this view, among others in those places where the designation is used for the people of God in the past. Cf. also below, n. 70 and the context.

[56] In PCH 1.342, at Vita Mos 2.189, B. Badt gives "befähigte."

[57] It alone practices the true worship of God; related to this should be mentioned Philo's conviction of the universal significance of the Jewish cult.

[58] On this cf. Quaes Ex 2.42, see above, p. 29.

[59] Cf. the designation (once more unanticipated in the context), "he who sees the One who is" (along with "he who sees God"), Leg All 3.172. Regardless of the figurative interpretation of Exod 15:8, the reflection on Israel through quotation of the Old Testament text remains clear.

[60] This is the primary seeing, as contrasted with seeing the starry heavens. Philo proceeds here from a translation of the name Reumah (concubine of Nahor, Gen 22:24), "who 'sees [only] something' (of the One who is)." In the LXX the form of the name is different; Philo's interpretations of names are not original.

priesthood and holy people" (Ex 19:6[61]; Abr 56); "its high position is shown by the name; for the nation is called in the Hebrew tongue Israel, which, being interpreted, is He who sees God" (57 [*PLCL* 6.33]; see above, Congr 51; further Somn 2.173, also Fuga 208; cf. "he who in the Hebrew is called Israel but in our tongue [Greek] the God-seer," Praem 44; *PLCL* 8.337–39). Mostly Philo spares himself the full formula, "which is interpreted"; occasionally he says, "the one who sees God, that is Israel" (Leg All 3.186, cf. above Quaes Gen 3.49). But it is clear that one should read a "that is" generally between the lines,[62] where the sequence "he who sees God, Israel," or a similar way of speaking[63] is found.[64] For Philo "Israel" and "the one who sees God" become in a particular way interchangeable designations or expressions, as is apparent many times.

In fact Philo in his own text, aside from citations from the LXX, uses the name Israel by far the majority of times in statements which either in essence or (most commonly) in full form relate to the meaning of the name as the one who sees God (in total 30 times out of 36[65]). Philo associates "seeing God" with "Israel."

If the analogy of the name Israel as "the man who sees God"[66] or "the God-seer" does not go back to Philo himself, then as far as its origin is concerned it is not connected specifically with Philonic concepts. A literal understanding of the received interpretation of the name in a sense of physical sight is, as has been shown, impossible for Philo; therefore he relates the name to the divine revelation transmitted through Moses to the race that is able to see, Israel.[67]

---

[61] The text is significant of the Diaspora and was inserted into the LXX of Exod 23:22. Philo uses it also in Sobr 66 with the same separation of the first two predicates (the third is not cited in Sobr 66). This division is found already in 2 Macc 2:17 (and in somewhat different form in the Targums; cf. further, Rev 1:6, but not 1 Pet 2:9).

[62] Occasionally exceptions suggest themselves; see the translation of Conf 56 on pp. 27–28.

[63] Cf. M. Adler in *PCH* 6.232 at Somn 2.44: "des Schauenden, d.h. Israels" (on this passage, see above); further, E. Stein, *PCH* 5.138 at Conf 146 (comma); A. Posner, *PCH* 5.163 at Migr 39: "in Israel, in den 'Sehenden.'" Cohn-Wendland, *PCW*, place a comma between the participle and the name in Conf 146, Migr 113, 125, 224, Somn 2.44 (in my view this would also be appropriate at Somn 1.114).

[64] Cf. the Greek word order at Heres 78: " . . . were called God-seeing, Israel" (note also the placement of the predicate, "seeing" or "the God-seer" after the name in Somn 1.129, 171).

[65] The name occurs 41 times in citations from the LXX. These figures are based on those writings extant in Greek, using the *index locorum* in Günter Mayer, *Index Philoneus* (Berlin: de Gruyter, 1974) 150.

[66] The Prayer of Joseph, see above. This form occurs less frequently, cf. Franz Wutz, *Onomastica Sacra* (TU 41:1 [3.11:1]; Leipzig: Hinrichs, 1914–15) 89.

[67] Another example of how Philo was able to put an inherited expression to theological use is his employment of the divine designation "the One who is" (Exod 3:14; see Vita

The interchangeability of "Israel" and "seeing God" became significant in particular for the relationship between God and his people. In
this connection we can refer to Post 92. In the context Philo refers here
also to Deut 32:8f.[68] When God divided out the nations under the angels,
as the all-sovereign ruler he kept for himself "the chosen race of Israel.
For he that sees God . . . has been allotted as His portion to Him Whom
he sees" (92; *PLCL* 2.379). This is certainly one of the most significant of
those sentences in which Philo, in the context of the meaning of the
name Israel, expresses his faith in the relationship of his people to God, a
relationship instituted once for all by God. Aside from this relationship
there is no seeing of God, no full knowledge of God.

IV.

Philo, for his own part, took over the interpretation of the name
Israel (as he did with the interpretations of other names). It is attested in
other texts which, while they were not composed before Philo,[69] are,
however, hardly dependent upon him.[70] One example is the so-called
prayer of Joseph in Origen, *Commentary on John* 2.189: "My name is
Israel, the one called Israel by God, a man who sees God." A further
example is the Coptic Gnostic tractate from Nag Hammadi entitled by
the English editors, "On the Origin of the World" (105.24–25):[71]
". . . called 'Israel,' i.e., 'the man, who sees God.'" This interpretation is

---

Mos 1.75; Somn 1.231; Mut 11; Quod Det 160). Friedrich Kuhr, "Die Gottesprädikationen
bei Philo von Alexandrien" (Dissertation, Marburg, 1944) 16, gives 24 occurrences in
which "the One who sees" is unquestionably a direct predicate; others, in which the participle stands in the genitive or dative and the type of predication is not clear from the
context, he lists under the neuter (p. 13, n. 1).

[68] Post 90f.; cf. above, p. 32 on Plant 60.

[69] At the end of the third century B.C.E. the biblical exegete Demetrius (Eusebius, *Praeparatio Evangelica* 9.21.7), who makes wide-ranging use of the vocabulary of the LXX,
reports the wrestling of an angel of God (sic) with Jacob, and even repeats the ritual etiol-
ogy given there (Gen 32:26, 33); he also mentions the re-naming of Jacob as such, but
gives neither the explanation of the new name according to Gen 32:29, nor any other. It is
possible, of course, that the interpretation of the name was omitted by Alexander
Polyhistor, who transmitted the quotation. On Demetrius, see Nikolaus Walter, "Untersuchungen zu den Fragmenten der jüdisch-hellenistischen Historiker" (Theologische
Habilitationsschrift, Halle/Saale, 1967) 15–37, 114–55.

[70] Dependence of the Prayer of Joseph on Philo should not be deduced from the fact
that individual epithets in Conf 146 (a highly specialized passage) correspond with the
Prayer of Joseph (*contra* E. Stein, "Zur apokryphen Schrift 'Gebet Josephs,'" *MGWJ* 81
[N.F. 45; 1937] 280–86, 282f). Here it is preferable to think of the use of traditional predi-
cates; they are used in various ways, and the interpretation of the name in the Prayer of
Joseph is structured differently, "a man . . . . "

[71] *The Nag Hammadi Library in English*, ed. James M. Robinson (San Francisco: Har-
per and Row, 1977) 166; also Alexander Böhlig and P. Labib, *Die koptisch-gnostische
Schrift ohne Titel aus Codex II von Nag Hammadi im Koptischen Museum zu
Alt-Kairo* (Berlin: Akademie-Verlag, 1962) 55.

also found in the *Constitutions of the Apostles* 7.36 (*ANF* 7.474): "a peculiar people, the true Israel, beloved of God, and seeing God," and 8.15 (*ANF* 7.491): "the God of Israel, Thy people which truly see, and which have believed in Christ." If the words "true" in 7.36 and "truly" in 8.15, as well as the conclusion, are to be deleted as Christian additions, then it is obvious that Jewish designations have been carried over intentionally and applied to Christianity.

Seeing God is, after all, not a particular gift to a selected circle within Judaism, but (as the name indicates) to all "Israel."[72] Philo does not mark off from the rest of Jewry an elite of those who see God, but rather the apostates (Praem 162, cf. Spec Leg 1.344), who forget the teachings transmitted from the Fathers (Praem 162), who for themselves choose blindness instead of keen seeing (they are thus specifically described in Spec Leg 1.54). God bestowed the seeing of God on the Jews in general, the Jews as the people of salvation.[73] "For the nation is called in the Hebrew tongue Israel, which, being interpreted, is, 'He who sees God.'" (Abr 57; *PLCL* 6.33; on this passage see above). It is simply the people to whom the revelation of God has been accorded, the revelation of the "one God who has taken all members of the nation for His portion" (Spec Leg 4.159; *PLCL* 8.107). The people as a whole, with the

---

[72] In contrast with the knowing of God from creation (cf. above, pp. 34–35), the "great mysteries" spoken of in Leg All 3.100–102 are the knowledge received from God (the creator). Accordingly Abr 122 declares that he who is yet "unable to perceive the Existent alone by Itself" (God), knows only "the minor rites" [*PLCL* 6.65]. Through Moses (by means of the Torah) one is initiated into the "great mysteries" (Cher 49). Even he who is least is initiated into the great mysteries by the "maker of all . . . and King of kings (2 Macc 13:4) and God of gods (Deut 10:17)"; God honors him, in that he refuses him "with the holy oracles and statutes" (cf. Deut 10:13), and offers them to him as nourishment (Dec 41; *PLCL* 7.27). In other words, the "great mysteries" or initiations are given in the biblical revelation (which is also the basis of figurative interpretation, Cher 47f.). Accordingly Moses is the "hierophant," through whom God has given the laws of the Torah (Dec 18; that such statements have to do with the text of the Torah is shown by Vita Mos 2.40, where its translators are described as "hierophants and prophets"). On the terminology, cf. Wis 2:22: "mysteries of God" here are nothing other than the Jewish teaching regarding the reward of the "righteous" in the hereafter. In 6:22 "Solomon" promises instruction in the secrets of truth. Later Clement of Alexandria (*Protrepticus* 120.1f.) lavishes expressions from the heathen mysteries on Christianity as the truly holy mysteries.

[73] Cf. Antonie Wlosok, *Laktanz und die philosophische Gnosis* (Abhandlungen der Heidelberger Akademie der Wissenschaften, Phil.-hist. Kl., 1960, 2; Heidelberg: Winter, 1960) 102: "Die Gleichsetzung der frommen Judenschaft mit den Gottschauenden ist für Philo selbstverständlich. Er kann, wenn von Israel die Rede ist, unvermittelt in die Wirform übertragen." ["The identification of pious Jewry with those who see God is taken for granted by Philo. In speaking of Israel, he can move directly into the first person plural and apply the charismatic traits of the racial ancestor to the contemporary community."] On the first person plural, see above, p. 28 on Conf 56, p. 33 on Plant 49.

exception of the apostates and those who are excluded,[74] constitute the "holy congregation" (*syllogos*, Spec Leg 1.344, 325), "the holy community" (Somn 2.184; Migr 69), "the holy company" (*taxis*) or "the company which sanctifies itself" (Spec Leg 1.114 or 1.5), "the congregation of God" (Leg All 3.81; Post 177), "the community of God" (Conf 144 on Deut 23.3).[75]

How much Philo thinks as a member of the Jewish nation is to be seen, among other evidences, in his use of the designation, "the people" (*to ethnos*), as well as in those places where the word "our" or something similar is to be supplied, as often in his absolute use of "the people." On the whole the brief designation, "the people," is suggestive in stories and reports, particularly in *Vita Mosis*, *De Decalogo*, and *De Specialibus Legibus*.[76] It should not be overlooked, as it often occurs specifically in *Ad Gaium*. It is in particular "the people," as distinguished from others (at times in *Ad Gaium* those who are oppressed), with whom Philo identifies himself—and with whom God identifies (Gai 196). In one series of passages an emphatic use is apparent throughout. Here Philo is able formally to distinguish "the people" from humanity in general (Spec Leg 2.171, 188, 190). The people "has been set apart out of the whole human race as a kind of first fruits (*aparchē*) to the Maker and Father" (Spec Leg 4.180 [*PLCL* 8.121]; cf. above Fuga 42). Further see on this emphatic usage (aside from *Ad Gaium*, see above) Somn 1.167; Flacc 124 (in the prayer); Praem 169.[77]

The weight of Philo's statements concerning the people of the God-seers is not diminished by the fact that in part they are found in the context of figurative explanations of Old Testament passages.[78] It has been seen again and again that as a whole they are anchored in a sphere which encompasses the past and present of the people of God found together with the name Israel in its double sense. As is shown in a series of striking passages, Philo understands the incident at the Jabbok as an event basic to the Jewish religion. In fact, the original referral of the meaning of the name Israel to the patriarch, or to the people of God, is recognizable even in the context of Philo's allegorical interpretations.

---

[74] Most of the following passages are concerned in the first instance with exclusion from the congregation.

[75] Literally, "Godly congregation" or "Godly community"; here, as frequently elsewhere, the adjective takes the sense of the genitive, see Ebr 213 (gen.) and LXX.

[76] However, see Spec Leg 4.159.

[77] I am not aware of such use of the word *laos* by Philo. Generally speaking he uses it much less often than *ethnos*, in half of these cases in citations from the LXX, i.e. some 40 times (he takes *ethnos* from the LXX 25 times, and uses it on his own accord about 150 times).

[78] The analysis of these allegorical interpretations would be a new task.

Even where Philo speaks allegorically,[79] he still speaks of religion—that of Israel. For Philo there is no other way to the knowledge of God than that of Israel.

In accordance with a firmly fixed biblical tradition which was inherited by Philo, the name Israel designates the ancestor of the people of God. According to a younger tradition, which also was in Philo's possession, the name indicates the relationship of the bearer to God. The declaration contained in the name was carried over from the forefather to the Jewish people. Whoever says "Israel," says "seeing God." The etymology of the name Israel opens the possibility for Philo to express that which is specific of the Jewish religion in a siglum that points to the special relationship between the one God and the Jewish people. For him it attests the uniqueness of the revelation of God and with it the uniqueness of knowing, of seeing God, that it accords.

[79] "A symbol (-word) for seeing is 'Israel'" (Conf 72).

ABRAHAM THE GENERAL IN JOSEPHUS

LOUIS H. FELDMAN

Yeshiva University

It is fitting that in a volume dedicated to the memory of Samuel Sandmel some attention should be given to the depiction of the figure of Abraham in Hellenistic literature, since this was the subject of his dissertation and of his first major published work. Having already discussed the portrayal of Abraham the philosopher and scientist in Josephus,[1] the writer wishes now to focus on Josephus' presentation of Abraham as king and general.

It is not surprising that Josephus, a military man himself in the Jewish war against the Romans, should be interested in military details, and that he often adds material not found in the Biblical narrative.[2] Thus, in his summary of the Torah, Josephus (*Ant.* 4.297), obviously drawing upon personal experience, adds that the Israelites are to go to battle under a single commander, since divided control is a hindrance to prompt action. It is this skill as a general that is likewise stressed in Josephus' portrait of Moses; and one of the highest points in Josephus' narrative is his extra-Biblical account of Moses' successful invasion (*Ant.* 2.238–53) of Ethiopia as commander of the Egyptian army. Moses likewise shows his mettle as a general in organizing his army against the Amalekites (*Ant.* 3.47), in his strategy (*Ant.* 3.42) in attacking them at the outset before they were too strong, in his preparations for the battle (*Ant.* 3.50), and in his ability to lead a good retreat (*Ant.* 4.9). We see him as a general inspecting his army (*Ant.* 3.287), and we appreciate his

---

[1] "Abraham the Greek Philosopher in Josephus," *Transactions of the American Philological Association* 99 (1968) 143–56. Cf. my companion studies of Josephus' reworking of the Bible: "Hellenizations in Josephus' Account of Man's Decline," in *Religions in Antiquity. Essays in Memory of Erwin Ramsdell Goodenough*, ed. Jacob Neusner (SHR 14; Leiden: Brill, 1968) 336–53; "Hellenizations in Josephus' Version of Esther," *Transactions of the American Philological Association* 101 (1970) 143–70; and "Josephus as an Apologist to the Greco-Roman World: His Portrait of Solomon," in *Aspects of Religious Propaganda in Judaism and Early Christianity*, ed. Elizabeth Schüssler Fiorenza (Studies in Judaism and Christianity in Antiquity 2; Notre Dame: University of Notre Dame Press, 1976) 69–98.

[2] E.g., *Ant.* 3.53, 3.289, 4.90–92, 5.5, 5.28, 5.46, 5.66, 5.157, 5.161, 5.206, 6.363, 7.142, 7.236, 9.221, 10.132.

achievements all the more when we realize the obstacles that he encountered as a general in the accusations directed against him by the Israelites (*Ant.* 3.11). He is depicted (*Ant.* 2.329ff.) as a fearless leader who leads the way into the Red Sea (*Ant.* 2.339); and, in fact, the events leading up to the miracle at the Red Sea are presented in terms of preparation for a battle (*Ant.* 2.334). He is confident (*kataphronōn*) of his powers of endurance (*karteria*); and, indeed, so gifted is he as a general that Pharaoh himself is envious of him (*Ant.* 2.255). Again, Moses shows good judgment as a general in resting his troops (*Ant.* 3.61) after the victory over the Amalekites. Moreover, the aim of Raguel's advice is presented as not merely a reorganization for the administration of justice, but also as a reorganization for military purposes (*Ant.* 3.70–71). Indeed, in selecting the three most memorable qualities in which Moses proved supreme, Josephus mentions first (*Against Apion* 2.158) that he was the best of generals. Aaron and his company are joined by Raguel in singing the praises of Moses as a general (*Ant.* 3.65); and even when he ascends Mount Sinai (*Ant.* 3.78) to receive the Torah, he is referred to as a general (*stratēgon*). In fact, he is constantly mentioned as a general (*stratēgos*) and leader (*hēgemōn*) by the Israelites (e.g., *Ant.* 2.268); and even after his death, when Joshua prays after the defeat at Ai, he recalls (*Ant.* 5.39) Moses the general to whom G-d promised "ever to ensure to our army superiority in battle over our foes" (Loeb ed. 5.19). Indeed, both his fearlessness (*Ant.* 3.21) and his hardihood (*Ant.* 2.267) in approaching the site of the burning bush, whither no one had previously gone because of its sanctity, are stressed. His ability as a general is furthermore magnified by exaggerating the stature of his opponent Og (*Ant.* 4.97–98). We see him, in an almost bloodthirsty extra-Biblical addition (*Ant.* 4.88), exhorting his soldiers, rousing them to gratify (*apolauein*) their lust (*hēdonēs*) for war. In addressing his people before his death, he refers to himself (*Ant.* 4.177) as their comrade in arms (*symmachos*). And when the Israelites realize that their leader is about to die, they shed tears (*Ant.* 4.194) for their general (*stratēgou*). In summarizing Moses' career, Josephus selects two aspects in particular on which to comment (*Ant.* 4.329), his ability as a general, where he had few to equal him, and his role as a prophet, where he was, indeed, incomparable. We may remark that Josephus significantly conceived of himself as possessing both these qualities, that of military genius and that of prophet in predicting that Vespasian would become emperor. Indeed, a major motif of the *War* is that of the general (Vespasian) who becomes king, precisely the motif which Josephus stresses in his portrait of Moses.

Again, Phinehas, who in the Bible (Num 31:6) is designated as the priest anointed for the war against the Midianites, becomes in Josephus (*Ant.* 4.159) the Israelites' general (*stratēgon*). Likewise, Joshua's courage (*Ant.* 3.49) is emphasized in the enumeration of his virtues, and he is praised (*Ant.* 5.118) as stout-hearted (*eupsychos*) and greatly daring (*megalotolmos*). The prime qualities of a military leader, to judge from Josephus' additions (*Ant.* 5.182) concerning Keniaz, are that he be vigorous and energetic (*drastērios*) and that he be noble-hearted (*to phronēma gennaios*); and it is precisely these qualities, as we see, that Josephus stresses as having been shown by Abraham in his campaign against the Assyrians and in his loyalty and good faith toward the Sodomites. Saul, like Joshua (*Ant.* 6.347–48), is praised as stout-hearted (*eupsychos*) and greatly daring (*megalotolmos*), and his stature as a general is magnified (*Ant.* 6.129), with praise for his brilliant exploits and particularly for his timing (*Ant.* 6.79–80). David's fearlessness is especially noted (*Ant.* 6.160, 6.198, 7.390). David's greatness as a general is magnified by Josephus' build-up of his enemy, the Philistines, who had a large army and who were joined by many other warlike nations (*Ant.* 7.74) and who, even after many defeats, returned to attack David with an army three times as large (*Ant.* 7.75). Likewise, in additions to the first book of Maccabees, which he generally follows very closely, Josephus stresses Judas Maccabaeus' courage and good fortune, the marks of a good general (*Ant.* 12.339), as well as Jonathan's courage (*Ant.* 13.195).

It was important for Josephus to stress the military excellence of his Biblical heroes since the Jews had been reproached with cowardice by such anti-Semites as Apollonius Molon (*ap. Against Apion* 2.148). Josephus answers such charges by citing the evidence of Choerilus (*Against Apion* 1.172–74) that the Jews had participated in the expedition of Xerxes and that of Hecataeus (*Against Apion* 1.200–204) that they had participated in the campaigns of Alexander and of his successors, and that one of the Jewish soldiers, a certain Mosollamus, was the best of bowmen, whether Greek or barbarian. Finally, he proudly points (*Against Apion* 2.49–52) to the fact that Ptolemy Philometor and his consort Cleopatra had entrusted their army to the command of the Jewish generals, Onias and Dositheus, who had proved loyal to the throne.

With this background to illustrate the importance that Josephus assigns to military qualities, we can better understand his motives in reinterpreting the character of Abraham in a similar vein. Josephus quotes Nicolaus of Damascus[3] as stating that Abraham was an invader

---

[3] Ben Zion Wacholder's theory, in his *Nicolaus of Damascus* (University of California Publications in History 75; Berkeley: University of California Press, 1962), that Nicolaus was Josephus' source not only for his account of Herod but also for the books of the *Antiquities* which parallel the Bible, rests chiefly on the four citations from Nicolaus (*Ant.* 1.94–95, 1.108, 1.159–60, 7.101–3) in these early books. But it seems highly questionable to erect such a theory on the basis of so few and such short fragments. Moreover, one may well wonder how a non-Jew could have been acquainted with the numerous midrashim which Josephus has incorporated in his history. And finally it would seem remarkable that the Byzantine excerpters, who are usually interested in Jewish matters and who are our

(*epēlys*) who had come from Chaldaea with an army and who had reigned in Damascus (*Ant.* 1.159), where his fame was still celebrated (*Ant.* 1.160) in Nicolaus' own day and where a village was pointed out named "Abram's abode" after him. Another non-Jew, the somewhat earlier Augustan historian Trogus Pompeius (*ap.* Justin, *Epitome* 36.2), likewise mentions an Abrahames as a king of Damascus. Philo (*Virt* 216), on the other hand, interprets allegorically the passage (Gen 23:6) in which Abraham is referred to as a prince, and comments that he is so designated because he possessed a kingly soul. The rabbis, to be sure, speak of coins struck by Abraham,[4] but their emphasis is hardly on Abraham the king; and, as Ginzberg[5] remarks, they note that scholars are called kings and stress Abraham's knowledge of the Torah even before its revelation.

As one who himself practiced the military art in Galilee, Josephus was much interested in military details. Thus we read (*Ant.* 1.172), in an extra-Biblical remark, that the military formation adopted by the Assyrians against the five kings of Sodom was to divide their army into four contingents, with one general in command of each. Again, we learn (*Ant.* 1.175), in another extra-Biblical detail, that the battle between the Assyrians and the Sodomites was a stubborn (*karteras*) contest. All of this leads up to the prowess in battle shown by Abraham. In a series of additions to the Biblical narrative, we are told (*Ant.* 1.177) that Abraham determined to help the Sodomites without delay, that he set out in haste and fell upon the Assyrians[6] on the fifth night in an attack in which he caught the enemy by surprise before they had time to arm. Then we are given the vivid details of his slaughter of the enemy: some he slew while they were still asleep, while he put to flight others who were not yet asleep but who were incapacitated by drunkenness.[7] The Bible (Gen 14:14) does not speak of the time and circumstances of the attack and says merely (Gen 14:15) that he continued his pursuit of the enemy, after night had fallen, with divided forces.[8]

---

chief source of fragments of Nicolaus, should have neglected to include a single fragment dealing with the Biblical period. Such a fragment as the one above about Abraham quoted by Josephus might have been included by Nicolaus as a passing reference in his account of the kings of Damascus, his native city, in which he took such pride.

[4] *Baba Kamma* 97b and GenR 12.11. See Louis Ginzberg, *The Legends of the Jews*, 5 (Philadelphia: Jewish Publication Society of America, 1925) 216, n. 46.

[5] Ginzberg, *ibid.*

[6] *Genesis Apocryphon*, col. 22, adds that Abraham surrounded the Assyrians on all four sides.

[7] In his description of David's surprise attack on the Amalekites and of his massacre of them, Josephus similarly adds (*Ant.* 6.363) that he fell upon some who, under the influence of strong drink, were plunged in sleep.

[8] Pseudo-Eupolemus (724 F 1, 4), as Wacholder (above, n. 3) 105, has noted, adds to the Biblical comment by reporting that Abraham captured the wives and children of the

Philo (*Abr* 233) says that Abraham attacked the Assyrians at night and, in a detail much like that of Josephus, adds that this was after the enemy had eaten and were preparing to go to sleep—presumably the best time to attack an enemy. Some were slain in their beds, while others who attempted to resist were similarly killed. To be sure, as Professor Sandmel[9] has commented, Philo does not speak of the drunkenness of the Assyrians or of those who flee, and, above all, Philo insists that Abraham trusted not in his small force but in G-d, whereas for Josephus it is a personal triumph of generalship by Abraham himself.

The rabbis are utterly divergent from this picture, for they speak (*Sanhedrin* 96a) of an angel named Night attacking the enemy, thus detracting from the picture of Abraham the general. Indeed, they stress the miraculous side of this whole episode, by noting that Abraham himself was actually a giant,[10] that the victorious battle with the kings took place on the fifteenth of Nisan (the night reserved for such miracles),[11] that all the weapons thrown at Abraham miraculously proved fruitless,[12] that the planet Jupiter made the night bright for him,[13] and that the 318 men who, according to the Bible (Gen 14:14), assisted him really consisted of his servant Eliezer alone, the numerical value of the letters of whose name adds up to 318.[14] Moreover, where Josephus' picture of Abraham is of one unafraid of blood and, in fact, ready to slay the enemy in their beds, the rabbis[15] depict Abraham as in deep anguish that he had violated the prohibition against the shedding of men's blood; and it is consequently necessary for the rabbis[16] to have G-d soothe Abraham's conscience in this matter. To them, in brief, Abraham's victory is really a victory for G-d, with the emphasis on the supernatural help that he had received. Josephus looks upon it as a human victory of a masterful general and sees in it lessons for the student of military science; Abraham's success, he says (*Ant.* 1.178), proves that military victory depends not on numbers (*plēthei*) and multitude of hands (*polycheiria*) but on the zeal (*prothymia*, "eagerness") and mettle (*gennaion*, "nobility, excellence") of the combatants.

Armenians (rather than the Assyrians), which aggrandizes further the picture of Abraham the general by implying that he invaded Armenia.

[9] Samuel Sandmel, *Philo's Place in Judaism: A Study of Conceptions of Abraham in Jewish Literature* (Cincinnati: Hebrew Union College, 1950) 64, n. 253.

[10] *Midrash Tanḥuma* B 1 (pp. 73–74, ed. Buber) and parallels cited by Ginzberg (above, n. 4) 225, n. 97.

[11] *Pirke d'Rabbi Eliezer* 17.

[12] GenR 42.3; *Midrash Tehillim* 110 (p. 466, ed. Buber).

[13] GenR 42.3 and parallels cited by Ginzberg (above, n. 4) 225, n. 98.

[14] *Midrash Tanḥuma* B 1 (p. 73, ed. Buber) and parallels cited by Ginzberg (above, n. 4) 224, n. 93.

[15] *Midrash Tanḥuma* B 1 (pp. 75–76, ed. Buber) and *Midrash Tanḥuma Lekh Lekha* 15.

[16] GenR 44.4–5.

There is further aggrandizement of Abraham in the fact that he is extolled by Melchizedek, the king of Salem (*Ant.* 1.181), upon his return from the military campaign against the Assyrians. Melchizedek hospitably entertains (*echorēgēse*—"furnish abundantly with a thing," used particularly of defraying the cost of bringing out a chorus) Abraham's army, providing abundantly for all their needs.[17] Later, to be sure, when, according to Josephus' addition to the Biblical narrative, G-d appears to Amram, who is to be the father of Moses, in a dream (*Ant.* 2.214), it is G-d's help to Abraham in this campaign that is recalled, though even there Josephus recalls all the prowess that Abraham displayed (*ēndragathēse*—"behave in a manly, upright fashion") in war. And again, in the war against the Romans, Josephus (*War* 5.380), urging the Jews to surrender by arguing that they were warring not against the Romans alone but also against G-d, cites the historical precedent of Abraham, who did not avenge himself on Pharaoh in connection with the abduction of Sarah, since he could not do so without G-d's help; but there, too, Josephus speaks of Abraham as being in command of 318 officers, each with a boundless army (*dynamin*).[18] In any case, in the main body of Josephus' presentaton of Abraham, the emphasis is on his own military qualities.

This stress on Abraham the general is continued in a remarkable addition to the Biblical narrative (*Ant.* 1.239), where we are informed that Abraham's tradition of generalship was continued by his grandson by Keturah, Eophren, who conquered Libya, and that his grandsons who settled there named the land Africa after him. Josephus then (*Ant.* 1.240–41) quotes the non-Jewish writer Alexander Polyhistor, who reports that, according to Cleodemus the prophet, also called Malchus, two of Abraham's sons by Keturah joined Heracles in his campaign against Libya and Antaeus, the giant son of Earth, and that Heracles actually married the daughter of one of them, who became the ancestor of the barbarians called Sophakes.[19]

---

[17] The relationship between Abraham and Melchizedek is hardly business-like, as Wacholder (above, n. 3) 106 would have us believe, in contrast with the relationship depicted in pseudo-Eupolemus. Melchizedek is the perfect host, giving an abundant feast and praising his guest; and Abraham, in turn, is the perfect guest, reciprocating with a gift of his own.

[18] Niese's index takes this to mean wealth, but more likely it refers to troops for war, and is so taken by Henry St. John Thackeray and Ralph Marcus, *A Lexicon to Josephus* (Paris: Geuthner, 1955) s.v. δύναμις, (6)(b). Karl Heinrich Rengstorf, *A Complete Concordance to Flavius Josephus*, 1 (Leiden: Brill, 1973), s.v., does not indicate the specific meaning in this passage.

[19] Perhaps there is some connection between this and the statement in 1 Macc 12:10, 20 and 14:20 and 2 Macc 5:9, and *Ant.* 12.226 (the letter of Areios, the Spartan king, to Onias), that the Spartans were regarded as descended from Abraham. Similarly, in the decree of the people of Perganum cited by Josephus (*Ant.* 14.255), there is mention that in the time of

Josephus' account of Abraham is to be understood in the light of his over-all aim in writing the *Antiquities*. It is in the hope that the whole Greek-speaking world will find it worthy of attention that he composed this work, as he himself (*Ant.* 1.5) says. Josephus' paraphrase of the Bible mirrors the defense against anti-Semitism to which Josephus found it necessary to devote his treatise *Against Apion*. If the Jews were accused of being unphilosophical or plagiarists or cowards, Josephus sought to correct the picture by emphasizing, as I have tried to show elsewhere,[20] that Abraham was a logician before the Greeks and a scientist from whom even the Egyptians learned and, as I have attempted to demonstrate here, a brave and resourceful general.

Abraham the ancestors of the Pergamenes were friends of the Hebrews. The only hint in Midrashic literature connecting Abraham with the Greeks is the statement (*Yalkut Reubeni* Gen. 26.2.36c) that Keturah was the daughter of Japheth, the traditional ancestor of the Greeks (perhaps to be identified with Iapetos, the father of Prometheus?). See Jacob Freudenthal, *Hellenistische Studien. Alexander Polyhistor und die von ihm erhaltenen Reste jüdischer und samaritanischer Geschichtswerke*, 1–2 (Breslau, *Jahresbericht des jüdisch-theologischen Seminars*, 1874–75) 130–36, 215. We may conjecture that this notion connecting Abraham with the Greeks may just possibly have contributed to the bracketing of the Jews and the Brahmans (Abraham would equal Brahman with a prothetic vowel) found in Megasthenes, *Indica* (*ap.* Clement of Alexandria, *Stromata* 1.15. 72.5; cf. Aristotle, *ap.* Clearchus of Soli, *De Somno, ap.* Josephus, *Against Apion* 1.179, who declares that the Jews are descended from the Indian philosophers).

[20] "Abraham the Greek Philosopher in Josephus" (above, n. 1).

THE EXEGETICAL CONTEXTS
OF PHILO'S INTERPRETATION OF CIRCUMCISION*

RICHARD D. HECHT

University of California at Santa Barbara

Samuel Sandmel's erudition covered a vast area and indeed, few of us could be said to have mastered even one or two of the many areas commanded by this one exceptional scholar. As teacher and scholar for almost four decades, he taught and published in the fields of Hebrew Bible, Hellenistic Judaism, early Christianity, and the history of Judaism. But as he taught and wrote, one concern, one passion dominated all others. Much of his work was characterized by an urgency which saw as the first priority the need to clarify and to resolve fundamental misunderstandings and misconceptions between Jews and Christians.[1] This existential concern, if it may be called that, was not absent from Sandmel's many studies of Philo. At one level, those Jews to whom Philo addressed much of his work were, according to Sandmel, the Jewish intelligentsia of Alexandria, who were infatuated with Greek thought and culture, and were similar to many Jews of the twentieth century. The similarity between the Alexandrian Jews of the first century and our century was unmistakable in Sandmel's view and he wrote, "it seems to me that I have encountered exactly such Jews in American universities as those to whom Philo is usually writing. It is a group of Jews who inherit some knowledge of Judaism, but most inexact and who are so allured by the prospects of social contacts with Gentiles that these take on not a normal relationship but appear to be the reward for an attained social status."[2] Sandmel wrote these words twenty-five years ago,

---

* Research for this paper was in part conducted under the auspices of the Regents of the University of California Junior Faculty Fellowship (1980). The author wishes to thank Professor Valentin Nikiprowetzky of the Université de la Sorbonne Nouvelle (Paris III) for his most helpful comments and corrections to an earlier draft of this paper.

[1] *A Jewish Understanding of the New Testament* (1956; augmented edition, New York: Ktav, 1974). *The Genius of Paul: A Study in History* (New York: Farrar, Straus and Cudahy, 1958), *We Jews and You Christians: An Inquiry into Attitudes* (Philadelphia: Lippincott, 1967), *Judaism and Christian Beginnings* (New York: Oxford, 1978), *The First Christian Century in Judaism and Christianity: Certainties and Uncertainties* (New York: Oxford, 1969), and *Anti-Semitism in the New Testament?* (Philadelphia: Fortress, 1978).

[2] "Philo and His Pupils: An Imaginary Dialogue," *Judaism* 4 (1955) 50.

but the dilemmas of particularism and assimilation are still very much a part of our time. At this level, the concerns of Sandmel the scholar overlapped the urgency and pedagogic interests which motivated much of Philo's work.

At a second and equally important level, the position of Philo in the most formative period of western thought dictated for Sandmel the need to understand him. His *Philo of Alexandria: An Introduction* attempted to outline a number of critical issues in Philonic studies and in so doing he hoped to present an honest review of what could be ascertained not only of Philo the man, but also various scholarly positions taken toward the Philonic corpus. Throughout this last major contribution, Sandmel underscored the importance of Philo for both Judaism and Christianity. He concluded his chapter on "Philo and Christianity" by quoting Henry Chadwick that "the history of Christian philosophy begins not with a Christian, but with a Jew, Philo of Alexandria . . . Philo's statements about the Logos were to have a notable future when adopted to the uses of Christian doctrine."[3] In reference to the achievement of Philo, Sandmel wrote, "the main accomplishment in Philo must stand out: he has blended *physis* and Torah so thoroughly that in his thought they are inextricably bound together."[4] Yet, Philo is more important than simply integrating the Greek concept of nature, with all the shades of meaning given to *physis* from Homer to the Stoa, and the specific idea of Torah. Indeed, we might extend in some small way Sandmel's thinking on the importance of Philo for Judaism by making a few simple observations, all the while paying due heed to his precautionary words: "Philo reflects Hellenized Judaism, but at the same time he is in many ways unique within the entity we can call Hellenistic Judaism. He is almost as remote from the Hellenistic Judaism of the Greco-Jewish writers whom we know from the fragments in Eusebius as he is from the Judaism of Midrash and Talmud. It is not wrong to regard Philo as representing a marginal *viewpoint*. But I have seen no evidence that Philo speaks for a segment of Jewry large enough to be called a *marginal Judaism*."[5] It may well be that Philo represents a "marginal viewpoint," but in sum total, the corpus of his work is the most extensive document of Hellenistic Judaism. As such, the corpus documents the first real, historic experience of Jewish life in what some commentators of our century would call the "open society." Certainly, open in Alexandrian society did not mean open and unlimited social mobility for this was one of the most hotly contested issues in the city during Philo's life and immediately after. Here, I use "open society" to mean that for the first time, distinctively Jewish values, ideas and concerns existed alongside and in competition with very

[3] *Philo of Alexandria: An Introduction* (New York and Oxford: Oxford, 1979) 163.
[4] Ibid. 124.
[5] Ibid. 147.

different values, ideas and concerns. There were of course very real dangers in this new situation; articulate critiques and evaluations of all ideas, values and concerns were made within this situation, and each group found itself necessarily in competition with other groups for civic rights, economic power and cultural legitimation. The evidence suggests that it was a period of immense ambition and as such, is similar to other great periods of Jewish enlightenment. Philo's Alexandria may have been very distinct from other periods of enlightenment in Jewish history. However, in one regard it is marked by one of the central concerns of the Golden Age of Spanish Jewry and the Haskalah—the examination of the entire content of culture and religion through an external system of value and thought. Philo's achievement and indeed his importance is that he documents this first Jewish confrontation with other intellectual horizons and attests to a variety of ways in which one external system of value and thought, completely integrated into his own thought at all levels, could be used to explicate that which was seemingly distinct and particularistic.

I. De Specialibus Legibus *in the History of Philonic Studies*

Central in Philo's examination of the content of his tradition is the four part treatise *De Specialibus Legibus*. Philo considered this treatise to be the focus of his exposition of the Law, in which following the pattern established in *De Decalogo*, he attempted to discuss all the specific injunctions and prohibitions of Mosaic legislation under the various commandments of the Decalogue. Émile Bréhier noted that within the treatises which he and Massebieau described as the Exposition of the Law, there was a parallelism between the treatises on the Patriarchs, *De Decalogo* and *De Specialibus Legibus*. He wrote that

> Les biographies édifiantes degagées . . . présentent un plan assez net. Bien que Philon y suive la chronologie des événements racontés par la Genèse, il fait correspondre chaque groupe successif de faits à une vertu particulière. On sait que, dans l'exposition des lois écrites, il groupe toutes les lois de Moïse en classes, dont chacune correspond à un précepte du Décalogue. Ces préceptes eux-mêmes commandent les différentes vertus, les cinq premiers la piété, et les cinq derniers les devoirs envers les hommes ou la justice. Ces deux vertus sont en somme les principales et parmi les nombreuses classifications, c'est elle qui revient le plus souvent chez Philon. Or, dans ses *Vies*, Philon, tout en conservant l'ordre chronologique, cherche un moyen de grouper les événements de la même façon qu'il groupe les lois dans les *Lois spéciales*.[6]

Bréhier's observation on the parallelism between Philo's treatment of the lives of the Patriarchs and his classification of the individual laws only

---

[6] *Les Idées philosophiques et religieuses de Philon d'Alexandrie* (1908; 3rd edition, Paris: Vrin, 1950) 27–28.

underscores the importance of *De Specialibus Legibus* within the corpus. Yet, as important as this treatise is within the corpus, it has not received the attention it merits. In some cases, this treatise has fallen prey to parochial interpretations which often creep into the study of religion. Goodenough remarked in his description of *De Specialibus Legibus* that "to many Jews these books *On the Special Laws* will be the most interesting in Philo, for here he is more concerned with Jewish law than in any other treatises. But to gentiles these books are quite slow reading."[7]

Valentin Nikiprowetzky has argued that in the history of Philonic studies two perspectives have dominated much of the research. These perspectives arise from Philo's own statements that he was a "disciple of Moses",[8] but from his youth had a thorough and authentic Greek education.[9] Nikiprowetzky describes these perspectives as "Philo Alexandrinus" and "Philo Judaeus," the former referring to Philo's literary personality being within the domain of Hellenistic thought and culture, and the latter, to Philo's essential Jewishness covered only by a thin veneer of Hellenic thought.[10] *De Specialibus Legibus* has consistently been seen as essential to resolution of the seeming contradiction posed by these perspectives. The attempt to demonstrate that Philo's thought is essentially Jewish extends back to his rediscovery by Jews in the Italian Renaissance.[11] In the nineteenth century, Philo and what was known of the varieties of Hellenistic Judaism were utilized to support both the claims of a scientific investigation of the Jewish past within the *Wissenschaft des Judenthums* and the goals of the classical Reformers. So, for example, to justify the translation of the Hebrew Bible into German, the Reformers mustered the examples of Philo's use of Greek and the LXX against the critiques of traditionalists that translation would inevitably lead to assimilation.[12] The resolution of the contradiction between the perspectives crystallizes in the attempt to reduce and minimize the differences between Philo and the rabbinic tradition. At one level, this effort

---

[7] Erwin R. Goodenough, *An Introduction to Philo Judaeus* (London and New Haven: Yale, 1940) 49.

[8] Quod Det 86, Heres 81 and Spec Leg 1.345.

[9] Cong 74–76.

[10] Valentin Nikiprowetzky, *Le Commentaire de l'Écriture chez Philon d'Alexandrie* (Leiden: Brill, 1977) 11–49.

[11] See Ralph Marcus, "A 16th Century Hebrew Critique of Philo," *HUCA* 21 (1948) 29–71, for a classic study of Philonic materials in Azariah de Rossi's *Meor Enayim* (first published in Mantua in 1573 and 1574). Samuel Posnanski, "Philo dans l'ancienne littérature judéo-arabe," *REJ* 50 (1905) 10–31, argued that Oriental Jews, such as Saadia, Benjamin al-Nahawendi and David ben Merwan in the 9th and 10th centuries, knew some of Philo through a Christian Syriac translation.

[12] See the comments of Abraham Adler (1813–1856) at the Second Rabbinical Conference (1845) on the use of the vernacular and Hebrew in the synagogue; W. Gunther Plaut, *The Rise of Reform Judaism* (New York: World Union for Progressive Judaism, 1963) 162–65.

introduces the question of whether or not Philo knew Hebrew and could use Hebrew texts. The evidence against the argument that Philo knew Hebrew and used the Hebrew Bible has now seemingly reached overwhelming proportion.[13] At a more important level, this effort introduces the issue of halakhic similarity between Philo and the Rabbis. Bernard Ritter introduced this question into scholarship in 1879 with his *Philo und die Halacha*,[14] but it was Samuel Belkin's work in this century which focused the question in its sharpest relief. Belkin stated, in perhaps one of his most famous passages, that Philo was an extension of Pharisaic Judaism in Alexandria.[15] Wolfson argued, of course, that Philo is the very pivot of western philosophy and also, a traditional Pharisaic Jew. Wolfson understood that both the Alexandrian and Palestinian Jewish communities were products of the Scribes, and the Jews who established themselves at the forefront of the Alexandrian intellectual community brought with them more than their baggage. They brought with them the oral tradition, inherited from the Scribes, which would later become identified with the central Pharisaic exegetical principles. The peculiarities of the Alexandrian Jews, which made them and their traditions unlike the Jewish traditions of Palestine, were only superficial and not substantive. An example of the similarity and overlap between the two communities was Philo's use of the technical terminology later identified with rabbinic Judaism such as *zētēsis*, which Wolfson believed to be a literal translation of the Hebrew *midrash*,[16] or the expression *agraphos nomos*, which he believed to be equivalent to the rabbinic Oral Law.[17] In reference to these discussions,

---

13 Samuel Sandmel, "Philo's Knowledge of Hebrew," SP 5 (1978) 107–12.

14 Ritter's study was in part based on Zacharias Frankel's *Ueber den Einfluss der Palästinensischen Exegese auf die Alexandrinische Hermeneutik* (1851) and *Ueber Palästinensische und Alexandrinische Schriftforschung* (1854).

15 *Philo and the Oral Law: The Philonic Interpretation of Biblical Law in Relation to the Palestinian Halakah* (Cambridge: Harvard, 1940) 27.

16 *Philo: Foundations of Religious Philosophy in Judaism, Christianity and Islam* (Cambridge: Harvard, 1947) 1.193.

17 Ibid. 1.188. The expression ἄγραφος νόμος occurs in Spec Leg 4.149–50 where Philo states "customs are unwritten laws, the decisions approved by men of old, not inscribed on monuments nor on leaves of paper which the moth destroys, but on the souls of those who are partners in the same citizenship" and then continues by stating that one who observes these unwritten laws should be praised for his obedience is freely willed. Sandmel, *Philo's Place in Judaism: A Study of Conceptions of Abraham in Jewish Literature* (2d ed., New York: Ktav, 1971) 8, argued against this parallelism and stated it was "for Wolfson another link in the chain binding Philo to the rabbinic halaka. But let anyone examine Aristotle's *Rhetoric* 1.14.7 and he will see that Philo is quoting that passage almost verbatim, and that the parallelism is not with the rabbis but with Aristotle. Or, more precisely, Aristotelianism is Philo's source, not rabbinic literature." Valentin Nikiprowetzky, *Le Commentaire*, 43–44, also questions this parallelism and suggests that in some cases where Philo used the expression ἄγραφος νόμος, especially Migr 89–90, the allusion may not be to the rabbinic Oral Law, but other Jewish traditions according to which many Mosaic

Sandmel stated, "there are overlaps in halacha between Philo and the Rabbis. Communication between Alexandria and Palestine need not be denied. Overlaps, however do not prove a dependency of Philo on the Rabbis, for often the overlap is between Philo and a Rabbi who flourished long after Philo. Independent, parallel developments seem the better explanation than that of major dependency in either direction."[18] The thrust of these efforts is always to reduce the difference between Philo and the "normative" rabbinic tradition. But, this narrowing of the gap between heterodoxy and orthodoxy, is not confined to matters of *halakhah*. In the nineteenth century, there were other efforts to demonstrate that Philo's ideas or his philosophic system were compatible with other great figures in the tradition.[19] In this century, there has been an effort to reduce dissimilarity by demonstrating that Philo made a substantial contribution to the mystical tradition within Judaism.[20]

A far more critical question is the place of *De Specialibus Legibus* in these efforts to minimize conflicts between Philo and the rabbinic tradition. Three positions have been taken in the evaluation of this treatise. First, *De Specialibus Legibus* contains or mirrors the judicial reflections of Jewish courts or tribunals within Roman Egypt. Second, *De Specialibus Legibus* reflects Greco-Roman legal traditions and any similarities between its specific interpretations and the interpretations of the rabbis is due in great part to similarities between Greco-Roman and rabbinic jurisprudence. Third, *De Specialibus Legibus* is essentially the *halakhah* of Alexandrian Jewry and is comparable to contemporary *halakhah* in Palestine. The first position that the *De Specialibus Legibus* reflects the judicial activity of Jewish courts in Roman Egypt is, of course, one of Goodenough's most controversial arguments advanced in *The Jurisprudence of the Jewish Courts in Egypt: Legal Administration by the Jews under the Early Roman Empire as described by Philo Judaeus* (1929) and one which has not won wide agreement. Already in this early volume, Goodenough had begun to consider whether the differences between Alexandrian Jews and

---

institutions were founded by the Patriarchs, and then abandoned before being reformulated by Moses. Nikiprowetzky cites the Book of Jubilees' interpretation of Noah's institution of Sukkot, Abraham's institution of circumcision, and the law of incest established after Reuben's incestuous relationship with Billah. It might also be argued that the term ἔθος, which is the subject of the ἄγραφος νόμος in Spec Leg 4.149–50 is too general to be parallel to the Hebrew *minhāg*.

[18] *Philo of Alexandria*, 133–34.

[19] Samson Weisse, *Philon von Alexandrien und Moses Maimonides* (Halle: H. Neubürger, 1884).

[20] For example, Samuel Belkin, "The Sources of Midrash ha-Ne'elam in the Ancient Alexandrian Midrashim," *Sura* 3 (1958) 25–92 (Hebrew) is an ingenious piece of scholarship, but R. J. Zwi Werblowsky, "Philo and the Zohar," *Journal of Jewish Studies* 10 (1959) 25–44, 113–35, offers a strong critique of efforts to trace direct lines from Philo to the *Zohar*.

Palestinian Jews might represent controversies between Sadducees and Pharisees.[21] Central in Goodenough's argument is the famous passage in Spec Leg 3.1–6 where Philo bemoans the situation he now finds himself in, no longer having the leisure for philosophy as he once had but being consumed by "civil cares" which poured in upon him from all sides. The general thrust of Goodenough's argument from this passage suggests that Philo was not a recluse, pursuing philosophy to the exclusion of all else. The passage seemingly supports the argument marshalled by Schwartz that Philo entered into political debates and judicial discussions as a young man.[22] However, the specific identification of these "civil cares" either with Goodenough's Jewish courts or only with the civil turmoil in Alexandria and the subsequent embassy to Caligula remains unproven.

While Goodenough's argument has not won great support among the specialists, the second and third interpretations of *De Specialibus Legibus* have proven to be more durable and more resilient to critique. The second position argues that *De Specialibus Legibus* reflects Greco-Roman legal traditions and was most forcefully presented in Isaak Heinemann's *Philons griechische und jüdische Bildung: Kulturvergleichende Untersuchungen zu Philons Darstellung der jüdischen Gesetze* (1932). Here, Heinemann took up *De Specialibus Legibus* from two vantage points, the history of classical philosophy and the history of Greco-Roman jurisprudence. His argument was that any similarities between Philo and the Rabbis in matters of legal interpretation can be explained either as a similar deduction from the biblical text or that both drew upon a common legal interpretation present in the larger Greco-Roman legal tradition. Further, Philo cannot be described as presenting *halakhah* in Heinemann's opinion for there does not seem to be a rationale for what Philo includes or excludes from his commentary and for what legal issues Philo chooses to treat allegorically or literally. But for Heinemann, *De Specialibus Legibus* is also a philosophical text, reflecting, albeit in different ways, the philosophical concerns of Philo in other treatises of the corpus. The third position that *De Specialibus*

---

[21] Erwin R. Goodenough, *An Introduction to Philo Judaeus* (Oxford: 1962) 88–89, states that Philo was closer to the Sadducees "but that was a suggestion which many rabbinists have not received. While specialists are debating this matter, we may well continue trying to understand Philo from his own writings." Despite Goodenough's efforts to place Philo among the Sadducees or "closer" to them and not among the Pharisees, his work made Philo understandable to us by situating him in some familiar category. On Goodenough's identification of Philo with the Sadducees, see Nikiprowetzky, *Le Commentaire*, 45–58, n. 17.

[22] Jacques Schwartz, "L'Egypte de Philon," *Philon d'Alexandrie. Lyon 11–15 Septembre 1966* (Paris: Centre Nationale de la Recherche Scientifique, 1967) 35–44. Schwartz suggests that Philo became active in the discussion of the *"question juive"* when the Alexandrian *ethnarch* was replaced by a *gerousia*, sometime between the years 11–13 C.E. This would mean that Philo was in his late twenties when he became active in the political dimensions of Jewish life in Alexandria.

Legibus reflects the *halakhah* of Alexandrian Jewry is, of course, the position taken by Samuel Belkin. Belkin's *Philo and the Oral Law: The Philonic Interpretation of Biblical Law in relation to the Palestinian Halakah (1940)* attempted to draw a series of parallels between what appeared to be legal interpretations in Philo and the vast corpus of rabbinic literature. Belkin argued that Philo's *halakhah* was essentially in agreement with Palestinian *halakhah*. If there were any disagreements, contradictions, or points of opposition, these could be explained and accounted for by later changes in the Palestinian traditions. Belkin based this argument upon Philo's knowing Hebrew, that he used the Hebrew text of the Bible, and that he had something far more than superficial familiarity with rabbinic hermeneutics and existing legal decisions.

We are thus confronted with three different interpretations of *De Specialibus Legibus*: (1) that it is a legal digest of the actual decisions and laws enacted by Jewish courts in Egypt (Goodenough); (2) that it is a synthesis of Greco-Roman jurisprudence and philosophy (Heinemann); (3) that it is a "code" of Jewish *halakhah* as practiced by Alexandrian Jews and is in agreement with early Palestinian *halakhah* (Belkin). Each of these interpretations is incorrect, but before advancing a counter hypothesis, there is need for a precautionary word and a brief examination of the weaknesses in each of the three existing interpretations of *De Specialibus Legibus*. The precautionary word comes in the form of Nikiprowetzky's study of the conclusion of *In Flaccum*, where Philo, beginning in paragraph 121 begins a long *Schadenfreude* at the fall of Flaccus. Both Colson and Pelletier were embarrassed by the malicious joy shown by Philo in his presentation of the misfortune of another. Colson stated that Philo "gloats over the misery of Flaccus in his fall, exile, and death, with a vindictiveness which I feel to be repulsive. While, as I have said in the preface, none of these treatises in this volume have any great value nor would probably have survived but for the high esteem given to his main work, this is the only one which those who admire the beauty and spirituality so often shown both in the Commentary and Exposition might well wish to have been left unwritten" (*LCL* 9.301). Nikiprowetzky demonstrates that the "emotional outburst" (which implies a psychological interpretation) described by both Colson and Pelletier is not that at all, but a carefully constructed presentation of the full meaning of divine justice. He concludes by pointing out "en effet, une information presque toujours inadéquate ou incomplète nous fait alors courrir le risque d'y projeter indûment une mentalité et des sentiments modernes ou anachroniques qui peuvent, parfois de façon grave, masquer la portée réelle d'un texte."[23] Indeed, Nikiprowetzky alerts us to the danger of reading our own religious

---

[23] Valentin Nikiprowetzky, "*Schadenfreude* chez Philon d'Alexandrie? Note sur *In Flaccum, 121 sq.,*" *REJ* 127 (1968) 19.

perspectives, philosophical concerns, and psychological realities into the corpus of Philo's work. While this is a simple observation and one any scholar would quickly agree with, it is precisely because we are not critical enough with our own perspectives that we misinterpret this specific treatise of the corpus.

Each interpretation of *De Specialibus Legibus* is subject to critique. Belkin's interpretation that *De Specialibus Legibus* is a "code" of *halakhah* depends upon a precise demonstration that Philo's supposed *halakhah* is in conformity with rabbinic decisions of a contemporary period. Belkin deduced a number of parallels between Philo and the Rabbis (which I believe are due to the nature of the biblical text and not Philo's dependence on the Rabbis), but he failed to demonstrate historical continuity or conformity with the Rabbis.[24] Heinemann's observation that the absence of any rationale for what Philo includes or excludes from his commentary or for what laws he treats literally and those he renders allegorically is a strong critique of both Belkin and Goodenough's positions in the interpretation of the treatise. However, it can also be turned against Heinemann. For example, *De Specialibus Legibus* 1, with the exception of paragraphs 32–50 in which Philo interprets Ex 33:13–23, lacks the philosophical precision that can be seen in other treatises. Likewise, the omissions in what Philo treats of the biblical text speaks against understanding the treatise as a digest of Greco-Roman law. Indeed, the omissions within specific biblical texts are as important in understanding what Philo was about in his Exposition of the Law and Allegorical Commentary as what he includes from the biblical text.[25] Further, there are blocks of material or specific issues which appear in all three genres of the corpus which cannot be satisfactorily accounted for within the corpus itself, not by reference to rabbinic traditions, nor by reference to the judicial traditions of the Greco-Roman world. An example is Philo's interpretation of the narrative of Nadab and Abihu in Lev 10:1–6. Although Philo does not mention this narrative in *De Specialibus Legibus*,[26] it indicates that elements within the corpus (and perhaps the corpus itself) must be understood within two exegetical contexts—one internal and related to the various themes *within* the corpus,

---

[24] In an earlier paper, "Preliminary Issues in the Analysis of Philo's *De Specialibus Legibus*," *SP* 5 (1978) 1–55, I compared Philo's treatment of the Red Heifer (Spec Leg 1.257–71) with the earliest strata of rabbinic discussion in *m. Parah* and *Sifre*. This comparison suggested that Philo's treatment of Numbers 19 was contradictory to rabbinic *halakhah* at a contemporary period (26–39).

[25] In "Patterns of Exegesis in Philo's Interpretation of Leviticus," *SP* 6 (1979) 77–155, I attempted to develop a method by which we might understand something of the manner in which Philo treated Leviticus across the three genres of the corpus. This study suggested that Philo's systematic omission of the details of specific sacrifices as presented in LXX (e.g., ὀσμὴ εὐωδίας) represents a component within his exegesis, which I described as an "anti-anthropomorphic interpretation by exclusion."

[26] See Som 2.67, 186, Leg All 2.57–58, Fuga 59, Heres 309 and Vita Mos 2.158.

and the other external, being directly related to specific issues *within* the intellectual, social and cultural environment of the first century. Philo's treatment of Nadab and Abihu makes them paradigms for the zealous pursuit of God. This interpretation is unlike any other treatment of this narrative in antiquity where the two sons of Aaron are consistently portrayed as being destroyed by fire as punishment for their revolt against the authority of God and Moses. Within the corpus and at the internal level of interpretation, Philo's treatment of the narrative reflects a common Middle-Platonic motif in which the body is viewed negatively. At the external level, Philo's interpretation and inversion of the narrative represents a polemic against "counter-histories" of Israel, in which revolts against Moses might have been construed as further examples of Moses' cruel and oppressive leadership and the desire among the Israelites to return to their original religious tradition, that of the Egyptians.[27] A counter argument might be formulated by considering the revolt of Korach from Num 16. Philo treats Korach and his followers as individuals not content with their position as gate-keepers and who overturned proper order in their aspirations to be kings (Fug 145–46), as the opposite of the man of gradual improvement (Som 2:234–37), as examples of blind presumptuousness (Praem 74–78), as examples of the confusion or inversion of proper order (Conf 50), the inroads of worse against the better (Quis Her 201–2), and the punishment of puffed up pride, which ultimately proves Moses' authority as prophet (Mos 2.257–89). In each case, Philo understands the revolt of Korach to be a revolt, although he interprets it to further explicate the greatness of Moses. This argument does not negate the above interpretation of the Nadab and Abihu narrative, for the expression *pyr allotrion*, "alien fire" (Lev 10:1), provides Philo with the opportunity of rendering Nadab and Abihu as having a zeal alien to the world and with the opportunity for inversion of the narrative's simple meaning. The biblical text did not provide a similar opportunity in the case of Korach, or Philo retained the original meaning of Num 16 in order to explicate more comprehensive issues (i.e., the perfection of Moses as prophet or Aaron as the man of gradual improvement).

Heinemann's effort to situate *De Specialibus Legibus* in the context of the larger Greco-Roman world was correct, although limiting it to a judicial and philosophical context may not have accurately rendered Philo's intention in this treatise. The overlaps with legal and philosophical issues only support a more comprehensive and encompassing purpose. The hypothesis which should be brought forward against the interpretations of Goodenough, Heinemann and Belkin is that *De Specialibus Legibus* is an analogy. As an apologetic text, it is not a "code" of *halakhah*, nor a digest of the laws enacted by Jewish courts, nor a judicial and philosophic text. A

---

[27] "Patterns of Exegesis," 115–28.

number of commentators have suggested that *De Specialibus Legibus* was intended for a Greco-Roman audience, the learned friends of the Jews as Goodenough suggested, and as having apologetic tendencies.[28] But, to the best of my knowledge, I am unfamiliar with any attempt to understand *De Specialibus Legibus* as an apologetic work from beginning to end. As an apologetic text, this treatise is similar to the genre of *ṭaʿamē hammiṣwôt*, "the rationale of the commandments." In the ancient world, the Middle Ages, and modern world, this literature attempted to explain the reasons for specific commandments, the division of the commandments into negative and positive commandments, the status of the commandments directly related to Temple worship after its destruction, the nature of the commandments before the theophany at Sinai, and why 613 commandments were necessary. This type of literature is almost exclusively apologetic, appearing in debates with other Jews or in disputations with Christians or Moslems. Heinemann suggested in his study of this issue that the rationale given by Hellenistic Jews for the commandments was absolutely different from the early efforts of the Rabbis. In rabbinic literature, the ratonale for the commandments is predicated upon the divine revelation of the Torah and the recognition that the primary purpose of the *miṣwôt* is the submission of the human will to the will of God. For Hellenistic Jews (and Heinemann's major examples are drawn from Philo and Josephus) the divine nature of Torah is affirmed, but because of similar ideas in the Greco-Roman world, divine revelation for a legal code was understood to be insufficient. They developed a three-fold rationale which encompassed divine revelation, but went further: (1) that the laws and the Torah are in harmony with the cosmos (this according to the rationale for law codes throughout the Hellenistic world); (2) that the commandments exercise an educative force on those who observe them; (3) that the commandments profit both the individual and society as a whole.[29] While Heinemann cites Philo for examples of this three-fold argument, he does not suggest that the intent of *De Specialibus Legibus* was to present a systematic apology for the Law. This hypothesis can be examined by consideration of Philo's treatment of circumcision.

---

[28] Bréhier, *Les Idées*, 7, argued that the apology begun in Vita Mos continues to inform other treatises, although he understood the Exposition of the Law to be directed at those Jews who reduced the Law to a simple mythological narrative (65–66). Goodenough, *An Introduction*, 33–34, understood Spec Leg to be addressed to the learned friends of the Jews. Jean Daniélou, *Philon d'Alexandrie* (Paris: Fayard, 1958) 70–71, argues that Spec Leg was intended for a non-Jewish audience during the decade of 30–40 C.E..

[29] Isaac Heinemann, *Ṭaʿamei Hammiṣvot be-Sifrut Yisrael* (Jerusalem: The Jewish Agency, 1966) 1.36–46; *La Loi dans la pensée juive*, trans. C. Touati (Paris: Albin Michel, 1962) 33–43.

II. *De Specialibus Legibus* 1.1–11

Philo begins the first book of *De Specialibus Legibus* with a brief discussion of circumcision (*peritomē*). He states that the argument, after the completion of the *deka logoi* (*De Decalogo*), dictates discussion of the special laws arranged under them. He states that "I will begin with that which is an object of ridicule among many people" (1; *PLCL* 7.101). The object of this derision is circumcision of the genital organs (*gennētikōn peritomē*) which, he admits, is practiced by other nations, most notably the Egyptians who are renowned for their populousness (*polyanthrōpotaton*), their antiquity (*archaiotaton*), and their attachment to philosophy (*philosophōtaton*) (2). The fact that great nations (*megalōn ethnōn*), like the Egyptians, practice this custom (*ethos*) should provide the detractors with reason to look for something more serious in its causes. To this, Philo adds a simple reason to consider circumcision further; thousands in each generation have undergone the operation and have suffered severe pains in multilating (*akrōtēriazousas*) their bodies and those of their nearest and dearest. Further, there are many circumstances which urge the retention and practice of a custom instituted by men of old. Philo then outlines four principal reasons (3). The first reason is that circumcision frees one from chronic inflammation of the prepuce (4). The second reason is that circumcision promotes cleanliness of the whole body which befits a priestly order. Therefore, the Egyptians, according to Philo, carry the practice to a further extreme and have the bodies of their priests shaved. This, he reasons, is because foreign substances which should be removed conceal themselves in the hair and in the foreskin (5). Thirdly, it assures the resemblance of the circumcised member to the heart. Both are intended for generation: thought (*noematōn*) being generated by the spirit (*pneuma*) in the heart and living creatures by the sexual organ. For, Philo tells us, the ancients found that the unseen and superior element to which the concepts of the mind owe their existence should resemble the visible and the apparent (6). The fourth and most important of the four principal reasons is that circumcision aids in fertility and therefore the nations which observe this practice appear most populous (7). These four reasons are the explanations given by divinely gifted men (*thespesiois andrasin*) who interpreted with great care the writings of Moses. Philo then states that he wishes to add that circumcision is a symbol for two things necessary for human well-being (8). First, circumcision represents the excision of pleasure which befuddles and confuses the mind. Since the mating of man and woman is the greatest of pleasures, the legislators (*nomothetais*) reduced the organ which ministers to such intercourse, thus making circumcision the figure or symbol of the excision of excessive pleasure (9).[30] Second, circumcision represents the banishment of conceit, for some assume that the ability to create another human being is a godlike quality. This blinds them to the real cause of all that comes into being, although they may find in their circumcised reproductive organ a corrective for this delusion (10). There are many men and women who are unable to reproduce and therefore this fatal opinion needs to be excised from the mind (11).

Philo's treatment of circumcision is striking not so much for what he says about circumcision, but for what he omits in his interpretation. There is no mention of convenant, which is central to the institution of circumcision in both M and LXX. Similarly striking is Philo's placement of the ritual at the beginning of the treatise and before he begins his discussion of the First Commandment of the Decalogue. Is it a special law? Philo seems to have thought not, for immediately after his discussion in paragraphs 1–11 he states: "We must now turn to the particular laws, taking those first with which it is well to begin, namely those the subject of which is the sole sovereignty of God" (12; *PLCL* 7.107).[31] The implication of this statement is that circumcision is a preliminary issue and once treated, Philo felt it was appropriate to begin with the First Commandment and the special laws arranged under it. If indeed *De Specialibus Legibus* was some form of halakhic text or digest of laws enacted by Jewish courts in Egypt or was intended to synthesize Greco-Roman law and philosophy as Belkin, Goodenough and Heinemann have suggested, we might expect Philo to spend some time with the details of circumcision. Indeed, Philo's discussion seems astonishingly lacking in the kinds of questions which might have been treated if the text was really what Belkin, Goodenough, and Heinemann argued it to be. Whose responsibility is it to have the child circumcised? If it is the father, what happens if the father neglects the responsibility or is absent? Does the responsibility for having the child circumcised then fall to another family member, such as the mother or an uncle, or does a third party outside of the family such as a *Bet Din*, take the responsibility? In this text Philo does not mention the eighth day, although in Quaes Gen 3.46–52 the number eight plays a significant role in his interpretation. When on the eighth day is the proper time for the circumcision? What credentials must the performers of the circumcision have and what instruments may

---

[30] Isaac Heinemann, *Philons griechische und jüdische Bildung: Kulturvergleichende Untersuchungen zu Philons Darstellung der jüdischen Gesetze* (Breslau: Marcus, 1932) 176–79, suggests that περιτομή is divided into *perittou ektomē*, "excision of excessiveness," and represents Philo's etymology of the term.

[31] Isaac Heinemann, *PCH* 2.15, perhaps offers the best translation of this passage with "Wir wenden uns nun zu den Einzelgesetzen, und zwar zuerst, wie es sich geziemen dürfte, zu denen, die Bezug auf die Alleinherrschaft (Gottes) aufgestellt wurden."

be used? What if the child is born without a foreskin or is born by
Caesarean section? Are alternate procedures called for in these cases? If
the eighth day falls on the Shabbat or a festival, do the commandments
pertinent to the Shabbat and festivals take precedence over the commandment of circumcision, or does the commandment of circumcision
take precedence over the commandments of the Shabbat and festival?
When does one begin counting for the eighth day if the child was born
during the twilight of Shabbat or a festival? Or, may the preparations
for circumcision be done on the Shabbat, if they have been previously
omitted? What if the child is ill on the eighth day and how is illness to
be ascertained and evaluated in this case?[32]

Some of the commentators have been aware of the difficulties posed
by this short section of *De Specialibus Legibus*. Goodenough was certain
that Philo did not understand circumcision under any of the commandments of the Decalogue, but the practice of circumcision was too important for him to omit altogether. Goodenough then stated,

> Philo argues that the rite should call for no ridicule, since it was
> practiced also by the Egyptians, whom he calls the most ancient, and
> populous, and philosophic of races, so far as I can recollect the only
> case in which he has a good word for a people who are generally
> with him a synonym for all that is bestial. But Philo is here defend-
> ing an actual Jewish practice, and must do so in any way he can. So
> he goes on to point out the sanitary value of circumcision, and then
> the importance of the operation in that it makes the penis resemble
> the heart, a most proper resemblance since the one generates living
> beings, the other thoughts. But most important of all its virtues in his
> opinion is the fact that he thought that circumcision promoted pro-
> lificness. These are the practical and immediate advantages of the
> rite. But it has also high symbolic value in being a gesture of con-
> tempt for merely human powers.[33]

---

[32] Philo's treatment of circumcision does not contain any of the motifs which appear in
aggadic treatments of circumcision: Abraham fears that circumcision may alienate pro-
spective proselytes (GenR 46); the circumcision removed Abraham's only blemish, and
thereafter he was perfect (GenR 46); Abraham was circumcised before the conception of
Isaac so that Isaac would issue from a pure and holy source (GenR 46); Abraham's circumcision preserved his virility, making him able to father Isaac at advanced age (GenR
46); before Abraham was circumcised his visitors were human, but after his circumcision
it was God who visited him (GenR 47); the visit in Gen 18:1ff. was God's visit to a sick
Abraham, suffering the aftereffects of his circumcision (TJI to Gen 18:1); Abraham's circumcision took place on Yom Kippur (PRE 29); Abraham's circumcision was only the
crowning achievement of a life already led in conformity with the commandments
(*Mekilta* Jethro 1). For a discussion of differences between Josephus, the Rabbis and Philo
in regard to the aggadic embellishments of circumcision see Sandmel, *Philo's Place in
Judaism*, 67–87.

[33] *The Jurisprudence of the Jewish Courts in Egypt: Legal Administration by the Jews
under the Early Roman Empire* (New Haven and London: Yale, 1929) 30–32. In his *An
Introduction to Philo Judaeus*, 206–7, he adds the following to his interpretation of

Goodenough was correct in underscoring that Philo in this passage treats the Egyptians in a way which is in sharp distinction from his other treatments of Egypt and the Egyptians. Here, Philo bluntly states that they are renowned for their populousness, their antiquity and their attachment to philosophy. This reversal of the interpretation of the Egyptians should only cause us to inquire further into his intention not only in this passage, but in the entire treatise. However, in the summary of the passage, Goodenough misunderstands Philo's argument. The first four reasons given for circumcision (4–7) are the reasons given by divinely gifted men (*thespesiois andrasin*) who have consulted the books of Moses. Philo apparently agrees with their reasonings, but his own reasons are the two things necessary for human well-being, the first of which may be dependent on the legislators mentioned in paragraph 9. Goodenough then continued and stated further,

> The passage is an excellent illustration of how Philo will resort to any frantic expedient to defend, when necessary, an actual practice of the Jews. He is not interested in the allegorical possibilities of the scriptural command, primarily, at all, but in finding by some hook or crook a rationalization of an actual custom of his people which will appeal to those who are criticizing it, or make those practicing it more comfortable in doing so. No better instance could be found to illustrate Philo's use of allegory in defense of an actual custom, in contrast with the use of allegory usually associated with Philo's name, where the motive is to obscure the original literal meaning and call attention to a teaching not otherwise found in the text. That is in the one case he is defending a group of sacred words into which he wants to put a new and appealing sense, but in the case before us he pays little attention to the form of the command, and is defending

---

Philo's discussion of circumcision: "For example, there is no trace of an initiatory rite for the Jews into the Mystery. Apprehension and experience of the deeper truth seem to have been sufficient. But for proselytes Philo changes circumcision into a sacrament, an outward sign of a mystic grace. When he explains circumcision to Gentiles in the *Exposition* he gives the traditional reasons for its practice: two reasons have to do with sanitation and a third with the fact that circumcision facilitates impregnation. The fourth is more fanciful: The rite makes the organ by which animate things are generated resemble the heart in which thoughts are engendered. These traditional and material explanations Philo characteristically keeps with respect. But to them he adds two mystic explanations. In mutilating the organ which is the source and symbol of material pleasure, circumcision becomes a symbol of that renunciation and belittlement of all pleasure which is the first step in spiritual emancipation. At the same time it pours contempt symbolically upon man's illusion of creative power, since it is the sense of independent power in man which most stands in the way of his mystic achievement. For only, Philo tells abundantly elsewhere, as man recognizes his own helplessness and unreality apart from God, his complete dependence upon God, can he hope to receive from God. That is, Philo has made circumcision into a mystic rite of abandonment of fleshly desire and confidence, as it is a rite of complete dedication to God. In the same spirit the mystic in Isis or Dionysis would have laid aside old robes and put on new ones to signify his renunciation of the old life and bodily commitments."

the practice itself. If we knew of Jewish circumcision from no other
source than this passage of Philo we should conclude that it was a
law actively enforced in Alexandrian Jewry, and from other sources
in abundance we know that such an inference would be quite correct. One could almost set it up as a criterion that the more remote
and anxious is Philo's defense of a Jewish practice the more likely
that the practice being defended was current among Jews in his
circle.

Goodenough understands Philo's interpretation of circumcision to be a
"frantic" effort to justify an existing ritual practice among Egyptian
Jews. Indeed, in Goodenough's opinion this passage is uncharacteristic of
Philo. The allegorical meanings attached to the ritual (9–11) are only
secondary and half-hearted explanations, the "hook and crook" used by
Philo to rationalize the ritual. Further, Goodenough's comment makes it
difficult to understand how Philo might have understood the relationship
between the issue of circumcision and all the rest of De Specialibus
Legibus. It would appear from what Goodenough has to say on the passage that Philo had no strategy and no real question in mind with this
passage, except that circumcision was a ritual which needed a rationale
and that those who practiced it needed some kind of support for their
practice. But this would mean a costly change of direction for Philo,
breaking the logical progression and coherence begun in De Decalogo
and continued in De Specialibus Legibus. If the matter was as Goodenough suggested, it would have been reasonable for Philo either to
place the matter of circumcision under one of the commandments of the
Decalogue or to place it in a context which would not impair the very
structure of the treatise. Lastly, Goodenough might have been correct in
suggesting that if we knew of no other document on circumcision, we
could conclude that it was a commandment enforced among Egyptian
Jewry. However, the meaning of the practice might have been quite
different from the description and meaning given to it in the other sources. In short, Goodenough recognized one of the problems suggested by
the text, namely that Philo did not consider circumcision to be a special
law, but his interpretation of Philo's intention with the passage is not
helpful. Certainly, Goodenough can give no specific reason other than
the explanation of the ritual for Philo's decision to begin the treatise with
circumcision rather than the First Commandment. It must be underscored that this would mean that Philo, in these paragraphs, has violated
his own structure of the argument, which he painstakingly attempts to
maintain throughout the treatise.

Belkin does not discuss our passage in his Philo and the Oral Law.
However, in Philo's discussion of peritomē at other places within the
corpus, Belkin attempts to demonstrate conformities between Philo's
interpretation of the ritual and that of the Rabbis. He indicates that the

LXX at Genesis 17:14 interpreted the term *nikretâh* (= *exolethreuthē-setai*) to mean that the child not circumcised on the eighth day was actually put to death. The Rabbis argued that *karet* is divine punishment and does not mean capital punishment exacted at the hand of man. Philo is in agreement with this interpretation in his argument with Alexandrian literalists who understood the text to mean human punishment (Quaes Gen 3.52). In this way, both Philo and the Rabbis mitigate against the severity of the biblical injunction.[34] Also, *peritomē* is directly related to Philo's interpretation of *prosēlytos*. Once again, Belkin attempted to show a basic conformity between Philo and the Rabbis on the issue of proselytes. He interpreted Spec Leg 1.51 (and 4.159) to mean Philo "did not require of proselytes circumcision and observance of the law, but only the belief in a monotheistic deity. He does not, however, consider them full-fledged Jews; he rather puts them in the same status with the Jews who lived in Egypt. This type of proselyte corresponds to the *ger toshab*, namely, a semi-convert who has embraced monotheism but has remained a stranger to the laws and customs of the Jews."[35] Belkin's observations are of little help with the passage from Spec Leg 1.1–11 and might lead us to think that Philo's understanding of circumcision was in large measure like that held by the Rabbis. Clearly, his comments do not aid us in understanding Philo's placement of the narrative at the beginning of the treatise; one might conclude that the problem of order or placement was unnoticed by Belkin. It is important to point out again that *diathēkē*, the LXX translation of the Hebrew *běrît* in Genesis 17, is nowhere present in Philo's treatment of circumcision.

The implicit problems presented by our text did not escape the attention of Suzanne Daniel. While she does not comment on the absence of what might be understood as *halakhah*, she does attempt to resolve the problems suggested by the placement of the passage at the beginning of the treatise and the absence of any direct reference to covenant. In regard to the placement of this material at the beginning of the treatise, she acknowledges that Philo has seemingly departed from the programmatic analysis anticipated by *De Decalogo* and which he reiterates in paragraph 1 of the treatise. However, by assigning to circumcision the two symbolic reasons (9–11), Daniel suggests, "ce qui laisse entendre qu'elle est comme un abrégé de toute la Loi, dont la fin suprême précisément est de donner à l'homme le bonheur intégral."[36] Circumcision, in her interpretation, functions as a paradigm for the acceptance of the Law. She resolves the absence of reference to *diathēkē* by stating "on peut admettre, dès lors, que le développement sur la

---

[34] *Philo and the Oral Law*, 15–17.
[35] Ibid. 47.
[36] Suzanne Daniel, *De Specialibus Legibus I–II*, PM 24.xiv.

circumcision, placé en tête du traité des *Lois Speciales*, répond en fait à
ce verset introductif, puisqu'elle symbolise précisément l'acceptation de
l'Alliance, l'appartenance au peuple élu."[37] It is possible to construe this
passage and the issue of circumcision as a paradigm for the acceptance
of the Law. The passage then becomes an introduction to the discussion
of the First Commandment and its special laws. However, it is a weak
argument to suggest that placement of circumcision at the beginning of
the treatise *implies* or symbolizes the covenant. If this were the case,
Philo would say it and might make reference to *diathēkē* in other passages where he takes up *peritomē*. He does not do this and speaks of
circumcision in isolation from covenant.

The commentators on our passage, then have not resolved the issues
implied by the text. They have not presented sufficiently the meaning of
circumcision whithin the corpus, which then leads them to misunder-
stand the argument in paragraphs 1–11. Nor have they resolved the
question of why Philo chose to begin the treatise with this issue. The
question of his strategy and his intention with this small block of material remains problematic. Both questions, the meaning of circumcision
and its placement at the beginning of *De Specialibus Legibus*, can be
resolved by considering the issue of circumcision within both the internal
and external contexts of interpretation.

III. *The Internal Exegetical Context of Circumcision*

The six reasons offered by Philo in Spec Leg 1.1–11 are of four different types. First, circumcision has a hygienic value (this corresponds to
his first reason in paragraph 4). Second, circumcision has a purificatory
value (this corresponds to his second reason in paragraph 5). Third, circumcision has a procreative value (this corresponds to his fourth reason
in paragraph 7). Fourth, circumcision has a symbolic value (this
corresponds to his third reason in paragraph 6 and to his two additional
reasons in paragraphs 9 through 11). Each of these reasons is drawn from
his exegesis of the Genesis 17:10–14 in Quaes Gen 3.46–52. The LXX for
this text reads as follows:

17:10   καὶ αὕτη ἡ διαθήκη, ἥν διατηρήσεις, ἀνὰ μέσον ἐμοῦ καὶ
         ὑμῶν καὶ ἀνὰ μέσον τοῦ σπέρματός σου μετα σὲ εἰς τὰς
         γενεὰς αὐτῶν. περιτμηθήσεται ὑμῶν πᾶν ἀρσενικόν, (and
         this is the covenant which you shall keep between me and
         you and between your seed after you for their
         generations: *every male of you shall be circumcized*).

17:11   καὶ περιτμηθήσεσθε τὴν σάρκα τῆς ἀκροβυστίας ὑμῶν, καὶ
         ἔσται ἐν σημείῳ διαθήκης ἀνὰ μέσον ἐμοῦ καὶ ὑμῶν (and
         you shall be circumcized in the flesh of your foreskin,

---

[37] Ibid. xv.

and it shall be for a sign of the covenant between me and you).

17:12   καὶ παιδίον ὀκτὼ ἡμερῶν <u>περιτμηθήσεται ὑμῖν πᾶν</u> <u>ἀρσενικὸν</u> εἰς τὰς γενεὰς ὑμῶν, <u>ὁ οἰκογενὴς τῆς οἰκίας σου</u> <u>καὶ ὁ ἀργυρώνητος</u> ἀπὸ παντὸς υἱοῦ ἀλλοτρίου, ὃς οὐκ ἔστιν ἐκ τοῦ σπέρματός σου (and an eight-day-old child shall be circumcized by you, every male for your generations, the one home-born in your house and the one bought with money, of every son of a stranger, who is not of your seed).

17:13   περιτομῇ <u>περιτμηθήσεται ὁ οἰκογενὴς οἰκίας σου καὶ ὁ</u> <u>ἀργυρώνητος</u> καὶ ἔσται ἡ διαθήκη μου ἐπὶ τῆς σαρκὸς ὑμῶν εἰς διαθήκην αἰώνιον (the one home-born in your house and the one bought with money shall be circumcized with circumcision, and my covenant shall be upon your flesh for an eternal covenant).

17:14   <u>καὶ ἀπερίτμητος ἄρσην, ὃς οὐ περιτμηθήσεται τὴν σάρκα</u> <u>τῆς ἀκροβυστίας αὐτοῦ τῇ ἡμέρα τῇ ὀγδόῃ,</u> ᾿εξολεθρευθήσεται ἡ ψυχὴ ἐκείνη ἐκ τοῦ γένους αὐτῆς, ὅτι τὴν διαθήκην μου διεσκέδασεν (and the uncircumcized male, who is not circumcized in the flesh of his foreskin on the eighth day, that soul be utterly destroyed from its generation, because it has broken my covenant).[38]

Philo only comments on those passages underlined in the above text. We see immediately that *diathēkē* has been consistently omitted in the interpretation of verses 10, 11, 13, and 14. This suggests that Philo is not concerned with *diathēkē* in his interpretation of circumcision. Indeed, *diathēkē* is not a common word in the entire corpus.[39] The reasons given for circumcision in Spec Leg 1.11 appear as abbreviations of the reasons offered in Quaes Gen 3.46–52, or at least, highly schematized versions of the longer interpretations. For example, in Quaes Gen 3.48, Philo develops the hygienic reason at some length, indicating not only the Jewish practice of circumcision, but also its practice among the Egyptians, Arabs, Ethiopians, and by all those "who inhabit the southern regions or near the torrid zone." It is then the heat in these areas which causes the inflammation avoided by circumcision. Further, he makes a comparative statement and suggests that those people living in the northern hemisphere, where the temperature is not as high as in the southern hemisphere, do not suffer this inflammation. He offers as proof that heat is

---

[38] John William Wevers, ed., *Septuaginta Actoritate Academiae Scientiarum Gottingensis* (Göttingen: Vandenhoeck and Ruprecht, 1974) 1.178–79.

[39] See J. Leisegang, *Indices ad Philonis Alexandrini Opera* in PCW 7.1.177 and G. Mayer, *Index Philoneus* (Berlin and New York: Walter De Gruyter, 1974) 73. David Winston, *The Wisdom of Solomon: A New Translation with Introduction and Commentary* (Anchor Bible 43; Garden City, New York: Doubleday, 1979) 62, n. 84, indicates that *diathēkē* is taken by Philo to mean "testament" or is allegorized by Philo to mean "grace" or "logos."

directly related to the inflammation, the observation that it never occurs in winter, but only in the summer. This represents a considerable expansion over the brief account presented in Spec Leg 1.4. Likewise, the procreative reason receives further embellishment and expansion in Quaes Gen 3.48. He once again indicates that the "ancients" gave thought to circumcision for the sake of populousness and that circumcision is enjoyed to ensure fertilization without obstacle. However, he expands this by comparing the Jewish circumcision of infants to the Egyptian circumcision at the age of fourteen years. He concludes this expansion by stating, "but it is very much better and more far-sighted of us to prescribe circumcision for infants, for perhaps one who is full-grown would hesitate through fear to carry out this ordinance of his own free will." The thrust of this expansion is to particularize circumcision (i.e., Jewish circumcision is not like Egyptian circumcision). This is not present in Spec Leg 1.7, where the reasoning is intended to universalize circumcision and where no distinction is made between the Jewish practice of the ritual and its form among other people. Indeed, Philo's interpretation in Spec Leg 1.7 seems more in line with the earlier tradition within Hellenistic Jewish texts which argues that Moses taught the Egyptians circumcision.[40]

Philo's treatment of circumcision in the *Quaestiones et Solutiones* is not limited to expansion of the reasons presented in our text. He also introduces new motifs which are not present in the reasons advanced in Spec Leg 1.1–11. Among these new motifs are sexual maturity, male and female circumcision versus exclusively male circumcision, and the importance of the number eight. For example, among the Egyptians circumcision is carried out on both men and women at the age of fourteen when they have reached sexual maturity. However, the Jewish injunction for circumcision is exclusively male. The first reason for this exclusivity is that "the male has more pleasure in, and desire for mating than does the female, and he is more ready for it. Therefore, Moses rightfully excludes the female and suppresses the undue impulses of the male by the sign of circumcision."[41] The second reason is that the female produces the fetus while "the male (provides) the skill and cause. And so, since the male provides the greater and more necessary (part) in the

---

[40] Artapanus, *peri Ioudaiōn* (Eusebius, *Praeparatio Evangelica* 9.27) portrays Moses as *euergetēs* who in addition to teaching the Egyptians philosophy and religion, the arts of building, shipping and weaponry, inventing hieroglyphic writing, dividing Egypt into the 36 nomes and assigning to each its god for worship, and founding the cult of the Apis bull, also instructs the Ethiopians on circumcision. On the various works preserved under the title *peri Ioudaiōn*, see Emil Schürer, *The History of the Jewish People in the Age of Jesus Christ* (175 B.C.–A.D. 135), ed. by Geza Vermes and Fergus Millar (Edinburgh: Clark Ltd., 1973) 1.41–42.

[41] Quaes Gen 3.47.

process of generation, it was proper that his pride should be checked by the sign of circumcision."[42] Both reasons represent common *topoi* in Philo's treatment of male and female throughout the corpus.[43] Similarly, Philo introduces the symbolic importance of the number eight. He suggests first that the number eight reveals many beauties (it is a cube; it contains the forms of equality; the composition of eight produces agreement; it is the pattern of an incorporeal, intelligible and invisible-corporeal substance; it is related to seven in the sum of its consecutive divisions in half). However, Philo suggests a second series of meanings attached to the number eight. It is related to the creation of the universe, it produces righteousness, through it the nation is adapted to righteousness, it represents the four elements, and most specifically the element earth.[44] The introduction of these new motifs is in part due to the structure of *Quaestiones et Solutiones* in which he must interpret the biblical text verse by verse. But, it is also a matter of different goals or intentions for the texts. The discussion in *De Specialibus Legibus* is devoid of any particularistic meanings of circumcision, while in *Quaestiones et Solutiones* Philo is intensely interested in the particular meanings of circumcision and in distinguishing it from other forms of circumcision.

Goodenough indicated in his comments on Spec Leg 1.1–11 that Philo was uninterested in the allegorical meaning of circumcision. However, Philo's comments in *Quaestiones et Solutiones* suggest quite the opposite. Here, again we find the expansion of the symbolic reason for circumcision and the introduction of new motifs as seen with the first through the third reasons. For example, in commenting on Gen 17:10–11 he introduces in Quaes Gen 3.46 two forms of circumcision (one of the male and the other of the flesh). This distinction arises from the phrase *peritmēthēsetai hymōn pan arsenikon*, "every male of you shall be circumcised," in verse 10 and the phrase *peritmēthēsesthe tēn sarka tēs akrobystias hymōn*, "you shall be circumcised (in) the flesh of your foreskin," in verse 11. This distinction is further developed in Quaes Gen 3.50 on the basis of the distinction made in the text between the home-born child and the purchased child. The literal meaning of the verse for Philo is that servants should imitate their masters. However, the deeper meaning is that "the home-born characters are those which are moved by nature, while the purchased ones are those who are able to improve through reason and teaching." Yet, the most interesting aspect

---

[42] Ibid.

[43] For example, in discussing the ὁλόκαυτον of Lev 1:3ff. in Spec Leg 1.200 he states that the animal must be male "because the male is the more complete, more dominant than the female, closer akin to causal activity, for the female is incomplete and in subjection and belongs to the category of the passive rather than the active." See Richard A. Baer, *Philo's Use of the Categories Male and Female* (Leiden: Brill, 1970) 41–42.

[44] Quaes Gen 3.49.

of the symbolic reason for circumcision in *Quaestiones et Solutiones* is
the development of his argument. In Quaes Gen 3.48, he suggests the
symbolic reason as the fourth reason after the hygienic, the procreative,
and the purificatory reasons. He first notes here the two generative
organs in the soul and body and how the ancients assimilated one to the
other. After stating this, which is of course the third reason in *De
Specialibus Legibus*, he states "now these are the widely known facts
concerning the problems we are inquiring into. But we must speak about
more symbolic things, which have their own status." The circumcision of
the foreskin is a symbol indicating that it is proper to cut off "superfluous
and excessive desires by exercising continence and endurance in matters
of the Law." He adds to this that circumcision also represents the
excision of arrogance. These are of course the fifth and sixth reasons
which he adds as his own in *De Specialibus Legibus*. Here, however,
they are not additions to a list of four reasons agreed upon by others, but
are deeper symbolic meanings of the fourth reason presented in the
Quaestiones et Solutiones. What is the great arrogance excised by
circumcision? Philo answers this question by stating the following:

> Very naturally does (Scripture) instruct those who think that they are
> the causes of generation and do not intently fix their minds on seeing
> the begetter of all things, for He is the veritable and true Father. But
> we who are called begetters are used as instruments in the service of
> generation. For as by a miracle of imitation all those things which
> are visible are inanimate, while that which activates them like pup-
> pets is invisible. The cause of this is the cause of the habits and
> movements of visible things. In the same way the Creator of the
> world sends out his powers from an eternal and invisible place, but
> we are wonderfully moved like puppets toward that which pertains
> to us, (namely) seed and procreation. Otherwise we might think that
> the shepherd's pipe is played by itself instead of being meant for the
> production of harmony by the artisan by whom the instrument was
> devised for this service and necessary use.[45]

The arrogance is that man should assume the power of generation. This
is an expansion of his statement in Spec Leg 1.10 that "there are some
who have prided themselves on their power of fashioning as with a
sculptor's cunning the fairest of creatures, man, and in their braggart
pride assumed godship, closing their eyes to the cause of all that comes
into being, though they might find in their familiars a corrective for
their delusion."

It is clear then that there is a direct relationship between Spec Leg
1.1–11 and Quaes Gen 3.46–52. It might also be suggested that Philo first
prepared his interpretation of circumcision by asking a series of questions of the biblical text and by constructing extended answers to each

[45] Quaes Gen 3.48 (*PLCL* 11.246).

question. He then summarized his answers to these questions and adapted them to his purposes in *De Specialibus Legibus*. In the process of adaptation he made a slight reorganization of the original four reasons, dividing them into six. Yet the interpretation in the *Quaestiones et Solutiones* (especially Quaes Gen 3.46 and 48) is also directly related to his interpretation of circumcision in other treatises. In Quaes Ex 2.2, he raises the question of why Scripture (Ex 22:21) prohibits the oppression of the sojourner and reminds that Israel was a sojourner in Egypt. The sojourner, like the Israelites in Egypt, is uncircumcised in the flesh, but is one who is circumcised in respect to the pleasures and passions of the soul. He continues and states that Israel lived with the Egyptians in self-restraint and endurance, as sojourners who are alienated from belief in many gods, but having "familiarity with honoring the one God and father of all." Cutting off all excessive pleasures and passions is presented again in Agr 39 where he develops Noah as the true *geōrgos*. The allegorical designation given to husbandry is that it cuts off (*peritēn*) all excessive and harmful luxuriance. Both interpretations are in conformity with the interpretation in *De Specialibus Legibus* and *Quaestiones et Solutiones*, and both, contrary to Goodenough, underscore the importance of the allegorical meaning of circumcision for Philo.

The two most important passages outside of Spec Leg 1.1–11 and Quaes Gen 3.46–52 are Somn 2.25 and Migr 86–94. In Somn 2.25, Philo develops the double circumcision of Quaes Gen 3.46 and 50 on the basis of Joseph's dream in Gen 37. In Joseph's first dream, he saw himself and the brothers binding sheaves. Philo indicates that reaping is the business of masters, while binding sheaves is the work of the unskilled. This leads him to consider the nature of reaping and especially Lev 19:9, which Philo quotes as *therizēte ton therismon*, "reap your reaping." In stating this, Philo understands that Moses "wishes the virtuous man to be not only a judge of things that differ, distinguishing and separating things which produce and their productions, but to do away with the very conceit that he has the power to distinguish . . . " (24). This *therizēte ton therismon* is the two-fold circumcision deduced from Gen 17:10, 11 and 13. These reduplicated phrases (to which he adds Num 6:2 as a third example) mean that they are "the purification of the very purification of the soul, when we yield to God the prerogative of making bright and clean, and never entertain the thought that we ourselves are sufficient apart from the divine overseeing guidance to cleanse our life and remove from it the defilements with which is abounds" (25). The double circumcision of Gen 17:10, 11 and 13 then means that the first circumcision is of the excessive appetites of the lower soul. This corresponds to the fifth reason given in Spec Leg 1.9. The second circumcision means that one cuts off the very ability and educated skill one had acquired in order to perform the first form of circumcision. This ensures the destruction of any conceit and corresponds to the sixth reason given in Spec Leg 1.10. In *De Migratione Abrahami*, Philo offers one of his most thorough accounts of the importance of the literal meaning of the Law. The literal commands are to be understood as *tamieias tōn phanerōn anepilēpton*, "stewards without reproach" (89). Circumcision is one of these "stewards" representing the excision of pleasure and all passions, and the putting away of the impious (*asebous*) conceit, under which the mind supposed that it was capable of begetting by its own powers (92).

These passages help us better understand why Philo chose to place the issue of circumcision at the very beginning of *De Specialibus Legibus* and why he did not understand it to be a special law. Philo's decision to set this matter where he did has nothing to do with an effort to justify or to rationalize the ritual as practiced by the Jews of Alexandria. Likewise, the interpretations in Quaes Gen 3.46–52 and their application and adaptation to the other treatises confirm the allegorical importance of circumcision in our text. The crucial meaning of circumcision is first the excision of the pleasures and passions which might potentially create confusion in the mind and second, the rejection of arrogant conceit. This explication given by Philo is anything but the frantic effort described by Goodenough and represents a thorough and deliberate interpretation of Gen 17:10–14. The arrogance that is excised by circumcision is the thought that man is the real generator and cause of being. Philo's response to this conceit is that circumcision is the means by which one should come to know himself (Spec Leg 1.10, *gnōnai tina heauton*).[46] Philo returns to this issue in Spec Leg 1.32 where he raises two questions: the existence of the *to on* and its essence. The existence of the *to on* is proven by the argument from design (33–35), but the essence cannot be apprehended (36–40). Philo then uses Ex 33:13–23 as an example of the incomprehensibility of the divine essence. God responds to Moses' request to be informed as to the divine essence by indicating that its comprehension is something beyond human nature (44). Rather, God tells Moses *gnōthi dē sauton* ("know thyself") (44). Here, Philo does not use the expression *gnōthi de sauton* in its Socratic sense, where philosophical introspection is central, but rather, the simple realization that man is totally dependent on God. Philo's use of the expression implies nothing of the classical Greek philosophical meaning. Indeed, *gnōthi dē sauton* is used by Philo in a thoroughly biblical sense,

---

[46] Spec Leg 1:10, ἑτέρου δὲ τοῦ γνῶναί τινα ἑαυτὸν καὶ τὴν βαρεῖαν νόσον, οἴησιν, ψυχῆς ἀπώσασθαι. F.H. Colson, *PLCL* 7.105, renders this passage, "The other reason is that a man should know himself and banish from the soul the grievous malady of conceit." S. Daniel, *PM* 24.17 renders it as "La seconde chose est la connaissance de soi et le rejet hors de l'ame de cette grave maladie, la présomption." I. Heinemann, *PCH* 2.15 renders the passage "Zweitens mahnt die Beschneidung den Menschen sich selbst zu erkennen und seine Seele vor der schweren Krankheit des Dünkels zu hüten."

encapsulating the most obvious aspects of the Hebrew Bible's anthropology. To presume that man is something more than a creature of God is the arrogance and conceit excised by circumcision. Spec Leg 1.1–11 is not Philo's desperate effort to rationalize a ritual. Philo shows no real interest in the actual ritual at this level of interpretation; his interests in the passage are far more important. The *nomos* in its entirety is at stake here, for without the banishment of this conceit, this specific form of arrogance, which stands above all others, it would make no sense. Consequently, circumcision, understood as the banishment of the most vain conception, properly belongs at the very beginning of a comprehensive interpretation of the Law. A proper understanding of each of the special laws is predicated upon what circumcision makes clear to man. Philo has selected the issue of circumcision with great deliberation and the passage is executed in the most precise fashion. Circumcision does not belong under any of the commandments of the Decalogue for it is properly the "vestibule" or portal through which one must pass if one is to understand properly the nature of the *nomos* and its special laws.

IV. *The External Exegetical Context of Circumcision*

The intricacies of Spec Leg 1.1–11 are not exhausted by the examination of περιτομή within the corpus. There are two further problems which cannot be resolved solely through the material on circumcision within the treatises of the corpus. First, Philo, as Goodenough saw, mentions the Egyptians with an uncommon respect in this passage as being populous, having great antiquity and most importantly, as being attached to philosophy. Second, Philo's treatment of circumcision in Quaes Gen 3.46–52 is a highly particularistic account in which he is concerned to indicate the unique qualities of the Jewish practice of circumcision. How is one to account for Philo's positive description of the Egyptians and the change from the particularistic account of circumcision to the univeral account in our text? Philo does not disagree with the four reasons given by those who have inquired into the Law of Moses and appends his reasons without critique of the foregoing explanations. The answer to both questions can only be gained by setting this passage in the context of what was said of circumcision in the ethnographies of the Jews produced in the ancient world. Here, the issue is not the very difficult problem of the legal status of circumcision within the Roman Empire either before or after Hadrian,[47] but the interpretations given to circumcision in descriptions of the Jews.

[47] On the question of the legal status of circumcision, see E. Mary Smallwood, "The Legislation of Hadrian and Antoninus Pius against Circumcision," *Latomus* 18 (1959) 334–47, "Addendum," *Latomus* 20 (1961) 93–96, and *The Jews under Roman Rule: From Pompey to Diocletian* (Leiden: Brill, 1976) esp. 464–73.

Greek and Latin literature in antiquity is of course replete with reference to the circumcision of the Jews. These references appear in everything from historiographical accounts to gossip. One of the common *topoi* found in the classical historiographies which touch upon the Jews is the observation that they learned circumcision from the Egyptians.[48] The association of similar ritual practices among both Jews and Egyptians is directly related to the issue of the origin of the Jews. For Diodorus, the presence of similar rituals in both national groups was a clear proof that the Jews were historically related to the Egyptians as colonists from Egypt. This observation, which is not unique to Diodorus, contains a subtle implication already present in Manetho's "counter-history" of the Jews. We can only guess whether Philo might have been sensitive to this in the construction of his interpretation of circumcision. If the Jews were historically related to the Egyptians, it might be argued that their religious institutions were either an Egyptian variant or some form of hybrid. In either case, this historical association might mean that the uniqueness of the Law of Moses could be challenged. One might imagine an argument in this way: Moses cannot be said to have been either a perfect or unique lawgiver since the law is a copy, extension or inversion of Egyptian law. Indeed, Strabo, Apion, Horace, Persius, Flaccus, Petronius, Martial, Juvenal, Tacitus, and much later, Rutilius Namantius all have something to say on the practice of circumcision. The Roman poets repeatedly portrayed circumcision as both ridiculous and humiliating. Petronius suggests in his *Satyricon* (68.8) that a certain slave would be perfect save his two faults, he snores and is circumcised.[49] Among the epigrams of Martial, the references to circumcision are only exceeded by his ridicule of the castrated priests of the cult of Cybele and Attis.[50] In Epigram 11.94, a poem of less than ten lines, circumcision is used as a pejorative adjective by which Martial disparages a Jewish poet. In Epigram 7.82, he mocks a Jewish actor whom he describes as attempting to conceal the shame of his circumcision under a large sheath, pretending that he covered his penis so as to abstain from sex and thereby to preserve the quality of his voice. He ends the epigram by stating that "in view of the people in the middle of the exercise ground,

[48] Herodotus, *Historiae* 2.104.1–3, Diodorus Siculus, *Bibliotheca Historica* 1.28.1–3, 1.55.5, and Origen, *Contra Celsum* 1.22.
[49] Menahem Stern, ed. and trans., *Greek and Latin Authors on Jews and Judaism* (Jerusalem: The Israel Academy of Sciences and Humanities, 1974) 1.442. In Fragment No. 37, he states, "The Jew may worship his pig-god and clamour in the ears of high heaven, but unless he cuts back his foreskin with the knife, he shall go forth from the people and emigrate to Greek cities and shall not tremble at the fasts of Sabbath imposed by the Law" (444).
[50] Ibid. 521.

the sheath unluckily fell off: lo, he was circumcised."[51] The satirist Juvenal suggests that circumcision is another step in the degeneration of the children of proselytes to Judaism and hence the corruption of Roman society.[52] Tacitus understood the purpose of circumcision among the Jews to mark their difference and ultimately, their hostility toward other nations (*Histories* 5.5).

The common element in all the observations produced by Greek and Latin authors is that circumcision is one of the primary examples of Jewish religous and social particularism.[53] While Jewish customs served only to underscore Jewish particularism in the minds of Greek and Latin writers, the writers of the second and third centuries of the Common Era registered a very different response to things Egyptian, as contrasted with Herodotus' comparative observation on how very different things were in Egypt. Juvenal's bitter attack upon the Egyptians, in which he bemoans the Egyptian inroads into proper Roman life and society when that "jumped-up Egyptian Pasha who's had the nerve to gate-crash Triumph Row" (Satire 1.129–30, here perhaps an allusion to Philo's nephew, Tiberius Julius Alexander), Chaldean and Egyptian success with oracles on the streets of Rome (Satire 6.557–65), Roman pilgrims in Egypt and the numerous Egyptian deities appealed to by seemingly proper Roman citizens (Satire 6.528–40), all suggest the popularity enjoyed by Egyptian religion and culture in Rome. His vigorous attack upon "that nation that has gods springing up in the kitchen garden" in the fourteenth satire, accusing them of cannibalism, suggests the "Egyptomania" which swept through the most fashionable circles of Roman society in the last half of the first century B.C.E. and the first century C.E. Philo's inclusion of the Egyptians and their practice of circumcision in his interpretation of the very same Jewish ritual then might be understood as the conscious exploitation of the historiographical tradition which had already made a similar connection. Those who ridiculed Jewish circumcision, while

---

[51] Ibid. 525.

[52] Juvenal, *The Sixteen Satires*, trans. by Peter Green (Middlesex: Penguin, 1967), Satire 14, lines 96–104:

> Some, whose lot it was to have Sabbath-fearing fathers,
> Worship nothing but clouds and the *numen* of the heavens,
> And think it as great a crime to eat pork, from which their parents
> Abstained, as human flesh. They get themselves circumcised,
> And look down on Roman law, preferring instead to learn
> And honour and fear the Jewish commandments, whatever
> Was handed down by Moses in that arcane tome of his—
> Never to show the way to any but fellow-believers
> (If they ask where to get some water, find out if they're foreskinless).

[53] Théodor Reinach, *Textes d'auteurs Grecs et Romains relatifs au Judaïsme* (Paris: Leroux, 1895) vii-xii, remains one of the best short discussions of Jewish religious and social particularism in the ancient world.

looking with more than favor on Egyptian religion, should understand its meaning. At the level of the external exegetical context, Philo's understanding of circumcision negates claims that it represents only Jewish particularism in the social world and hostility toward others. Circumcision is practiced by many nations, among them, the one most praised in Roman society for its attachment to philosophy. In this way, Philo is able to universalize a specific ritual practice, along with the Law itself. It is no mere accident that Philo chose to begin the treatise with this issue. One of the most particular characteristics of the Jews is shown not only to have parallels among other peoples, but also to have universal meaning. The interpretation of the particular ritual of circumcision is in perfect harmony with the central intention of the entire treatise, the universalization of the *nomos*. Philo's universalization of circumcision, against the observations which saw it only as a prime example of Jewish particularism, is further underscored by his statement that other legislators (νομοθέταις) reached the same conclusion arrived at by Moses (Spec Leg 1.9). This is a striking statement, but against the tradition found in Juvenal, and perhaps against others like it, in which circumcision is an eccentric stipulation in the "arcane tome" of Moses, it is a most forceful response. Philo's argument is that other wise legislators saw in circumcision a representation of the excision of excessive pleasure.

Spec Leg 1.1–11 is a critical passage in arriving at a proper understanding of the entire treatise. Philo's discussion of circumcision in this passage is devoid of anything which might be construed as halakhic distinction and qualification, anything which might reflect the actual proceedings of Jewish courts in Egypt, and anything which reflects the thorough synthesis of Greco-Roman law and philosophy. The text must be considered in two interrelated contexts, the first being the meaning of περιτομή in this text and other treatises of the corpus, and the second being the background of circumcision in Greek and Latin authors. Goodenough did not have the benefit of the *Quaestiones et Solutiones*, but if he would have compared Philo's treatment here with the interpretations in *De Somniis*, *De Agricultura*, and *De Migratione Abrahami*, he might have been more careful in evaluating Philo's argument and the allegorical importance of circumcision. Within its internal context, circumcision is the destruction of the arrogance and conceit which stands as a major impediment to a proper understanding of the *nomos*. Here, Philo has introduced a thoroughly biblical meaning to *gnōthi dē sauton*. Through circumcision man learns limitations and that he is *just* a man. The two circumcisions implied by Genesis 17 in Philo's interpretation of the text, suggest that within the corpus circumcision is directly related to the ascension of the soul. Sense perception is to be utilized, but in order to progress beyond it, appetites of the body must be pruned. Circumcision becomes the symbolic vestibule to the Law and the entrance for the ascension of the soul within the Law or in conformity with it. Within the external exegetical context, Philo demonstrates, by exploiting both Greek and Roman romanticism for Egypt, that it is not unique to the Jews. Many legislators saw it as a symbol for that which is fundamental to human life. The genius of Philo in this passage is that both arguments are advanced simultaneously.

This two-fold argument is important in determining the intention of *De Specialibus Legibus*. In both arguments, within the internal and external contexts of circumcision, Philo's primary concern is with demonstrating the reasonableness of this specific ritual practice. Again, this overlaps with his desire in the entire treatise to show that all of the special laws are reasonable. This is the very nature of the *nomos*. We should not assume that he was unable to find a place for circumcision under one of the commandments of the Decalogue. The placement of circumcision at the beginning of the treatise is not by accident or an unexplained deviation from the plan set forth in *De Decalogo*. Philo selected this issue in order to accomplish his larger purpose of offering a systematic apology for the Law. Our text is an apologetic in the genre of literature which is solely intended to rationalize the commandments. This observation should not be misunderstood to simply present another example of the apologetic *Tendenz* in Philo. Many commentators have pointed to an apologetic tendency within specific texts of the corpus and have set aside an entire genre of the corpus for identifiable apologetic treatises. The implication of this brief study of Philo's interpretation of circumcision is that *De Specialibus Legibus* is an apology and that either this four-part treatise should be included within that genre or far better, that the division of the corpus into a variety of genres be dispensed with in favor of understanding Philo as being exclusively engaged in deducing the reasonableness of the Law. Perhaps further support for this implication might be generated by considering other blocks of material from *De Specialibus*.

DECODING THE SCRIPTURE:
PHILO AND THE RULES OF RHETORIC

BURTON L. MACK

Claremont Graduate School

Proem

I shall never forget a delightful weekend as house guest with Sam and Frances Sandmel in Cincinnati. I had recently written a dissertation on Philo, and was teaching New Testament at the Methodist Theological School in Delaware, Ohio. Sam took note and invited me and BJ down for conversation about things of mutual interest. It was my first experience of the Sabbath rituals and my first serious talk with a Jewish colleague about early Judaism and Christianity. Sam was magnificent as he conversed and probed, rummaged through the books and rooms and gardens, and shared with me his learning. He helped me phrase some questions then which, in the course of time, reshaped my quest and concerns with Philonica. I am deeply indebted to him for that and many other occasions of collegiality and scholarly conversation. I have pursued the present study with Sam in mind.

Introduction: Philo in the School of Rhetoric

Philo's acquaintance with Hellenistic culture has been noted and explored by every major writer in the history of scholarship dealing with his works. His language was Greek. And his world of thought was etched in conceptualities drawn from the traditions of Greek philosophy. He understood the *polis* and its peoples and its institutions. And he was read, well-read some would say, in the canons of Greek literature as well. About all of that there can be no disagreement.

But to make precise Philo's place in the history of Hellenistic literature and philosophy has been another matter. There is now some agreement that, in general, his view of the world and the order of things can be called middle-Platonic.[1] But none will deny that he prefers the Stoa for his ethics, and that he speaks as well, on occasion, with Aristotle,

---

[1] See now John Dillon, *The Middle Platonists* (Ithaca, New York: Cornell, 1977) 139–83.

Pythagoras, or some Socratic school. And there is considerable debate as to whether one dare speak about Philo as a systematic philosopher at all.[2] As for his dependence upon Greek literature, there is also no clear placement possible in any special tradition or traditions. Scholars have pointed out some of Philo's literary precursors, of course. He used the famous Tropes of Aenesidemus,[3] crafted his lives on the model of Hellenistic biography,[4] employed terminology and methods usually associated with Stoic allegorization, cited a full range of Greek poets, and formed his commentaries in ways reminiscent of Hellenistic commentaries on Homer and Plato.[5] But how Philo read his Hellenistic precursors, and what he intended by his appeals to their authorities, are questions which have not yet found their answers.

In recent scholarship, two lines of investigation have emerged which hold some promise for our quest. The first is based upon the simple observation that Philo intended his treatise-commentaries to be just that—explications of the text of the Five Books of Moses.[6] The suspicion is that the books of Moses have been read and understood by Philo in certain ways reflective both of Jewish and Hellenistic concerns. If we were able better to understand Philo's view of these scriptures, and his methods of interpreting them, we might be able to understand as well his employment of Hellenistic thought and literature in his commentaries. Perhaps it is even so that Philo's reading of the books of Moses, not

---

[2] The last major work proposing that Philo was a systematic, philosophic theologian was H. A. Wolfson, *Philo* I, II (Cambridge, MA: Harvard, 1945–48). Critical appraisals may be found in: E. R. Goodenough, "Wolfson's Philo," *JBL* 67 (1948) 87–109; J. Daniélou, "The Philosophy of Philo: The Significance of Professor Harry A. Wolfson's New Study," *TS* 9 (1948) 578–89; K. Borman, *Die Ideen-und Logoslehre Philons von Alexandrien. Eine Auseinandersetzung mit H. A. Wolfson* (Diss: Köln, 1955); H. Thyen, "Die Probleme der neueren Philo-Forschung," *TR* N.F. 23 (1955) 230–46.

[3] Hans von Arnim, "Quellenstudien zu Philo von Alexandria," in *Philologische Untersuchungen*, ed. A. Kiessling and U. von Wilamowitz-Moellendorff, XI (Berlin: Weidmann, 1888).

[4] Anton Priessnig, "Die literarische Form der Patriarchenbiographien des Philo von Alexandrien," *MGWJ* N.R. 37 (1929) 143–55.

[5] See the preliminary study and call to investigation by P. Borgen and R. Skarsten, "*Quaestiones et Solutiones*: Some Observations on the Form of Philo's Exegesis," *Studia Philonica* 4 (1976–77) 1–16.

[6] See V. Nikiprowetzky, *Le commentaire de l'écriture chez Philon d'Alexandrie* (Leiden: Brill, 1977); B. L. Mack, "Philo Judaeus and Exegetical Traditions in Alexandria," in *Aufstieg und Niedergang der römischen Welt*: Religion II (Berlin: de Gruyter). Since 1977 a team of scholars has collaborated on Philo's exegetical methods, working on "The Philo Project" at the Institute for Antiquity and Christianity at Claremont. See the call-paper by B. Mack, "Exegetical Traditions in Alexandrian Judaism: A Program for the Analysis of the Philonic Corpus," *Studia Philonica* 3 (1974–75) 71–112.

his reading of the Greek philosophers, provided whatever structure, systematic, or coherence there may be in his voluminous works.[7] But how, indeed, has he read Moses?

The second line of investigation in recent scholarship may help us with this question. Reading and writing were learned at school. And Philo certainly learned to read and write. But where, in what school? And with what advancement? These are the topics now being explored in studies on Philo's education, his knowledge of the system of Hellenistic *paideia*, and his skillful use of the canons of Hellenistic rhetoric.[8] It is not Philo's place in some school tradition of Hellenistic philosophy which is at issue here. What we seek to know is whether and how he was trained in *paideia*—that system of education (*paideia*) which was understood to produce Hellenic culture (*paideia*). We need not argue the point that Philo appears to have been well-versed in the subjects and skills of Hellenistic general education. He mentions repeatedly the encyclical curriculum, discusses the virtues of its various courses, cites or borrows from its canons of literature, and draws heavily upon its lore and learning. The schema of the two stages, one of Philo's principle themes—first the discipline of toil, practice and correction, then the joys and rewards of accomplishments—is taken from common Hellenistic notions of the nature of *paideia*.[9] The analogy from agriculture which Philo uses so frequently, first patient labor, at last the produce, was also a favorite among the Greeks as an image of education.[10] His considerable linguistic skills, his general knowledge of Greek literature, and his position on the purpose of education, i.e. for virtue, all bespeak a rather thorough experience in Hellenistic learning. What is not so clearly understood is the degree to which that education may have been predominantly and formally rhetorical in nature. If Philo learned to read and write in the system of Greek *paideia*, and if he was trained in the schools of rhetoric, his reading of Moses and his writing of commentaries may actually have been an exercise in the achievement of the definitive Hellenistic virtues—the virtues of literacy and how one fared with words.[11]

[7] This is the thesis of V. Nikiprowetzky. See n. 6.

[8] On Philo and Hellenistic education in general, see now A. Mendelson, *Secular Education in Philo of Alexandria* (Cincinnati: Hebrew Union College, 1982). Major works on Philo's knowledge and use of Hellenistic rhetorical theory are now in process by Thomas Conley, University of Illinois, and Manuel Alexandre, University of Lisbon.

[9] Readers of Philo will be familiar with his notion of the two stages. The major monograph on the topic is W. Voelker, *Fortschritt und Vollendung bei Philo von Alexandrien* (Leipzig: Hinrichs, 1938).

[10] A clear example of its usage in Hellenistic education as metaphor for *paideia* is given with the text from Hermogenes, to be discussed below. Philo uses the same metaphor in Sacr 35, the treatise under investigation in this essay.

[11] A preliminary study on the concept of authorship in Hellenism, and its reflection in the literature of Hellenistic Judaism, including Philo, is given in B. Mack, "Under the

It is the purpose of this essay to propose such a thesis. We want to suggest that Philo was not only trained in the Hellenistic school through its secondary curriculum. We seek to demonstrate that he was trained in the art of rhetorical composition as well. In order to make precise the nature of such training, a first section of the essay will describe a single, basic exercise in rhetorical education of the time. This exercise, on the *chreia*, is common to all handbooks and discussions on the "preliminary exercises" (*progymnasmata*) and reveals a great deal about the way in which rhetorical analysis of texts and composition of these were practiced. In a second section of the essay Philo's commentary of Gen 4:2 in the treatise *De sacrificiis* 1–10 will be shown to follow the rhetorical principles outlined in the *chreia*-exercise. This will be given as an example of Philo's training in, and practice of, basic rhetorical skills. In a final section conclusions of a more general nature will be drawn. There it will be argued that Philo regarded all of Moses' writings to be crafted according to canons of rhetorical composition, and that his commentaries on Moses' writings were intended to elaborate upon Moses' own authorial intention according to the several genres of literary and rhetorical composition found to be employed in the scriptures.

The essay does not intend to account for all we need to know about Philo's place in Hellenistic Judaism, nor about the function of the scriptures within the pre-Philonic (school?) traditions of Jewish interpretation. But it may serve to make precise one important factor at work in the construction of Philo's commentaries. That factor will be the lens of rhetorical theory through which Philo viewed his work as scholar and author. If Philo was trained in the Hellenistic schools of rhetoric, an implicit theory of argumentation will have determined his way with words and conventional *topoi* in the composition of his treatises. It is an important aspect of this theory of argumentation in the exercise known as "the elaboration of the *chreia*" which we now seek to understand.

I. The *Chreia*-Exercise in the Progymnasmata

A. *The Chreia in the Classroom*

The *progymnasmata* were teachers' handbooks for guiding classroom exercises at the introductory level of training in rhetoric. This training presupposed the secondary level of encyclical education and served as formal preparation for the more advanced levels of the professional schools in civics and the practice of law. The first extant *progymnasmata* is that of Theon of Alexandria (first century C.E.).[12] But in his

Shadow of Moses: Authorship and Authority in Hellenistic Judaism," in *Society of Biblical Literature, 1982 Seminar Papers* (Chico, CA: Scholars, 1982) 299–318.

[12] The best edition is still that of C. Walz, *Rhetores Graeci* I (Stuttgart: Cotta, 1832) 137–256. A critical text and English translation is in preparation at Claremont by James Butts.

introduction Theon refers to a handbook tradition; and it is now accepted that both the *progymnasmata* and the institution it assumes were current as early as the first century B.C.E.[13]

The handbook consists of a number of sections, each devoted to a specific speech-form ranging from the *chreia*, fable, and short narrative, through exercises in description and characterization through speech, to the composition of encomia, theses, and legislation. The lessons were graded, beginning with small units of speech and advancing to longer and more difficult compositions. At first, students were provided with already composed units and taught to analyze them in terms of rhetorical theory. Gradually, students were led from analytic exercises to assignments which required compositional skills.[14]

The earlier exercises took up small forms of literary composition familiar to students from their encyclical education. This meant that rhetorical theory was first experienced in the process of analyzing excerpts from literary traditions in general, thus tending to erase the distinction between literature proper and the speech-forms more closely identified with rhetorical theory.[15]

One of these smaller units of traditional literature, apparently of singular importance in the *progymnasmata*, was the *chreia*. The *chreia* was a brief account of something which a certain person had said or done, usually told of a well-known person, and frequently understood to have been a response to a specific situation.[16] One of the traditional examples of *chreia* is the following: "Diogenes, on seeing a youth in the marketplace misbehaving, struck the tutor and said 'Why do you teach him to do that?'"[17] Many other examples can be found in Plutarch, Diogenes Laertius, the *progymnasmata*,[18] and elsewhere. There is evidence of their use in the secondary schools for instruction in grammar.[19]

---

[13] On the existence and use of *progymnasmata* in the first century B.C.E., see: S. F. Bonner, *Education in Ancient Rome* (Berkeley: University of California, 1977) 250–51; G. Kennedy, *The Art of Persuasion in Greece* (Princeton, NJ: Princeton University, 1963) 270.

[14] For a general discussion of the *progymnasmata* see D. L. Clark, *Rhetoric in Greco-Roman Education* (New York: Columbia, 1957) 177–212.

[15] For a general discussion of "Literary Rhetoric" see G. A. Kennedy, *Classical Rhetoric and its Christian and Secular Tradition from Ancient to Modern Times* (Chapel Hill, NC: University of North Carolina Press, 1980) 108–19.

[16] In the *chreia*-chapters of the *progymnasmata* a definition is regularly given. Theon's definition is: "The *chreia* is a concise statement or action with pointedness which is attributed to some specific character . . . , " C. Walz, *Rhetores Graeci* I, 201.

[17] The example is taken from Hermogenes' chapter on the *chreia*. See H. Rabe, *Hermogenis Opera* (Stuttgart: Teubner, 1969) 6.

[18] A group of scholars at the Institute for Antiquity and Christianity, Claremont, is preparing a volume of texts and English translations of the *chreia*-chapters in the early *progymnasmata*: R. F. Hock and E. N. O'Neil, *Ancient Discussions of the Chreia: The Principal Texts* (to be published by Scholars Press, Chico, CA, in the series *Texts and Translations*).

[19] The evidence is, unfortunately, available only for the second and third centuries. See

The *chreia* was distinguished by the rhetors from maxims, in that the *chreia* always attributed the saying to a specific person. It was this characteristic of a *chreia* which interested the rhetors, and determined its usefulness for the very first exercise in rhetorical analysis. Because the *chreia* combined speaker, speech, and circumstance, it could be viewed as a micro-example of the rhetorical speech situation itself. As early as Anaximenes and Aristotle, rhetorical theory had focused upon just these three components as basic to any rhetorical situation. Persuasion occurred when the *ethos* of the speaker, the *logos* of the speech, and the *pathos* of the situated hearers conjoined.[20]

We turn now to a description of the way in which the *chreia* was used in the classroom. We shall analyze the *chreia*-chapters in the two earliest *progymnasmata* extant—those of Theon (first century), and Hermogenes (third century).[21] In Theon we will see that the *chreia* was used for very basic exercises in a wide variety of primary skills of importance for the practice of rhetoric. A description of these will serve us well as an introduction to the cluster of assumptions about language and its rhetoricity which prevailed in the Hellenistic school. But we need to include Hermogenes' discussion, because it is there that a fully developed elaboration of the *chreia*-exercise is given which can serve as a text for comparison with Philo. The third century date for Hermogenes presents us with a slight problem in historical methodology. But as we shall see, the elaboration outline in Hermogenes is an application of discussions of the arrangements of arguments which occur already in authors of the first centuries B.C.E.-C.E., i.e., the *Ad Herennium*, Cicero, and Quintilian.[22] There is reason to believe that the development in the form of the *progymnasmata* from Theon to Hermogenes reflects an upgrading of instruction to address the needs of students at a more advanced level of composition. The combination of Theon and Hermogenes, then, will provide us with a picture of rhetorical education through several grades of instruction, all of which, in one form or another, must have been practiced during the time of Philo. It is important to keep in mind the distinction between the technical handbooks of rhetorical theory (*technē*)

---

the discussion of teachers' handbooks for primary education in H. I. Marrou, *A History of Education in Antiquity* (New York: Mentor Books, 1964) 218, n. 8; 238.

[20] For a succinct statement see Aristotle, *Ars Rhetorica* 1.2.3.

[21] The best critical text of Hermogenes is now H. Rabe, *Hermogenis Opera* (Stuttgart: Tuebner, 1969). The *progymnasmata* is found on pages 1–27.

[22] For discussions of the essentials of a "complete" argumentation see: (Cicero), *Ad Herennium* 2.18.28; 2.29.46; 4.43.56; Cicero, *De Inventione* 1.34.58–61; 1.37.67; Quintilian, 5.10. Quintilian resists a rigid codification of the "topics" for building an argument, because he understands the process as creative and free. But a careful reading shows that he has discussed the manifold possibilities as combinations of major and minor (or sub-) types of arguments. The major types are closely related to the small lists of "arguments" found in Cicero and the *Ad Herennium* cited above.

on the one hand, and the *progymnasmata* on the other. In the technical handbooks for professionals and scholars rhetorical theory and practice is organized logically. In the *progymnasmata* paedagogical concerns determine the organization. It is in these that we are able to catch sight of the way in which rhetorical skill was achieved through learning, and understood to function in practice.

B. *The Exercises in Theon of Alexandria*

In his chapter on the *chreia*,[23] Theon lists the exercises (*gymnazein*) which one may perform as follows: (1) Recitation (*apaggelia*), (2) Inflection (*klisis*), (3) Commentary (*epiphōnēsē*), (4) Critique (*antilogia*), (5) Expansion (*epekteinein*), (6) Condensation (*systellein*), (7) Refutation (*anaskeuē*), and (8) Confirmation (*kataskeuē*).[24] The list consists of eight exercises which, however, may be reduced to four sets of complementary pairs. Of these four sets, two sets have to do generally with basic skills in style and delivery (Recitation/Inflection; Expansion/Condensation), and two sets have to do with basic skills in analysis and argumentation (Commentary/Critique; Refutation/Confirmation). The first pair (Recitation/Inflection) may appear at first glance to repeat merely customary exercises in memorization and grammar practiced at the level of general secondary education. But they are quite appropriate as well for training in rhetoric where skills in delivery were telling. Theon emphasizes that the Recitation should aim at clarity—a mark of good delivery frequently mentioned in discussions on style—and that the student is free to paraphrase the *chreia* if it would be helpful—another common stylistic device. The Inflections-exercise is illustrated at some length, and amounts to a series of recitations in which (1) the main verbs are conjugated by changing the number of the persons referred to in the *chreia*, then (2) the proper nouns are declined into the five cases by changes which can be made in the phrasing by which the *chreia* is introduced. The ability to do this well is a stylistic skill appropriate to the insertion of a bit of traditional material into a longer speech context with its demands upon stylistic variations. Expansion and Condensation are also skills related to composition and style. If the larger speech-context demands it, a brief *chreia* may thus be expanded by adding descriptive details of the circumstance, or explaining in more detail who the characters were, or even expanding the dialogue into a little story with dramatic traits of its own. But if the larger speech-context requires a pointed and poignant *chreia*, one must also be able to reduce longer stories (*apomnēmoneumata*) in order to make the point.

---

[23] In C. Walz, *Rhetores Graeci* I, 201–16.
[24] C. Walz, *Rhetores Graeci* I, 210.

Classroom practice was probably quite demanding, both for teacher and students. The teacher was responsible for supplying appropriate materials and knowing how best they might lend themselves to various exercises. He also had to be capable of giving precise and technical critique of student performance. A *chreia* would be selected for a certain exercise, and a student would be called upon to perform. Correction, explanation, and performance by the teacher might intervene. Then another *chreia* and another student, and so forth. Memorization and repetition were basic, and the codes of style were firm. But the skills necessary to apply the prescribed techniques to these small bits of speech-material could only have been achieved through long and difficult practice.

For the first exercises in argumentation an even more difficult and demanding set of skills was necessary. In order to perform here, the student was required to have some knowledge of the major types (*topoi*; *kephalaia*) of rhetorical arguments or "proofs," and their arrangements (*taxis*). Discussions of these were available to teachers in the advanced handbooks of rhetorical theory. For the beginning student, various lists were probably copied out, judging from the itemized discussions given in the *progymnasmata*. Argumentation theory was extremely complex, and facility in rhetorical logic would have required a very long and detailed study. First steps would have to do with a few of the more obvious, general, and single ways of making a telling point. Theon's lists of arguments, for instance, for use in the first exercises on the *chreia*, are brief composites of various classifications and kinds of proofs. There is also a tendency to include the most general and easily recognized proofs capable of illustrating the several technical classifications. One gets the impression that the student was provided with only a basic introduction to the main types of proof, and how they were to be used in constructing an argumentation. The emphasis in the *chreia*-exercises, moreover, seems to have been at first inductive and analytical. A *chreia* would be proposed, and the student would run down the list of proofs, showing whether and how the speaker of the chreia had made use of them, and how well.

For the Commentary/Critique, Theon suggests that the *chreia* be looked at to see whether it is true (*alēthes*), honorable (*kalon*), and expedient (*sympheron*), and whether its thought had been expressed in a similar saying by some other person of distinction.[25] This list of four items combines proofs taken from two separate classifications. The first three are recognizable as a short list of the so-called "chief ends" (*telika kephalaia*) used primarily in deliberative argumentation and speech. In the technical handbooks one encounters standard listings of these consisting of about eight items.[26] They expressed general, conventional values

---

[25] C. Walz, *Rhetores Graeci* I, 212.
[26] The earliest list is given by Anaximenes (Pseudo-Aristotle), *Rhetorica ad Alexandrum*

and became "proofs" when it could be shown that a given proposal, or thesis, or legislation agreed with them. The three categories suggested by Theon, moreover, are a version of the standard triad which was used to define the ultimate objectives of the three major speech types themselves. According to Aristotle the forensic speech as a whole was an argument determined by the category of "what was right" (*dikaion*); the deliberative speech by "the expedient" (*sympheron*), and the epideictic speech by "the honorable" (*kalon*).[27] Theon has substituted "true" for "right" because the *chreia* will be treated as a maxim or philosophical judgment, not as a forensic judgment. He has thus provided the student with a list of the three most general categories belonging to rhetorical persuasion. To them he has added another kind of "proof," namely, the citation of an ancient authority. Such a citation was known as a "witness" or a "previous judgment" and functioned as an argument from precedence in a standard list of types of supporting arguments.

The list of four categories could be memorized easily. But the application to a given *chreia*, whether to point out that it could be supported or that it could not, would have required considerable ingenuity. The worked-out example Theon gives for the Commentary on a saying of Euripides, "that the mind of each of us is a god," illustrates just how difficult this exercise was intended to be. Not only must reasons be given to show how the saying was true, expedient, and honorable. A theme had to be found which could unite all of the considerations together in a small paragraph. This paragraph-Commentary can be reconstructed from his discussion of the exercise and the illustrations given for each of the four items. Bracketing Theon's own statements which introduce each of the "comments" one might make by using the categories listed, the paragraph reads as follows:[28]

> "Euripides the poet said that the mind of each of us is a god.
> For the mind in each of us is *really* a god, encouraging us toward things that are *advantageous* and keeping us away from things that are injurious.
> For it is *noble* that each considers god not to reside in gold and silver but in himself.
> So that, by supposing that punishment is not far distant, we might not have much tolerance for wrong doing.
>   'Such is indeed the mind of earthly men.
>   To what a day the father of men and gods may
>   lead it.'"

1.1421b–22b, 12. It consists of the following eight categories of persuasion (*protropē*): (1) Just (*dikaion*); (2) Lawful (*nomimon*); (3) Expedient (*sympheron*); (4) Honorable (*kalon*); (5) Pleasant (*hēdy*); (6) Easy (*hradion*); (7) Feasible (*dynaton*); and (8) Necessary (*anagkaion*).

[27] Aristotle, *Ars Rhetorica* 1.3.5.

[28] C. Walz, *Rhetores Graeci* I, 212–13. The quotation which is cited is from the *Odyssey* 18.136–37.

One can see from my emphasis how the categories have been used. The theme of the god within as a conscience has been used to string the statements together. Because this exercise combines analytical operations with "invention" or composition and treats the *chreia* as a thesis to be supported, it is clearly a precursor of the more elaborate *ergasia* in Hermogenes. In Theon, however, the composition-aspect is minimal and not emphasized.

For the exercises in Refutation and Confirmation, Theon provides a much larger list of nine items which now combine dictional, logical, and ethical categories. The list is given only for the refutation, and is therefore composed of "fallacies." For confirmation the list would be given in terms of their "opposites." The dictional are: (1) obscure (*asaphon*), (2) loquacious (*pleonazon*), (3) elliptical (*elleipon*). The logical are: (4) impossible (*adynaton*), (5) implausible (*apithanon*), and (6) false (*pseudos*). The ethical are: (7) unsuitable (*asympheron*), (8) useless (*achrēston*), and (9) shameful (*aischron*).[29] From the discussion which follows, it is clear that the student is to have this list clearly in mind when presented with a *chreia*. His task is to run down the list, analyzing the *chreia* with each in mind, and say whether and how the category might apply. The exercise is purely analytical and the procedure *ad seriatim*. There is no indication here that one is to construct a coherent paragraph by using this list of topics.

Theon does suggest at the end of the chapter on the *chreia*, that advanced students may be asked to take a *chreia* as a thesis and develop it as a thesis-exercise.[30] Turning to the chapter on the thesis, we find that not only *chreiai*, but maxims, proverbs, apophthegms, stories (*historiai*), and encomia may be used. Here a very long list of twenty-three categories is given which includes (1) a full set of the "chief ends" (*telika kephalaia*), (2) a fairly full set of traditional items known as supporting arguments, plus (3) random selections from other, less organized, frequently lengthy lists of argumentative *topoi* and devices found in the handbooks on rhetorical theory and technique.[31] As it appears, the more advanced student has been confronted with fuller lists of ever more specialized and intricate categories for inventing arguments, and is now expected to come up with a sizable number of telling arguments which could be used to support the *chreia* as a thesis-statement. It should be noted that the discussion and illustrations which Theon gives in the thesis-chapter indicate that the exercise is still primarily analytical, and the procedure *ad seriatim*. The list is merely a list, and not the outline for a composed speech. And there is no suggestion that the student is expected to do more than produce a respectable list of supporting arguments for a given thesis.

[29] C. Walz, *Rhetores Graeci* I, 214.
[30] C. Walz, *Rhetores Graeci* I, 216.
[31] C. Walz, *Rhetores Graeci* I, 243–44.

The time must come for a student to present a full and polished speech in support of a thesis, of course. And all of the necessary ingredients for the construction of a coherent and comprehensive argumentation are there in the list of twenty-three topics. But Theon has not, either in his discussion or in his illustrations of the exercise, said that this was to happen or what such a *chreia*-thesis-speech might have looked like. At the end of the *chreia* chapter he does mention that, if the *chreia* is used as a thesis, there should be an appropriate "introduction" (*prooimion*) after which the *chreia* itself should be "set forth," followed by "the arguments in order" (*taxis*), and the use of elaborations, digressions, and character delineations as opportunity presented itself.[32] This notice contains references to most of the major parts of what was known as a "complete argumentation," and it presents them in a sequence which correlates rather closely with the standard arrangement (*taxis*).[33] We are very close here to the outline for the elaboration of the *chreia* in Hermogenes. For Theon, however, this is to be an advanced exercise for which there is considerable opportunity for variation. The particular list of "proofs" to be used is still to be made up by the teacher, it seems. And the use of various rhetorical devices, such as elaborations and digressions, are still matters left to the discretion and ingenuity of the student. It may even be that this suggestion about using the *chreia* to compose a little self-contained speech, coming at the end of the *chreia*-chapter as it does, is a later addition to Theon's manual reflecting developments which took place sometime between the first and third centuries.

The evidence from Theon, then, is that the *chreia* was found to be helpful for a wide range of preliminary exercises in basic rhetorical skills, graded as it appears from very elementary practices to quite advanced compositions. The saying which the *chreia* contained was viewed primarily as a rhetorical statement itself, and could be subjected to analysis and critique in keeping with rhetorical theory. There is a decided emphasis upon Refutation of *chreiai* in Theon, even though the list of exercises strikes an even balance between negative and positive analyses. For the most part one has the impression of *ad hoc* and *ad seriatim* procedures, *chreiai* tossed up one after the other, in order to be analyzed as to their rhetoricity in keeping with the prescribed topics and categories of persuasion. But in the case of the Commentary, and in the chapter on the Thesis, we can see that *chreiai* were also used as statements for which several supporting arguments were to be invented. And at the end of the *chreia* chapter it seems that a speech-outline is in the making.

Before turning to Hermogenes, it should be noted that Theon seems to be concerned that only certain kinds of *chreiai* be used for the exercises in

---

[32] C. Walz, *Rhetores Graeci* I, 216.
[33] See above n. 22.

Commentary and support of a Thesis. The Commentary, he says, "is possible for those who approve (*apodechesthai*) of what has been said 'properly' (*oikeiōs*)."[34] The sayings (*apophthegmata*) to be used as theses are to be "useful" (*chrēsimos*),[35] and when used as supporting citations, they should be the sayings of "approved" persons (*dedokimasmenoi*).[36] Some *chreiai* cannot be critiqued, because "many have been expressed properly and faultlessly." And some can't be praised at all, because they involve "outright absurdity."[37] The distinctions which are being made here may have to do merely with judgment about the logics of rhetoricity. But judging from other indications, one suspects that more is at stake. In the list of topics for the Refutation, Theon has included decidedly moralistic categories as we have seen. In the first section of the *chreia* chapter he has made the distinction between the *chreia* which is *not* always "useful *for life*," and maxims and *apomnēmoneumata* which are.[38] There are also other curious remarks and interpretations throughout the chapter which seem to indicate that some *chreiai* are considered "wholesome," and therefore appropriate for confirmation; others are considered less so, and are probably not to be selected for confirmation. These, however, may be used for rhetorical analysis and refutation. The "usefulness" of the *chreia*, then (*chreia* means "useful"), may be of two kinds. One would be its "usefulness" for rhetorical training; the other would be its value as vehicle of conventional cultural ethics.

If we note the high incidence of Socratic-Cynic *chreiai* used as illustrations in the chapter, a datum which may very well reflect the original provenance and characteristics of the *chreia*-form itself, the suspicion would be that *their* "usefulness" for rhetorical training lay precisely in the sophistic and forensic qualities of their sayings. Theon's emphasis upon "helpful" sayings from approved persons, however, seems to reflect another concern altogether. It is the moral concern about influence, shared generally by teachers and authors of the first century. This concern was closely related to ideas about the effectiveness of words to manifest character and influence behaviour. Various attempts were made to counteract what was understood to be unhelpful ethically in the literary traditions, and to propose principles by which morally respectable selections and interpretations could be made.[39] That Theon chose a religious-philosophical maxim from Euripides for the Commentary, for instance,

---

[34] C. Walz, *Rhetores Graeci* I, 212, 12–13.

[35] C. Walz, *Rhetores Graeci* I, 243, 16.

[36] C. Walz, *Rhetores Graeci* I, 212, 24.

[37] C. Walz, *Rhetores Graeci* I, 213, 8–11.

[38] C. Walz, *Rhetores Graeci* I, 202, 7–9.

[39] An excellent example of this is the Ps-Plutarchian treatise on "How the Young Man Should Study Poetry" (*Quomodo alolescens poetas audire debeat*). The concern to be selective in the authors one reads is also strongly expressed in Seneca.

and selected the proposition "that a sage should participate in govern-ment" for the thesis-chapter, may reflect just such a concern. If so, we may be looking at the very end of the history of the use and usefulness of the predominately Cynic-type *chreia* in rhetorical education. With Hermogenes, Libanius, Aphthonius, and beyond, it appears to be the domesticated *chreiai* of approved teachers and philosophers which were preferred. It is, in any case, the type chosen by Hermogenes to exem-plify the exercise in elaboration which became standard.

C. *The Elaboration in Hermogenes*

The shift in emphasis which occurs with Hermogenes can be observed by noting that there is no longer any mention of separate exercises in Recitation, Inflection, Expansion, Condensation, Critique, or Refutation. Instead a single exercise in support of the *chreia* as thesis is outlined in a strictly sequential order of argumentation which is intended to produce a full and coherent confirmation. It is called the elaboration, and manifests considerable interest in matters of style and composition. The text of this section of Hermogenes' chapter on the *chreia* reads as follows:[40]

> But now let us move on to the next matter, and this is the elabo-ration. Let the elaboration be then as follows: (1) First, in a few words, an *encomium* of the one who spoke or acted; (2) then a para-phrase of the *chreia* itself; (3) then the rationale. For example: *Isocrates said the root of education is bitter, but the fruit is sweet.*
>
> (1) Praise: "Isocrates was a wise man. . .," and you amplify the topic slightly.
>
> (2) Then the chreia: "He said . . . and so forth." And you do not present it without embellishment, but you amplify the recitation.
>
> (3) Then the rationale: "For the greatest matters usually succeed because of toil, and their successfull accomplishments bring plea-sure."
>
> (4) Then a statement of the opposite: "For things that happen by chance do not require labors, and their end is most unpleasant; but in the case of worthwhile matters it is just the opposite."
>
> (5) Then the elaboration from analogy: "For just as farmers must work with the soil before reaping its fruits, so also must those who work with words."
>
> (6) Then the elaboration from example: "Only after Demosthe-nes had confined himself to his room and toiled long did he reap the rewards: wreaths and public acclamations."
>
> (7) It is possible also to give an argument by means of a state-ment from an authority. For example: "For Hesiod said,
> 'For gods in front of virtue ordained sweat.'
> And another poet says,
> 'Gods sell us every good, our toil their price.'"

[40] H. Rabe, *Hermogenis Opera* 7–8. The translation is mine.

> (8) At the end you are to add an exhortation, to the effect that it
> is necessary to heed the one who has spoken or acted.
>> So much for now; you will learn the more advanced teaching
> later.

The *chreia* chosen as an example is a saying of Isocrates, a founder figure with whom the practice of rhetoric and the formation of the Hellenistic school were combined. The saying is about *paideia*:

> "Isocrates said that the root of education is bitter, but the fruit is sweet."

The elaboration of this *chreia* consists of making eight statements. These are indicated by shorthand technical designations for various rhetorical tropes and arguments as follows: (1) Praise for the author, (2) Paraphrase of the *chreia*, (3) Statement of the rationale, (4) an Argument by contrast, (5) an Analogy, (6) an Example, (7) a Citation of an authority, and (8) an Exhortation. The set as a whole follows very closely what had come to be known as "the complete argument." There are fine discussions of the complete argument in the *Ad Herennium*, Cicero, and Quintilian.[41] A study of these discussions shows that the manifold lists of topics and arguments possible had been reduced to a single set of the basic and major types of proofs, arranged in a logical order, and correlated with the standard outline of the forensic speech itself. It was the mini-speech outline resulting from these theoretical endeavors which Hermogenes used for the elaboration of the *chreia*. Technically, the term "elaboration" should apply only to items 4 through 7, the first three items having to do with introducing and establishing the thesis, not elaborating it. Neither should it refer, technically, to the last item, which functions rather as the conclusion of the speech. But the discussions of "the complete argument" had produced a full speech outline, beginning with the statement of the proposition, and ending with a conclusion. It was in keeping with this view of the argumentation-speech as a unit that Hermogenes could designate the whole as an elaboration. We may look now at Hermogenes' suggestions for the elaboration of the saying of Isocrates.

First there is to be *a brief word of praise* for Isocrates. This corresponds to the introduction of a speech and is in keeping with the usual considerations about the establishment of a speaker's *ethos*, as well as winning audience-appeal, which are appropriate to it. It also tips us off to the author-ity of the *chreia* to be considered.

Then the *chreia* is to be given, perhaps paraphrased, making sure that its recitation enhances its meaning. This is important, because its recitation amounts to a statement of the "case" or "proposition" to be investigated.

---

[41] See above n. 22.

Then *the rationale* (*aitia*) must be given:

> "For the greatest matters usually succeed because of labors, and their successful accomplishments bring pleasure."

This is a most significant move, for with it the *chreia* is restated in the form of an assertion which can be argued. There is an interpretive aspect to this move which corresponds to the determination of the "issue" in a forensic case, or the isolation of the telling point or side to be taken in a thesis-proposal. In our case the rationale advances the *chreia* for argumentation in two ways. One is that the figural mode of the *chreia* is transposed into descriptive discourse. The other is that the theme of labor is made explicit, as that which will be at issue and in need of argumentation. It is achieved by combining the two figures of the metaphor ("vine" as symbol for agriculture, and "paideia") under the more generic category of "greatest undertakings" (*pragmata*), and by translating the sequence "bitter root"/"sweet fruit" into the staged sequence of hard labor at first/pleasant success afterward. The notion of labor or toil is won (1) by association with the term "bitter," (2) the decision to take the vine as a symbol of agriculture, and (3) the correlation of agriculture and *paideia* as "undertakings." The notion of pleasure is won by association with the term "sweet," and with the ideas of success and accomplishment which are the goals of great undertakings. But pleasure (*to hēdy*) is also one of the conventional values included in the standard lists of the "chief ends" (*telika kephalaia*)![42] This means that Hermogenes has already made a claim for the validity of the *chreia*, and proposed a very forceful thesis. If it can be sustained throughout the elaboration, the claim will be supported. This will mean that the *chreia* is right about the achievement of education as worthwhile.

The argument which follows is called a statement of "*the opposite* (*enantion*)." This is a standard argument, and a test of the validity of arguments. There were several ways in which it could be employed. In our case it inverts the terms of the proposed rationale. If the opposite set of relationships makes sense, or is recognized as a plausible statement, this serves to support the original contention:

> "For everyday occurrences do not require labors, and their end is most unpleasant, but in the case of worthwhile matters it is just the opposite."

By itself, this might not appear as a convincing statement. But it has succeeded in stating a set of relationships which contrast with the rationale and describe an eventuality "most *un*pleasant." This is achieved by contrasting labors with "everyday occurrences." There is a considerable bit

---

[42] See the list above in n. 26.

of sleight-of-hand here. The intentional aspect of labor has been assumed in order to find the contrast, and the happenstance (*tychē?*) of chance-events (*tychonta*) has been turned into a purely negative factor. But in the context of the speech-situation, the cleverness of the inversion probably would have been telling. The occasion has been taken, it should be noted, to advance the discussion about labors as well. Not only is labor now defined as "undertaking with purpose," it is also specified that the "greatest undertakings" are "worthwhile" (*spoudaios*). The category of the "worthwhile" is closely related to that of "the noble" (*kalon*), and thus evokes surreptitiously yet another of the conventional values as an argument. The effect would not have been lost on third century ears.

With *the analogy* (*parabolē*) which follows we come to an even more basic means of making a supporting argument. Discussions of the importance of the analogy for this purpose can be found in the technical handbooks on rhetoric, beginning with the earliest extant by Anaximenes and Aristotle. By definition the analogy may be taken from any of the orders of reality, but preference seems to have been given to the natural and social orders. It must be a general statement having to do with a class of objects, illustrating a principle or a relationship which has the potential for being universalized. It makes its rhetorical point by showing that the principle operates not only in the arena of relationships addressed by the thesis, but in some other order of reality as well. The correlation by analogy achieves the illusion of the universal truth of the thesis by expanding the contexts in which it can be shown to apply:

> "For just as it must be that farmers reap the fruit only after working
> the earth, so it must be also in the case of working with words."

Here the analogy of the farmer is taken from the metaphor given with the *chreia* itself, in keeping with the earlier move which established that the vine was to be understood as a symbol of agriculture. The significance of that earlier move can now be seen. By making it, Hermogenes set himself up for this telling analogical "proof." It is especially telling because agriculture itself is an arena in which both human endeavor and natural process must be conjoined. By developing just this analogy, then, Hermogenes has succeeded in correlating not just two, but three orders of process—the natural, the agricultural, and the arena of rhetorical education. The point is that the principle of the sequence effort/produce is constitutive in all arenas. The mention of the farmer makes of the analogy a new and additional argument, because the class is specified against which the correlation may be tested. Hermogenes has also taken the opportunity to specify the arena of labor indicated by the other pole of the metaphor of the *chreia*. *Paideia* is now defined precisely as "working with words." This, of course, has been the understanding of *paideia* all along, but it is allowed to come into focus only after stacking up the several implicit analogies which have been in play: natural process, greatest endeavors, worthwhile matters, farming. Now, at the appropriate place—argument by analogy—the several arenas of the analogous are combined in the analogy proper, and the labor of *paideia* is specified.

The example (*paradeigma*) which follows continues this movement toward specificity. The paradigm and the *enthymeme* (rhetorical syllogism) are, according to Aristotle, the two primary forms of rhetorical logic and proof. By definition, the paradigm is to be taken from the arena of history and be about some well-known person. Its function is to show that the general principle at issue has been actualized in a particular instance. If the example is well-chosen and telling, the argument confirms the validity of the general rule in terms of specific and precedent cases:

> "Only after Demosthenes had confined himself to his room and toiled
> long, did he reap the rewards: wreaths and public acclamations."

The famous rhetor is chosen as the example. The stories about his long hours at the desk are well-known. Allusion to these is combined with an allusion to the equally well-known passage of his famous oration "On the Crown."[43] This bit of erudition would not have damaged the argument at all. But the telling force of the argument is just that the thesis which has been developed pertains in a specific and notable case. The clever inclusion of an allusion to the canons of literature is a special touch, introducing as it does the next category of argumentation.

Other *authorities* may now be cited. In a forensic case the citation of authorities functioned as precedent judgments or decisions. In the speech in support of a thesis the citations were still called "judgments" (*krisis*) or "witnesses" (*martyria*), but the authorities were taken from the canons of literature and philosophy, not law. The purpose of the citation was to confirm the truth of the developed proposition by showing that recognized authorities had said much the same thing.

> "For Hesiod said,[44]
>   'For gods in front of virtue ordained sweat.'
> And another poet says,[45]
>   'Gods sell us every good, Our toil their price.'"

To find a telling citation from Hesiod would have been considered fortunate indeed. His authority ranked with that of Homer, and his teachings in general about the importance of work would add weight to an appropriate maxim on the subject. The one selected turns out to be

[43] Demosthenes, *De corona* 18.58.
[44] Hesiod, *Works and Days* 289.
[45] Epicharmus, frag. 287 (Kaibel).

quite significant. Not only can Hesiod's authority be claimed in support of the *chreia*-thesis. Two additional specifications are achieved. The first is that the necessity of labor is grounded in the ordinance of the gods. The second is that the pleasurable goal at the end of the time of toil can now be spoken. It is none other than *arete* itself, the mark par excellence of the highest human achievements. With this citation, then, the climax of the speech is reached, not only in the confirmation of the thesis, but in its development as a theme. The next citation from Epicharmus, then, serves as a slight denouement before the concluding exhortation is given. It continues the idea of the divine ordinance and sums things up around two terms: "our toil"/"good things" (*agatha*)!

The *exhortation* (*paraklēsis*) forms the period by referring again to Isocrates: "It is essential to heed him." This is so because the argument has confirmed the truth of his saying. It is also true because the saying, if heard, demands imitation.

The force of the argument as a whole may now be analyzed briefly. Basic rhetorical modes of inventing arguments have been used to establish the *chreia* as a thesis and support it. The establishment of the thesis is achieved by translating the *chreia's* metaphor into an assertion, and introducing categories from the "chief ends" (*telika kephalaia*) of persuasive speech. They function now as designations for commonly accepted values, the point of which is to claim them for the proposition of the thesis. This is the first move in the argumentation: "*Paideia* is like all great undertakings. It requires labor, but brings pleasure."

The second move is made with the series of supporting arguments, the elaboration in the narrower sense. Their function is to show that the proposition is in agreement with conventional and accepted judgments about the way things go in the several arenas of human observation, experience, and discourse. These include logic or dialectic (argument from the opposite), natural and social science (analogy), history and the institution of rhetoric (example), literary and cultural tradition (authority), as well as theology and ethics (citations). Taken together, there is precious little space left upon which to stand in dissent.

The third move is more subtle, but also more telling. It is the way in which the thesis has been developed thematically. This was achieved by the clever choice of terms which pick up on previous statements and move the topic ahead toward ever greater specificity and concretion. This was correlated with the sequence of arguments which moved toward the example as that argument which could use the particular instance in the form of the most basic rhetorical "proof."

Analyzed in this way, it is clear that the elaboration of the *chreia* in Hermogenes was a very difficult and demanding exercise. One wonders what has happened to the beginning exercises where skills would have been learned necessary for such an assignment. For the recitation-paraphrase of the *chreia*, and its insertion into a speech setting, something similar to Theon's exercises in Recitation, Inflection, Expansion and Condensation would have been necessary. For the rationale, Theon's exercises in Commentary and Confirmation, and so forth. As it appears, the *chreia*-exercise now seems to assume quite an advanced level of rhetorical training.

There is also much more emphasis on style, composition, and facility with the functions of *figura*. Moralizing is no longer merely a matter of caution and advice. It is built into the structure of the speech as its express intention. And the moral to be supported has precisely to do with the work at hand: a rhetoric in support of rhetorical training! It is Isocrates now whose saying is to be confirmed. And in what way, ultimately? By heeding him! We are dealing here, then, with the mimetic mentality of the Second Sophistic. Rhetoric has come full circle, from its origination in the individual's critique of social convention, to its domestication as *apologia* for social convention itself.

II. The Elaboration Pattern in Philo

A. *The Discovery of the Theme in Gen 4:2*

We turn now to a section of Philo's exegesis on a scriptural pericope in order to compare it with Hermogenes' elaboration of a *chreia*. It is important to remind ourselves that Philo is not performing a student's classroom exercise. According to rhetorical theories on style and composition, no theoretical discussion of a speech form, much less a classroom exercise, was to be taken woodenly as a model. The professional writer and speaker was to be distinguished by the skill with which he crafted his own composition. Points of entrée, arrangement and order of arguments, selection of themes, turns of phrase, amplifications, clarifications, expanded descriptions, pacing, clever allusions—all were understood to be his own "invention"—even with a given subject, theme, or text for elaboration. And every reader of Philo knows about the erudition and complexity, if not sophistication, of his dense and intricate discourse. No one has accused him of following woodenly any predetermined outline.

It is therefore all the more surprising to discover that it is the pattern of elaboration which gives structure and movement to section after section in his commentaries. In the section we have chosen as an example, an elaboration of Gen 4:2, it is even the case that seven of the eight parts of the *chreia*-elaboration are present, and in the order in which they occur in Hermogenes! There are several moves which Philo makes to complicate the pattern, one of which is a replication of the last four items in order to develop the second half of a double theme discovered in the text. But even here the items are in order, and the two themes are brought together forcefully in the final period.

De sacrificiis is a commentary-treatise on the verses in Gen 4:2-4, where Eve gives birth to Abel, a shepherd, and he, together with his brother Cain, a tiller of the soil, bring their offerings to the Lord. The treatise is divided into sections by taking up the several phrases of the pericope separately in turn, and treating them as *lemmata*. Each section, then, serves as a commentary upon, or as we would now say, an elaboration of, the particular *lemma* at hand. The trick was to craft a coherent treatise by combining the several elaborations. This could be done by a sustained development of a common theme.

The first section of the treatise (1-10) takes up the statement that "Again she gave birth, to his brother Abel" (καὶ προσέθηκε τεκεῖν τὸν ἀδελφὸν αὐτοῦ τὸν ᾿Αβελ). If our thesis is correct, this rather straightforward bit of narrative information will have been viewed by Philo in much the same way as the *chreia* was viewed upon which Hermogenes' elaboration was constructed. Philo must discover its theme and state it in the form of a thesis. The theme, moreover, must be that very one which can sustain development throughout the treatise, i.e., be rediscovered in each of the remaining *lemmata* of the pericope.

As mere beginners in such matters, we should probably confess resignation immediately. We have before us a verse which does not appear to be figural, rhetorical, or *chreia*-like at all. In the *chreiai* of the handbook there are sayings of aphoristic quality, pungent rhetoricity, clever word plays, and usage of figural language. In the saying of Isocrates, the metaphor of the vine and the theme of *paideia* were given as clear invitations to thesis- and thematic development. Where, in our bit of scripture, could a point of entrée be found?

As Philo read it, the clue was given with the term *prosethēke*, which we, poor novices, have translated by "again." According to Philo it should be translated as "he/she/it *added*." This, of course, is the basic and conventional meaning of the Greek word. It does not appear to be followed usually by an infinitive as we have it in our verse, except in LXX and the New Testament, a usage which reflects the syntactical possibilities of the term *ysp* in the Hebrew which it translates. In order to read it as Philo does, he must violate this Hebraism, as well as the Greek syntax which results from the more conventional reading of the term, because the subject of the infinitive *tekein* is now unexpressed. This, however, he finds advantageous, as we shall see. By taking *prosethēke* as "he added," and *tekein (autēn)* as "she bore," he has discovered not one, but two subjects encoded in the curious Greek syntax.

We need to pause here, and offer a brief observation on this procedure. It is not unlike other exegetical moves which Philo must make time after time as he encounters Moses' text. He can make them because of three assumptions which he holds about the nature and intention of Moses' books. The first is programmatic, namely that Moses has carefully constructed all of his writing with significant rhetorical intention. We shall return to this point in the last section of the essay. The second assumption is that the purpose of the five books is to instruct the reader in the quest for the knowledge of God. How this notion came about in the pre-Philonic traditions of scriptural interpretation, and thus could be assumed by Philo, cannot be charted here. But we can note that Philo does not find it difficult to imagine at all, least of all not in conjunction with his Hellenistic learning. If, in the system of Hellenistic-rhetorical education, texts were being exegeted with the "path toward virtue" in mind, the assumption that his Jewish texts teach the soul the path toward God cannot have appeared to be all that strange.

But just at this point a serious problem emerges. In the Hellenistic tradition, texts can be found which articulate expressly the notions and themes of the "way of *paideia.*" In the books of Moses the path to the knowledge of God is not articulated expressly. Only the overriding contours of the grand scheme of the epic can be traced out. For the rest, the manifold narrative moments do not appear, at first, to offer the soul the instruction it needs. The solution, however, is at hand. And it is fully in keeping with the first assumption. Moses' rhetorical skill was such, so the solution runs, that he could encode the epic to contain as well the story of the soul. If one is rhetorically astute, the clues may be found in Moses' text by which it can be decoded. Moses has left them there intentionally, it seems, providing for just that enigmatic quality which calls for investigation. The *lemmata* of the text, then, are *chreia*-like as to their (now assumed) figurality; but they are not *chreia*-like in respect to their lack of thematic expression. With Moses' text one must work harder. Not only must the figural intentions be discerned; the themes themselves will have to be discovered. As Philo read the text before us, then, the slightly unusual syntax given with the construction προσέθηκε τεκεῖν offered the clue. If we read ahead to see how Philo developed his interpretation of Gen 4:2–4 in the treatise as a whole, we discover that he wanted to work toward the notion that true, sacrificial offering must be the gift of oneself to God. This, of course, is in keeping with his concern to trace out the story of the soul. It would be the explication of a chapter, episode, moment, or perspective of that "story" in psychological terms.

In order to achieve the reading of the text there are two basic moves which Philo had to make. The first was to identify the persons in the narrative text as figures of psychological qualities or processes. This could be achieved quite easily through the use of etymologies, symbol identifications, word-plays, and so on, as every reader of Philo knows.

The second move, however, would have been more difficult. Philo had to discover in the text some clue appropriate for the development of his theme. Reading through the treatise, one is struck by the repetition of two contrasting sets of terms which form clusters of associations of loosely related meanings. The one set contains such words as gift, offering, return, attribution, referral, and addition; the other contains terms as possession, keeping, separaton, rejection, and subtraction. Following these through the treatise as a whole, one can see that they provide for its thematic development (elaboration). By using them, all of the *lemmata* with their elaborations and intricate amplifications can be used to explore the complex theme of "offering" to the full.

When one notices, then, that the names of Abel and Cain, decoded etymologically, correlate curiously with this theme (Cain means "possession"; Abel means "refers to God"), we are about ready to begin. Here the figural and the thematic aspects of the text as *"chreia"* conjoin. And with the discovery of Moses' intention in the use of *prosethēke* the elaboration is on.

B. *The Pattern of Elaboration in Sacr 1–4*

1. The Text Reconstructed

We want now to analyze Philo's commentary of Gen 4:2. In order to do that it will be helpful to set the text before us in its form as an elaboration. We have therefore deleted or bracketed material which serves as clarification or amplification of the main points in the elaboration. We can do this because the logic of the thematic development is present in the major moves and arguments given with the elaboration outline. To demonstrate Philo's use of this outline we need reproduce a reconstructed text only for Sacr 1–4, because the first pattern of elaboration is completed within these paragraphs. The sections of the elaboration-pattern are given in parentheses. Quotation marks are used to indicate terms understood by Philo to be encoded, and waiting for decoding. We shall see that most terms in the scriptural text are regarded as encoded, but that decoding occurs gradually in the course of the elaboration. The text, then, is as follows:

1. (Brief word of praise)
   (missing)
2. (*Chreia*)
   "and 'He' 'added' to this that 'she' 'brought forth' 'Abel' his brother."
3. (*Ratio*)
   The addition of one thing implies the subtraction of another.
   (Rationale)
   If we must say that "Abel" was "added," we must imagine that "Cain" was "subtracted."

4. (Contrast)

It turns out then, that there are two opposite and contending views of life—

[One which ascribes all things to the mind; the other which attributes all things to God. The first is figured by Cain, whose name means "possession"; the second is figured by Abel, whose name means "refers to God."]

5. (Analogy)

Both of these lie in the "womb" of the single soul; but when they are "brought to birth" they are separated.

6. (Example)

This will be shown more clearly in the case of Rebekah, who conceived two natures of good and evil, received a vivid impression of the character of both, and perceived them contending. She asked God what had happened, and how it might be remedied.

7. (Witness-Authority)

God answered her question by saying two things:

'Two nations are in your womb,'

and

'Two peoples shall be separated from your womb.'

8. (Epilogue as partial period)

The first oracle states what had befallen her—to bear both good and evil.

(Epilogue as exhortation)

The second gives the remedy—that good and evil be separated and occupy no longer the same abode.

(Epilogue as period)

So then, when God added the good conviction Abel to the soul, he took away the foolish opinion Cain.

2. The Composition of the Elaboration

(1) A Brief *Word of Praise*. The elaboration, according to Hermogenes, is to begin with a brief word of praise for the author. Philo has not made mention of Moses' authorship in the text before us. But every reader of Philo knows that this is assumed. Philo mentions and discusses Moses' authorship of the five books in many places throughout his works,[46] and frequently introduces the elaboration of *lemmata* by "then he (Moses) says," or "how well Moses has written this," or some such brief acknowledgement of skillful composition. That he does not provide a brief word of praise in our case is therefore inconsequential to our thesis. The commentary form prohibits the repetition of such a notice at every verse. And the context of the treatise itself, presupposing as it does the preceding treatise, *De cherubim*, does not require it even here at the beginning.

[46] Among the many references to Moses as author of the Five Books which he has carefully conceived and wonderfully written, two fine sections may be mentioned: *Opif* 1-6; *Abr* 1-6. They are thoroughly encomiastic.

(2) *Chreia*. The scriptural verse is cited simply as that which is to be analyzed and elaborated. This is Philo's customary procedure, and it is given, presumably, in the form in which Philo has read it in the text before him. This substitutes for the "recitation" customary in the rhetorical schools, and prohibits any paraphrastic embellishment at this point. But the "reading" intended, and to be clarified in the elaboration, is Philo's own. Whether aspects of recitation are involved in the writing and reading of the citation is difficult to determine. But it is conceivable that something analogous to the Hellenistic practices of memorization and "meaningful" recitation was also at work in some way. Philo assumes, in any case, that the citation of the verse automatically sets the stage for its analysis. We have already discussed the procedure for finding a point of entrée to this difficult *"chreia."* Philo's readers will have understood that that had happened, and read (hear) the verse as significant and full of "meaning," i.e., "to be elaborated."

(3) *Ratio*. The move from a *chreia* to a statement of its thesis in the rationale could be made in one step. In Philo's elaboration two steps are required, which we have designated as *ratio* and *rationale*. This actually accords with accepted rhetorical practice in the development of a thesis from some narrative or aphoristic text. According to the *Ad Herrenium*, the *ratio* is to "set forth the causal basis for the proposition by means of a brief explanation subjoined." The *propositio* itself, then, sets forth "what we intend to prove."[47] In our text the *ratio* is given with the statement that "the addition of one thing implies the subtraction of another." We might consider this irresponsible rhetoric, were it not for the fact that it does agree with conventional Hellenistic logic in mathematics and dialectic theory. That Philo knew this, and wished to remind his readers of the fact, is noted expressly: ". . . as in the case of arithmetical quantities, or of our successive inward thoughts."

This intervening step is necessary, because Philo intends to set up the contrast between Abel and Cain. In the verse at hand only Abel is mentioned. But with the term *prosethēke* translated as "he *added*," Philo is able to infer the contrast logically by means of the *ratio*. The appeal to logic here is not inconsequential. With it a primary concern of rhetorical argumentation is addressed.

The rationale can now be given, that namely, "If Abel was added, Cain was subtracted." This may appear to be a most curious statement of the thesis to be developed. But it is problematic only because the terms are not yet decoded. Philo was fully aware that this was the case, because he immediately adds the notice about the "unfamiliar terms" possibly causing perplexity, and notes his intention to clear this up in the course of the elaboration. With the statement of the rationale, Philo has

---

[47] *Ad Herennium* 2.18.28.

accomplished the first major move in the elaboration of the text. He has transposed the *chreia*'s enigmatic expression into a discursive statement. And he has presented the statement as the *chreia*'s thesis which may now be analyzed and supported as to its meaning and validity, i.e. elaborated. That this is the thesis statement is demonstrated further by the fact that it is restated at the end of the elaboration as the period, i.e., that point which has been proven. By then, of course, the reader will have been led through a complete decoding procedure, as well as a complex development of the theme as it applies to this particular thesis.

(4) *The Contrast*. The category of the opposite (*enantion*) was used in rhetoric in a number of ways. In Hermogenes' elaboration it was used to invert the thesis statement and show that a logical relationship also pertained when the terms of the thesis were changed into their opposites. But other ways to test the thesis by inventing some kind of dialectic logic were also in order. Philo has already introduced an opposition in his statement of the thesis. He uses the *topos* of opposition, then, to explicate that contrast further. He makes three significant moves at this point. The first is that "Abel" and "Cain" are decoded at this point by means of etymologies. The second is that each is taken to symbolize a view of life (*doxa*). The third is that the opposition between these views is expressly stated, then made precise by means of the term "contending."

This is a rather complex argumentation, encompassing much more than one might expect under the heading of the contrast. But it is fully appropriate to the theme of the thesis, and necessary to its development. The meaning of the names "Abel" and "Cain" advance the elaboration in two respects. They show that the verse of scripture was encoded; and, now that they are decoded, they show that the theme suggested is correct. They do this by revealing that in addition to the term *prostithēmi*, two other figures in the verse also have to do with matters of "addition," namely "attribution" and "referral." A set of terms begins to cluster around the theme of "addition" at this point. The entire treatise will be required in order to develop all of the dialectics involved in the several relationships which must be explored (God—soul—two contrasting opinions possible). Here it is enough to establish the correctness of the thesis of the first *lemma* in such a way as to prepare for what follows. In that Abel and Cain now are seen to refer to two contrasting opinions or views of life, the stage is set for an exploration of each in relationship to the contrast between "addition" and "separation" as it may apply to the *chreia* itself. This will be elucidated in the analogy which follows.

(5) *The Analogy* states that "separation" occurs at "birth." The amplification of this argument which Philo offers is extremely convoluted, and does not appear to be very helpful. There is mention of enemies not being able to live long together, Cain as self-loving principle being in the soul until Abel is born, and Cain being abandoned at that

point. This is difficult to imagine in terms of the story at hand, although it does anticipate aspects of the Rebekah paradigm to follow, which may have been in Philo's mind all along. The analogy, however, is proper according to the canons of rhetoric, taken as it is from the orders of natural and human events. It is also *a propos* to the elaboration, given with the scripture verse itself, and lending itself as illustration to the theme of "separation." This move corresponds exactly to the way in which Hermogenes "invented" his analogy. To find a way to do that would have been considered skillful indeed. "Separation" had, we may remember, been "inferred" by Philo as "implied" in the use of the term *prostithēmi*. Now he has demonstrated that the analogy suggested by the verse itself supports that implication. The plot thickens. The procedure thus far (steps 1–5) is very similar to that found in the elaboration of Hermogenes.

One additional observation should be made here. Philo has taken the occasion to begin the process of thematic specification. The use of the term "enemies" heightens the sense of contention, and moves it in the direction of hostility. The contrasting opinions are now specified more narrowly as "God-loving" and "self-loving." This is not merely a superfluous shift to the language of piety. The notion of "love" is earmarked as that toward which the development of the themes of addition, referral, and gift must move, if the true meaning of "offering" is to be grasped. Another specification of significance is the usage of the term doctrine (*dogma*) for Abel's view of things. This begins to distinguish Abel's view from that of Cain as to its validity. Cain's view continues to be called a *doxa*. Abel's dogma is also indicated. It is the view which confesses that there is a single cause of all things.

(6) *The Example* is taken from the epic history, and is the well-known story of Rebekah's conception of Jacob and Esau (Gen 25:21–23). It is quite a singular "example" to be sure, but one most striking and, just because of its epic significance, telling. By choosing it, Philo is able to identify who it is ultimately who makes "additions" and "subtractions," thus decoding the last cipher still encoded in the scripture verse. (It is God who made the addition.) He is also able to tie up several strings still loose in the development of the theme. The two views of things are now "good" and "evil." These, in turn, are capacities given with the *pathos* of the soul as it experiences perception and contention. Only by asking God for help can a remedy be found. All that and the force of a classic example of Jewish piety from the foundational epoch of Jewish history beside! Can all of that really be thought while reading that single verse about Eve? And what, after all, is the remedy?

(7) *The Witness* is taken from the scriptural account of the story of Rebekah's conception, supplied by the words of God to Rebekah's query. This is clever, and first century listeners would have taken note. Not only

is a firm connection established between the two headings of the elaboration (Example and Witness of an authority). The authority for the witness is none other than the Lord himself. Four statements are made by the Lord in Gen 25:23. Philo uses two of them, the one to answer Rebekah's query about what had befallen her, and the other to indicate the remedy. In each a further bit of decoding is necessary to make the point, of course. But in their decoded form, the oracular witnesses of the Lord can be seen, marvelously, to supply the epi-logic necessary to close the elaboration.

(8) *The Epilogue* for Philo's elaboration is a bit complex, and we have divided it into three parts. In rhetorical elaboration both exhortation and periodization were appropriate. Philo has included both functions, couching the exhortation between two statements which function as periods. The first statement decodes the oracle about the "two nations" Rebekah has conceived, indicating that they refer to the "good and evil" which the soul must bear. This psychologizes the story of Rebekah, aligns it with the analogy and the scriptural text, and produces a partial period for the argumentation. The text is about the soul which bears both good and evil.

The Exhortation is a restatement of the second oracle about the remedy. The reader is prepared to hear that the "two peoples" are also ciphers for "good and evil." The reader is also prepared to understand the oracle from the Lord about the remedy as an exhortation, even though it is not addressed directly to the reader. What comes as a bit of a surprise is that the remedy involves a "separation." The occurrence of just this term in the oracle suddenly appears as the key which unlocks all of the still undisclosed mysteries of the interconnectedness of the various parts of the elaboration. It is there in the text of the oracle of remedy which addresses the situation of Rebekah (the example), clarifies the meaning of the analogy (birth), picks up on the themes of "opposition" and "subtraction" in the rationale, and aligns them all as explication of the scriptural *lemma* about Eve. By discovering just this oracle (witness) in conjunction with a telling example, Philo has succeeded in composing a very impressive elaboration.

The *Epilogue as period* can now be given. Here, finally, the last bit of decoding also occurs. The subject of the verb *prosethēke* may now be expressed. It is none other than God. "So then, when God added the good conviction Abel to the soul, he took away the foolish opinion Cain." With this statement the elaboration is complete, the thesis sustained, and the *lemma* exegeted, i.e., transposed into that order of significance claimed for it in the first thesis-statement itself.

3. The Thematic Development

Philo's composition of an elaboration has now been analyzed with respect to the major headings of the elaboration pattern. It has not been possible to discuss matters of style, sources for ideas and imagery, or Philo's use of tropes and clever rhetorical devices—all of which do have significance for the persuasiveness of the composition. But we do need to make a few observations about the thematic development of the elaboration as a unit.

As with Hermogenes' composition, one can chart the thematic development in Philo by noting how the selection of terminology and imagery is handled as moves are made from heading to heading. In some cases connotations of associated terms need to be expanded in the direction of that order of reality to which the theme is moving. In Philo's composition this order of reality is ethical psychology. But as earlier terms of more general application are expanded in this direction, a kind of specificity also occurs. Thus the movement from *doxa*, through *dogma*, *physis*, *agathos*, and back to *dogma*, as designations for "Abel," functions as a study in the specification of a certain psychology.

But thematic development must be achieved in tandem with another developmental function of the elaboration. We have seen in Hermogenes that all of the "arguments" selected for the elaboration are derived from or have immediate association with, some aspect of the *chreia* itself. The elaboration does not move away from the *chreia* and its imagery at any point, but continually returns to it in order to find there clues for the intention of the appropriate argument for the next heading. This, in fact, defines the elaboration as a particular form of rhetorical argumentation. It is, in this respect, thoroughly "exegetical." The same is true for Philo's commentary, of course. This means that the scripture verse is not fully elucidated in the first move (the statement of the rationale as thesis), even in respect to a clear explication of what the theme will be. The entire elaboration is required in order to explicate the significance of all aspects of the verse, in regard to the theme which has been suggested.

Since Philo is dealing with the double problem of deriving a theme, as well as establishing the "*chreia's*" figurality, the process of decoding the scripture's figurality is sequential. Each heading of the elaboration is taken, not only to develop the theme, but also to render yet another figural aspect of the verse into decoded significance. We must wait until the very end, for instance, to learn that it is God who makes the "additions" and "subtractions" for the soul. Thus the earlier decodifications are also thematically unspecified. Only by combining exegetical elucidation and thematic development can Philo end with a fully coherent statement.

We may chart this sequential process by identifying each move of the elaboration with that particular aspect of the text which is thereby decoded. The encoded text reads as follows:

> 'And "He" "added" to this that "she" "brought forth"
> "Abel" his brother. (And "Cain" was "subtracted.")'

The sequence of decodification unfolds one step at a time:

> The Ratio decodes "added."
> The Rationale decodes "subtracted" (implying "Cain").
> The Contrast decodes "Abel"; "Cain."
> The Analogy decodes "She"; "brought forth."
> The Example decodes "brought forth"; "subtracted."
> The Witness decodes "subtracted."
> The Epilogue decodes "He."

This combination of sequential exegesis and thematic development results in the curiosity that the argumentation succeeds ultimately by establishing its own claim to be the correct reading of the text. And the correct reading of the text is simply the decoded statement of the encoded text. So the elaboration has merely established the text itself-as-thesis. It is this curiosity which invites the reader to read on. Surely there is more to be said, more to learn. And there is. But, as we shall see, it too will merely be a further elaborative amplification on the text. The *lemma* at hand has not yet been exhausted, even at the level of primary thematic elucidation. Both "addition" and "subtraction" are in play. But we have learned, after all, only that such is the case, namely that "subtraction" really is implied, and that "subtraction" is what must happen to Cain. As for the "addition" of "Abel" we are less informed. And as for the full significance of the themes of "giving to" and "taking away" as they apply to the story of the soul and God, much more needs to be said.

So the first elaboration of the treatise has merely established (1) that the first verse of the pericope gives the theme, and (2) what that theme is. It has been completed within the first four paragraphs. And there are still six paragraphs to go before the next *lemma*. What more might be said about this first verse? And will the pattern of elaboration be left behind?

C. *The Elaboration in Sacr 5–10*

A complete analysis of the argumentation in Sacr 5–10 will not be possible here. It will be sufficient to indicate (1) that the pattern of elaboration continues to provide the outline, and (2) that the theme for the treatise is developed and advanced by this means.

At first glance it appears that Sacr 5–10 merely sets forth a series of examples having to do loosely with the theme of "addition." Abraham, Jacob, Isaac, and Moses are set forth as models of piety, and their deaths are described as transitions in which some things are left behind, others gained. Coming as they do on the heels of the Rebekah story, they appear to add other examples to that of Rebekah, on the general notions of "separation" and "addition."

A series of examples is not uncommon in Hellenistic literature, and finding that Philo has constructed such a series is not surprising. The question is whether and how the series of paradigms relates to the elaboration in paragraphs 1–4, and how it continues the development of the theme. The place to begin is with the observation that the *example* does have a place in the elaboration pattern Philo has been using. If we look for indications of other components of the pattern in Sacr 5–10, we can determine (1) a fine period as *epilogue* ("Such is the meaning of the words that God added to the mind the birth of the perfect good. The good is holiness and the name of holiness is Abel," Sacr 10; *PLCL* 2.101); (2) a rather heightened and eulogistic description about God's spiritual gifts, a passage which applies the examples to the experience of "the soul," and thus borders on *exhortation* (Sacr 10); and (3) the citation of God's words to Moses ("I give thee as god to Pharaoh," Sacr 9; *PLCL* 2.101) which could function as a *witness* within a pattern of elaboration. At this point we have retraced the steps of the elaboration in reverse order, beginning with the epilogue, and arriving at the examples before us. It does appear that the pattern of elaboration is in evidence from the example through the epilogue.

When we notice now that the theme of the three examples is that of "addition," we can see that, thematically, the discussion of the examples presupposes the first steps of the earlier elaboration about the importance of "addition" and the contrast between "addition" and "subtraction." Since the analogy of the elaboration in Sacr 1–4 was birth and the point of the paradigm there was "separation," the introduction of the analogy of death in Sacr 5–10, and the discussion of "addition" there, appear to invert the immediately preceding emphases and refer back to the *rationale* and *contrast* as an alternative elaboration. If this is correct, two elaborations have been produced which share in common the first three steps. The outline appears as follows:

Sacr. 1–2

Chreia	And he added to this that she brought forth Abel his brother.
Ratio	The addition of one thing implies the subtraction of another.
Rationale	If we must say that Abel was added, we must imagine that Cain was subtracted.
Contrast	There are two opposite and contending views. . . .

	Sacr 3–4	*Sacr 5–10*
Analogy	Birth	Death
Example	Rebekah's conception of	Patriarch's deaths as
	two contenting natures	transitions to the better
Witness	Separation at birth	Addition at death
Epilogue	God took away Cain	God added Abel

Setting Sacr 3–4 and 5–10 side by side in this way, it can be seen that each has taken up one of the aspects of the contrast for elaboration. Sacr 3–4 elaborates the thesis that the "addition of Abel" follows on the separation of Cain. Taken together, the two elaborations function to validate the single thesis: that the scriptural verse is about the story of the soul, the contrast of good and evil, and God's remedy—"putting away" evil; "adding" good. The *lemma* has been established as thematic; it contains clues for the reconstruction of a complete description of the significant moments in the story of the soul ("birth"–"death"). And it provides clues for thematic categories by which that story can be fully explored ("separation"–"addition"). This discovery and verification can provide a very firm foundation for additonal elaborations. That is because the elaboration has really only established the thesis, *that* the *lemma* is *about* the story of the soul's contentions. Much more can be said about it.

The clever dialectic which Philo sets up within and between the two elaborations is indicative of the direction in which the treatise will be developed. The analogy for "separation" is not death, but birth; the analogy for "addition" is not birth, but death. And so the inversions of contrasting symbols begin to produce such interesting notions as the following: the one who takes is taken away; the one who gives is added to; the one who gives himself is both taken away and added to—all studies in reciprocity which continue throughout the treatise and eventually allow the statement to be made, that "a soul wholly complete in all its parts, should be given in their entirety as a burnt-offering to God" (Sacr 139; *PLCL* 2.195). "Gift" finally wins as the preferred term for the theme of the treatise. Philo discovered it lurking there under the term *prostithēmi* in the first *lemma* of the pericope, used the first elaboration to develop the contrasts involved, and introduced the possibility of a dialectic in the exchange of gifts by setting those contrasts up dialectically in the second elaboration.

The plays on scriptural references to births, deaths, offerings, and gifts which this now makes possible provides for the development of innumerable schemata and full discussion of intricate interrelationships among the various figures and events in the story of the soul. Not only does the elaboration of the first *lemma* set the stage for the elaboration(s) of the pericope as a whole; the requirements of elaboration expand the text ultimately to include the scriptures as a whole. The scripture provides the resources from which the analogies and examples must come. It substitutes for the literary traditions of Hellenistic lore and learning by which the *chreia* is elaborated. It becomes Philo's field of quest and play. The soul's quest and Philo's quest are ultimately one and the same. And as the theme of gifting is worked out for Gen 4:2–4, so the theme of gifting is discovered in all the scriptures, and so the soul of the exegete is gifted and returns the gift—in a marvelous linguistic fiction. The fiction resides in the assumption of the scripture's rhetoricity. We may ask, now, about the assumption, whether it may have been justified, and how it may have influenced Philo's commentaries as a whole.

Conclusion: Philo in the School of Moses

We have theorized that Philo was trained in the Hellenistic schools of rhetoric. We have sought to demonstrate that he knew and followed the rhetorical pattern for elaborating narrative and aphoristic material. But in place of the Hellenistic *chreia*, Philo sets the successive *lemmata* of the scriptures at the beginning of his exercises, and derives from Moses his theses. Thus the logic of thesis-derivation from narrative and aphoristic material is learned from rhetorical theory. And the logic of argumentation as exegetical elaboration of narrative and aphoristic material is learned from Hellenistic practice. Much of the imagery, patterns of thought, conceptualities and *topoi* in Philo is also clearly Hellenistic. Thus the question: How can Philo seriously have thought that the intention of Moses' scripture could be disclosed by this means?

The answer must begin with the observation already made about Philo's assumption of Mosaic authorship. If Moses were truly skilled as an author, as becomes the cultural significance of his books, they must be carefully crafted. And the marks of the craft of that skillful composition must be available to those who know rhetoric. For rhetoric deals in the analysis of texts, in order to disclose their intentions and persuasions.

If such were the assumption in general, it would not have been difficult for Philo, or others before him, to have made a start. There are, after all, many obvious genres of material in the five books which literary critics with rhetorical training could easily recognize. Philo has some fine passages about Gen 1–2 as "cosmogony,"[48] Gen 3–10 as "primeval history,"[49] the patriarchal narratives as "epic history,"[50] the giving of the

---

[48] Examples: *Opif* 3; *Abr* 1–2.
[49] An example: *Vita Mos* 2.45–65.
[50] Cf. *Abr* 1–2; *Vita Mos* 2.45–65.

laws as "legislation,"[51] the words of the Lord as "oracles," and so on. He discusses the sequence in which Moses has ordered his materials.[52] And he explains that literary form determines rhetorical intentionality, and therefore exegesis as well.[53]

It is therefore not insignificant that Philo treats the cosmogony as cosmogony, the patriarchal narratives as encomia, and the laws as legislation—all forms of discourse with which the Hellenistic rhetor would have been familiar. To begin with, then, the genre of the text puts some constraints upon the genre of its commentary. If a patriarchal narrative is encomiastic, the commentary should produce at least an encomium, and so forth. It may even be the case that the various types of material in the five books are distinguished as to their need for decoding, weighted as to their rhetorical intentions and clarity, and thus as to their employment according to the headings of the elaboration pattern used in the allegories.

We have noted that the "oracles" of the Lord occur as witnesses. This may be significant as a clue to Philo's understanding of their rhetorical form and appropriate function. Further investigation may show that the book of Leviticus enjoys a particular status, is interpreted peculiarly with respect to its literal and symbolic signification, and that its laws may be cited in the allegorical commentaries as having innate legal precedence. The same may be suspected for Deuteronomy. Citations from this book appear repeatedly in the allegorical commentaries with little need for decoding. Has Philo read it as a compendium of Moses' gnomological and philosophical teaching? And is it significant that the allegorical commentaries are limited to the books of Genesis and Exodus? Is a rhetorical judgment in play here as well?

Our thesis has been that the text of Gen 4:2 was regarded as a "*chreia*," i.e., an aphoristic narrative. What about this view of the text? And what about the elaboration it invited? A remarkable case is given with the story of Sarah's laughter in Gen 18:9–15. The stories of Abraham and Sarah are generally taken by Philo to be encomiastic (witness *De Abrahamo*); but they also are found to yield marvelous points of departure for allegorical commentary. In the case of Sarah's laughter, a pivotal and problematic theme is given from which various encomiastic

---

[51] *Vita Mos* 2.12–20.

[52] Cf. *Vita Mos* 2.46–51.

[53] The treatise *De Abrahamo* is an excellent example of Philo's view of the significance of the literary form of the patriarchal narratives. They are, according to Philo, encomia. Cf. *Abr* 4, 9, 31, 36, 52, 60, 89, 114, 167, 183, 190–91, 208, 217, 247, 255, 262, 275. This view in turn determines the encomiastic exegesis both at the "literal" level of paraphrastic embellishment, and at the "allegorical" level of decoding as the story of the excellent "soul." The several encomiastic episodes taken together form, according to Philo, a "life" (*bios*). Cf. *Abr* 276; *Jos* 1.

traits can be developed by some form of denial of, or apology for, the incident. But just because it is a remarkable notice on Moses' part, and because it is relatable to the meaning of the name "Isaac" (by etymology), the passage can also be read as a "*chreia*," inviting decoding and allegorical elaboration. This is also a rhetorical judgment. And it means that the scriptural text has been read at this point from at least two rhetorical points of view. Were these two points of view to be taken together, compared and contrasted as Philo does, one form of interpreting scripture from scripture would be given. The basic assumption would be that the scripture is complex, crafted rhetorically in such a way as to invite layered exegesis.[54]

If we now recall the elaboration of Gen 4:2 in Sacr 1–10, another form of interpreting scripture from scripture is illustrated. Gen 4:2 is treated mainly as a "*chreia*," i.e., a statement by Moses which was intentionally encoded and is therefore enigmatic. The logic by which its thesis was derived is fully Hellenistic; and the pattern of argumentation by which it could be fully decoded is also Hellenistic. But once the thesis has been stated in the rationale, the examples and the witnesses are taken from scripture, and the conclusion reveals a strong and peculiarly Jewish theological concern, also based upon the teaching of Moses.

The procedure here consists in stacking up a series of scriptural citations and narrative events, each of which contributes to the elaboration by expanding the connotations of all of them. The scriptural citations are selected because of the incidence of terminology which can be taken to belong to a common word-cluster—a phenomenon which we have called the theme. This results in the enrichment of nuances as the theme is developed. It also gives the illusion that all of the scriptural citations are referring to the same phenomenon. It is the same with the stacking up of examples. One gets the impression that all of the scriptural accounts of e.g., conception, birth, death, etc. are encoded narrative events referring to the story of the soul in its quest for God.

Thus the procedure of using scripture to interpret scripture in this way functions in the elaboration of any given *lemma* by supporting the basic assumption of its encoded rhetoricity. The stacking succeeds in building a case for the figurality of the *lemma* (that it is indeed encoded), while at the same time working for its decodification. Movement from one heading to the next is made possible by the fact that the several illustrations, and the poignant discourse (citations) which attends them, are not really analogous in every respect. The slippage caused by difference among the citations and illustrations taken to be analogous creates the possibility of word-plays, contrasts, rankings, and so forth. Schemata can be developed for staged ascents, dialectical inversions, and

---

[54] Cf. *Abr* 111–13, 200–207; *Leg All* 3.217f.; *Mut* 166; *Spec Leg* 2.54.

significant sequences. Thus the scripture as a whole becomes a field of play. And it is the curious logic of the elaboration pattern which facilitates this amazing exegesis.

The five books of Moses, then, are understood by Philo to be a complete and sufficient scripture for the disclosure of all aspects of the story of the soul. As such it is understood as a unit. It is the complete and unifying vehicle for the transmission of Jewish cultural and theological heritage. It is authoritative in terms of Moses' authorship and his privileged position of having had discourse with God. But because he was skilled in his writing, it must be read with that skill in mind. That skill, according to Philo, was the mastery of rhetorical technique. Trained in rhetoric himself, Philo claims to be able to master the master. The elaboration we have analyzed shows that his claim was not unfounded. His commentaries as a whole show the extent to which his mastery was complete. And the validity of his reading of Moses? Does it matter as long as the rules of rhetoric pertained?

"MOYSES PALPANS VEL LINIENS":
ON SOME EXPLANATIONS OF THE NAME
OF MOSES IN PHILO OF ALEXANDRIA*

VALENTIN NIKIPROWETZKY

La Sorbonne

The sudden and cruel recurrence of an illness which several years' remission had accustomed us to believe to be conquered, struck down Samuel Sandmel at the beginning of November, 1979. Appointed to the University of Chicago after a long and distinguished career at Cincinnati, Samuel had spent that year in the joy that his teaching and the pursuit of his work afforded him.

He died with pen in hand, so to speak. He had just published an introduction to Philo of Alexandria and had finished revising the manuscript of an extensive novel on the Apostle Paul. The diagnosis of his disease, of which he was fully aware, in no way lessened his courage nor caused him to give up the project he had in mind of a biographical work in which he would retrace the history of his family, from the Ukraine to the United States, as well as his own spiritual itinerary.

The work of Samuel Sandmel is worthy of a study in itself. I will content myself with emphasizing that ten years of close friendship gave me the opportunity of appreciating Samuel's erudition, his critical judgment, his sense of the movement of history, his reasoned capacity for resisting the fashionable, more tyrannical and deranging in the realm of the mind than in any other area. As a man he was as impressive as he was as a scholar. In him the dynamic of his great integrity was tempered by authentic humanity, a warm openness to others which transformed every *rencontre* into a celebration. Faithful to his religious convictions, he knew the history of Christianity in depth and clearly evaluated its dimensions. Making no facile concessions, he yet built a bridge between the "two living faiths" and won the respect of both Jews and Christians. His editorship of the Oxford Study Edition of the *New English Bible with the Apocrypha* is an enduring testimony to this.

Though hastily and all too insufficiently recalled, such are some of

* Valentin Nikiprowetzky died December 19, 1983. This article was translated by Elvire and Earle Hilgert.

the personality traits, unique in their kind, of an uncommon man whose absence we mourn and whose presence continues among us.

Samuel Sandmel devoted one of his compositions to the solitude of the prophet Moses on Mount Sinai. I would wish that the memory of this work would be sufficient reason for offering its author this handful of remarks on the name of the hero whom he praised so diligently, attentively, and fervently.

The following lines are intended as a complement to Jaroslaw Černy's article published in 1942 in the *Annales du Service Archéologique de l'Egypte* 41, 349–54, entitled "Greek Etymology of the Name of Moses."

I.

A reader of the *Liber Interpretationis Hebraicorum Nominum* of Jerome or of the Greek *Onomastica Sacra* cannot help but be struck by etymologies, either semi-obscure or totally enigmatic in appearance, which these collections propose almost insistently for the name of the Lawgiver.

We give them here according to Paul de Lagarde,[1] who lists them without comment:

14.1 *Moyses vel Moses adtrectans vel palpans aut symptus ex aqua siue adsumptio* [Moyses or Moses, who handles or indeed feels for or was taken up from water, or reception].

65.8 *Moyses adsumptus vel palpans siue contrectans aut urgens sed melius est ex aqua* [Moyses, who is received or who feels for, or handles, or who urges; but what is better, from water].

73.20 *Moyses palpans siue liniens* [Moyses who feels for or who anoints].

74.20 *Moyses adtrectans siue liniens* [Moyses who handles or anoints].

75.24 *Moyses palpans siue liniens* [Moyses who feels for or anoints].

78.9 *Moyses palpans vel liniens* [Moyses who feels for or anoints].

79.18 *Moyses palpans vel contrectans* [Moyses who feels for or handles].

173.60 Μωϋσῆς νοῦς ἢ εὐσεβῆς ἢ ἔρευνα κυρίου. [Moses, mind or pious or inquiry of the Lord].

179.15 Μωϋσῆς ὕδατος ἀναίρεσις ἢ νοῦς εὐσεβῆς ἢ ἔρευνα κυρίου. [Moses, taking up from water or pious mind or inquiry of the Lord].

183.33 Μωϋσῆς ὕδατος ἀναίρεσις. [Moses, taking up from water].

---

[1] Paul de Lagarde, *Onomastica Sacra*, 2d ed., Göttingen: Horstmann, 1887; repr. Hildesheim: Olms, 1966.

195.82   Μωσῆς ἐξ ὕδατος ἀναίρεσις. [Moses, taking up out of water].
195.82–83 Μωυσῆς ἔρευνα κυρίον. [Moses, inquiry of the Lord].

II.

We must admit that the pages F. Wutz devotes to these singular etymologies of the name Moses in his classic work on the *Onomastica Sacra*[2] appear to be confused, and in fact, all the more so in that Wutz mentions a reference which should have been decisive, in part at least, in evaluating them.

Wutz writes as follows:

> What is remarkable here is that particularly in this etymology *nous* also is used: Μωυσῆς ὕδατος ἀναίρεσις ἢ νοῦς εὐσεβῆς ἢ ἔρευνα κυρίον [Moses, taking up from water or pious mind or inquiry of the Lord], 179.15; Lactantius, Ms. b, only *Moyses sec. aegyptiaca de aqua susceptus* [Moses, according to the Egyptian, taken up from the water]: ὕδατος ἀναίρεσις [taking up from water] goes through all the groups, 183.33 (= Vaticanum Gr. s. §7); 195.82: Μωσῆς ἐξ ὕδατος ἀναίρεσις. Μωϋσῆς ἔρευνα κυρίον ἢ ἀπὸ σωτηρίας [Moses, taking up out of water. Moses, inquiry of the Lord, or from salvation] and 203.16: Μωϋσῆς ὕδατος ἀναίρεσις [Moses, taking up from water] (both = Philonic-Origenistic group of onomastica). On the other hand, we find in Vatican Onomasticon Fragment 1 simply Μωϋσῆς νοῦς ἢ εὐσεβῆς ἢ ἔρευνα κυρίον [Moses, mind or pious or inquiry of the Lord] 173.60.
>
> The etymology *hydatos anairesis* [taking up from water] could easily be found in all the groups because it is biblical: Exod 2:10: "And she called his name משׁה, ותאמר כי מן המים משׁיתהו [Moses, for she said, 'Because I drew him from the water']." Hence Philo, Vita Mos 1.4 [i.e. 1.17]: εἶτα δίδωσιν ὄνομα θεμένη Μωυσῆν ἐτύμως διὰ τὸ ἐκ τοῦ ὕδατος αὐτὸν ἀνελέσθαι· τὸ γὰρ ὕδωρ μῶς ὀνομάζουσιν Αἰγύπτιοι. [Therefore she gave him a name, Moses, derived etymologically from his having been taken up from the water; for the Egyptians call water *mōs*.] Thus Philo holds that *Mōsēs* is derived from *mōs*, as do Clement of Alexandria, *Stromata* 1.23 (sec. 152) and also Ambrose, *Hexaemeron* 1.1. Similarly in another passage Philo quite correctly emphasizes *anelesthai*: Mut 22 [i.e. 126] (Mangey 597) μεταληφθεὶς γὰρ Μωυσῆς καλεῖται λῆμμα: משׁה [For Moses, translated, is called "reception"]: *mšh*, "to draw out." Apparently Philo was unclear concerning the character of the biblical etymology. Flavius Josephus, *Antiquities* 2.228, also explains concerning Moses: "τὸ γὰρ ὕδωρ μῶ οἱ Αἰγύπτιοι καλοῦσιν, ὑσῆς δὲ τοὺς ἐξ ὕδατος σωθέντας [For the Egyptians call water *mō* and those who are saved from water *ysēs*]; the name is compounded from these two words." Even Jablonski (*Opuscula* 1.152ff.) maintains that [Coptic] *mō* [water] and *ouje* ([Eg.] wd3; ["to be safe"]) are the components of the etymology. The extraordinary spread of this etymology forced Jerome to

2 F. X. Wutz, *Onomastica Sacra* (TU 41, 1914) 89–91.

adopt it; ignorance may also have played a part here, as with *Som-thomfanech*. Otherwise Jerome rejects biblical etymologies that are not explicable by his usual etymological procedure, e.g. *Abraham* as "father of many nations" is sought in vain in his *Onomasticon*. On the other hand we have *Moyses* or *Moses adtrectans vel palpans aut sumptus ex aqua sive adsumptio* [Moses who touches or feels for or was taken up from water, or reception], 14.1. That we have genuine ignorance on Jerome's part seems clear from 65.8: *Moyses adsumptus vel palpans sive contrectans aut urgens, sed melius "est ex aqua"* [Moses, who is received, or who feels for, or handles, or who urges; but better, "(who) is from the water"] ([Heb.] *my, yš* placement!); 73.20, 75.23, 78.9: *adtrectans sive liniens* [who touches or anoints], 74.20; *palpans vel contrectans* [who feels for or handles], 79.18. [Heb.] *mwš* and *mšḥ* or *mšš*, cf. Assyr. *mašâšu*, "to besmear."

Cf. *Mosi* (Exod 6:19 *mwšy*) *adtrectator sive palpator meus* [the toucher of Moses or my feeler], 14.4. Presumably Lactantius, Ms. *a*: *Omonsi* (= [Heb.] *mwšy*) "my fountain," corrupted from a similar etymology: *pal-pans, trec-tans*. [Heb.] *mwš*, "to touch"; urgens = *myṣ*, "to press" (*mṣṣ*)?

Nous eusebēs, in terms of the second component of the etymology, could then = *Israēl*: *'iš, yerē' 'ēl*; in the LXX cf. Isa 11:2: *eusebeia = yr't yhwh*; *is = nous* is then an admirable equivalent of the *nous* of the Philonic-Origenistic group of onomastica. At this point, however, it is not clear how this agreement is to be explained. Another possible origin of the etymology *Moysēs nous eusebēs* [Moses, pious mind], on the basis of Philo, Mut 11 [i.e. 208] Μωσῆς μέν ἐστι νοῦς ὁ καθαρώτατος [Moses is the purest mind] is hardly to be brought into consideration, since its counterpart, *Aarōn logos* [Aaron, reason] appears in no passage where we encounter *nous eusebēs*: 181.81: *Darōn* (= *Aarōn*) *kibōtos* ([Heb.] *'rwn*) [Aaron, ark] and *Aarōn horōn horasin* [Aaron, the one who sees a vision], 173.61.

Ereuna kyriou [searching (or inquiry) of the Lord] pertains to Moses as well: in the LXX, *mšš = ereunan* (Gen 31:27); *kyriou* would then not be etymologically legitimate; this explanation is otherwise unknown and in any case must have come into the Philonic-Origenistic group of onomastica (Lagarde 172.44–174.4; 185.84–200.12) from another source; perhaps from the Lactantian group of onomastica?

The general complaint we would bring against these comments of Wutz is that they seem to multiply uncertainties and obscurities at will. When he writes that Philo, in Mut 22 (Mangey 597) in explaining the name of Moses by the word *lēmma* [reception], justly puts emphasis on *anelesthai* [to take up], one has the impression that he is placing the idea of *anelesthai* in opposition to that of *hydōr* [water]. The verbal form is taken, in fact, from the phrase in Vita Mos 1.4 which he has just cited: διὰ ἐκ τοῦ ὕδατος αὐτὸν ἀνέλεσθαι [because of his having been taken up from the water].

However, such a connection would prove either that Wutz had not read the context of the sentence in *De Mutatione Nominum*, or that he had not analyzed this important text sufficiently, which brings out that the etymology of the name Moses on the basis of *lēmma* [reception] has nothing to do with the episode of the child saved from the waters of the Nile.

This passage would have provided him the origin, in no way hidden in this philological perspective, not only of the etymology of Moses *adsumptio* [reception], but also of relationships such as *adtrectans, palpans, contrectans, urgens* [who handles, feels for, handles, urges] or their Greek equivalents. At the same time greater attention to other texts which in Philo concern themselves with Moses would have allowed Wutz to note more precisely or more exactly other etymological explanations such as *liniens, nous, eusebēs*, or *nous eusebēs* [who anoints, mind, pious, or pious mind].

We will not address here the problem of the scientific etymology of the name of Moses. Concerning this question which at present remains unsatisfactorily resolved and may be impossible to resolve, we will have to be satisfied to refer to existing literature on the subject.[3] Černy, in the article we have mentioned at the beginning of these notes, has treated the Nile episode with unusual clarity, in spite of a rather equivocal title. "Greek Etymology of the Name of Moses" does not mean, in fact, that there have been etymologies of the name of the prophet on the basis of the Greek language, but only that learned Greeks—essentially Philo and Josephus—have used their ingenuity to find in the Egyptian language some confirmation of the statement in Exod 2:10.

We will also leave aside everything that concerns itself with the Nile episode.[4] We will expend our efforts on etymologies from Hebrew or

---

[3] See R. de Vaux, *Histoire Ancienne d'Israël* (Paris: Lecoffre Gabalda, 1971) 1.312 and the bibliography given there in the note; Werner K. Schmidt, *Exodus* (Biblischer Kommentar; Neukirchen-Vluyn: Neukirchener Verlag, 1979) 73–75: Excursus 3: "Zum Namen Mose," with bibliography, p. 73.

[4] It is difficult to resolve the question of whether the etymologies of the Onomastica edited by Paul de Lagarde and those such as *Moyses . . . aut sumptus ex aqua* [Moses . . . or taken up from the water] (14.1), *adsumptus* [received] (65.8), *Mōysēs hydatos anairesis* [Moses, taking up from water] (179.15, 183.33, 195.82) are simply references to Exod 2:10 or whether they derive from the Egyptian etymology cited by Philo in Vita Mos 1.17 or to that alleged by Josephus, *Antiquities* 2.228.

A form, *mōy, mōyêy*, "water," exists also in Aramaic: Targ Ps 1:3, etc. As for the expression in 65.8, *sed melius est ex aqua*, it is not certain that Wutz is correct in understanding it as *sed melius "est ex aqua"* [but better, "who is from the water"] and in seeing in terms of this etymology a compound of *mêy + yēš* in the name of Moses. Lagarde adds no punctuation. The old edition of Victor Marianus, *Divi Hieronymi Stridoniensis Epistolae et Libri contra Haereticos . . . Loca Sacrae Scripturae a D. Hieronymo explicata* (Paris: 1587) fol. 489b gives, it would seem with reason, *sed melius est, ex aqua* [but what is better, from water]. This etymology, *ex aqua*, is cited again in A. Jones, *The Proper Names of the Old Testament Scriptures Expounded and Illustrated* (London: n.d.) 259, col. *a*, "from water," and is justified on the basis of the Coptic. Finally, neither is it certain from other sources, which the learned men of Alexandria advocated in order to explain the name of the Lawgiver. In this sense, our study could also be entitled "Greek Etymology of the Name of Moses," as it completes, as we have mentioned, the article by Černy.

III.

The key passage in Philo to which Wutz alluded is found in Mut 125–29. Philo notes that the greatest prophet bore several names.[5] The

_____

that _Moyses . . . sive adsumptio_ [Moyses . . . or reception] (14.1) must be related to the episode at the Nile and to the Heb. root _mšh_, as Wutz would have it. It appears probable to us that we have here to do with the Latin equivalent of the Greek etymology on the basis of _lēmma_ [reception], which, as we shall see, related to something quite different than the saving of the child Moses.

[5] Philo declares that God, Wisdom, the Potencies, the Logos, and the human wise man bear multiple names (_polyōnymon onoma_). In regard to Wisdom, he writes (Leg All 1.43): τὴν μετάρσιον καὶ οὐράνιον σοφίαν πολλοῖς ὀνόμασι πολυώνυμον οὖσαν δεδήλωκε· καὶ γὰρ ἀρχὴν καὶ εἰκόνα καὶ ὅρασιν θεοῦ κέκληκε. [He has made manifest that the sublime and heavenly Wisdom was polyonymous in designating it by many names: he calls it "principle," "image," and "vision of God"]. According to Somn 2.254, the name Jerusalem would also be a designation of Wisdom since, signifying "vision of peace," it is equivalent to "vision of God," for peace is not only a member of the choir of the polyonymous Potencies of God, but is in fact its leader: μηδὲν οὖν διαφερέτω σοι ἢ ὅρασιν εἰρήνης ἢ ὅρασιν θεοῦ τὸ αὐτὸ ὑποκείμενον ὀνομάζειν, ὅτι δὲ τῶν πολυωνύμων τοῦ ὄντος δυνάμεων οὐ θιασῶτις μόνον, ἀλλὰ καὶ ἔξαρχός ἐστιν εἰρήνη. [Let it make no difference to you whether the same object is named "vision of peace" or "vision of God," because peace is not only a member of the company of the polyonymous Potencies of the Existent One, but indeed its leader]. Conf 146 enumerates several designations for the Logos of God, his first-born son who bears multiple names (_polyōnymon hyparchonta_): καὶ γὰρ ἀρχὴ καὶ ὄνομα θεοῦ . . . καὶ ὁ κατ᾽ εἰκόνα ἄνθρωπος καὶ ὁ ὁρῶν, Ἰσραήλ, προσαγορεύεται, "for he is called 'principle' and 'name of God' . . . and 'man in the image' and 'the Seer Israel.'" Ebr 92 applies the term _polyōnymos_ to the wise man, which it associates with its equivalent _polyphēmos_ [many-voiced] (which appears only here in Philo): πάντα γὰρ ταῦτα ὁ πολύφημος ὡς ἀληθῶς καὶ πολυώνυμος σοφὸς κεχώρηκεν, εὐσέβειαν, ὁσιότητα, φυσιολογίαν, μετεωρολογίαν, ἠθοποιίαν, πολιτείαν, οἰκονομίαν, βασιλικήν, νομοθετικήν, ἄλλας μυρίας δυνάμεις, καὶ ἐν ἁπάσαις ἓν εἶδος καὶ ταὐτὸν ἔχων ὀφθήσεται. "The wise man, who truly deserves the names 'polypheme' [that is, by a kind of play on the ordinary meaning of _polyphēmos_, 'famous,' the man 'of many titles'] and polyonymous, contains in himself all these: piety, sanctity, knowledge of nature, meteorology, ethics, politics, economics, king-craft, the gift for legislation, and countless other talents, and in all of these he will appear as having one and the same character." It may be noted in passing that neither the English edition (_PLCL_) nor the French (_PM_) offers an acceptable translation of ἓν εἶδος καὶ ταὐτὸν ἔχων with either "to have one and the same form" or "comme n'ayant qu'une seule et même forme [as having but one single and the same form]." Maximilian Adler gives the correct meaning when he writes, "nur ein einziges und das gleiche Wesen" [only a single and the same nature]. We have here, in fact, a stylistic reminiscence of Plato, _Meno_ 72c: ἕν γέ τι εἶδος ταὐτὸν ἅπασαι ἔχουσιν δι᾽ ὃ εἰσιν ἀρεταί [they all have one single nature, by which they are virtues]. On the polyonymous name of God, see E. Bréhier, _Les Idées Philosophiques et Religieuses de Philon_ (Paris: Vrin, 1930) 112f.; E. R. Goodenough, _By Light Light_ (New

scripture designates him at times by the name Moses, at times by the term "man of God," at times by the word "god," and Philo gives the reason for this. It is essential to quote the text in its entirety.

Haven: Yale University Press, 1935) 227; H. A. Wolfson, *Philo* (Cambridge, MA: Harvard University Press, 1948) 2.122, 127. Without question, as far as the divine polyonymy is concerned, Bréhier exaggerates the influence of Stoicism and the Isiac or Orphic circles, and takes insufficient account of scriptural statements. The idea of the polyonymous name of God that one finds with Wolfson appears unacceptable in the sense that the abstract attributes which he enumerates on pp. 126–27, such as *agenētos* [uncreated], *adekastos* [unbribed], *akatonomastos* [unblamed], *aoratos* [unseen], *aperigraphos* [undefined], *arrētos* [ineffable], *asygkritos* [incomparable], can hardly qualify as *klēseis* [names] or make room for the abuses of the polyonymous name of God of which Philo complains in Dec 94. Wolfson's argument appears to us particularly unfounded when he accords an almost objective reality to Philo's "abstract mythology," to use Bréhier's expression. In fact, since God is unknowable, the whole system of the Potencies, of which Wisdom and Logos are constituents, must be seen in the perspective of an infinitely plastic *nominalism*. In themselves, all these names are but *flatus vocis* which have meaning only in relation to the degree of intellectual and spiritual advancement of the mind that conceives them. They participate in the nature of the Glory that the Israelites perceived in the great fire at Sinai: a supreme illusion, the reflection of a supreme truth.

As for Moses, the polyonymy with which he is privileged is not an indication that the Prophet occupies a place on the scale of being which puts him beyond or above humanity in bringing him near to Wisdom, the Logos or God. Although, according to Vita Mos 1.158, in common with the Father and Creator of the Universe he has the name of *theos*: ὠνομάσθη γὰρ ὅλου τοῦ ἔθνους θεὸς καὶ βασιλεύς [for he was named god and king of the whole nation], and even if he represents the supreme point of perfection of which *nous* is capable, yet Moses remains a man. The multiple names with which Scripture designates him have no other purpose than to signify, as in the case of the wise man of Ebr 92, his *dynameis* [powers] or his three great historic functions.

The multiplicity of the names of Moses is a particular case of the phenomenon of the change of names to which the entire treatise *De Mutatione Nominum* is dedicated. When they reach a higher level of perfection, Abram and Jacob *abandon* their former names to take those of Abraham and Israel. Moses, on the contrary, throughout his career never ceases to bear his three titles.

It is appropriate to note, moreover, that the polyonymy of the characteristics of the soul may apparently be ambiguous. According to Quaes Gen 4.144, "when one analyses Abraham and Isaac one discovers that they are one and the same." The change of name can indicate not a progression, but a spiritual regression. Such is the case with Jacob who, when he backslides, becomes Joseph, according to Quod Deus 120. The particularities of the scriptural text on which Philo comments oblige him at times to emphasize that *non-polyonymy* can be the mark of a particular perfection. Such is the case with Isaac, who according to Mut 88, in contrast with his father and his son, did not have to change his name, because he was by nature the incarnation of wisdom, always equal to itself. Conversely, it also occurs that polyonymy is the mark of multiple imperfection, as in the case of Joseph and Benjamin (Mut 89–91, 92–94), or that it characterizes the negative and positive aspects of the same figure, as with the father-in-law of Moses, which the text sometimes names Jethro, "the infatuated," and sometimes Ruel (Raguel) when he shepherds the flock of God and becomes a witness to the "pastoral care of God" (Mut 103–6).

A. The Polyonymous Prophet

[125] Τὸν δὲ ἀρχιπροφήτην συμβέβηκεν εἶναι πολυώνυμον. ὁπότε μέν γὰρ τοὺς χρησμῳδουμένους χρησμοὺς ἑρμηνεύων ὑφηγεῖται, προσαγορεύεται Μωυσῆς· ὁπότε δ᾽ εὐχόμενος εὐλογεῖ τὸν λεών, ἄνθρωπος θεοῦ (Deut 33.1)· ἡνίκα δὲ Αἴγυπτος τὰς ὑπὲρ τῶν ἀσεβηθέντων δίκας ἐκτίνει, τοῦ βασι-
[126] λεύοντος τῆς χώρας Φαραὼ θεός (Exod. 7:1). διὰ τί δέ;

(125) "It is the case that the supreme prophet is designated by several names. When he interprets and reveals the oracles that are given, he is called Moses. When he prays and blesses the people, he is named Man of God (Deut 33:1). Finally, when Egypt suffers punishment for its impieties, he is designated as the god of Pharaoh, the king of that country (Exod 7:1).
(126) And why is this?"

B. Moses

ὅτι τὸ μὲν νόμους μεταγράφειν ἐπ᾽ ὠφελείᾳ τῶν ἐντευξομένων ψηλαφῶντός ἐστι καὶ διὰ χειρὸς ἔχοντος ἀεὶ τὰ θεῖα καὶ ἀνακεκλημένου ὑπὸ τοῦ θεσπιῳδοῦ νομοθέτου καὶ εἰληφότος παρ᾽ αὐτοῦ μεγάλην δωρεάν, ἑρμηνείαν καὶ προφητείαν νόμων ἱερῶν· μεταληφθεὶς γὰρ Μωυσῆς καλεῖται λῆμμα, δύναται δὲ καὶ ψηλάφημα διὰ τὰς εἰρημένας αἰτίας.

"Because to transcribe the laws for the use of future readers is the portion of one who constantly *feels for* (psēlaphōntos) and handles the divine realities, who, commanded by the oracular Lawgiver, has *received* (eilēphotos) from him as a signal endowment the gift of interpreting and transmitting the holy laws. In fact, translated, Moses is called *reception* (lēmma), which can also be *feeling for* (psēlaphēma), for the reasons indicated."

C. Man of God

[127] τὸ δέ γε εὔχεσθαι καὶ εὐλογεῖν οὐκ ἔστι τοῦ τυχόντος, ἀλλ᾽ ἀνθρώπου τὴν πρὸς γένεσιν μὴ ἑωρακότος συγγένειαν, προσκεκληρωκότος δὲ ἑαυτὸν τῷ πάντων ἡγεμόνι καὶ πατρί·
[128] ἀγαπητὸν γάρ, εἴ τῳ ἐξεγένετο εὐλογιστίᾳ χρῆσθαι, τὸ δέ γε καὶ ἑτέροις περιποιεῖν τὸ ἀγαθόν, τοῦτο μείζονος καὶ τελειοτέρας ψυχῆς καὶ ὡς ἀληθῶς θειαζούσης ἦν ἐπάγγελμα, ἧς ὁ τυχὼν εἰκότως θεοῦ κεκλήσεται.

(127) "As for praying and blessing, this is not at the disposal of anyone by chance, but the privilege of a man who, paying no regard to his

relations with the future,[6] has made of himself the portion consecrated to the Sovereign and Father of the universe."

(128) "It would have been a sufficient good to find oneself the object of a blessing,[7] but to be capable also of communicating this blessedness to

---

[6] Colson (*PLCL* 5.207, n. *c*) refers correctly to the benediction of Levi in Deut 33:9. This benediction is recalled in its literal sense in Fuga 88: οἱ Λευῖται . . . ἕνεκα ἀρεσκείας θεοῦ γονεῖς καὶ τέκνα καὶ ἀδελφοὺς καὶ πᾶσαν τὴν θνητὴν συγγένειαν ἀπολελοιπότες. [the Levites . . . having, for the sake of being well-pleasing to God, forsaken parents and children and brothers and all their mortal kindred (*PLCL* 5.57)].

Moses is a Levite. It is striking that the Pentateuch never mentions the relationship that he would have had with Amram or Jochebed. He acts as a Levite, in spite of appearances, when he calls Aaron and his sons to the priesthood. Vita Mos 2.142 emphasizes that in doing this Moses was not moved by consideration of his family and chose his brother and his nephews only with regard to the piety and sanctity that he saw in them. On the other hand, he excluded his two sons, whom he judged to be unworthy.

We have here an *allegorical interpretation* of the benediction of Levi. Moses repudiates everything in his being that attaches himself to the future. From this point forward, there is place in himself only for God, a fact that explains and justifies his title, "Man of God."

[7] In Philo the verb *eulogistein* often serves as a commentary on the verb *eulogein*, of which it can be an equivalent pure and simple. Such is the case in Leg All 3.190 where, in connection with the episode of Jacob and Esau, the words ἔν τε τοῖς πρωτοτοκίοις καὶ ἐν τῷ εὐλογιστεῖν [both in the matter of the birthright and in the blessing (*PLCL* 1.431)] correspond with τότε τὰ πρωτοτόκιά μου εἴληφε, καὶ νῦν εἴληφε τὴν εὐλογίαν μου [then he took my birthright, and now he has taken my blessing (*PLCL* 1.431)] cited from Gen 27:36 in the following paragraph. The sense is again the same in 192: εἴληφε γὰρ καὶ <τὸ> εὐλογιστεῖν σὺν εὐχαῖς τελείαις [for he has received the blessing also accompanied by perfect prayers (*PLCL* 1.431, 433)].

In Leg All 3.215 the sense in which the verb is used is less clear. The words of Exod 20:24 ἥξω πρὸς σὲ καὶ εὐλογήσω σε [I will come to you and I will bless you] are given the following allegorical commentary: ἐὰν γὰρ ἔλθῃ εἰς τὴν διάνοιαν ἔννοια θεοῦ, εὐθὺς εὐλογιστεῖ τε καὶ πάσας τὰς νόσους αὐτῆς ἰᾶται [For if a thought of God come into the soul, He immediately blesses it and heals all its sicknesses]. It appears that we have here a definition of what Philo understands by "blessing." "Blessing" is to heal the soul of its passions; it is the power of a healthy, and consequently a holy mind. This idea is well presented in Sobr 18. It is constant in all the uses of the noun *eulogistia*. In Conf 66 *katadysis eulogistias* [the setting of reasonableness] is contrasted with *anatolē aphrosynēs* [the rising of folly (*PLCL* 4.47)]. Migr 71 explains *eulogistia* as a happy functioning of the mind, after it has been given right thought served by efficacious utterance.

As for the adjective *eulogistos*, it has the double meaning of "reasonable" and of "blessed" in Leg All 1.17–18, 3.210. It means "reasonable" in Somn 1.155.

Here we probably have the same play on meaning. As for Philo the priest is a designation of the Wise Man, so in the exercise of his priestly functions Moses communicates to the people access to the wisdom which distinguishes him. He heals souls into whom he places, instead of the passions, a right mind and a holy reason. But the religious coloring of the passage and the superhuman dimension which it attributes to Moses' action precludes, it seems to us, one's being content with a translation such as that of the French edition (*PM*): "On doit s'estimer heureux qu'il soit possible à un homme d'user de réflexion" [he should consider himself fortunate if it is possible for a man to make use of reflection]. It would be preferable to keep the term "benediction," even though it may be ambiguous.

others, such was the office of a higher soul, one more accomplished, *actually under the rule of God* (*hōs alēthōs theiazousēs*), whose possessor justly would be called, 'of God.'"[8]

D. God of Pharaoh

[129]

θεὸς δὲ ὁ αὐτὸς οὗτος ἅτε σοφὸς ὢν καὶ διὰ τοῦτ' ἄρχων παντὸς ἄφρονος, κἂν εἰ τοῖς βασιλείοις σκήπτροις ἐκεῖνος ἐφιδρύοιτο μεγαλαυχῶν. καὶ διὰ τοῦτο οὐχ ἥκιστα· βούλεται γὰρ ὁ τῶν ὅλων ἡγεμών, κἂν ἀφόρητα ἀδικοῦντές τινες μέλλωσι κολάζεσθαι, παραιτητὰς ἔχειν τοὺς ἐντευξομένους ὑπὲρ αὐτῶν, οἱ τὴν τοῦ πατρὸς ἵλεω δύναμιν ἀπομιμούμενοι μετριώτερον καὶ φιλανθρωπότερον χρήσονται ταῖς τιμωρίαις· θεοῦ δὲ τὸ εὐεργετεῖν ἴδιον.

"But he himself is *a god* (*theos*) in his quality of wise man, which makes him the prince of every fool; even though the latter should depend,[9] in

---

[8] Colson's correction (*PLCL* 5.208), replacing the *theos* of the MSS by *theou*, to us seems necessary and excellent. The change must have been brought about by the word *theos* which appears at the beginning of the following phrase.

The genitive is necessary, because it serves to explain Moses' second title, "Man of God." The word *theos* in the following phrase belongs to a development independent of what precedes and relates to the third title of the Prophet, a fact which the French editor, as shown by his note (*PM* 18.90, n. 2), seems not to have seen clearly.

Colson's correction is much preferable to that proposed by Wendland, who wished to read *anthrōpos theou* here. The simple *theou* is clearly an allusion to a complete expression, but serves also to explain it. It indicates that the title "Man of God" means that the prophet belongs entirely to God. It may be, moreover, that we have to do here with an implicit citation of Gen 50:19, where Josephus declares: τοῦ θεοῦ εἰμι ἐγώ [I am of God]. Cf. Migr 22: τὸ ὁμολογεῖν ὅτι "τοῦ θεοῦ ἐστι," τῶν δ' εἰς γένεσιν ἐλθόντων οὐδενός [To confess that "he is of God," not one of those who have come into created being]; see also 160, and Somn 2.107: "τοῦ θεοῦ" ἐστιν, ἀλλ' οὐδενὸς ἔτι τῶν εἰς γένεσιν ἡκόντων αἰσθητοῦ τὸ παράπαν [He is of God, and no longer at all of anything sensible that has come into created being]. In Jos 265–66, the expression is interpreted as meaning that God, to whom Joseph belongs, is witness to his intimate thoughts.

[9] W. Theiler (*PCH* 6.134 and n. 1) follows Wendland when he translates incorrectly: "Wenn dieser sich prahlend auf königlichen Thron setzen sollte" [If this one should sit boasting on a royal throne] and justifies this translation by a note which seems to us to be particularly wide of the mark: "It is traditional that one cannot sit on a royal scepter; in place of *ephidryoito* [though he should place himself], one would expect a word such as *semnynoito* [though he should affect dignity] (cf. Leg All 2.66; Spec Leg 1.311), *brenthyoito* [though he should bear himself haughtily], or similar. Or, instead of *skēptrois* [scepters] one should introduce—as in the translation—a word for "throne," *thakois* rather than *thronois* (Wendland): cf. Cyril, *Adversus Julianum* 664d (*MPG* 76): τῆς βασιλείας θάκοις ἐνιδρυμένος καὶ αὐχήμασι κατεστεμμένος [established on the thrones of the kingdom and having sat down with boastings]."

Actually, no change is necessary here; *ephidryesthai* is employed at times by Philo in a figurative sense and with the meaning of "to lean upon," "to establish oneself upon." See, for example, Abr. 8: ὡς μόνου πρὸς ἀλήθειαν ὄντος ἀνθρώπου τοῦ τὰ ἀγαθὰ προσδοκῶντος καὶ foolish pride, on his royal scepter, such a circumstance would change absolutely nothing.[10]

(129) The sovereign of the universe desires that even though certain perpetrators of intolerable transgressions must be punished, they yet have available intercessors who will speak in their favor, and who, in imitation of the favorable power of the Father, will inflict the penalties with greater moderation and clemency. Beneficence is the portion *of a god* (*theou*)."

This text, which has never been well understood, appears to us, however, as being very clear and rigorously composed.

We will now return to the paragraph (126) which demonstrates the correctness and the well-founded basis of the name Moses, by which the Lawgiver is designated.

Paragraph 127 and the half of paragraph 128 are devoted to giving a rational basis for the second of the terms for Moses, "Man of God." Moses is, first of all, a Levite and an example of the levitical spirituality which is the great religious ideal of Judaism as Philo understands it. Moses has no concern for his earthly relatives. He has consecrated his person to the Lord. Such a commitment makes the expression "Man of God" perfectly understandable and appropriate. What is more, at the instance of God Moses is able to bless the people effectively. His soul returns to the divine domain, and the participle *theiazousēs* announces and justifies the genitive *theou* which follows.

The end of paragraph 128 and paragraph 129 are concerned with elucidating the third name of the Lawgiver, who is presented as "god of

---

ἐλπίσι χρησταῖς ἐφιδρυμένου [With the idea that he alone is truly a man who expects the good and bases himself on excellent hopes]. The French translation (*PM*) here is misleading. Cf. Abr 268: ψυχῆς . . . ἐφιδρυμένης τῷ πάντων αἰτίῳ [of the soul . . . which rests upon the cause of all things. . . .]; Aet 99, where Philo compares food to a staff on which the seed of the world leans: ᾧ καθάπερ βάκτρῳ τινὶ τὴν σπερματικὴν ἀρχὴν ἐφιδρύεσθαι συμβέβηκεν [which the originating seed takes as a staff for its support (*PLCL* 9.255)].

10 The notes in the editions here are worthless. The translations: "And he is a god for this reason in particular" (*PLCL*), "und nicht zum wenigsten auch aus folgendem Grunde" [and not the least also for the following reason] (*PCH*), "et dans ce cas surtout" [and in this case above all] (*PM*) reflect a misunderstanding. The French editor (p. 90, n. 4), who gives correctly, word-for-word, "Et pour cette raison (qu'il serait roi), cela n'en serait pas du tout moins vrai" [And for this reason (that he would be king), this would be none the less true], nevertheless leads the reader astray in the rest of the note.

Frequently one finds in Philo the expression *ouch hēkista* taken in the sense of "none the less," "no less for that reason"; see for example, Agr 2.39, Ebr 181, Conf 22, Mut 233, Jos 94.

In our text διὰ τοῦτο οὐχ ἥκιστα [and for this reason nevertheless] is to be taken in relation with ἄρχων παντὸς ἄφρονος [prince of every fool]. As such, the wise man is the master of every fool, and in the case where the fool hangs on to the kingship, the wise man remains master nevertheless, the kingly quality changing nothing in regard to the relationship between the two figures.

Pharaoh."[11] Philo offers a double reason. The words of Exod 7:1: "Behold, I have made of you a god for Pharaoh," are comparable to those of Exod 4:16, where Moses is "as a god" for Aaron. It is probable that in these two cases Moses is designated thus because he is God's substitute to the people and to Pharaoh. He transmits the divine thoughts; Aaron is content with putting them into words and proclaiming them.

Philo begins by interpreting the expression "god of Pharaoh" in accord with the Greek doctrine of the kingliness of the wise man: "god" designates the man who has power to command (archōn) every fool, even though he be a king, by "greatness of establishment." "God" thus signifies simply "master." But theos is still the name of the "Favorable Power" of the Supreme Being.

The scriptural story places Moses as the intermediary between the king of Egypt and the divinity because the dramatic movement of the narrative excludes direct intervention by God. It is through the manifestations of the divine intrepidity—which he will be forced to acknowledge at his own expense—that Pharaoh, who has been boasting that he does not know YHWH, will come to recognize the dynamic presence of the great and terrible God. Basing himself on the equation theos = hileōs dynamis [god = favorable power], Philo conjures up a kind of midrash which nothing in the text of Exod 7 suggests.[12] He supposes that in the presence of Pharaoh Moses plays the role of the hileōs dynamis due to the mercy of God, as no creature would be able to bear punishment administered directly by Him. Acting as hileōs dynamis in the case of Pharaoh, Moses thus well deserves being designated as Pharaō theos [god of Pharaoh].

Paragraph 126, concerning the name of Moses, appears to have been the least clearly understood. To sense this, it is sufficient to turn to this passage in the major editions.

The confusion is most visible in PLCL 5. In spite of the use of the

---

[11] The expression "God of Pharaoh" is commented on by Philo several times and provides an opportunity for important developments concerning the allegorical value of Moses as symbolizing the nous, as well as the entirely metaphorical sense of the divinity of Moses; see Leg All 1.40, Sacr 9, Quod Det 161–62, Somn 2.189, Quod Omnis 43–44. In Mut 19 one finds another interpretation of the necessary intercession of the wise for the evil man. God is willing to be theos only of the one who progresses. In the case of Pharaoh, who is at the extreme limit of impiety, God delegates this title to the wise man.

[12] According to Vita Mos 1.97, the first three plagues are administered by Aaron, the next three by Moses, the seventh by Aaron and Moses in common; the last three have God himself as their agent.

The scriptural account appears more concerned with the triumph of God over Pharaoh than with the moral progress of the king of Egypt, whose heart God has "hardened," or with how he is to be handled. One should not seek precise justification in scripture for the interpretation Philo gives here of Moses' function.

term *metalēphtheis* [translated], which is an irrefutable indication, F. H. Colson, the editor, does not appear to see that Philo intends to explain the name of Moses etymologically when he writes: μεταληφθεὶς γὰρ Μωυσῆς καλεῖται λῆμμα, δύναται δὲ [127] καὶ ψηλάφημα διὰ τὰς εἰρημένας αἰτίας. [For translated, Moses is called "reception," which can also be "feeling for," for the reasons indicated.]

On p. 206, n. *b*, Colson observes:

> The meaning is obscure. Perhaps the fact that Moses "handled" the law shews that his name of "receiving" must also be understood to include the kindred meaning of "handling." The derivation here given applies only to the last part of the name. The common ancient derivation that "Mo" represented the Egyptian μῶυ, "water," is given by Philo, *De Mos.* i.17. In *Leg. All.* iii.231 ψηλάφημα was used for "groping" (in darkness).

In all justice one can describe this note as confused, and this for several reasons. A judgment such as "his name of 'receiving' must also be understood to include the kindred meaning of 'handling'" rests on an imprecision and a misinterpretation. Colson does not see that the translations *lēmma* [reception] and *psēlaphēma* [feeling for] are based on two etymologies from Hebrew, and that the second is certainly not derived *ad sensum* from the first.

The allusion to "the common ancient derivation" and the reference to Vita Mos 1.17 show that Colson was victim to the same uncertainty as was Wutz in the pages of the *Onomastica Sacra* which we cite above.

Wutz, it will be remembered, related the *lēmma* [reception] of Mut 126 to the [*dia to ek tou hydatos auton*] *anelesthai* ["because he had been *taken up* from the water"] of Vita Mos 1.17. The remark of Colson—who however did not know what Wutz had written—that "the derivation here given applies only to the last part of the name," goes in the same direction. It presumes that *lēmma* corresponds to [*Mōy*]*sēs*, which actually has nothing to do with it.

Finally, Wutz, who relates *Moses palpans, adtrectans* [Moses, who feels for, handles], etc.[13] correctly to the root *mwš* [to touch], seems never to have had a sense that this etymology is contained in the same passage of Philo as the etymology via *lēmma* ["reception"]. As for Colson, he never doubts for a moment that *psēlaphēma* ["feeling for"] is an etymology independent of the name of Moses attached to the root *mwš*. J. W. Earp's note[14] does not change this situation: "He derives 'Moses'

---

[13] It is probably useless to relate *Moyses . . . urgens* (65.8) to the root *myṣ* or *mṣṣ*, as Wutz (p. 90) does. The participle *urgens*, just as *palpans* or *contrectans* (to touch, to test by touching, to feel, to search) must be a translation of *mwš—mšš* and mean "to touch," "to press," as in Judg 16:26, the object always being the divine realities.

[14] See *PLCL* 10.386.

from Hebrew to mean 'handling' (*ib.* 126 and n.), or from Egyptian to mean 'water' (*Mos.* i.17)."

Wutz's work is from 1914; the translation by Colson dates from 1934 and was reprinted in 1949. That of Willy Theiler,[15] published first in 1938, was reproduced photomechanically in 1962. Theiler saw very well the relationship *psēlaphōntos* [one who feels for] = Moses[16] = *mšh* from *mwš*, "to touch," but his reference to Acts 17:27, *to psēlaphan*, is as inappropriate as that of Colson to Leg All 3.231. Furthermore, Theiler offers no explanation for the statement, "Translated, Moses is called 'reception.'"[17]

The French edition of *De Mutatione* (*PM* 18), published in 1964, translates: "Car, en traduction, Moïse veut dire: 'acquitision,' mais ce nom a aussi le sens de 'palpation' pour les raisons que nous avons dites" ["For, in translation, Moses means: 'acquisition,' but this name has also the meaning of 'to feel for,' for the reasons which we have mentioned"].

The translation of *lēmma* by "acquisition" is not a particularly happy one. It has the disadvantage of obliterating the relation of the term to the words *eilēphotos . . . megalēn dōrean* [having received . . . a great gift], which announce and explain *lēmma*. Furthermore, the editor did not choose to offer a word of explanation to clarify the etymological relationship of the terms "acquisition" and "to feel for" to the name of Moses.

---

15 *PCH* 6.104ff.

16 *PCH* 6.133, n. 3.

17 "Übersetzt ñamlich heisst Moses 'Empfangen.'" In Paul's Areopagus speech, the idea of a search for the divine εἰ ἄρα γε ψηλαφήσειαν αὐτὸν καὶ εὕροιεν ["That they might feel after him and find him" (Acts 17:27)], a hesitant undertaking—according to which men grope for God who attracts them while yet remaining the Unknown God—is basically different from that which Philo attributes to Moses. Moses knows God and constantly holds in his hand, feels, examines, inspects, the divine realia.

It is less appropriate still to bring in the passage in Leg All 3.221, 225, where the Moabites are called, as in Scripture, the "People of Chemosh." The name of the god of Moab is related to the root *kms*, or, as in Philo, analyzed into *k* + *mwš* (see P. de Lagarde, *Onomastica* 17.12–13, 32.4, 41.15, 54.2, 114.5). According to Philo (225), Moab is lost because he has lost the truth in order to occupy himself with obscurities that have a semblance of truth. Leg All 3.231: "λαος Χαμώς" τουτέστιν ὁ λαός σου καὶ ἡ δύναμις εὕρηται πηρὸς καὶ τετυφλωμένος· Χαμὼς γὰρ ἑρμηνεύεται "ὡς ψηλάφημα"· ἴδιον δὲ τοῦ μὴ ὁρῶντος τὸ ἔργον τοῦτο ("The people of Chemosh," that is thy people and its power has been found to be maimed and blinded; for "Chemosh" means "as a groping," and . . . [this action] is characteristic of one who cannot see [*PLCL* 1.459]).

Colson, moreover, could have added Deut 28:29: καὶ ἔσῃ ψηλαφῶν μεσημβρίας, ὡσεί τις ψηλαφήσαι τυφλὸς ἐν τῷ σκότει [and you shall be groping at noon-day, as a blind man gropes in the darkness], on which Philo comments in Heres 250. Finally, the palpable darkness, *psēlaphēton skotos*, which fell on Egypt (Exod 10:21) reminds Philo (Somn 1.114) of the darkness into which the mind is plunged when the divine illumination disappears: δύντος γάρ, ὡς πᾶσα Αἴγυπτος, ψηλαφητὸν ἕξεις σκότος [For, when (that light) has set, you, like "all Egypt," will experience . . . a darkness that may be felt (*PLCL* 5.357)].

To speak in a general way, it is regrettable that Wutz practically ignored the Philonic corpus, that the reprint of Colson's translation took no notice of the relationship indicated by Theiler, whose explanations themselves should have been carried to completion, and finally that the French editor saw no need to add to the work of his predecessors.[18] Thus it is appropriate to take up once more and complete the explication of Mut 126.

A preliminary observation is necessary. One seriously obscures Philo's thought when one seeks to relate the etymology based on Egyptian, which Philo himself and then Josephus mention in connection with the child Moses' being saved from the Nile, to the etymologies of the name Moses advanced in the present passage. It is incorrect, we repeat, to conclude that since *mo* means "water," the etymologies *lēmma* [reception] and *psēlaphēma* [feeling for] are intended to explain only the

---

[18] The result is that Philo's text remains basically misunderstood. To cite but one recent example, we refer to the thesis of Lala Kalyan Kumar Dey, *The Intermediary World and Patterns of Perfection in Philo and Hebrews* (Missoula, MT: Scholars Press, 1975) 162–63. Kalyan Dey analyzes the passage in Mut 125–26 with greater precision than do the editions, but he finds no relation for the etymologies of the name of Moses alleged in 126. He translates: "Translated Moses can mean both 'receiving' and 'handling,'" and adds: "The etymological basis for this is unclear." On p. 163, n. 8, he makes no difference between *lēmma* [reception] and *psēlaphēma* [feeling for] and thinks that this term may be applicable to the gift of exegetical prophecy that Moses receives on the top of Sinai. A careful rereading of 126 shows that only the word *lēmma* is logically appropriate to and recalls this episode. The term *psēlaphēma* constitutes a much more general description of the activity of the "man of God." It is clearly impossible to follow Dey when he writes in the same note: "This unusual term [*psēlaphēma*], not attested in the LXX, which describes Moses' receiving of the law when he was called up to Sinai, is used in Hb 12, 18 and points to the fact that it is such tradition which is bearing the brunt of the author's polemic in 12, 18ff." As a matter of fact, the text of Heb 12:18 appears to have no connection with the "tradition" of Mut 126.

Furthermore, the statement, "not attested in the LXX," is unclear. Does the author mean that the LXX does not use this word to describe Moses' receiving the law?

But in the text of Heb 12:18, *psēlaphōmenō* [that which might be touched (tentatively or gropingly)] does not apply to Moses, but rather to the fire on Sinai: *psēlaphōmenō kai kekaomenō pyri*, a phrase that one oridinarily understands as meaning the "palpable and burning fire," *psēlaphōmenō* having the vaule of *psēlaphētō*.

The idea would be to place, over against the material and terrifyingly dramatic scene of the giving of the law, the mountain of Zion and the heavenly Jerusalem. In fact, certain MSS have *psēlaphōmenō orei* [palpable mountain], which would contrast with Σιὼν ὄρει καὶ πόλει θεοῦ ζῶντος, Ἰερουσαλὴμ ἐπουρανίῳ [to Mount Zion and to the city of the living God, the heavenly Jerusalem] (Heb 12:22).

On the other hand, the "giving of the Law," as we have noted and as we will see again below, is indicated in Philo by *lēmma* and not by *psēlaphēma*. Thus it is more probable that the "tradition" that Philo offers on the subject of Moses is totally absent from Heb 12:18–24. It would indeed be impossible to understand it as saying, "You have not come near to him who received the Law (*psēlaphōmenō*) and to the blazing fire," since *psēlaphasthai* nowhere means "to receive the Law."

second part of the Prophet's name, as Wutz and Colson would have it. As for Philo, when he explains the multiple name of Moses, if he does not have in mind either the reference in Exod 2:10, or the explanation based on Egyptian, of which he is not ignorant, this is due neither to forgetfulness nor illogic. It has rather to do with a *deliberate procedure* which throws particularly vivid light on his theological method and on the way he conceives the scripture.

Philo remains essentially a moralist and a theologian, even in those treatises which are commonly termed "historical." Much in advance of being historical chronicles, *In Flaccum* and *Ad Gaium* are treatises concerning *Providence*. As for the exegetical treatises properly so called, it is not too much to say that here Philo's feeling for history borders on zero. The episodes described in the Pentateuch are not made up of a pure and simple recounting of events which occur and pass on. Nor do they engage in any way other events which would appear to relate to them.

To be more concrete, we will illustrate this judgment in terms of the question under consideration.

Certainly it is true that when the Egyptian princess named the child she had adopted *Moses* it was because she had taken him from the water, and the Egyptian language attests to the sound basis of the scriptural statement. But, considering the real nature of scripture, when it calls the prophet presented in his *lawgiving* function *Moses*, this can hardly be simply with reference to the haggadic episode related to his beginnings. In the context of his name being polyonymous, *Moses* functions as a correlative of "man of God" and "god of Pharaoh." From this perspective the meaning "saved from the waters" has no relation to the holy laws nor any theological value comparable with that of the other two names. With his habitual plasticity of thought, however, Philo supposes that the name given by the princess, perfectly realistic and legitimate in terms of the story where it is mentioned, has nothing to do with the name of Moses which the prophet bears in his maturity when he fulfills his role of intermediary between the living Lawgiver and humanity.

First of all, Moses is presented as a writer (*metagraphein* [to transcribe]).[19] Charged by God with transcribing the laws, he is always in

---

[19] The verb *metagraphein* means "to transcribe," "to recopy." Philo uses it two more times, in Spec Leg 4.61, where he describes the activity of certain Greek legislators who borrowed legal provisions from the Law of Moses: τῶν παρ' ῞Ελλησιν ἔνιοι νομοθετῶν μεταγράψαντες ἐκ τῶν ἱερωτάτων Μωυσέως στηλῶν [. . . some Grecian legislators did well when they copied from the most sacred tables of Moses (*PLCL* 8.45)] and Spec Leg 4.163, where he remarks on the obligation placed on the king to recopy Deuteronomy (Deut 17:18): ὅπως αὐτὰ ἐν βιβλίῳ γράφων εὐθὺς εἰς τὴν ψυχὴν μεταγράφω [writing them in a book, I thus recopy them immediately into my soul].

close contact, both through his mind (*psēlaphōntos*)[20] and his hand (*dia cheiros echon*),[21] which is that of an inspired scribe, with the divine realities which he sets forth through these laws. Thus his name indicates his function, for *Moses* must then be derived from the Hebrew *mwš*, a secondary form of *mšš* "to touch."[22]

Philo then recalls the origin of this function of Moses. Bidden to the top of Sinai, he received from the Lawgiver, who speaks in oracles, the gift of interpreting and proclaiming the laws. His name also reflects this situation, as *Moses* is explained by *lēmma*, "a thing received," a word which itself is anticipated and explained by *eilēphotos*, a form belonging, as does *lēmma*, to the verb *lambanein*, "to receive."

But with Philo this explanation has something entirely strange. The word *lēmma* has a favorable meaning only in our passage;[23] everywhere else, in accord with good Greek usage, it designates disreputable or

---

In regard to Moses, the verb *metagraphein* refers to his publication of the Laws, and it is evident that this activity goes beyond the episode on Sinai and that it continues throughout the career of the prophet. But it is on the summit of the holy mount that Moses receives, so to speak, his ordination and the authority necessary for him to write as vicar of God. It seems essential, then, to be clear that *psēlaphēma* indicates in a general manner the whole function of Moses as a sacred writer, while *lēmma* designates specifically the origin of this function and relates to the gift received on Sinai, and only to that gift.

[20] The verb *psēlaphan* is used in both literal and figurative senses. In a figurative sense, it can mean "to look closely," "to examine," "to search." Liddell-Scott-Jones give various examples of it and cite the derivative noun *psēlaphētēs*, "a searcher," used in a scholion on Oppian, *Halieutica* 2.435. It is thus more than probable that the etymology of the name Moses from *ereuna kyriou* [inquiry of the Lord] (P. de Lagarde, *Onomastica* 173.60; 195.82–83) is also related to the root *mwš—mšš*. See further Wutz, *Onomastica* 91 in regard to the pursuit of Laban, Gen 31:7. In its literal sense *psēlaphan* can have the meaning of "to handle." Zech 9:13 LXX: ψηλαφήσω σε ὡς ρομφαίαν μαχητοῦ "I will handle you like the sword of a warrior."

[21] If the participle *psēlaphōntos* is taken in its literal sense in this paragraph and means that Moses "handles" the divine realities when he reduces them to writing, the expression *dia cheiros echon* [I hold by the hand] can only extend and clarify its meaning.

[22] One must simply relate the name of Moses to the root *mwš* without asking to what form of the verb the name of the Prophet may correspond. The "etymologists" were never so scrupulous or meticulous. Thus the name *mwši*, Moshi, is explained sometimes as *adtrectator vel palpator meus* [my toucher or feeler] (14.4–5), sometimes simply as *psēlaphēma* [a feeling for or groping]: F. Wutz, *Onomastica* 600, 913. One recognizes the root *mwš* again in proper names such as *Misahel*, *tactus dei* [touch of God] (14.5), *psēlaphēsis theou* [touch of God] (195.81), or *Namsi* (Nimšî, father of Jehu according to 1 Kings 19:16, or his grandfather according to 2 Kings 9:2) *tangens, adtrectans sive palpans* [the one who touches, handles or feels for] (43.1).

[23] See Gig 39 in regard to those who betray philosophy "for a meager profit" (*mikrou lēmmatos*); Quod Deus 170, "vanquished by cupidity" (*lēmmatos hēttōmenon*). In Plant 105 and Spec Leg 1.280 *lēmma* designates the pay of prostitutes. In Virt 10 it refers to the shameful profit that one receives for denouncing the men of merit. According to Vita Cont 66, in the course of their prayers, the Therapeutae raise their hands to heaven to attest "that they are pure of profit-taking": ὅτι καθαραὶ λημμάτων εἰσίν.

dishonest gain. But above all the word *lēmma* seems imprecise and quite incapable of bearing by itself alone what Philo wants to make it say: εἰληφότος παρ᾽ αὐτοῦ μεγάλην δωρεάν, ἑρμηνείαν καὶ προφητείαν νόμων ἱερῶν (Mut 126) [. . . has received from him as a signal endowment the gift of interpreting and transmitting the holy laws]. Finally, it is impossible to relate the name *Moses* to the Hebrew roots *lqḥ* or *qbl*, which would correspond to *lambanein*.

It therefore appears to us that we have to do here with an etymological tradition that Moses = *lēmma*, one which Philo knew and had received from the Jewish circles of Alexandria.[24] This tradition was based on a rapprochement between the names of Moses and the Hebrew word *maśśā'*, "oracle," "vision," which derives from the root *nś'*, "to lift," "to carry," "to take." Indeed, in the LXX, *maśśā'* is translated by *lēmma* in a whole group of texts where it plays a role similar to those of *hrēma* [that which is spoken], *horama* [that which is seen], *horasis* [seeing] elsewhere;[25] these latter offer a good indication of the sense in which the translators took *lēmma*.

To cite first texts in prose, we can refer to 2 Kgs 9:25: וַיהוה נָשָׂא עָלָיו הַמַּשָּׂא הַזֶּה: καὶ κύριος ἔλαβεν ἐπ᾽ αὐτὸν τὸ λῆμμα τοῦτο "Yahweh will pronounce this sentence against him."[26]

We find the translation *maśśā'* = *lēmma* in the following texts from the Prophets:

1. In the well known passage, Jer 23:33, 34, 36, 38, where *maśśā' Yhwh* means "the oracle of God": *to lēmma kyriou* (33, 34, 36, 38) and the "burden" that those people of Judah, who use this expression, are for

---

[24] In the preceding note we say that in Philo *lēmma* never designates the abstract act of receiving. It is even possible to maintain that the equation Moses = *lēmma* is *contrary* to his usage. Most probably, then, we have to do here with a tradition that Philo received from elsewhere. The etymologies of names such as Mosi (Moshi), Namsi, Misahel, which are not found in the Philonic corpus, strengthen this impression.

We should note that Wutz, *Onomastica Sacra*, 264 in regard to Massa, came very close to the truth as to the origin of the etymology Moses = *lēmma*. He writes, "Cf. the seemingly obscure Massa (*myš*, 2 Kings 3:4), *onus vel adsumptio* [burden or reception] 46.12: *lēmma* = *onus vel sumptio* [burden or taking up] (*mš*); but for *adsumptio* one might rather think of *mšh* [to draw out], LXX *proslambanein* [to take hold of], since Jerome also gives the explanation *Moyses vel Moses* (*mōšeh*) *adsumptio* [Moyses or Moses, reception] 14.2."

Wutz is thrown off here because he does not see that the etymology Moses = *adsumptio* [reception] has no relation to the event at the Nile. Contrary to Wutz' suggestion, far from thinking of *mšh* rather than *mš* as the explanation of the name of the king of Moab as meaning *adsumptio*, one can find in the equation Maase = *adsumptio* the confirmation that Moses = *adsumptio* goes back, as does Maasa, to *lēmma*, i.e. to the noun *mśś'*.

[25] One finds *horasis* in Isa 13:1; 19:1; 30:6; *horama* in 21:1, 11; *hrēma* in 14:28; 15:1; 17:1; 22:1; 23:1.

[26] In 2 Chron 24:27, *hammaśā'* appears to have been *ḥămišāh*, "five."

God (33, 36).

2. In the Minor Prophets, as introductory formulas:

Nah 1:1: מַשָּׂא נִינְוֵה: λῆμμα Νινευή [an oracle concerning Nineveh].

Hab 1:1: הַמַּשָּׂא אֲשֶׁר חָזָה חֲבַקּוּק: τὸ λῆμμα ὃ εἶδεν Ἀμβακούμ [the oracle which Habakkuk saw].

Zech 9:1: מַשָּׂא דְבַר־יְהוָה: λῆμμα λόγου κυρίου [an oracle, the word of the Lord].

Zech 12:1: מַשָּׂא דְבַר־יְהוָה עַל־יִשְׂרָאֵל: λῆμμα λόγου κυρίου ἐπὶ τὸν Ἰσραήλ [an oracle, the word of the Lord concerning Israel]. This expression is found again in Mal 1:1.

The term *maśśā'* appears finally in certain poetic texts; thus Lam 2:14: וַיֶּחֱזוּ לָךְ מַשְׂאוֹת שָׁוְא: καὶ εἰδοσάν σοι λήμματα μάταια [they have seen for you vain oracles].[27]

As for Philo, we resist supposing, as certain critics do too willingly, that he paid little attention to the Greek of the LXX and hence—as far as our passage is concerned—to the meaning of *lēmma* as "oracle" or "vision." We are persuaded of the contrary. It is sufficient to observe with some attention the way in which Philo cites the text of the LXX to be convinced that it was impossible for him here to use the word *lēmma* in the sense of "oracle," "prophecy," "vision." Philo, in fact, never hesitates to conform the language and syntax of the LXX to the norms of the classical Greek of his time, as long as such corrections as he makes do not alter what appears to him to be the meaning of the verse—even though the meaning seems strange—and confine themselves to purely formal matters. Contrary to what H. A. Wolfson at times maintains, Philo never loads a Greek word he is using with meanings which normally are foreign to it. This was precisely the case with the terminus technicus *lēmma* = "oracle," "vision," "prophecy." Philo could use it only with the meaning which he knew in current Greek, that is, "something taken or received." This was so much so that while the Alexandrian etymological tradition of Moses: *maśśā'* = *lēmma* doubtless meant that the name of the prophet could be translated by "oracle" or "prophecy," Philo felt constrained to explain it with reference to the normal sense of *lambanein*, as "something taken or received." At the same time he was able to preserve the Alexandrian tradition almost completely through a paraphrase by which he specified that the "thing taken or received" was none other than the gift of prophecy: εἰληφότος παρ᾽ αὐτοῦ μεγάλην δωρεάν, ἑρμηνείαν καὶ προφητείαν νόμων ἱερῶν· μεταληφθεὶς γὰρ

---

[27] In Ezek 12:10 הַנָּשִׂיא הַמַּשָּׂא הַזֶּה בִּירוּשָׁלַ͏ִם is translated by the LXX ὁ ἄρχων καὶ ὁ ἀφηγούμενος ἐν Ἰερουσαλήμ: "the prince and the chief in Jerusalem." Nothing in the LXX appears to correspond with Prov 31:1. On the problem of the root of *maśśā'*, see P. A. H. De Boer, "An Inquiry into the Meaning of the Term מַשָּׂא," *Old Testament Studies* 5 (1948) 197–214.

Μωυσῆς καλεῖται λῆμμα [(he) has received from him as a signal endowment the gift of interpreting and transmitting the holy laws. In fact, translated, Moses is called *lēmma*].

We may conclude, then, that the name of Moses, as a component of the polyonymous name of the prophet, in Mut 126 is related to the root *mwš* and to the word *maśśā'*.

IV.

We cannot presume to be as certain in regard to the etymology *"Moses liniens"* [Moses who anoints] which is never cited as such by Philo, but which, we believe, can be explained by reference to scriptural details whose presence is certain in the Philonic corpus.

Contrary to Wutz' proposal, *liniens* [who anoints] is not to be related to *mšš* [to touch]. In fact, in spite of the word *mašāšu* to which he refers, *mšš* does not have in Hebrew the meaning of "anoint." Rather, the etymology *Moses = liniens* relates the name of the prophet to the root *mšḥ* [to anoint], and to it alone.[28]

As for what this etymology signifies, this is not difficult to explain. *Moses liniens* refers to Moses' action which the Priestly Writer describes when he recounts that Moses ordained Aaron and his sons by anointing them with the sacred oil which God commanded him to prepare and to which, according to one text, he added the blood of the ram of consecration. See Exod 28:41; 29:7, 15–21; 30:25, 30; 40:14–15; Lev 7:36 (according to this text Moses was but the instrument of Yahweh, who is presented as the real author of the unction); 8:12.

Moses also anointed the tabernacle and all its vessels and accessories, the tent of meeting, the ark of the covenant, the table, the candlestick, the altar of burnt offering, the laver and its base. See Exod 29:36; 30:26–28; 40:9, 10, 11; Lev 8:10–11; Num 7:1.

These actions of Moses, which made him the direct and unique intermediary between God, the priesthood and the sanctuary, and the dispenser of holiness in Israel, in the eyes of the priestly redactors must have been seen as the supreme prerogative of the prophet. More generally, if—to borrow the concluding phrase of Vita Mos (2.292)— Moses was king, lawgiver, high priest and prophet, his delegation of the high-priesthood to the Aaronids by means of anointing was a sufficiently important and sublime act in the career of the Man of God to give rise to the temptation to explain his name in terms of the root *mšḥ* [to

---

[28] Wutz, in fact, writes (*Onomastica Sacra* 601): "*Moyses liniens* [Moyses who anoints] 73.20; 74.20; 76.24; 78.10: *mōšĕaḥ* [one who anoints]." He does not indicate *mšš* [to touch] as a possible alternative. On the anointing of Aaron by Moses (ἔχρισεν αὐτὸν ἐν ἐλαίῳ ἁγίῳ), see Joseph Ziegler, *Sapientia Iesu Filii Sirach* 45:15 (Göttingen: Vandenhoeck & Ruprecht, 1965).

anoint]. *Moses liniens* was a reminder that in Israel he was the source of levitical holiness.

The question that now confronts us is to determine whether the tradition of *Moses liniens* exists with Philo and is derived from him.

The passages of scripture to which we have referred above are not cited explicitly by Philo, but one finds a detailed paraphrase of them in Vita Mos 2.146–52. To this may be added a text such as Quaes Ex 2.33 on Exod 24:6, a verse that forms part of the description of a covenant ritual and mentions only a sprinkling of blood. But according to the translation of Ralph Marcus, Philo interprets it as "a sacred unction (*chrisma*) in place of oil for sanctity and perfect purity, and, if one must speak the truth, in order that (men) may be inspired to receive the holy spirit" (*PLCL Sup.* 2.73–74).

Having said this, one can only confirm that in Philo there is no explanation of the name of Moses in terms of the anointing which he administers. Nowhere in his writings does one find such a phrase as μεταληφθεὶς γὰρ Μωυσῆς καλεῖται (κατά)χρισις, (κατά)χρισμα, or (κατα)χρίων [for translated, Moses is called an anointing, an ointment, or one who anoints].[29] Thus it is probable that the etymology *Moses liniens* derives from biblical events, but, even though Philo describes Moses as *liniens*, he did not use the etymology.

The case is different with the explanations for Moses as *nous, eusebēs,* or *nous eusebēs* [Moses, mind, pious, or pious mind]. If the adjective *eusebēs* by itself has no compelling weight, the interpretation of the name of Moses on the basis of *nous* has an unmistakable Philonic flavor.

Let us add that in contrast to the relationships which we have analyzed up to this point, neither *nous* [mind] nor *eusebēs* [pious], properly speaking, constitutes an etymology of the name of Moses. They are, rather, moral or allegorical equivalents, not of the name of the prophet but of that of which he is a figure.

If, as Earp has observed,[30] "Philo makes comparatively little use of Moses as a symbolical figure," this allegorization exists nonetheless. We will concern ouselves here only with that which gives to Moses the quality of *nous.*

---

[29] In Conf 105 the verb *katachriō* refers to Noah's application of asphalt to the ark; in Vita Mos 2.146–52 to the anointing of the vessels of the sanctuary and the smearing with blood, while in Vita Mos 2.150 the simple form (*chriō*) is also used for the latter procedure. *Chriō* is also used in Fuga 110 in reference to the head of the high priest anointed with oil, i.e. crowned with intelligible light. In Vita Mos 2.146, 151, *chrisma* designates "the oil of holiness." One should note an error, among others of the same kind, in Günther Mayer's *Index Philoneus* (Berlin: De Gruyter, 1974): the references to *chriō* in Spec Leg 2.141, Virt 84, Praem 166, Gai 73, have to do rather with the word *chrēstotēs*, which of course has no relation to *chriō*.

[30] *PLCL* 10.386.

The explanations offered by Wutz, who once more practically ignores Philo and attempts to explain the significance of *nous eusebēs* [pious mind] in terms of the name Israel interpreted as "a man fearing God"—"man" being the equivalent of *nous* and "fearing God," according to Isa 11:2, that of *eusebēs*—have nothing in particular to recommend them.

In reality, the equation Moses = *nous* [mind] was suggested by Exod 4:16 and 7:1, which we have cited above. Moses conceives the thoughts with which God inspires him. He transmits them to Aaron, who proclaims them. In Leg All 1.40 Philo is really citing Exod 7:1. He does not set Moses in opposition to Aaron, but to Pharaoh considered as representing the irrational part of the soul. In contrast to the king of Egypt, Moses is the *nous*: ὡσανεὶ γὰρ θεός ἐστι τοῦ ἀλόγου ὁ νοῦς, παρὸ καὶ Μωυσῆν οὐκ ὤκνησεν εἰπεῖν "θεὸν τοῦ Φαραώ" [it is as if the mind is the god of the irrational part, and this is why he did not hesitate to call Moses "god of Pharaoh"] (Leg All 1.40). But in Migr 169–70, it is indeed Aaron whom Philo places in contrast to Moses: Ἀαρὼν μὲν γὰρ προφήτης λέγεται Μωυσέως ἐν τοῖς νόμους, ὁ γεγωνὸς λόγος προφητεύων διανοίᾳ. . . . εἰσὶν αἱ τοῦ βασιλεύειν ἀξίου νοῦ δορυφόροι δυνάμεις [For Aaron is called a prophet of Moses in the Laws, the articulate language prophesying to the understanding. . . . But these (that is, in addition to Aaron the powers symbolized by Nadab, Abihu and the seventy elders of Israel) are the satellite powers of the *nous*, which is worthy of exercising the kingly power]. In this passage Moses is indifferently designated by *nous* or by its equivalent, *dianoia* [understanding]. Elsewhere Philo calls it either *logos* [reason], *orthos logos* [right reason], or *logikon eidos* [rational form]. Thus in Mut 208, Moses, who is the human mind that has attained all the purity of which a human mind is capable, under the name of *nous* is again placed over against Aaron, on the basis of Exod 4 and 7: ἐπειδὴ γὰρ Μωυσῆς μέν ἐστι νοῦς ὁ καθαρώτατος, Ἀαρὼν δὲ λόγος αὐτοῦ, πεπαίδευται δὲ καὶ ὁ νοῦς θεοπρεπῶς ἐφάπτεσθαι καὶ ὁ λόγος ὁσίως ἑρμηνεύειν τὰ ὅσια [For since Moses is purest mind, and Aaron is its word, both have been trained—the mind to grasp holy things in a manner worthy of a god, and the word to interpret them worthily].[31]

---

31 For other examples, see Quod Det 29–40, Ebr 99, Migr 83, 169, where *nous* is replaced by its synonym, *dianoia*: Ἀαρὼν μὲν γὰρ προφήτης λέγεται Μωυσέως ἐν τοῖς νόμοις, ὁ γεγωνὸς λόγος προφητεύων διανοίᾳ [For Aaron is called a prophet of Moses in the laws, the articulate language prophesying to the understanding].

In Agr 80, Moses, directing the male voices in the Song of the Sea, is set over against Miriam, conducting the women's choir, representing the perfect *nous* contrasted with purified sense perception: χρήσεται δ᾽ ὁ μὲν τῶν ἀνδρῶν χορὸς ἡγεμόνι Μωυσεῖ, νῷ τελείῳ, ὁ δὲ τῶν γυναικῶν Μαριάμ, αἰσθήσει κεκαθαρμένῃ [The choir of the men shall have for a leader Moses, the perfect mind, while that of the women shall have Miriam, purified sense perception].

But in the same treatise, 117–20, one finds an interpretation that makes Moses the mind, somewhat in the sense suggested by Wutz, without taking, however, the detour via Israel; and here the mind is designated by *logos*. This passage has to do with the story of the daughters of Reuel (Raguel) (Exod 2:19), who symbolize the sense and who, in speaking of Moses to their father call him *anthrōpos Aigyptios* [an Egyptian man], that is, the reason which they imagine is bound to sense perception: διὰ μὲν τοῦ "ἄνθρωπος" τὰ μόνῳ λόγῳ θεωρητὰ μηνύουσαι, διὰ δὲ τοῦ "Αἰγύπτιος" παριστᾶσαι τὰ αἰσθητά. [By the word "man" they point out the world which reason alone discerns, by "Egyptian" they represent the world of sense (Mut 118; *PLCL* 5.203)]. Reuel reproaches his daughters, who hesitate between the things perceived by the mind and those by the senses, for having met the "man," i.e. *to logikon eidos* [the rational form] and having let him go away.

In Sacr 50–51, Moses is presented as the shepherd of Jethro, whose vain thoughts he guides toward the good. Philo notes also that if the Egyptians hold every shepherd in abomination, it is because like all lovers of the passions, they detest right reason, our pilot and guide to the good: τὸν γὰρ κυβερμήτην καὶ ὑφηγητὴν τῶν καλῶν ὀρθὸν λόγον βδελύττεται πᾶς φιλοπαθής [For the right reason which is our pilot and guide to things excellent is an abomination to all who love the passions (Sacr 51; *PLCL* 2.133)]. The juxtaposition of these two verses, Exod 3:1 and Gen 46:34, shows that when Moses watches over the flocks of Jethro, it is as the *orthos logos* [right reason]. The same interpretation of the same event is found in Agr 43, but there Moses is simply designated the shepherd and keeper of the confused thoughts of an infatuated soul.

The equation Moses = *nous* or "pious" *nous* is found also in the *Quaestiones in Exodum*. From Ralph Marcus' translation we cite the following examples: "For Moses is the most pure and God-loving mind" (2.27; *PLCL Sup* 2.67); "the most perfect and prophetic mind" (2.28; *PLCL Sup* 2.69); "prophetic mind . . . the prophetic mind . . . divinely inspired and filled with God" (2.29; *PLCL Sup* 2.69–70); "The allwise and God-beloved soul" (2.31; *PLCL Sup* 2.71); "but as for the deeper meaning, there are two brothers in one—the mind and the word. Now Moses, who is called by another name, mind, has obtained the better part, (namely) God, whereas the word, which is called Aaron, (has obtained) the lesser (part, namely) that of man" (2.44; *PLCL Sup* 2.88); "the holiest mind" (2.45; *PLCL Sup* 2.90).

One can see, therefore, that Wutz was wrong in avoiding a Philonic origin for Moses = *nous—eusebēs*. The equivalents Moses = mind or pious mind or pious (man) are amply represented in Philo and the contrast between Moses "the mind" and Aaron "articulate language" is found here explicitly as well. It is true that the epithet *eusebēs* does not occur alone to designate Moses; it is as infrequent as the other predicates used to qualify the *nous*, of which the prophet is the symbol.

This concept, of course, is deduced easily from the other ordinary attributes used to describe the moral nature of Moses, such as *teleios* [perfect], *hierōtatos* [most consecrated], *theophilos* [beloved of God], *theophilēs* [beloved of God], *philos theou* [friend of God], *philotheos* [lover of God], etc.[32] But there remain two texts where Moses is depicted almost explicitly as *nous eusebēs*.

The first is Vita Mos 2.66, where Philo writes: ὃ τοίνυν μέγιστον καὶ ἀναγκαιότατον ἀρχιερεῖ προσεῖναι δεῖ, τὴν εὐσέβειαν, ἐν τοῖς μάλιστα οὗτος ἤσκησεν [Certainly the highest quality of the high priest, that which is most indispensable to him, that is, piety, he (i.e. Moses) practiced to the highest point]. The other is found in Praem 53: πᾶσαι μὲν οὖν αἱ ἀρεταὶ παρθένοι, καλλιστεύει δὲ ὡς ἐν χορῷ παραλαβοῦσα τὴν ἡγεμονίαν ἡ εὐσέβεια, ἣν ἐκληρώσατο διαφερόντως ὁ θεολόγος Μωυσῆς, δι' ἣν μετὰ μυρίων ἄλλων, ἅπερ ἐν τοῖς γραφεῖσι περὶ τοῦ κατ' αὐτὸν βίου μεμήνυται, τεττάρων ἄθλων ἐξαιρέτων τυγχάνει, [τυχὼν] βασιλείας, νομοθεσίας, προφητείας, ἀρχιερωσύνης. [All the virtues are virgins, but she who exceeds in beauty and who, as in a choir, has taken the lead, is piety, with which Moses, the spokesman of God, was endowed in an eminent manner. It is this virtue along with numberless others set forth in what has been written concerning the life of Moses, which made it possible for him to gain four choice rewards: kingship, legislative power, prophesy, high priesthood].

Thus it is clear, according to this passage, that the principal virtue of Moses, the one which rules all others and explains par excellence the career and the prerogatives of the prophet, is piety. Consequently it is not illegitimate to affirm that Philo's Moses is above all an *eusebēs* or a *nous eusebēs*.

V.

It is clear then that all the traditions[33] reported and commented on

---

[32] A complete listing of the titles and attributes of Moses is given by Earp, *PLCL* 10.386, n. *a*; 387–88, nn. *a–h*; 388, nn. *a–i*.

[33] Apparently with the exception of that given in *Onomastica Sacra* 42.24: *Mose salvificator sive a salvatore* [Moses, savior or from the savior] and *apo sōtērias* [from salvation] (195.83). These etymologies certainly must not be related to the present participle of the root *mšh*. Here the name of Moses has been attached to *yš'*: *salvificator* [savior] is *môšia'*; *a salvatore* [from the savior] and *apo sōtērias* [from salvation] are derived from the preposition *m(n)* [from] + *hôšea'* [salvation]. Note Lagarde's correction in *Onomastica* 173.63, *Osēe sōzōn* [Hosea, saving] with the support of Jerome: cf. *Osee saluator aut saluans* [Hosea, savior or saving] 19.27; *saluans vel saluatus aut saluator* [saving or saved or savior] 51:15; *saluator* [savior] 74.24. Thus the *Onomastica Vaticana* and Jerome furnish proof that the noun *hôšea'* = "salvation" could be interpreted as *salvator* [savior]. In Mut 121 *sōtēria* [salvation] is related to *Yešûa'* (Joshua), and the name

by Wutz in regard to the name or the figure of Moses may be explained quite easily by reference to the writings of Philo. Other than the "Egyptian" etymology of the name of Moses, which he confines strictly to the story of the prophet's infancy and aside from explanations such as *nous eusebēs* which are not, as we have seen, etymologies strictly speaking, Philo relates the name of Moses to the root *mwš* and the noun *maśśā'*. In spite of his description of the rites of anointing and investiture carried out by the prophet, Philo does not make use of the explanation of the name on the basis of the root *mšḥ* [to anoint]—which is a further proof that the etymologies that he offers are second hand.

A further observation should be made. It is that the approximate nature, even the arbitrary crudeness with which these supposed etymological derivations are imagined, can suprise only the reader who has never cast an eye on the *Onomastica Sacra*. On the other hand, one who has worked with them a bit cannot be ignorant of the fact that many of the etymologies defy the most elementary laws of Hebrew philology with an amazing lack of concern. The explanation of the name of Moses by the roots *mwš* or *nś'* is neither more nor less inadmissable, depending on the way in which one views matters, than that of the name of Abraham by the root *rḥm* [to have mercy] (see *Abraam patēr oiktirmōn* [Abraham, merciful father], 172.49; 177.76) or by *r'h* + *'m* [he who sees + people] (*Abraham, pater videns populum* [Abraham, the father who sees the people], 3.3); or than the derivation of *Kabasaēl* (*[ye]qabṣe'ēl*), Josh 15:21; 2 Sam 23:30 = 2 Chr 11:22; Neh 11:25 (Jerome, on the other hand, gives a correct etymology: *Cabseel congregatio dei* [Cabseel, the congregation of God], 31.10) from the root *qwh* [to wait, to hope] (*Kabaseēl, hypomonē theou* [Kabasael, the patience of God], 171.21), etc.

This finding should lead anyone to exercise extreme prudence who, like Edmund Stein or Anthony T. Hanson, seeks to draw arguments for or against Philo's knowledge of Hebrew from an evaluation of his etymologies. No one has yet been successful in showing that any of the etymologies used by Philo were imagined by him. Those we have studied here in regard to the name of Moses are no exception to the rule. They were received by Philo from elsewhere rather than being conceived by him. Furthermore, the most fantastic or the most "barbarous" of them do not prove that their real authors were ignorant of Hebrew, but only that they were concerned with other matters than an exercise in philology and that they were not under the same constraints as we are today. The least assonance could be taken as

---

is explained as *sōtēria kyriou* (salvation of the Lord). Thus it is not ruled out to think of the same Hebrew word as the explanation of the equation Moses = *apo sōtērias* [from salvation].

sufficient basis for an etymology. In the case of Philo, consideration of the etymologies can, à fortiori, prove nothing at all. Their interest lies elsewhere. Whether plausible or grammatically absurd, Philo's etymologies are vehicles for theological concepts.

Those which he offers for the name of Moses are of this nature. Their correct understanding permits nothing other than a more exact approach to the thought of the Alexandrian exegete.

FURTHER GREEK FRAGMENTS
OF PHILO'S *QUAESTIONES*

JAMES R. ROYSE

San Francisco State University

The publication by Aucher in 1826 of the ancient Armenian version of Philo's *Quaestiones*[1] enabled scholars to attempt to locate within their original context the hundreds of Greek fragments attributed to Philo in various sources. Aucher himself began this task of identification,[2] and was followed by others, notably Harris[3] and Wendland,[4] whose work was summed up by Marcus for the Loeb edition of Philo.[5] Most recently, Petit has produced an even fuller collection, based on a critical examination of a superior range of manuscript evidence.[6]

This process of localization varies considerably in difficulty according to the source of the Greek involved. The exegetical chains on Genesis and Exodus,[7] which provide a substantial portion of the known Greek of

---

[1] J. B. Aucher, *Philonis Judaei Paralipomena Armena. libri videlicet quatuor in Genesin. libri duo in Exodum* . . . . (Venetiis: Typis coenobii PP. Armenorum in insula S. Lazari, 1826).

[2] Aucher is not, it seems, given credit for these identifications by Harris or by later authors, but in fact Aucher localized Greek fragments from 30 sections of the *Quaestiones*: Quaes Gen 1.21, 1.51, 1.55 (a), 1.64 (b-d), 1.77, 1.93, 2.9 (actually 1.94), 2.59, 2.62, 3.30 (b), 4.51 (a), 4.52 (b), 4.64, 4.99, 4.198, 4.202 (a), 4.227, 4.228; Quaes Ex 1.1, 2.1, 2.2, 2.3 (a), 2.9 (a-b), 2.17, 2.24 (b), 2.25 (d), 2.38 (a), 2.45 (a), 2.47, 2.49 (a). (Four of these, Quaes Gen 3.30, 4.52, 4.64, and 4.99, are made on the page [non-numbered] following p. 443; the others are cited ad loc.)

By the way, Aucher cites both the chains and the *Sacra parallela* for Quaes Gen 4.228, but J. R. Harris, *Fragments of Philo Judaeus* (Cambridge: University Press, 1886) 46, cites only the chains, as does R. Marcus, *PLCL* Supplement 2.232–33 (left column). (See F. Petit, *PM* 33, 212, n. *a*.) Furthermore, Aucher correctly ascribes to Quaes Ex 2.9 both the fragment from the chains and the second fragment from the *Sacra parallela*; Harris ascribes the fragment from the chains to Quaes Ex 2.9 (*Fragments*, 51–52), but prints the first fragment from the *Sacra parallela* as unidentified (*Fragments*, 75). Marcus repeats this dual citation (*PLCL* Supplement 2.242 and 262 [no. 22]), as noted by Petit (*PM* 33, 244, n. *a*).

[3] *Fragments*.

[4] P. Wendland, *Neu entdeckte Fragmente Philos* (Berlin: Georg Reimer, 1891).

[5] *PLCL* Supplement 2.179–263.

[6] F. Petit, *Quaestiones in Genesim et in Exodum: fragmenta graeca* (*PM* 33, 1978).

[7] See R. Devreesse, "Chaînes exégétiques grecques," *DBS* 1.1084–1233.

the *Quaestiones*, simply follow the order of the Biblical text in citing extracts from various exegetical works. Since Philo, of course, also follows the order of the Biblical text in his *Quaestiones*, it is a rather straightforward matter to see whether a Greek text ascribed to Philo in these chains comes from the appropriate portion of the *Quaestiones*. In fact, since it happens that quite a few fragments of the *Quaestiones* are assigned to someone other than Philo or are simply anonymous, a more thorough analysis can be accomplished by comparing *all* the exegetical extracts with the appropriate places of the *Quaestiones*. Such an analysis is laborious but remains a straightforward method of locating Greek fragments of the *Quaestiones* contained within these chains, whatever their ascription may be.[8] It is similarly uncomplicated to locate the Greek extracts from the *Quaestiones* found in Procopius,[9] who also follows the Biblical order in his comments. Procopius does not name his sources, but a comparison with the Armenian enables us to see when he is in fact quoting from the *Quaestiones*.[10]

The other sources of Greek fragments from Philo pose more formidable problems of localization. Within the florilegia the extracts from various authors are arranged not according to the Biblical order but according to subjects,[11] and the task of identification is consequently much more difficult. In general, the only way to localize them is simply to read through the *Quaestiones*, hoping to find the Armenian portion which corresponds to a given Greek text. An additional, but not infallible, guide for many of these fragments found in the florilegia is that they are ascribed not only to Philo but to Philo's *Quaestiones*, and even to specific books of the *Quaestiones*. And in fact the vast majority of the texts ascribed to the *Quaestiones* have been located within the Armenian text (or the Latin version[12]).

This process of identification, though, is beset with several problems. For one thing, it is difficult enough to keep the various Greek texts in mind while reading the Armenian. Furthermore, the Greek texts themselves may have been altered somewhat when removed from their original context, and may also have been corrupted in the course of manuscript transmission. The Armenian, too, may have mistranslated the Greek in the first place, or have suffered corruption in subsequent copying. And, finally, the task of reading the Armenian amounts in most cases to reading the Latin

---

[8] See Petit, *PM* 33, 16.

[9] Devreesse, "Chaînes," 1087–88.

[10] See Petit, *PM* 33, 18–19.

[11] See M. Richard, "Florilèges spirituels, III. Florilèges grecs," *Dictionnaire de Spiritualité* 5 (Paris: Beauchesne, 1964) 475–512.

[12] Three Greek fragments are located in the Latin version of the original sixth book of Quaes Gen, which preserves a portion of the *Quaestiones* missing in the Armenian. See Petit, *PM* 33, 199–201.

translation of Aucher or the English translation of Marcus.[13] It is clear that these factors may combine to make the localization of a Greek fragment practically impossible, especially if the fragment is fairly brief.

A further difficulty is that the Greek fragments ascribed to the *Quaestiones* may come from a portion of that work which is not extant in Armenian or Latin. Such may indeed be the case with many of the unidentified Greek fragments of the *Quaestiones*, and for such texts the precise localization will almost always be impossible.[14] It is also, of course, possible that a Greek text ascribed to the *Quaestiones* in fact comes from some other work of Philo,[15] or is not even from Philo at all.

Unfortunately, the list of difficulties in identifying the Greek remains of the *Quaestiones* is not yet at an end. Many of the texts in the florilegia (and in some other miscellaneous sources) are simply ascribed to Philo, and they may come from the *Quaestiones*. Moreover, since the lemmata are often erroneous not only as to work but even as to author, texts which are ascribed to other writers may nevertheless be fragments of the *Quaestiones*.[16] But the possibility of locating such texts is indeed remote, since we are dealing with literally thousands of Greek texts. A similar problem arises with the citations from Philo to be found in the works of early Christian writers. These citations range from lengthy verbatim transcriptions, as in Eusebius, to the incidental use of Philonic terms and phrases, often not accompanied by an explicit reference to Philo.[17] In the latter

---

[13] The first volume of the French version by C. Mercier (*PM* 34A, 34B, 34C) has also appeared.

[14] Of course, the content of the fragment may allow a conjecture as to its original location. Thus, there is a Greek text ascribed to Philo in an exegetical chain on Hebrews which appears to be taken from Philo's comment on Gen 14:20, which would come from the lacuna between the present books 2 and 3 of the Armenian Quaes Gen. See my "The Original Structure of Philo's *Quaestiones*," *SP* 4 (1976–77) 49 and nn. 63–64 (on pp. 71–72). Petit (*PM* 33, 227–28) prints this text from Harris (*Fragments*, 71–72), noting that it is not to be found, as Harris claims, at p. 580 of Cramer's edition of this chain. In fact, it is found on p. 549, and in the manuscript itself, Parisinus 238, is found at f. 335ᵛ 21–23 and 336ʳ 1–6. The lemma there (335ᵛ 21–22 margin) is simply Φίλωνος, and so the ascription to the *Quaestiones* is, as Petit thinks probable, a hypothesis of Harris.

Another example of the possible localization of a fragment without the use of the Armenian (or Latin) is a text which relates to Ex 13:2, Philo's comment on which is again lost because of a lacuna in the Armenian. See "The Original Structure," 54 and n. 85 (on p. 74). Incidentally, the emendation of the lemma referred to there (p. 54 and n. 86 [on p. 74]) is unnecessary. A re-examination of the microfilm of Vat. 1553 and a later examination of the manuscript itself made clear that the ascription is actually to the first (A) book of Quaes Ex, and not to the fourth (Δ) book. Petit (*PM* 33, 299 and n. *a*) also reads *first*. (By the way, the lemma is in uncial script, and so the A and Δ would be similar.)

[15] See n. 20 below.

[16] Cf. Petit, *PM* 33, 22.

[17] The citations found by K. Staehle in Johannes Lydus are of this sort.

case, the eventual localization of a citation in terms of the Armenian (or Latin) will be rather problematic.

As a consequence of all these difficulties, it is likely that we will never have a complete identification of all the Greek texts extant in some source or other which in fact come from those portions of the *Quaestiones* now preserved in Armenian (or Latin), not to speak of those portions lost entirely. The pleasant aspect of this subject, however, is that scholars from Aucher to Petit have had considerable success in locating Greek fragments, and it certainly seems reasonable to believe that comparatively few Greek texts which can be identified at all have not already been identified.

A further regrettable feature of the study of the Greek fragments of Philo is that a good deal of the discoveries and identifications have been made repeatedly. The complexity of the textual tradition of Philo and the extent of the secondary literature devoted to his works have combined to make it difficult to be confident that one has not missed relevant points already made. It is also the case that earlier scholars have not always presented their findings in the most perspicuous manner. This is true in particular of an article by Früchtel concerned with the Greek fragments of the *Quaestiones*.[18] He there printed the Greek of eleven newly identified fragments (three of which had previously been located by Bréhier), but then noted other identifications in passing in his text or in a footnote. Furthermore, Früchtel printed nine other Greek texts from Clement which are not genuine fragments of the *Quaestiones* at all.[19]

It is thus perhaps not surprising that Marcus and Petit do not fully utilize the discoveries noted in Früchtel's article.[20] Indeed, Marcus shows

---

[18] L. Früchtel, "Griechische Fragmente zu Philons Quaestiones in Genesin et in Exodum," *ZAW* 14 (1937) 108–15.

[19] Accordingly, in his unpublished collection of Greek fragments of Philo (cf. "The Original Structure," n. 6 [pp. 65–66]) Früchtel did not include any of these nine, although he did give a passing reference to *Strom.* 6. 145.5 in connection with Quaes Gen 1.1 (cf. "Fragmente," 114, no. 8).

[20] We may especially note the fate of two of the "unidentified" fragments from Quaes Gen printed by Marcus, *PLCL* Supplement 2.234–35. His no. 4 is taken from Harris, *Fragments*, 69, but was in fact already recognized as coming from Somn 1.177, 176 in *PCW* 3.242–43, as was explicitly cited by Früchtel, "Fragmente," 112. Not only does Marcus miss this identification, but Petit (*PM* 33, 214 and n. *a*) makes the correct identification of the text and notes: "Identifié par Enzo Lucchesi (lettre du 10 novembre 1975)."

Marcus' no. 5 is taken from Harris, *Fragments*, 69–70, and was recognized as coming from Quod Deus 27 in *PCW* 2.62, as was cited by Früchtel, "Fragmente," 112. Marcus misses this identification, and Petit made the identification independently: cf. her *L'ancienne version latine des Questions sur la Genèse de Philon d'Alexandrie* 1: *Édition critique*, TU 113, 1973, 6, n. 4 (where the reference to no. 4 should be to no. 5), and also *PM* 33, 214.

The history of even those two small texts proves to be involved, but one hopes that they will not need to be located again. (See also "The Original Structure," n. 79 [p. 74].)

acquaintance only with the eleven Greek texts numbered by Früchtel, and Petit cites only these eleven and then makes three other localizations independently. All of this can be seen in the following table, where the texts are arranged according to the order of the *Quaestiones*.

Quaes Gen 1.41	Früchtel, p. 113, note 1: previously identified by Wendland;[21] not in Marcus or Petit.
Quaes Gen 1.82	Früchtel, p. 112: not in Marcus or Petit.
Quaes Gen 1.100(a)	Früchtel, p. 110 (no. 6): cited by Marcus and Petit.
Quaes Gen 2.22	Früchtel, p. 112: identified by Wendland as Quaes Gen 1.99, followed by Marcus; Petit correctly identifies the text independently.
Quaes Gen 2.34(b-c)	Früchtel, p. 110 (no. 4): cited by Marcus and Petit.
Quaes Gen 2.41	Früchtel, p. 111 (no. 9): cited by Marcus and Petit.
Quaes Gen 3.38(b)	Früchtel, p. 110 (no. 7): cited by Marcus and Petit.
Quaes Gen 3.48	Früchtel, p. 111 (no. 8): cited by Marcus and Petit.
Quaes Gen 4.8(c)	Früchtel, p. 109 (no. 2): previously identified by Bréhier;[22] cited by Marcus and Petit.
Quaes Gen 4.74	Früchtel, pp. 109–10 (no. 3): cited by Marcus and Petit.
Quaes Gen 4.100	Früchtel, p. 111 (no. 11): cited by Marcus and Petit.
Quaes Gen 4.179	Früchtel, p. 109 (no. 1): previously identified by Bréhier; cited by Marcus and Petit.
Quaes Gen 4.211	Früchtel, p. 110 (no. 5): previously identified by Bréhier; cited by Marcus and Petit.
Quaes Ex 2.9(a)	Früchtel, p. 109: Harris cites as unidentified,[23] as does Marcus;[24] Petit identifies the text independently.[25]

---

21 As Früchtel cites: *Neu entdeckte Fragmente*, 140, n. 1. In fact, Wendland merely quotes the text and inserts after ἡδονή: "(S. Quaest. in Genes. I 41)."

22 E. Bréhier, *Les idées philosophiques et religieuses de Philon d'Alexandrie* (Paris: J. Vrin, 1908) vii, n. 2.

23 *Fragments*, 75.

24 *PLCL* Supplement 2.262 (no. 22).

25 *PM* 33, 244–45. This is the first fragment from the *Sacra parallela* at this text, and it was remarked above (n. 2) that the second fragment from the *Sacra parallela* was already placed here by Aucher. Petit brings together the fragment from the chains and both fragments from the *Sacra parallela*, as indeed Früchtel had also done in his unpublished manuscript.

Quaes Ex 2.15(b)   Früchtel, p. 111 (no. 10): cited by Marcus and
                    Petit.
Quaes Ex 2.64   Früchtel, p. 109: Harris cites as unidentified;[26]
                    Petit identifies the text independently.

Früchtel's efforts to locate still more Greek fragments of the *Quaestiones* did not stop with this article, and in fact he succeeded in identifying ten more Greek texts.[27] Six of these have subsequently been located by Petit,[28] and they are simply noted here: Quaes Gen 1.49, 3.20, 3.21, Quaes Ex 2.38 (b), 2.44, 2.71. The four others are printed below, along with two texts identified in Früchtel's 1937 article but not repeated by Marcus or Petit; and yet three more fragments are here located for the first time.

In the citations of these fragments the following sigla are used:[29]

A   Athous Iberorum Monasterii 382, f. 171^r–197^r (*Sacra parallela*)[30]
K   Vaticanus 1553 (*Sacra parallela*)[31]
L^a Laurentianus pluteus VIII 22, f. 1^r–45^v (*Sacra parallela*)[32]

---

[26] *Fragments*, 101. This is the citation from the *Sacra parallela* which overlaps with the fuller extract in Vaticanus 379. Marcus does not print this citation, since Harris had claimed: "Referred to *De Ebrietate*, perhaps the lost book on this subject which may have preceded our present one." Wendland (*Neu entdeckte Fragmente*, 24, no. 9) also refers this citation to the lost book περὶ μέθης. However, the lemma here in R is (as Petit notes) simply τοῦ αὐτοῦ, which equals Φίλωνος. Both Harris and Wendland evidently misinterpreted the lemma as referring to both the author and the book of the previous lemma: τοῦ αὐτοῦ περὶ μέθης (R, f. 191^r 15), which itself refers to Φίλωνος (R, f. 191^r 13). Früchtel says that the source of the error was "die Umstellung der beiden Sätze im cod. Rup.," but this should not affect the reading of the lemmata. By the way, in "The Original Structure," 56 and n. 98 (p. 75), this fragment of Quaes Ex 2.64 in the *Sacra parallela* was overlooked.

[27] These are all noted in his unpublished manuscript; however, Früchtel knew of these fragments only from the then published sources and not from the manuscripts themselves. Incidentally, Früchtel did not include the fragment from Quaes Gen 1.49 among the fragments of the *Quaestiones*, but did identify it in his table giving the locations of the fragments edited by Mangey and Harris.

[28] The last five are found in *PM* 33. The fragment from Quaes Gen 1.49 (Τοῦ φαύλου-ἀνακέκραται) was later identified by Petit in her review of *PM* 34A in *Le Muséon* 92 (1979) 404.

[29] For access to microfilms of the five manuscripts cited here I am grateful to the Institut de Recherche et d'Histoire des Textes, Paris. Petit uses the symbol A for Atheniensis Metochion 274, which is probably just a copy of H (Hierosolymitanus S. Sepulcri 15); see *PM* 33, 25, n. 5. However, the Florilegium Hierosolymitanum (the recension of the *Sacra parallela* surviving in these two manuscripts) is itself a mixed recension, and it appears that its textual value is minimal; cf. Richard, "Florilèges," 483–84.

[30] Ibid., 479. A is not only, as it appears, the only witness to Quaes Gen 1.41 within the *Sacra parallela*, but also contains several other extracts from Philo not known elsewhere among the florilegia.

[31] Ibid., 478.

[32] This manuscript contains three different florilegia: f. 1^r–45^v (L^a) f. 46^r–73^v (L^b), and and f. 74^r–189^v (L^c). Cf. ibid., 482 and 495.

R Berolinensis 46 (*Sacra parallela*)[33]
T Thessalonicensis Blateon 9 (*Sacra parallela*)[34]

Also cited are the florilegium attributed to Antonius[35] and the editions of Mangey,[36] Mai,[37] Harris,[38] Lewy,[39] Marcus, and Petit, as well as the Stählin-Früchtel edition of Clement's *Stromateis* (*GCS* 52).

Quaes Gen 1.41

Δοκεῖ μὲν λεία τις εἶναι κίνησις ἡ ἡδονή, τὸ δὲ ἀληθὲς τραχεῖα εὑρίσκεται καὶ ἔστιν.

A, f. 185ᵛ (28 margin) 28–29: Φίλωνος
Antonius, 824B4–5: Philonis
λεία τις εἶναι: δολεῖ τὶς ἔσται A
Mangey, 674.1 (from Antonius)

Located by Wendland (*Neu entdeckte Fragmente*, 140, note 1) and by Früchtel ("Fragmente," 113, note 1): ". . . although the movement of pleasure seems to be somewhat slippery and smooth, nevertheless in truth it proves to be rough, . . ." (Marcus, *PLCL* Supplement 1.24). Marcus (*PLCL* Supplement 2.183) and Petit (*PM* 33, 52) print a text which is, as Petit says, a "simple écho philonien."

Quaes Gen 1.82

Τί δέ; οὐχὶ καὶ ὁ θεὸς μετὰ τὴν ἐπὶ τῷ Κάϊν συγγνώμην ἀκολούθως οὐ πολλῷ ὕστερον τὸν μετανοήσαντα Ἐνὼχ εἰσάγει δηλῶν ὅτι συγγνώμη μετάνοιαν πέφυκε γεννᾶν;

Clemens Alexandrinus, *Stromateis* II 70,3
R, f. 252ᵛ (30) 30–31: Φίλωνος (συγγνώμη - γεννᾶν only)
Antonius, 1145A12: Philonis (συγγνώμη - γεννᾶν only)
συγγνώμη μετάνοιαν R Antonius (Klostermann conjectured in Clem.): συγγνώμην μετάνοια L (sole manuscript of Clem.)
Mangey, 672.2 (from Antonius)

---

[33] Ibid., 481–82. The importance of this manuscript (Codex Rupefucaldinus) is seen from the fact that it contains six of the nine fragments printed here.
[34] Ibid., 483. This is Petit's S.
[35] Ibid., 492–94; cited from *MPG* 136.
[36] T. Mangey, *Philonis Judaei opera quae reperiri potuerunt omnia* (London: Bowyer, 1742), Vol. 2 (cited by page and the order on that page).
[37] A. Mai, *Scriptorum veterum nova collectio* 7 (Romae: Typis Vaticanis, 1833).
[38] *Fragments* (cited by page and the order on that page).
[39] H. Lewy, "Neue Philontexte in der Überarbeitung des Ambrosius. Mit einem Anhang: Neu gefundene griechische Philonfragmente," *Sitzungsberichte der Preussischen Akademie der Wissenschaften*, Philosophisch-Historische Klasse (1932) 23–84.

Located by Früchtel ("Fragmente," 112): " . . . (Scripture) reveals the ordering of things. For not very long after the forgiving of Cain it introduces the fact that Enoch repented, informing us that forgiveness is wont to produce repentance" (Marcus, *PLCL* Supplement 1.51). The first six words cited from Clement do not correspond to the Armenian.

Quaes Gen 1.98

Σωτήριον ἐν τοῖς μάλιστα δικαιοσύνη καὶ ἀνθρώπων καὶ τῶν τοῦ κόσμον μερῶν, γῆς καὶ οὐρανοῦ.

R, f. 148ʳ (25) 28–29: τοῦ αὐτοῦ (Φίλωνος, 1. 24)
Mangey, 664.4
Harris, 101.1

Not previously located: " . . . deliverance from this in particular is justice both for men and for the parts of the world, (namely) heaven and earth" (Marcus, *PLCL* Supplement 1.65).

Quaes Gen 3.3 (b)

Συγκρύπτεται διὰ κολακείας φιλία, νόθου πράγματος καὶ ἀδοκίμου τὸ γνήσιον καὶ δοκιμώτατον.

K, f. 191ʳ (15) 16–17: (Φίλωνος, 1. 13) ἐκ τοῦ δ᾽ τῶν ἐν Γενέσει ζητημάτων
Mai, 103b (=*MPG* 86².2084C(6)7–8)
Harris, 71.3
Marcus, *PLCL* Supplement 2.237 (unidentified no. 13)
Petit, *PM* 33, 220 (unidentified no. 7)

Located by Früchtel (in his unpublished manuscript[40]): " . . . they are also hidden, as love (is hidden) by flattery, (and as) natural and genuine things are subjected to tests (by comparison with) foreign and untested things" (Marcus, *PLCL* Supplement 1.179). Petit suggests that the final word of this text has been lost and proposes "ἐπαινοῦσα, vel sim." However, the Armenian is also missing a verb, as noted by Aucher (*Paralipomena*, 170, note 3): "Verbum deest in Arm. unde pendet sensus."

Quaes Gen 3.42

Ἐπεὶ καὶ πρότερον εἶπεν "διαθήκην", <λέγει>· μὴ ζήτει αὐτὴν ἐν γραφῇ.

Clemens Alexandrinus, *Stromateis* I 182,2

---

[40] Cf. "The Original Structure," 72, n. 69.

<λέγει>· μὴ ζήτει from the Armenian: <ἐπιφέρει> μὴ ζήτει Früchtel: μὴ ζητεῖν Clem.: <παραινεῖ> μὴ ζητεῖν Früchtel conjectured in Clem.

Located by Früchtel (in his unpublished manuscript): "Since He had earlier spoken of the covenant, He says, 'Do not seek it in writing , . . .'" (Marcus, *PLCL* Supplement 1.231). Früchtel's conjecture of ἐπιφέρει was based on Aucher's rendering of the Armenian: " . . . inducit: Ne quaeras . . . . " But the word translated as *inducit* is simply *asē*, which corresponds to λέγει.[41]

Quaes Ex 2.13 (c)

Τῷ ἔνδον οἰκείῳ δικαστηρίῳ πᾶς ἄφρων ἁλίσκεται.

R, f. 196ᵛ (33) 33–34: τοῦ αὐτοῦ (Φίλωνος, 1. 31)
Antonius, 1213B4–5: Philonis (A9)
Harris, 109.12 (from R and Antonius)

Located by Früchtel (in his unpublished manuscript): " . . . he within whom it [conviction] is, is apprehended by his own judgment as being altogether foolish" (Marcus, *PLCL* Supplement 2.51). Aucher translates the Armenian as: "quia eo qui intus est, judice proprio omnis insipiens reprehenditur." This appears to be an adequate rendering of the Armenian, and fits the Greek better than Marcus' version does.

Quaes Ex 2.19 (b)

Εὔπαιδες οἱ τῶν καλῶν καὶ ἀγαθῶν ἐπιστήμονες.

R, f. 266ʳ (30) 30: Φίλωνος
Antonius, 1052B2: Philonis
Mangey, 673.5b (from Antonius)
Lewy, 82 (no. 24) (from R)
Not previously located: "those who are learned in the knowledge of good and excellent things have good children" (Marcus, *PLCL* Supplement 2.58).[42]

Quaes Ex 2.110

Τὸ λέγειν ἄνευ τοῦ πράττειν ἀτελές.

R, f. 30ʳ (35) 35–36: Φίλωνος
Lᵃ, f. 34ʳ (31) 31: Φίλωνος

---

[41] R. Marcus, "An Armenian-Greek Index to Philo's *Quaestiones* and *De Vita Contemplativa*," *Journal of the American Oriental Society* 53 (1933) 256.

[42] This text is discussed in my "Philo and the Immortality of the Race," *JSJ* 11 (1980) 33–37.

T, f. 21ʳB (28) 29–30: Φίλωνος ἐκ τῶν ἐν ᾽Εξόδῳ ζητημάτων
Τὸ R Lᵃ: τοῦ T
Harris, 108.4 (from R)
Petit, *PM* 33, 303 (unidentified no. 27) (from R and T)

Located by Früchtel (in his unpublished manuscript): " . . . for
everything without workmanship is imperfect and lame" (Marcus, *PLCL*
Supplement 2.160). As Marcus notes, "workmanship" is literally "working," and so the final four words of the Greek fit the Armenian perfectly.
The first two words are a resumption from the previous clause.

Quaes Ex 2.115

Θυμοῦ μάλιστα δεῖ κυβερνήτῃ χρῆσθαι <τῷ λόγῳ>· καταλειφθεὶς
γὰρ ἀκυβέρνητος ἄνω καὶ κάτω κυκώμενος ὑπὸ σάλου καὶ κλύδωνος τὴν
ψυχὴν ὅλην καθάπερ ἀνερμάτιστον σκάφος ἀνατρέψει συνανατρέψας
καὶ τὸ σῶμα.

R, f, 247ʳ (3) 3–6: Φίλωνος
Antonius, 1173C13–D2: Dionysii Alex. (C8, on previous text)
Θυμοῦ Früchtel: θυμῷ R Antonius <τῳ λόγῳ> from the Armenian:
om. R Antonius ἀνερμάτιστον Antonius: ἀνορμάτιστον R συνανατρέψας
Antonius: συναναστρέψας R
Harris, 110.6 (from R)

Not previously located: "anger especially has need of the controlling
and directing reason. For when it is left without a controller and director, it is borne hither and thither in confusion and tossed about as though
by stormy waves, and overturns the entire soul like a ship without a
ballast, the body being overturned with it" (Marcus, *PLCL* Supplement
2.166).

Früchtel included this text (cited from Harris only) among his
"Fragmenta dubia," and made the conjectures of θυμοῦ and of the addition of <τῷ λογισμῷ> after χρῆσθαι. The Armenian, however, has *ban*,
which corresponds to λόγος.[43] It may be noted, though, that among the
fragments of the Oxyrhynchus Papyrus of Philo occurs the phrase
λογισμῷ γὰρ μόνῳ χρῆται κυβερνήτῃ,[44] and Früchtel may have had this
in mind as a parallel for his conjecture.

Is it possible that still more Greek fragments of the *Quaestiones* will
be located? Many of the sources of these fragments await a critical and
systematic exploration, and increased understanding of the Armenian

---

[43] According to Marcus, "Index," 258, *ban* renders λόγος 23 times, and does not render any
other Greek word at all.
[44] *P. Oxy.* 1356, f. 4ʳ 10–11. I believe that this fragment probably comes from the original
first book *De ebrietate*; see "The Oxyrhynchus Papyrus of Philo," *BASP* 17 (1980) 155–65.

version is certainly possible. And so the patient researcher may yet be rewarded with small successes in the task of rediscovering the original Greek of Philo's *Quaestiones*.

PHILO'S PRIESTLY DESCENT

DANIEL R. SCHWARTZ

Hebrew University

In his recent critical review of J. Schwartz's speculations regarding Philo's life and career,[1] S. S. Foster has again raised the question of whether the philosopher was indeed of priestly descent as St. Jerome reports (*De viris illustribus* 11). Schwartz had offered a complicated theory which supported Jerome's notice, but Foster, in my opinion correctly, showed that the facts could be accounted for by a much simpler explanation (see below, IId). As for the Father's report, Foster comments that "it seems reasonable to class this account with other such legends developed by Christians who used the literature of Philo."[2] While some scholars who accepted Schwartz's theories followed him regarding Philo's priestly descent as well,[3] it appears that Foster's skepticism echoes the dominant note: Schwartz himself did not explicitly repeat this detail in a later restatement of his views, and it is also ignored by scholars who otherwise followed him.[4]

Furthermore, it may be noted that such skepticism has been prevalent for almost a century, since the publication of the second edition of Schürer's *Geschichte*, wherein he emphasized the fact that no authority prior to Jerome reports Philo's priestly descent.[5] Schürer's doubts were seconded by such prestigious scholars as L. Massebieau[6] and O. Stählin,[7]

---

[1] "A Note on the 'Note' of J. Schwartz," *SP* 4 (1976–77) 26, 28–29. Schwartz's articles are referred to in nn. 4 and 34, below.

[2] "A Note," 28.

[3] J. Daniélou, *Philon d'Alexandrie* ("Les temps et les destins"; Paris: A. Fayard, 1958) 15; followed in turn by A. Jaubert, *La notion d'alliance dans le Judaïsme aux abords de l'ère Chrétienne* (Patristica Sorbonensia 6; Paris: Editions du Seuil, 1963) 294, n. 167.

[4] Schwartz, "L'Égypte de Philon," *PAL* 43; L. Feldman, *Scholarship on Philo and Josephus (1937–1962)* (Yeshiva University Studies in Judaica 1; New York: Bloch, 1963) 4; C. Mondésert, "Philon d'Alexandrie ou Philon le Juif," *DBS* 7.1288–89.

[5] E. Schürer, *Geschichte des jüdischen Volkes im Zeitalter Jesu Christi* (2 vols.; Leipzig: Hinrichs, 1886–90) 2.832. The same statement may be found in the third and fourth editions of Schürer's work, 3.489 and 3.636 respectively.

[6] "Chronologie de la vie et des oeuvres de Philon," *RHR* 53:3 (May-June, 1906) 30, n. 1.

[7] In *Wilhelm von Christs Geschichte der griechischen Literatur* (2 vols. in 3; 5th ed., by W. Schmid; Munich: Beck, 1908–13) 2/1.478, n. 8.

among others, while H. Leisegang[8] specifically made the same pro-
nouncement as Foster: since Jerome reports Christian legends about
Philo, this unparalleled detail must also be classified among them. These
pronouncements have had their effect, and very little attention has been
given the question; it is not even mentioned in most major and minor
studies regarding Philo, nor even in the only special study I have found
which is devoted to Philo's family background (apart from those by
Schwartz and Foster).[9] Since Schürer, the most Jerome's notice usually
gets, if mentioned at all, is a passing mention with a non liquet.[10]

Prior to the second edition of Schürer, on the other hand, it is difficult to find anyone who doubts that Philo was of a priestly family. Most
scholars seem to have believed that he was,[11] while a few confine themselves to reporting Jerome's statement without passing judgement upon
it[12] or omit reference to it altogether, as Schürer did in the first edition
(1874) of his handbook. Such acceptance of Jerome's testimony is not
very surprising, of course, given the prestige which the Fathers then
more routinely enjoyed. But doubts as to the truth of Jerome's Christianizing legends about Philo were already rampant.[13] T. Mangey, for
example, who believed that Philo was a priest, argues just a few pages

---

[8] "Philon. 41," *PW* 20:1, columns 1–2.

[9] A. Fuks, "Marcus Julius Alexander: On the History of Philo's Family," *Zi* 13/14
(1948–49) 10–17 (Hebrew); the article appeared in English, in altered form, as "Notes on
the Archive of Nicanor," *Journal of Juristic Papyrology* 5 (1951) 207–16.

[10] So, for example, O. Zöckler, "Philon von Alexandrien," *Realencyklopädie für protes-
tantische Theologie und Kirche* (3rd. ed.; 24 vols.; Leipzig: Hinrichs, 1896–1913) 15.349;
N. Bentwich, *Philo-Judaeus of Alexandria* (Philadelphia: Jewish Publication Society,
1910) 46; E. Zeller, *Die Philosophie der Griechen in ihrer geschichtlichen Entwicklung*
(5th–7th ed.; 3 vols. in 6; Hildesheim: Olms, 1963 [reprint of 1923]) 3:2.385–86, n. 2; H.
Box, *Philonis Alexandrini In Flaccum* (London-New York: Oxford University, 1939) xxxi;
and, more recently, R. Arnaldez in *PM* 1.18. Apart from Schwartz's followers mentioned
in n. 3 above, I have noted only two post-Schürer scholars who believe Jerome's notice: M.
Stein, *Dat VeDaʿat* (Cracow: "Miflat," 1938) 103 (Hebrew) and idem, *Philon HaʾAlex-
androni* (Warsaw: Stybel, 1937) 50 (Hebrew), and P. Seidensticker, *Lebendiges Opfer*
(*Röm. 12,1*): *Ein Beitrag zur Theologie des Apostels Paulus* (NTAb 20:1–3, 1954) 115.
Neither cites any argument apart from Jerome's testimony. In *PW* 9.2515 (1916), W. Otto
promised to write a study proving, inter alia, that the priest who authored one of
Josephus' putative sources was none other than Philo. However, he never published such a
proof, as far as I have been able to ascertain.

[11] Apart from the many to be mentioned below in connection with specific arguments,
the following believers may be cited: Thomas-Pope Blount, *Censura Celebriorum
Authorum* (London: R. Chiswel, 1690) 72–73, and A. F. Dähne, *Geschichtliche Darstellung der jüdisch-alexandrinischen Religions-Philosophie* (2 vols.; Halle: Buchhand-
lung des Waisenhauses, 1834) 1.104–5.

[12] So A. F. Gfrörer, *Philo und die alexandrinische Theosophie* (Kritische Geschichte des
Urchristentums 1:1; Stuttgart: Schweizerbart, 1831) 1.1–2.

[13] See F. Conybeare's review of opinions, in his edition of *Philo About the Contemplative Life* (Oxford: Clarendon, 1895), especially pp. 320–26. Cf. n. 74, below.

later that chronology rules out the possibility that *De vita contemplativa* describes early Christians or that Philo met Peter in Rome.[14] So it is somewhat surprising that Schürer's rejection of Philo's priesthood won such overall acceptance, given the fact that it was not based on any new evidence or argument but rather only upon the previously recognized lack of authority prior to Jerome.

Moreover, former scholars had not contented themselves with Jerome's notice alone; they had assembled a number of arguments in order to corroborate it. While some of these do not stand up under examination, others, which can be supplemented, do seem to be worthy of consideration. Especially in this post-Qumran generation, which has recognized the persistence of special priestly traditions even centuries after the work of priestly circles in the formation of the canon,[15] the question of Philo's relation to the priesthood is not one which should lightly be dismissed.

I.

First, let us look at Jerome's statement. He begins his entry on Philo with the words, "Philon Iudaeus, natione Alexandrinus, de genere sacerdotum. . . . " He then proceeds to explain that Philo is included in this catalogue of Christian writers because of his book praising early Christian monks of Alexandria, and he reports Philo's meeting with Peter. Since the latter two reports, which Jerome took from Eusebius (*Hist. eccl.* 2.17), are plainly Christian legends, Leisegang, Foster, and others have assumed that the ascription of priestly descent was too, as mentioned above.

Christian legends about Philo, however, must have a purpose, and the purpose, undoubtedly, must be to glorify him, exaggerate his importance, and so add to the value of his early testimony to the truth of Christianity.[16] Thus, when he first mentions Philo's book on the Christian monks of Alexandria, in the course of his entry on Mark (*De vir. ill.* 8), Jerome introduces Philo as "dissertimus Iudaeorum." Eusebius too (*Hist. eccl.* 2.4.2–3) takes pains to point out that although Philo was "Hebrew by birth, he was inferior to none of those who held high dignities in Alexandria," which statement is followed by praise for his knowledge of both Jewish and Greek wisdom. The latter corresponds to Jerome's report, at the end of his entry on Philo, that a Greek proverb held

---

[14] See his "Praefatio ad Lectorem," reprinted in *Philonis Iudaei Opera Omnia graece et latine* . . . (ed. A. F. Pfeiffer; 2nd. ed.; Erlangen: Heyder, 1820) ii and v-ix.

[15] See nn. 81–82, below.

[16] Cf. Mondésert, "Philon d'Alexandrie," 1289: "Ce que nous raconte Eusèbe . . . d'une rencontre de Philon avec S. Pierre . . . appartient déjà à cette légende chrétienne qui voulait faire de lui un prophète, une sorte de crypto-chrétien, et presque un 'Père de l'Église.'"

"either Plato philonized or Philo platonized."

It is interesting to note, however, that Jerome did not reproduce Eusebius' statement about the superiority of Philo's station. He passed up this opportunity to glorify the philosopher. Instead of Eusebius' concession that Philo was a Hebrew, compensated for by the fact that he was nonetheless inferior to no Alexandrian dignitary, Jerome has confined himself to reporting two successive data: Philo was born in Alexandria, and he was of a priestly family. While Eusebius clearly implies that Hebrew birth is a handicap which requires compensation, Jerome has not implied any evaluation at all. This should already make us suspicious of the claim that "de genere sacerdotum" is a glorifying legend.

But, sentence structure aside, does not the simple ascription of priestly family imply prestige? I do not think so, as investigation of two parallels in Jerome's writings will show. In this same De vir. ill., chapter 2, Jerome recounts Josephus' report of the death of James (Ant. 20.197–203); the main antagonist is introduced as "Ananus . . . pontifex, adulescens Anani filius, de genere sacerdotali . . . . " The most obvious explanation of the last three words is that they are a summary reference to Josephus' report (198) that Ananus himself and all five of his sons achieved high priesthood, which never occurred in any other family.

It may be this same family, furthermore, which is mentioned in Acts 4:6, where, along with Ananus, Caiaphas, Jonathan (Ananus' son?), and Alexander, "those of the high priestly family" met to examine Peter and John. Jerome translated hosoi ēsan ek genous archieratikou with the same words he used of Ananias in De vir. ill. 2: "de genere sacerdotali." Here we have confirmation that the latter phrase is used by Jerome of high priestly families. Of Philo, on the other hand, we read only "de genere sacerdotum," "of a family of priests," and it may be that the distinction indicates that Jerome did not want to give the impression that Philo was of a high-priestly family.[17] That distinction, in any event, was picked up by the early Greek translator of De vir. ill.,[18] who gave genous hieratikou = "of priestly family" for chapter 2's "de genere sacerdotali," but only genous hiereōn = "of a family of priests" for chapter 11's "de genere sacerdotum," of Philo; and the latter is echoed in the later medieval renditions of Jerome's entry on Philo, by Photius and the Suidas, where too Philo's is left a family of plain priests.[19]

---

[17] But the Vulgate of Lev 6:29 (=Massoretic 6:22) and 7:6 has "de genere sacerdotali" for the simple "any male priest."

[18] Edited by O. von Gebhardt in TU 14:1b; this translation, according to its editor (pp. vii-x), dates from the fifth or sixth century. Tradition assigns it to Sophronius.

[19] Photius, Bibliotheca 105: esti de to genos ex hiereōn katagomenos; Suidas, s.v. genous hiereōn. A twelfth-century edition of Josippon similarly paraphrases Jerome's entry, including the opening mention of Philo's priestly descent, but it oddly concludes with the statement that Philo was a descendant of the high priest Joshua ben Jehozadak. See The

Moreover, it should be underscored that Jerome has not even called Philo a priest, but only specified his priestly descent. The comparison with Jerome's entry on Josephus (*De vir. ill.* 13) is instructive: while Philo is "natione Alexandrinus, de genere sacerdotum," Josephus is "ex Hierosolymis sacerdos."[20] Jerome is in effect telling us that while Philo lived in Alexandria and could thus be termed a priest by family only— cf. II Maccabees 1:10, where the Alexandrian Jew Aristobulos is similarly called a priest by descent alone—Josephus, of the temple city, could be termed a priest without qualification.

Jerome has thus doubly demoted Philo: his was not a high-priestly family, as was Ananias', but one of lesser rank, and he was not even a real priest himself, as was Josephus, but rather one by family alone. Is this the procedure of a glorifying legend-maker? He omitted Eusebius' words as to Philo's superiority, affiliated him with a family of simple priests rather than high priests, and avoided the impression that Philo was himself a priest. Any prestige which this left Philo seems to have been lost on Jerome himself, for he did not mention it in any other of his references to Philo, including the two others in *De vir. ill.*: in chapter 8, where he rather glorifies Philo by calling him "dissertimus Iudaeorum," as mentioned above, and in chapter 13, where no praise is added at all. But if Jerome did not use Philo's priestly lineage, why should we assume that he made it up? Finally, we may note that while there are many cases of *high* priesthood being falsely attributed to a hero by late glorifiers—Moses, Jeremiah, Ezra, Judah Maccabee, Eleazar the martyr (of 2 Macc 7), and Jesus come to mind[21]—I know of no case in which mere priestly descent has been shown to be falsely ascribed.

It therefore seems to me that whatever the channels through which he received his information, Jerome's statement does constitute a prima facie case for Philo's priesthood; it is not the only datum in *De vir. ill.* whose source can no longer be ascertained.[22] Its off-handed condemnation as a late legend is to be rejected, for it is not written in the way a legend is written, nor used as one. This, I suppose, is what led pre-Schürer

---

Josippon (*Josephus Gorionides*) (ed. D. Flusser; Jerusalem: Bailik, 1978) 434–35 (Hebrew).

[20] "Sophronius": *Hierosolymōn hiereus* (p. 16).

[21] Of the many sources which could be cited, see for example: on Moses—Philo, Vita Mos 2.66–186; on Jeremiah—*Paraleipomena Jeremiou* (ed. and trans. by R. A. Kraft and A. E. Purintun; SBLTT 1, 1972) 25 (note on 5:17); on Ezra—1 Esdr 9:40, 49; on Judah Maccabee—Josephus, *Ant.* 12.414,419,434; on Eleazar the martyr—the references given by C. L. W. Grimm, *Kurzgefasstes exegetisches Handbuch zu den Apokryphen des Alten Testaments*, 4. Lieferung (Leipzig: Hirzel, 1857) 114; on Jesus—Heb 5:1–10.

[22] See J. H. Robinson, "The Sources and Composition of Jerome's De viris illustribus," Essay entered in competition for the Hitchcock Prize in Church History, Dec. 1910 (typescript in the Library of the Union Theological Seminary, New York, N. Y.) 49–51, for a list of the biographies for which no source is known. To these may be added many details of other biographies.

scholars to maintain their confidence in this detail of Jerome's report even while rejecting the Christianizing legends he transmitted a few lines later.

II.

As noted above, many arguments have been proposed over the past three centuries in order to corroborate Jerome's statement out of yet earlier literature. Before examining some which seem to be fairly convincing, I will briefly mention several which seem either unprovable or definitely improbable.

(a) John Pearson, Bishop of Chester (d. 1686), was apparently the first to suggest that the Alexander of Acts 4:6 (quoted above) was Philo's brother, Alexander the alabarch;[23] as the verse apparently implies that he was a member of the high-priestly family, it would follow that his brother Philo was too. In defense of this imaginative suggestion, we may note that the verse's author assumed that Alexander was known and needed no further identification, but Philo's brother is the only contemporarily prominent Jewish Alexander of whom we know. Pearson's suggestion had the same fate as Jerome's notice itself; while it was repeated by various scholars through the late nineteenth century, including Mangey[24] and F. W. Farrar,[25] almost no one bothers to mention it today, apart from the occasional commentator who takes the trouble to reject it. And rightly so: even apart from our suggestion regarding *sacerdotum* and *sacerdotali*, the plain fact is that the verse gives no basis at all for the identification of this Alexander.

(b) N. Brüll, in 1865, taking Jerome's report at face value, found confirmation in the similarity of the roles of the Egyptian Jewish alabarchs and the Jerusalem Temple officials known as *'ămarklîn* (e.g.: *Mishnah Sheqalim 5.2*);[26] identification of the two again results in Alexander (and so too Philo) being a priest. But the rapprochement of the functions of alabarchs and *'ămarklîn* lacks evidence, and Brüll's explanation of how the two words are really variants of the same demands too much credulity.

(c) H. Graetz, a decade later,[27] postulated that (1) rule of the region of

---

[23] See "Lectiones in Acta Apostolorum," in his *Opera Posthuma* (ed. H. Dodwell; London: S. Roycroft and R. Clavell, 1688) 41–42.

[24] "Praefatio" iii.

[25] *The Life and Works of St. Paul* (2 vols.; New York: Dutton, 1902) 1.106–7.

[26] "Alabarchen," *Jüdische Zeitschrift für Wissenschaft und Leben* 3 (1864–65) 279, 284–86. On *'ămarklîn*, cf. A. Büchler, *Die Priester und der Cultus im letzten Jahrzehnt des jerusalemischen Tempels (Jahresbericht der israel.-theol. Lehranstalt*, 1894–95; Vienna: Israel.-theol. Lehranstalt, 1895) 93–103.

[27] "Die judäischen Ethnarchen oder Alabarchen in Alexandria," *MGWJ* 25 (1876) 209–24, 241–54, 308–20, especially 245–46. Graetz's study, liberally sprinkled with the editor's question marks and comments, was reprinted in the fifth edition of his *Geschichte der Juden* 3:2 (ed. M. Brann; Leipzig: Leiner, 1906) 631–51, especially 642.

Leontopolis, where Onias' Temple was found, was hereditary in the family of its high-priestly founder; (2) that this region was known as Arabia and its ruler therefore "arabarch"; (3) that the titles "arabarch" and "alabarch" are identical; and (4) therefore Alexander the alabarch, and thus his brother Philo as well, was an Oniad priest. This was the study which elicited Schürer's insertion of his doubts on Philo's priestly descent in the second edition of his handbook. But Graetz's argument does have some merits, and B. Ritter[28] indeed thought it made Philo's priesthood probable: there is some evidence for hereditary rule of Onias' land by his descendants,[29] and most scholars agree that alabarchs and arabarchs are identical.[30] The problem is with the second step of Graetz's argument: there is no reason to believe that the term "Arabia," which had a very wide meaning,[31] should have been restricted to the area around Leontopolis, or that the rulers of Leontopolis were granted control of Arabia. And there is reliable evidence showing that the arabarchs were tax officials, not rulers of a Jewish colony.[32] Moreover, it is difficult to believe that Philo, as virtually all Alexandrian Jewish writers, would have omitted all reference to Onias' Temple if his family were its ruling line.[33]

(d) J. Schwartz, to whom we alluded at the outset of our study, reasonably suggested, in 1953, that the fact that Josephus uses virtually idential terms to describe the families of the only two Jewish alabarchs known to us implies that they were members of the same family.[34] He further speculated, however, that since both became linked by marriage

---

[28] *Philo und die Halacha: Eine vergleichende Studie unter steter Berücksichtigung des Josephus* (Leipzig: Hinrichs, 1879) 9, n. 4.

[29] See Josephus, *Ant.* 13.284–87. Cf. Graetz, "Judäischen Ethnarchen" 241–43 (*Geschichte* 639–40) and my "The Priests in *Ep. Arist.* 310," *JBL* 97 (1978) ᵯ70, n. 17. We will posit below (IId) that the only two Jewish alabarchs known were of the same family. For a summary of the evidence on ancient Jewish dynasties, including several among priests, see E. Stauffer, "Zum Kalifat des Jacobus," *ZRGG* 4 (1952) 194–97.

[30] See, for example, Schürer, "Die Alabarchen in Aegypten," *Zeitschrift für wissenschaftliche Theologie* 18 (1875) 31–40; idem, *Geschichte* (4th ed.) 3.132–34 (n. 42). An isolated case of opposition is that of M. Rostovtzeff and C. B. Welles, "A Parchment Contract of Loan from Dura-Europos on the Euphrates," *Yale Classical Studies* 2 (1931) 50.

[31] See Schürer, "Alabarchen," 17–18.

[32] See the reference in n. 30, above, also J. Lesquier, *L'armée romaine d'Égypte d'Auguste à Dioclétien* (Mémoires publiés par les membres de l'Institut français d'archéologie orientale du Caire 41; Cairo: Inst. fran. d'arch. or., 1918) 421–27.

[33] See S. Belkin, *Philo and the Oral Law: The Philonic Interpretation of Biblical Law in Relation to the Palestinian Halakah* (Cambridge, Mass.: Harvard Univ., 1940) 4, n. 1; S. Safrai, *Pilgrimage at the Time of the Second Temple* (Tel-Aviv: Am HaSepher, 1965) 62–63 (Hebrew).

[34] "Note sur la famille de Philon d'Alexandrie," *Mélanges Isidore Lévy = Annuaire de l'Institut de philologie et d'histoire orientales et slaves* 13 (1953) 600; the reference is to *Ant.* 20.100 and 20.147, to be cited in IIIa, below. Others too, such as Graetz ("Judäischen Ethnarchen" 317 = *Geschichte* 650), have similarly concluded that Alexander and Demetrios were of the same family.

with Agrippa I, while Herodians otherwise usually limited their mar-
riages to either royalty or relatives, it must be that the alabarchs were in
fact related to the Herodians. While this is tenuous enough, his further
guess that such a relation was via Mariamne the Hasmonean—one of
Herod's nine wives (*Ant.* 17.19–21)!—is positively groundless.[35] Furthermore, as Foster points out,[36] the links of financial obligation between
Agrippa and Alexander are more than enough to account for the
former's willingness to match their children.

(e) Finally, we should mention the suggestion that Philo's statement
in Provid 2.64 (apud Eusebius, *Praep. evang.* 8.14.398), that he once
went to the Jerusalem Temple "to pray and sacrifice" (*euxomenos kai
thysōn*), should be taken very literally.[37] Coupled with Philo's assumption that only priests may sacrifice, which apparently coincides with the
actual Temple practice,[38] one could conclude from this that Philo was
himself a priest. It seems, however, that although Philo does at times use
thyein in the specific meaning of sacrifice (as opposed to the *bringing* of
sacrifice) or even slaughter, as in Vita Mos 2.224, he very often uses
"pray and sacrifice" or "offer prayers and sacrifices" simply as general
terms for "worship," without having any specifically priestly functions in
mind. Confining ourselves to examples using the roots *euch-* and *thy-*, as
in the passage from *De providentia*, we may refer to Mut 8, Plant 161,
Spec Leg 1.97, 1.229, 3.131, Somn 1.215, Vita Mos 2.133, 2.147, 2.174,
etcetera. Compare especially Spec Leg 2.17 [PLCL 7.317], where Philo
states that "to such persons I would give the advice which I gave the
former class, that they should propitiate God with prayers and sacrifices . . . "; in the antecedent (ibid. 2.15), however, only the general
"supplicate God" (*potniasthō ton theon*) is mentioned.

III.

But if the above five arguments appear to be inconsequential, others
do better.

---

[35] Although Daniélou, summarizing Schwartz's argument (see n. 3 above), turns his suggestion into a certainty; if there was a family connection between the alabarchs and the
Herodians, he writes, "Cela ne pourrait se faire que par les Hasmonéens . . . ." For
Herod's wives, see the tables inserted in the back of A. Schalit, *König Herodes: Der Mann
und sein Werk* (Studia Judaica 4; Berlin: de Gruyter, 1969) and between columns 16 and
17 of *PWSup* 2 (by W. Otto).

[36] "A Note," 28–29.

[37] Brüll, "Alabarchen," 279; Graetz, "Judäischen Ethnarchen," 246 (*Geschichte* 642),
more tentatively. Schwartz, "Note," 600–601, n. 9, suggests that if Jerome concocted
Philo's priesthood, this could have been the reason.

[38] Ritter, *Philo und die Halacha* 110–13; Belkin, *Philo and the Oral Law* 61–64; Safrai,
Pilgrimage, 235–36.

(a) J. Robinson, who apparently disbelieved Jerome's notice, suggested that it resulted from Jerome's hasty inference from Eusebius' remark, quoted above, to the effect that Philo was inferior to no Alexandrian dignitary.[39] While we have already emphasized the difference between Eusebius' and Jerome's presentation of this point, it is now time to turn to Eusebius' statement itself. It is based upon Josephus' comment on Alexander the alabarch (*Ant.* 20.100: *genei te kai ploutǭ prōteusantos*). We have already approved J. Schwartz's inference that the similarity of this comment with Josephus' notice regarding Demetrios, the only other Jewish alabarch known (*Ant.* 20.147: *prōteuonti genei te kai ploutǭ*), means that the two were of the same family.[40] The question is: Does the prestige of Philo's family indicate that he was a priest? Phrased differently, we may ask whether, if Robinson is correct that Jerome's statement represents not received tradition but rather inference, such inference was reasonable.

I believe so. While it would be rash to assume that all notables of Jewish Alexandria were priests, it should not be overlooked that most of those of whom we know in fact were. I have recently collected the evidence for this statement,[41] and it need not be repeated here. For our specific question, however, it is most noteworthy that while we do not know the names of other prominent Alexandrian Jews of the first century, we do know that all the members of Philo's family were well-known and important: Philo himself, Alexander, Alexander's sons Tiberius and Marcus,[42] and (probably) Demetrios. Although the alabarchs were not identical with ethnarchs, as earlier scholars often thought,[43] it seems clear that Philo's position at the head (so Josephus, *Ant.* 18.259) of the delegation to Caligula was no fluke; E. R. Goodenough, referring to Spec Leg 3.3 and to other considerations, long ago argued that Philo regularly held an official position in the administration of the Jewish community of Alexandria.[44] If we had to suggest the

---

[39] "Sources and Composition," 61.

[40] See above, n. 34.

[41] "Priests in *Ep. Arist.* 310," 569–71.

[42] On him, see the references in n. 9, above.

[43] E.g., L. Herzfeld, *Geschichte des Volkes Israel von Vollendung des zweiten Tempels bis zur Einsetzung des Mackabäers Schimon zum hohen Priester und Fürsten* (2nd ed., 2 vols.; Leipzig: Wilsserodt, 1863) 2.527; Brüll, "Alabarchen"; Graetz, "Jüdaischen Ethnarchen," 213–17 (*Geschichte* 633–35). Cf. n. 32.

[44] "Philo and Public Life," *Journal of Egyptian Archaeology* 12 (1926) 77–79; cf. idem, *The Jurisprudence of the Jewish Courts in Egypt: Legal Administration by the Jews Under the Early Roman Empire, As Described by Philo Judaeus* (New Haven: Yale, 1929) 9 and passim; E. G. Turner, "Tiberius Iulius Alexander," *JRS* 44 (1954) 55–56. In his doctoral dissertation, S. S. Foster reviews the opinions and leans toward the conclusion that Philo was a teacher, rather than a judge of the Jewish community; but he in any case admits that the evidence points toward Philo having been a "leader" of the Jewish community ("The Alexandrian Situation and Philo's Use of *Dike*" [Ph.D. dissertation, Northwestern University, 1975] 86–90, 106).

single characteristic most likely to account for this concentration of positions in one family, the evidence on Jewish Alexandria points to priestly descent.[45]

Furthermore, even apart from the evidence regarding Alexandria, Josephus' repeated statements extolling Philo's family (*Ant.* 18.259, 20.100, 147) must be considered in light of this historian's prejudices, which are priestly.[46] A historian who opens his autobiography with the notice that "different races base their claim to nobility on various grounds; with us a connection with the priesthood is the hallmark of an illustrious line" (*Vita* 1) probably has the same principle in mind when ascribing noble birth to Philo's family. We may note in this connection that, apart from the alabarchs Alexander and Demetrios, Josephus links the two characteristics of distinctive wealth (*ploutos*) and family (*genos*) with respect to only two other characters: Korah (*Ant.* 4.14) and Mary of Bethezuba (*Bellum* 6.201). The former vied for the high priesthood, and the latter was most probably the daughter of a priestly family, as is indicated by her father's name, Eleazar.[47]

(b) Another line of argument leading to the same conclusion,

---

[45] Although Foster emphasizes that there is no need for J. Schwartz's assumption that Alexander's closeness to the imperial family was inherited from his (and Philo's) father ("A Note," 27–29; "Philo's Use of *Dike*," 72–74), this does not effect the presumption that Philo's family's prominence in the Alexandrian Jewish community was indeed hereditary (cf. ibid., 66).

[46] See J. Schwark, "Matthäus der Schriftgelehrte und Josephus der Priester: Ein Vergleich," *Festgabe für Karl Heinrich Rengstorf zum 70. Geburtstag = Theokratia* 2 (1970/72 [1973]) 137–54; Foster, "The Alexandrian Situation," 62–64. For the Judaean reality which generally corresponded to Josephus' prejudice, see M. Stern, "Aspects of Jewish Society: The Priesthood and Other Classes," *The Jewish People in the First Century* (2 vols.; ed. S. Safrai and M. Stern; Compendia Rerum Iudaicarum ad Novum Testamentum, 1–2 Assen/Amsterdam: Van Gorcum, 1974–76) 2.580–618.

[47] See M. Stern, "The Relations Between Judea and Rome During the Rule of John Hyrcanus," *Zi* 26 (1961) 21 and n. 119 (Hebrew), also idem, "Aspects of Jewish Society," 568–69 (n. 46). Our Eleazar of Bethezuba is no. 23 in a list of twenty-four Eleazars mentioned by Josephus, according to the index supplied by L. Feldman in LCL *Josephus* 9.657–58; these may be reduced to twenty-two, if nos. 16 and 18 and nos. 19 and 20 are identical. Of these, eight are specifically said to be priests (nos. 2, 5, 7, 9, 10, 11, 16, 18); no. 1 was Moses' son, a Levite; no. 4 Josephus terms his "fellow tribesman"; Stern (as cited above) argues that no. 6 was a priest; no. 22, Eleazar ben Jair, is consistently called "Eleazar the priest" in the Venice edition of Josippon (ed. A. J. Wertheimer; Jerusalem: Hominer, 1956/7) 355, 397–402 (but cf. Flusser's edition, 385, n. 1). Other priestly Eleazars (or Eliezers) not mentioned by Stern include "Eleazar the priest" on some Bar Kokhba coins and the rabbis E. ben Zadok, ben Jacob, ben Hyrcanus, and ben Azariah; cf. "Lazarus the priest," mentioned by the Pseudo-Clementines among Peter's early followers (*Hom* 2.1.2 [*MPG* 2.77–78 = GCS 42.36]), a fact noted and developed by R. Eisler, *The Messiah Jesus and John the Baptist* (English trans. by A. H. Krappe; New York: Dial, 1931) 103.

advanced already by Mangey,[48] is from the fact that Philo is very favorable toward priests in his accounts of Israel's laws and history. One thinks, for example, of his conception of the sinless high priest,[49] the exclusiveness of his priestly marriage laws,[50] his claim that Israel's chief judges are priests (Spec Leg 4.191),[51] his care to point out that even the holy Therapeutae recognized the priests as their betters (Vita Cont 82), as do the Levites as well (Spec Leg 1.157), his failure to mention any of the usual charges of corruption then current against the Judaean priesthood.[52] One passage in particular, Spec Leg 1.124, leads us to infer that its author was not only an extoller of the priesthood but also a member of it:

> No one at all of the alien race (*allogenei*) even though he be nobly born and of the original stock (*eupatridēs* . . . . . *tōn autochthonōn*), without flaw either on the male or the female line, is permitted by the law to share in the sacred things, in order that the privileges may not be tainted with bastardy (*hina hai timai mē notheuōntai*) but remain the securely guarded possessions of the priestly order.

From Josephus' testimony we are sure that Philo was himself "nobly born"; cf. De Animalibus 8, "nobilem, nobilibusque natum" (of Alexander). Are we to assume that he would use such a nasty word as "bastardy" of the sharing of priestly perquisites by even the noblest of nonpriests, if he were himself included in the prohibition?

   (c) It should be emphasized, moreover, that Philo not only extols

---

[48] "Praefatio," ii, referring to Spec Leg 1.152–59 and 3.128–33; so too H. Ewald, *Geschichte des Volkes Israel* (3rd ed.; 7 vols.; Göttingen: Dieterich, 1864–68) 6.258–59, n. 3, referring to Leg All 3.82.

[49] See the references in my "The Priests in *Ep. Arist.* 310," 570, n. 22; also Belkin, *Philo and the Oral Law*, 79–80.

[50] See L. Blau, *Die jüdische Ehescheidung und der jüdische Scheidebrief: Eine historische Untersuchung* (2 vols.; supplements to *Jahresberichte der Landes-Rabbinerschule in Budapest*, 1910–11 and 1911–12; republished Farnborough, England: Gregg, 1970) 1.40–42; Blau speculates that Philo's version of these laws may have been taken from a priestly code. Cf. Ritter, *Philo und die Halacha*, 72–74, who shows Philo's frequent agreement with Josephus (a certain priest) on these points, and Büchler, *Priester und Cultus*, 88–90. Büchler, who shows that Philo's exclusiveness probably conformed to priestly practice, opens his discussion with the general comment that Philo "über viele den Tempel und die Priester berührenden Fragen ziemlich gut unterrichtet ist."

[51] Cf. I. Heinemann, *Philons griechische und jüdische Bildung: Kulturvergleichende Untersuchungen zu Philons Darstellung der jüdischen Gesetze* (Breslau: Marcus, 1932 [reprinted Hildesheim: Olms, 1962]) 181–82; Belkin, *Philo and the Oral Law* 190–91.

[52] A failure noted by R. A. Stewart, "The Sinless High-Priest," *NTS* 14 (1967–68) 133. For a possible exception (Quaes Ex 2.105), which however concerns not the priests themselves but rather a detail of the cult they perform, see H. A. Wolfson, *Philo: Foundations of Religious Philosophy in Judaism, Christianity and Islam* (2nd ed.; 2 vols.; Cambridge, Mass.: Harvard, 1948) 2.344–45, n. 151.

priests: he is also, apparently, both better informed about[53] and more interested in precisely those matters regarding the Temple and the sacrificial cult, matters one would expect priests to prefer. A disproportionate part of *De Specialibus Legibus* is devoted to the cult, as Philo discusses it under both the first commandment, on worship, and under the fourth, on the Sabbath; here we find the same degree of detail which Josephus, the priest of Jerusalem, often promised to include in a special composition.[54] As I. F. Baer has recently commented, such matters were "close to Philo's heart";[55] he returns to discussions of the cult in almost every book. We should also note, in this connection, his brother's gift of the silver and gold for nine of the Temple's gates (Josephus, *Bellum* 5.205). Furthermore, Philo's legal opinions most frequently agree with Palestinian ones precisely in this field, while his civil and criminal jurisprudence tend more often to favor Roman law.[56]

(d) Finally, we should note the complex of arguments which tend to show that Philo was a Sadducee or a Boethusian;[57] as these sectarians

---

[53] So Goodenough, *By Light, Light: The Mystic Gospel of Hellenistic Judaism* (New Haven: Yale, 1935) 78–79, referring to Heinemann. Cf. Büchler's comment cited in n. 50, above. We have already noted two cases of Philo's accurate knowledge of priestly practice (above, nn. 38, 50); for other cases, see Belkin, *Philo and the Oral Law*, 48–88 and G. Alon, *Jews, Judaism and the Classical World* (Engl. trans. by I. Abrahams; Jerusalem: Magnes, 1977) 89–137.

[54] See the references supplied by L. Feldman in LCL *Josephus* 9.531, n.d. D. Altshuler has recently argued that Josephus at least partially fulfilled these promises via certain additions to the early books of *Ant.* and by composing *Contra Apionem*: "The Treatise ΠΕΡΙ ΕΘΩΝ ΚΑΙ ΑΙΤΙΩΝ 'On Customs and Causes' by Flavius Josephus," *JQR* 69 (1978–79) 226–32. Cf. the abstract of his paper, "The Constitution of Moses: Law and Apologia in Josephus' Antiquities," *AJS Newsletter* 22 (March 1978) 9, where he points out that although Josephus omits a good deal of biblical cultic law, still over half of the law he retains deals with the cult.

[55] "The Service of Sacrifice in Second Temple Times," Zi 40 (1975 [1978]) 112 (Hebrew): "The details of this (*scil.* Day of Atonement) sacrificial service are near to Philo's heart, for they allow him, as a philosopher tending toward spiritual mysticism, to interpret and plumb the depths of its meaning" (my translation from the Hebrew—D.S.). When Stewart ("Sinless High-Priest," 134) comments that Philo's "interest in the earthly priest was very slight—he is a mere peg for allegorization," he has noted the same interest as did Baer; the point for us is not what Philo does with his subject, but that it is so important to him as to warrant frequent interpretation.

[56] See above, n. 53; on Philo's civil and criminal jurisprudence, see Goodenough, *Jurisprudence*, along with Belkin's arguments (*Philo and the Oral Law*) on various details.

[57] That Philo was a Boethusian was suggested in the sixteenth century by Azariah de Rossi, *Me'or 'Eynayim*, *'Imrei Binah*, chap. 5 (ad fin). While Mangey ("Praefatio," xi) roundly states that "A Sadducaeis mores eius et dogmata toto distabant coelo," Goodenough (*By Light, Light* 78–80) argued in detail a that Philo was indeed a Sadducee, an argument skeptically reviewed by Belkin, *Philo and the Oral Law*, 10–11, n. 14, and by J. Le Moyne, *Les Sadducéens* (EB, 1972) 60–62. Le Moyne's arguments were adopted and in part expanded by V. Nikiprowetzky, "Note sur l'interprétation littérale de la loi et sur l'angélologie chez Philon d'Alexandrie," *Mélanges André Neher* (Paris: Adrien-Maisonneuve, 1975)

were, by general agreement (see below), generally members of the upper priesthood, it would follow that Philo was as well.

Before examining the evidence for this, however, we must first consider two methodological difficulties: (1) There is no report that there were Pharisees, Sadducees, and Boethusians outside of Judaea; although Philo does refer to some "sects" among Alexandrian Jewry, these are not among them; (2) It is not certain that all Sadducees and Boethusians were priests.

While these are worthy of notice, they do not appear to invalidate the method of argument; they suffice only to reduce the syllogism to one of probabilities, rather than certainties. But this is no novelty when it comes to discussions of the Sadducees, about whom we possess so little reliable and unambivalent evidence. As for the first argument, we may note three points in rebuttal: (1) Schwartz's argument that Philo's family had recently emigrated from Palestine to Alexandria,[58] a part of Schwartz's case which has won general approval,[59] would explain his Sadduceeism even if such were rare in Alexandria; (2) Herod's father-in-law Boethus, from whose name the term "Boethusian" most probably stems,[60] was an Alexandrian Jewish priest of great note, according to Josephus (*Ant.* 15.320); (3) since 2 Maccabees seems to reflect an anti-Sadducee polemic, as some scholars since A. Geiger have argued,[61] it seems reasonable to infer that its Greek-speaking audience included readers who leaned toward the views of that sect.

As for the second objection, I admit that it would be rash to assume that all Sadducees and Boethusians came from the ranks of the aristocratic priesthood alone. It nevertheless appears true that there is no source which refers to Sadducees or Boethusians who were demonstrably not priests.[62] Those who deny the assumption that Sadducees were priests usually do so by emphasizing that some notable Pharisees (such as

---

181–91, and Sandmel, in one of his last works, depended upon Nikiprowetzky for his denial of Philo's Sadduceeism: *Judaism and Christian Beginnings* (New York: Oxford University, 1978) 439, n. 4. In the following discussion of the Sadducees, I will generally refer to Le Moyne alone, where references to the sources and the literature may easily be found, although at times I disagree with his conclusions.

[58] "Note," 601; "L'Égypte de Philon," 43.

[59] See above, nn. 3–4.

[60] Le Moyne, *Sadducéens* 335–37.

[61] Geiger, *Urschrift und Übersetzungen der Bibel, in ihrer Abhängigkeit von der innern Entwicklung des Judentums* (2nd ed., by N. Czortkowski; Frankfurt a. M.: Madda, 1928) 219–30; Th. Nöldeke, *Histoire littéraire de l'Ancien Testament* (Paris: Sandoz et Fischbacher, 1873) 96–97; R. Leszynsky, *Die Sadduzäer* (Berlin: Mayer & Müller, 1912) 176–78.

[62] Le Moyne (*Les Sadducéens* 131) argues that the "high priests and elders" of Acts 23:14 are identical with the Sadducees of vv. 6–8. This may well be, but it does not (as he thought) necessarily refer to lay elders, for there were elders among the priesthood as well (e.g. *Mishnah Yoma* 1.5, *Tamid* 1.1).

Josephus) and early rabbis were priests,[63] which is, however, the converse of what is needed. Nor is it true that the only argument linking Sadduceeism with high priesthood is the syllogistic combination of Josephus' statement (*Ant.* 13.298, 18.17) that the Sadducees were drawn from the aristocracy with the assumption that the Judaean aristocracy was drawn largely from the high priesthood. This is in fact not a bad syllogism, and has been restated and defended lately by G. Maier.[64] But it is not the only argument. In addition, we may note that (1) the name of the sect points to Solomon's high priest,[65] and (2) the period in which the sect arose—the early Hasmonean period, when the Zadokite high priesthood was usurped by the Hasmoneans—hints, as does the sect's name, that it was at least originally a party of legitimist priests and their supporters;[66] (3) the name of the Boethusian sect or party, which is closely associated with the Sadducees if not identical with them, also points to a high-priestly connection, and this in the first century, two hundred years after the Hasmonean usurpation;[67] (4) most of the recorded legal differences between the Sadducees (or Boethusians) and the Pharisees are in the fields of cult and ritual purity,[68] which indicates that it was in the Temple that they made their stand; and (5) we know of several high priests who were Sadducees,[69] and indeed find some rabbinic sources assuming that all high priests were.[70]

Having thus concluded that it is legitimate to consider the possibility

---

[63] Leszynsky, *Sadduzäer*, 16–17; Le Moyne, *Les Sadducéens*, 348. Some rabbis who were priests are mentioned in n. 47 above. Regarding Josephus, we should note M. Hengel's suggestion that Josephus in fact tended to Sadduceeism, at least as late as the beginning of the revolt (*Die Zeloten: Untersuchungen zur jüdischen Freiheitsbewegung in der Zeit von Herodes I. bis 70 n. Chr.* [Arbeiten zur Geschichte des antiken Judentums und des Urchristentums 1; Leiden-Cologne: Brill, 1961] 378, n. 3). Such doubts as to Josephus' early Pharisaism have been developed by J. Neusner, *From Politics to Piety: The Emergence of Pharisaic Judaism* (Englewood Cliffs, N. J.: Prentice-Hall 1973) 45–66, and most recently by S. J. D. Cohen, *Josephus in Galilee and Rome: His Vita and Development as a Historian* (Columbia Studies in the Classical Tradition 8; Leiden: Brill, 1979) 144–51.

[64] *Mensch und freier Wille nach den jüdischen Religionsparteien zwischen Ben Sira und Paulus* (WUNT 12; 1971) 133–35; cf. G. Hölscher, *Der Sadduzaismus: Eine kritische Untersuchung zur späteren jüdischen Religionsgeschichte* (Leipzig: Hinrichs, 1906) 37.

[65] Le Moyne, *Sadducéens* 160–62.

[66] The sects are first mentioned in the context of the reign of Jonathan the Hasmonean (Josephus, *Ant.* 13.171–73); cf. V. Tcherikover, *Hellenistic Civilization and the Jews* (Philadelphia: Jewish Publication Society, 1959) 491, n. 30.

[67] Le Moyne, *Sadducéens* 334–37, 347.

[68] Ibid. 177–218, 236–38, 249–94.

[69] Ibid. 347–48.

[70] As Le Moyne concludes, ibid. 348, referring back to his discussion of *Mishnah Yoma* 1.5–6 (ibid. 260–62); cf. the rabbinic traditions (*Babli Yoma* 19b and parallels; ibid. 251–54) which have a priest tell his son, who is apparently the high priest, that "although we are Sadducees," the Pharisaic practice is still to be followed.

of the Alexandrian Philo being a Sadducee, and that proof of the latter would constitute a probable case for his priestly descent,[71] we must now turn to the evidence that he indeed was a Sadducee. Most of the evidence, it must be admitted, is negative: Philo makes no reference to bodily resurrection, to angels, to the Davidic messiah, or to the oral law; denial of each of these seems, with varying degrees of certainty, to have characterized the Sadducees.[72] Similarly, he very seldom refers to the latter two divisions of the Bible, and when he does introduce them, as Goodenough notes,[73] it is in a manner which distinctly shows their lack of authority as compared to the Pentateuch; it has often been thought that the Sadducees denied the inspiration of the extra-Pentateuchal writings.[74] Finally, in his discussion of nasty but legal oaths (as opposed to oaths which conflict with the laws), Philo shows that he knows of no possibility of their remission (Spec Leg 2.16–17); Leszynsky has convincingly argued that the latter was a Pharisaic innovation rejected by the Sadducees,[75] and Heinemann indeed thinks that Philo polemicized against the practice.[76]

On the positive side, we may note that his high social position, his emphasis upon free will, and his preference for severe penalties match

[71] The latter has recently been shown in detail by M. Stern, "Aspects of Jewish Society" 609–12 (n. 46).

[72] See the literature cited in n. 57, above. On Philo's lack of Davidic messianism, see Jaubert, *Notion d'alliance*, 382–85; cf. Leszynsky, *Sadduzäer*, 93–96.

[73] *By Light, Light*, 75–78. On Philo's use of the Bible outside of the Pentateuch, see the studies by W. L. Knox ("A Note on Philo's Use of the Old Testament") and F. H. Colson ("Philo's Quotations from the Old Testament") in *JTS* 41 (1940); Colson (p. 239) suggests that, for Philo, "the non-Pentateuchal books were, compared to the Pentateuch, what the Apocrypha is to the Protestant compared with the O.T. or at any rate what the Old Testament is to the New."

[74] Le Moyne, *Sadducéens*, 358–59; he notes that this opinion of the Church fathers, including Jerome, was usually rejected in the nineteenth century but has found some recent supporters.

[75] *Sadduzäer*, 48–51, 113; Le Moyne, *Sadducéens*, 205–6.

[76] *PCH* 2.112, n. 2. In *Philons griechische und jüdische Bildung* (p. 88), however, Heinemann writes that "Auch Gelübde der Ungeselligkeit darf und soll man nach Philo § 16 übertreten und Gott wegen des Eidbruches um Verzeihung bitten." Belkin (*Philo and the Oral Law*, 159) similarly holds, in connection with the same passage, that "Philo regards such passive oaths as not binding, for they could not be taken with reason and deliberate purpose, but only in anger and hatred." I believe that both of these scholars are mistaken; it seems that Philo recognizes the validity of such oaths, but calls upon those who make them to pray to be cured of their "spiritual distempers," so they will not repeat such errors. As for the passage from the *Hypothetica* (apud Eusebius, *Praep. evang.* 8.7.5), which Belkin refers to on p. 166, his translation is misleading in that it implies that Philo allows the priest to dissolve all vows. Actually, the passage deals only with property dedicated to the Temple, which a priest is allowed to decline; no one could expect a mortal's oath to force God to accept (through His agents) any given piece of property. Cf. F. H. Colson's translation (*PLCL* 9.425–27).

what we otherwise read about the Sadducees.[77] In addition, his explanation of some laws on the basis of Moses' own motives and personality[78] is
precisely what the scholion to *Megillat Ta'anit* attributes to the Boethusians or Sadducees;[79] H. D. Mantel rightly notes that such a mode of
argument is so distant from rabbinic norms that it is difficult to imagine
a late scholiast concocting it out of whole cloth.[80]

While many of the above-mentioned characteristics of both Philo
and the Sadducees (and Boethusians) are debatable, such a number of at
least apparent agreements calls for an explanation. The likeliest is that
Philo was either a Sadducee himself or inherited most from that brand
of Palestinian Judaism. From here it is not far to the inference that the
Palestinian forebears of this aristocratic family were Sadducees, and so,
as I have argued, priests.

IV.

In summary, we have argued that Jerome's statement that Philo was
of a priestly family should likely be believed, for it is neither written the
way a legend would be nor exploited as one. Furthermore, while several
arguments offered in support of Jerome's statement prove to be incorrect
or improbable, those based upon Philo's family and social status (along
with Josephus' appreciation of them), his position in the Alexandrian
Jewish community, his references to the priesthood along with his interest in and knowledge of the priestly cult, and the possibility that he was
a Sadducee, all tend to corroborate the attribution of priestly descent.
While none of the arguments taken alone is probative, I believe that,
taken together with Jerome's explicit testimony to the same effect, they
constitute a case as solid as that which historians of antiquity can usually
hope to attain.

The importance of this conclusion, apart from the clarification of
Philo's lineage, is largely heuristic. While Philo has usually been studied
along the axes of Jewish versus Graeco-Roman influences, the latter
being broken up among its various components and the former also
refined, at times, by distinction of earlier from later halakhah and midrash, his priesthood would suggest that the Jewish axis should be further

---

[77] See Goodenough, *By Light, Light*, 79; cf. Blau, *Die jüdische Ehescheidung*, 1.40–42.

[78] Noted by Heinemann in *PCH* 2.7, referring to *De spec. leg.* 2.104 and to the panegy-
ric of Moses as legislator in *Vita Mos.* 2.8–65.

[79] In the edition by H. Lichtenstein (*HUCA* 8–9 [1931–32]) see pp. 324–25 (= baraita in
Babli Menaḥot 65a) and 338.

[80] "*Megillat Ta'anit VeHakitot*," in *Studies in the History of the Jewish People and the
Land of Israel in Memory of Zvi Avneri* (ed. A. Gilboa et al.; Haifa: Univ. of Haifa,
1970) 62, 65 (n. 78), and 67 (Hebrew). Cf. Ch. Albeck, "On the Pharisees' and Sadducees'
Disputes Regarding the Temple and the Holy Things," *Sinai* 27 [52] (1962–63) 6–7
(Hebrew).

subdivided. For the separate category of priestly traditions in the Second Temple period, which was first discerned by E. Stauffer,[81] has lately been the object of deserved attention, especially since the discovery of the literature of the priestly community at Qumran.[82] It may well be that herein lies the key to the provenance of much which has been difficult to assign to Graeco-Roman interests and influences but also unparalleled in rabbinic literature; such, for example, are the conception of the sinless high priest and many of Philo's allegorical explanations of sacrifices and related rites. While some of the latter may be of his own creation, it seems likely that many ultimately depend upon a Judaean source, as Baer has recently argued.[83] But if the latter was not preserved by the rabbis, it is logical to seek its origin in priestly circles. In short, therefore, recognition of the probability that Philo was of a priestly family should encourage us to compare his writings specifically with the other remnants of the literature of the priestly tradition.[84]

[81] *Die Theologie des neuen Testaments* (3rd ed.; Stuttgart: Kohlhammer, 1947) 25–27.

[82] See especially idem, "Probleme der Priestertradition," *TLZ* 81 (1956) 135–50. Cf. Schwark, "Matthäus der Schriftgelehrte," and, among other studies which have utilized this category of tradition: O. Betz, "Le ministère cultuel dans la secte de Qumrân et dans le Christianisme primitif," *La secte de Qumrân et les origines du Christianisme* (Recherches bibliques 4; ed. J. van der Ploeg; Paris: Desclée de Brouwer, 1959) especially 170–72; W. Grimm, "Die Preisgabe eines Menschen zur Rettung des Volkes: Priesterliche Tradition bei Johannes und Josephus," *Josephus-Studien: Untersuchungen zu Josephus, dem antiken Judentum und dem Neuen Testament, Otto Michel zum 70. Geburtstag gewidmet* (ed. O. Betz, K. Haacker, M. Hengel; Göttingen: Vandenhoeck & Ruprecht, 1974) 133–46; R. G. Hammerton-Kelly, "The Temple and the Origins of Jewish Apocalyptic," *VT* 20 (1970) 15; J. A. Huntjens, "Contrasting Notions of Covenant and Law in the Texts from Qumran," *RQ* 31 (8:3; March 1974) 379–80.

[83] This is a major theme of the article mentioned in n. 55, above. (It need not entail the assumption that Philo knew Hebrew; the evidence rather shows that in fact he knew little or no Hebrew at all. See D. Rokeah, "A New Onomasticon Fragment," *JTS* 19 [1968] 75–77, 82, and the literature he cites.) In his *Cult and Conscience: The* Asham *and the Priestly Doctrine of Repentance* (SJLA 18; 1976), J. Milgrom frequently notes Philo's agreement with aspects of what the subtitle of his book terms "priestly doctrine"; see especially pp. 111–14, also the other references on p. 169.

[84] I would like to thank my friend and colleague Joshua Schwartz (Bar-Ilan University), who was kind enough to read and comment upon the draft of this paper. Also, my thanks to the National Foundation for Jewish Culture, whose assistance in 1978–79 helped allow me the time to do the research involved.

A PHILONIC FRAGMENT ON THE DECAD

ABRAHAM TERIAN
Andrews University

In the course of translating some of Philo's works which survive only in Armenian, it became necessary to develop an Armenian-Greek glossary based on his works which are extant in both Greek and Armenian versions and which could therefore be compared. But the Armenian text of Philo published by the Venetian Mechitarists[1] needed dividing into sections and enumeration of sections following the Greek text. While I was thus working on the Armenian text, I came to the two pages reproduced below for which there was no Greek parallel.[2]

I. Text and Translation[3]

Յաննեկի չարագրութիւն թիւ,
ծնանի գՀինկն և գյիսունն, պանչելի յիմբեան ու-
նելով գեղեցկութիւն. քանզի նախ առաջին գո-
յացաւ ի քունէից , ի կրկնակէ և յերեքնակէ
5 յայնցանէ որ մի րատ միոջէ չարագրեցան․ իր-
րու թէ որպէս. ի կրկնակին ա. ք. դ. ր. լինին
սորա Հինգբատասան․ երեքկինք, և յերեքկնէն, ա.
գ. ր. իէ. որ են քառասուն, և են սորա չարա-
գրելով ծէ. գորս և Պղատոն ի Տիմէոսին յիշէ յա-

---

[1] *Works of Philo Judaeus Translated by Our Ancestors, the Greek Original of Which is Extant* (Armenian), (Venice: The Mechitarist Press, 1892). According to the postscript (p. 286), the editorial work was supervised by F. C. Conybeare.

[2] From ibid., 222.8–223.17, where an asterisk indicates the omission of these lines in the Greek text.

[3] The underlining indicates additions in this passage when compared with a strikingly similar passage in Anatolius 39.21–40.19, reproduced below from Heiberg's edition (see n. 22 below); the underlining in the comparable Greek text of Anatolius indicates omissions in the Philonic passage (and vice versa). Parentheses ( ) are used to indicate interpolations; brackets [ ] for editorial additions in the course of translating; braces { } for variant readings in the respective texts; and angular brackets < > to indicate emendations.

10   դագս ողեծէնութեան , սկսեալ այսպէս ։ Մի ի բաց
      երարձ յամենայնէ մասն , և որ գՀետ այտրիկ ։
      երկրորդ՝ ծև թիւն տանեկին է չարագրութիւն .
      իսկ յ ՛ն. ձև ՛ն, գաւրութեամբ տանեկին է ։
      քանզի եթէ իւրաքանչիւր որ ի սոցանէ, ի մի-
15   եկէն մինչև ի տանեակն բազմապատիկ արա-
      րեալ չարագրեսցես գարարեալ թիւն, գյոցն,
      գ. ձ. և Հնգին. իսկ յձեն, ծևին եւթնպատիկ
      է. երիցս ծև, երեքանկինի է, որպէս գ ՛ն, և
      որպէս նոյն ինքն տանեական. յորիցս եթէ թու-
20   եսցես գմին , գոցես գրատ բազագրութեանն
      տանեակ գծևն ։ Հինգերորդ, սերականագոյն .
      վեցակ իՊ բազմապատիկ յինքեան եղեալ, գաւ-
      րութիւն որ ձնանի գերեսուն և գվեց, որոյ է
      երկիցս չորք. սորա մասունքն ձնեալ այսպէս ։
25   երկիցս ութումատն, գմր. դր. գգ. րդ. ձք.
      գ. ձր. ք. երեսուն և վեցիցս մի, մրանգամայն
      լինին մասունքք ր թիւ յիսուն և Հինկ. մակ
      եռանկինիքք Հինկ. որք մի բատ միոՀէ ձնանին
      գյիսուն. և գՀինկ. դարձեալ յորեքանկիւնքք և.
30   որք մի բատ միոՀէ ձնանին գՃ և գՀինկն։ իբ-
      րու թէ որպէս. գ. գ. ձ. ձե. իա- լինի ծև.
      դարձեալ յորեքանկիւնիքք Հինկ, որք մի բատ միո-
      Հէ ձնանին գյիսուն և գՀինկն. որպիսի. ա. դ.
      ք. ձգ իե. լինի յիսուն և Հինկ. իսկ յերեք-
35   անկինիցն, բոլորին է ձնունդ. քանզի ի գու-
      գագողմանգն կրկնակաց երեքանկինիցն, երեք
      տառք րաղկանան. Հուր, և վուղձ և ուժանիւ-
      տրն. քանզի է որ Հրոյ ձև է, և է որ աւդոյ, և
      է որ Ջրոյ, իսկ ի յորեքանկիւննացն՝ քուբային
40   է. և սա է ձև երկրի ։

The number generated by the sum of the decad is 55,[4] which
of itself is marvelously beautiful. First, it is constituted of the sum

---

[4] The text here has numeral words. The use of numeral letters, however, is more frequent in the fragment. Such interchangeable use of numerals is common in the Armenian
corpus of Philo's works; cf., e.g., the notes of R. Marcus on Quaes Gen 1.83 (*PLCL* Suppl.
1.51–52), which has much in common with the opening lines of this fragment.

5   of doubles and triples taken successively, *in the following manner*: the doubles 1, 2, 4, 8 make 15, and the (threefolds)[5] triples 1, 3, 9, 27 equal 40, and when added up, these make 55, which Plato men-

10   tions in the *Timaeus* with reference to the construction of the soul, beginning thus: "He took one portion from the whole," and what follows this.[6] Second, [as] the number 55 is the sum of the decad, 385 is the product of the decad: for if you multiply *every [number]*

15   from 1 to 10 [by itself and] add up [the products], the number obtained [will be] 385—and 385 is the sevenfold of 55. Third, 55 is a triangular [number]—*like the [number] 6 or the decad itself.*[7]

20   Fourth, if you add up the numerical value of the letters in [the word] ἕν,[8] you will discover what amounts to the sum of *the decad*,[9] [namely], 55. Fifth, the most productive [number], 6, when multiplied by itself, generates 36—*of which it is the square root.*

25   The factors of this[10] are generated in the following manner: by 2 = 18, by 3 =12, by 4 = 9, by 6 = 6, by 9 = 4, by 12 = 3, by 18 = 2, *by 36 = 1.* The sum of the {8} *factors* is the number 55.[11] Taken successively, 5 triangular [number]s generate 55 (likewise, 5 quad-

30   rangular [number]s, taken successively, generate 55),[12] as follows: 3, 6, 10, 15, 21 make 55; likewise, 5 quadrangular [number]s, taken successively, generate 55, as follows: 1, 4, 9, 16, 25 make 55. For

35   out of the triangles <and the quadrangles>[13] is everything gener-ated.[14] Out of the parallel equilateral triangles three {elements} are

---

[5] A modified *duplus*.

[6] Plato *Timaeus* 35B: *mian apheile [ho theos] to prōton apo pantos moiran, ktl.* Note the omission of *to prōton* here and in the comparable Greek text of Anatolius (at 40.2); nonetheless, the Philonic passage with its Armenian text is closer to the text of the *Timaeus*.

[7] For illustrations of triangular numbers, see Colson, *PLCL* 6.607; Marcus, *PLCL* Suppl. 1.52 and n. *h*; quadrangular numbers are those which can be arranged in the form of a square.

[8] The Armenian text is meaningless at this juncture, since it translates the Greek word which means "one" and omits *en grammasin* (cf. Anatolius 40.8).

[9] Although omitted in Anatolius 40.9, "the decad" appears in a certain MS of Ps.-Iamblichus' *Theol. arithm.* (see n. 10 in the apparatus of the Greek text below).

[10] The comparable Greek text has "the 7 factors of this" (40.10).

[11] As of this line, the two texts differ considerably. In keeping with the preceding note, the Greek has "7" instead of "8"; omits the last of the eight divisions (thus falling short of generating 55) and the word "factors"; and adds the ordinal "sixth" before the next state-ment (40.13).

[12] Clearly an error of doubling (cf. lines 32–33).

[13] The omission is due to *homoioteleuton* (cf. Anatolius 40.15).

[14] The comparable Greek text adds "according to Plato" (40.16).

contrived: {fire, moisture},[15] and the octahedron;[16] for there is a
figure for fire, a figure for air, and a figure for water. Whereas out
40   of the quadrangles, the cube, is the figure for earth.[17]

II. The Locus of the Fragment

Throughout the Armenian manuscript tradition of the Philonic corpus there is a certain disruption at Spec Leg 3.7: it is followed by this
fragment and the *De decalogo* before the text of Spec Leg 3.8–63 is
resumed. Judging from the fragmentary condition of the *De specialibus
legibus* in the Armenian version (1.79–161, 285–345; 3.1–7, 8–63), the
transposition of the *De decalogo* into the third book of the latter work,
and other partial translations of Philo's works, it would seem that this
fragment was part of a poorly preserved Greek exemplar from which
the Armenian translation was made. The two-page fragment is the
equivalent of a loose, transposed *folio*, and because it deals with the
decad, it was inserted immediately before the *De decalogo*—itself a
transposed book. The latter—whether before or after our fragment was
placed before it—was inserted immediately after Spec Leg 3.7 since the
section deals with the decalogue: Philo is about to begin his discussion of
the second five of the ten commandments. The words "ten" and "five" in
a context dealing with the decalogue on the one hand, and the *De
decalogo* on the other, created a logical place for the insertion of the
loose *folio* with its emphasis on "ten" and "fifty-five" (the apparent
digression into discussing the number fifty-five, triangles, and quadrangles, is but an elaboration on the essence of the decad). It is therefore
understandable how the fragment was interpolated into the text and how
it was transmitted unnoticed by the translator, who was not fluent in
Greek and depended systematically on a Greek-Armenian lexicon.[18]

The ascription of this arithmological "loose-leaf" to Philo becomes
more certain when we probe beyond its locus of discovery in a disjointed

---

[15] D. T. Runia, with whom I had shared a preliminary translation of this fragment,
perceives a corruption here on the basis of the parallel passage in Anatolius: "The word
puramis was thus split into *pur* and *atmis*, which accounts for the unexpected 'moisture'
in the translation." See his *Philo of Alexandria and the Timaeus of Plato* (Diss.: Vrije
Universiteit, Amsterdam 1983) 255. Consequently, the word *eikosaedron* was dropped
from the text lest there be four "elements" (i.e., *stoicheia* instead of *schēmata*).

[16] I.e., air; see Plato *Tim.* 55C; cf. Quaes Gen 3.49.

[17] Cf. Plato *Tim.* 55E, 56A.

[18] See A. Terian, "Syntactical Peculiarities in the Armenian Translations of the Hellen-
izing School," in *First International Conference on Armenian Linguistics: Proceedings*
(*The University of Pennsylvania, Philadelphia, 11–14 July, 1979*) 197–207, edited by J.
A. C. Greppin (Delmar, N.Y.: Caravan Books, 1980); cf. Idem, *Philonis Alexandrini De
Animalibus: The Armenian Text with an Introduction, Translation, and Commentary*,
Supplements to *SP* 1 (Chico, Calif.: Scholars Press, 1981) 9–14.

and mutilated Philonic codex, written in Greek, and dating from before the fourth quarter of the sixth century—the date of the Armenian translation.[19] A closer look at the passage itself leaves no doubt about its Greek authorship: (1) the Greek syntax awkwardly maintained by the translator; (2) the numerical significance of the Greek word *hen* in lines 19–21, which are altogether meaningless in Armenian; and (3) corrupt readings behind the Armenian translation which could occur only in the Greek text, such as noted on line 37. Moreover, the fragment cannot be ascribed to any extant Armenian translation from Greek, particularly to a work translated by the so-called Hellenizing School of the Early Middle ages, which is noted for its strict adherence to the Greek syntax as is readily discernible in the Armenian corpus of Philo's works and other philosophical writings translated from Greek.[20] And since the fragment cannot be ascribed to any of Philo's known works, its ascription to one of his lost works becomes very tempting indeed. Of such works the *Peri arithmōn* (*De numeris*), on which more will be said later, seems to be the most likely. But before any such identification of the fragment, we must consider the possibility of its belonging to one of the arithmological compilations extant in Greek literature.

III. The Non-Philonic Origin of the Fragment

The quest for comparable passages in non-Philonic works leads to later arithmological compilations by Peripatetic and Neoplatonic writers, whose works abound with common Neopythagorean speculations on numbers punctuated with occasional, dogmatic references to Plato's *Timaeus*.[21] From among these compilations a strikingly similar passage is found in Anatolius' account on the decad (39.21–40.19)[22] which dates

---

[19] Terian, *Philonis Alexandrini De Animalibus*, 6–9; Idem, "The Hellenizing School: Its Time, Place, and Scope of Activities Reconsidered," in *East of Byzantium: Syria and Armenia in the Formative Period* (*Dumbarton Oaks Symposium, 1980*) 175–86, edited by N. G. Garsoian, *et al.* (Washington, D.C.: Dumbarton Oaks, 1982).

[20] For a catalogue of these works, see the pages in the preceding note.

[21] A list of such writers and their works is found in K. Staehle, *Die Zahlenmystik bei Philon von Alexandreia* (Leipzig und Berlin: Teubner, 1931) vi, and a survey in his introduction, 1–18. For a survey of ancient scholarship on the *Timaeus*, see the excellent discussion by Runia, *Philo of Alexandria and the Timaeus of Plato*, 27–39; see also the exhaustive notes by H. Cherniss to Plutarch's *De animae procreatione in Timaeo* (*Mor.* 1012B-1030C) in LCL. On the question of sources, see below, n. 29.

[22] *Peri dekados kai tōn entos autēs arithmōn*, edited by J. L. Heiberg, "Anatolius sur les dix premiers nombres," *Annales internationales d'Histoire* (Paris: A. Colin, 1901) 5.27–57. A brief biography of Anatolius, who flourished in the third century C.E., is provided in the *Oxford Dictionary of the Christian Church*, edited by F. L. Cross and E. A. Livingstone (2nd ed.; London: Oxford University Press, 1974) 50.

I am indebted to D. T. Runia for bringing the parallel passage in Anatolius to my attention.

from the third century C.E. and is utilized in Pseudo-Iamblichus' *Theolo-goumena arithmeticae* (86.10–87.11)[23] along with a compilation of the same name attributed to Nicomachus of Gerasa (*ca.* 50–150 C.E.). The comparable passage in Anatolius, with a critical apparatus showing certain variants in Ps.-Iamblichus' *Theol. arithm.*, is reproduced here from Heiberg's edition.[24]

39.21   ἔτι ἡ δεκὰς ἀριθμὸν γεννᾷ τὸν
ἔ καὶ ν' θαυμαστὰ περιέχοντα κάλλ(η)[15]. πρῶτον μὲν
συνέστηκεν ἔκ τοῦ διπλασίου καὶ τοῦ τριπλασίου τῶν κατὰ τὸ
ἑξῆς συντιθεμένων, <διπλασίων μὲν[16]> α' β' δ' η'· (ταῦτα[17]) δ'
ἐστὶ ιε'· τριπλασίων δὲ[18] α' γ' θ' κζ, ἅπερ ἐστὶ μ'· ταῦτα
40.1   συντιθέμενα <ποιεῖ τὸν'> νε'. ὧν καὶ Πλάτων ἐν Τιμαίῳ[2]
μ(έ)μνηται τῆς ψυχογονίας ἀρχόμενος οὕτως· μίαν ἀπὸ
παντὸς μοῖραν καὶ τὸ ἑξῆς. δεύτερον <ὁ[3]> μὲν νε' ἀριθμ(ὸς)
δεκάδος ἐστὶ σύνθεσις, ὁ δὲ τπε' τῆς[4] δυνάμει δεκάδος· ἐὰν γὰρ
5   ἀπὸ μονάδος ἄχρι δεκάδος πολυπλασιάσῃς, συνθήσεις[5] τὸν
προειρημένον[6] ἀριθμὸν <τὸν'> τπε'· τὰ δὲ τπε' τοῦ νε' τὸ
ἑπταπλάσιον. τρίτον δὲ ὁ νε' τρίγωνόν ἐστι. τέταρτον, ἐὰν
ψηφίσῃς τὸ ἔν[8] ἐν γράμμασιν, εὑρήσεις τὸν[9] κατὰ σύνθεσιν
τὸν[10] νε'. πέμπτον ἡ γονιμωτάτη ἑξὰς ἐφ' ἑαυτὴν
10   πολυπλασιασθεῖσα δυνάμει ἐπιγεννᾷ τὸν λς', ἔστι δὲ ζ
τούτου μέρη γεννώμενα οὕτως· δὶς ιη', τρὶς ιβ', τετράκις θ',
ἑξάκις ς', θ'[11] δ', ιβ' γ', ιη' β'[12]· γίνονται μὲν ζ, ἀριθμὸς δὲ ὁ νε'.
ἕκτον τρίγωνοι[13] πέντε κατὰ τὸ ἑξῆς γεννῶσι τὸν νε'[14], οἶον
γ'[15] ς' ι' ιε' <κα'[16]>. πάλιν τετράγωνοι ε ' οἱ κατὰ τὸ ἑξῆς α' δ' θ'
15   ις' κε'[17] γίνονται[18] νε'· ἐκ δὲ τριγώνου καὶ τετραγώνου ἡ τοῦ
ὅλου γένεσις κατὰ Πλάτωνα[19]. ἐκ μὲν γὰρ ἰσοπλεύρων
τριγώνων τρία σχήματα[20] συνίσταται, πυραμίς[21], ὀκτάεδρον,
εἰκοσάεδρον, τὸ μὲν πυρὸς σχῆμα, τὸ δὲ ἀέρος, τὸ δὲ ὕδατος,
ἐκ <δὲ[22]> τετραγώνων ὁ κύβος, τοῦτο δὲ τὸ σχῆμα γῆς ἐστιν.

39.21   15. τριῶν]—ῶν sustulit lac. chartae M, ut infra 15—η,17 ταῦτα, p. 40, 1.1
-ἔ-, 1. 3—ός. —16. διπλασίων μέν] Theol., *nam dupli primi sunt* V, om. M.
—17. ταῦτα] Theol., p. 64, 3; *qui* V.—18. δέ] Theol., δὲ ὁ M.

40. 1   1. ποιεῖ τόν] Theol., *efficiunt* V, om. M.— 2. Τιμαίῳ] 35 b.—3. δεύτερον ὁ]
Theol., δευτεροῦ M.—4. τῆς] Theol., τῇ M.—5. συνθήσεις] Theol., ὃ συνθ́σις M.
—6. προειρημένον] Theol., πρῶτον εἰρημένον M.—7. τόν] Theol., om. M.—
8. τὸ ἔν] Theol., τὸν νε' M.—9. τόν] Theol., τήν M.—10. τόν] Theol., δέκα
τόν M.— 11. θ'] h.e. ἐννάκις; similiter ιβ' et ιη'.—12. ιη' β'] Theol., νβ' M. 13.

[23] Edited by V. De Falco (Leipzig: Teubner, 1922).
[24] See above, n. 22. On p. 28 Heiberg provides the following sigla: M = *cod. Monac.* gr. 384; V = Giorgio Valla, *De exp. et fug. reb.*; *Theol* = *Theologoumena arithmeticae*, ed. Ast (cf. De Falco's edition, cited in the preceding note).

τρίγωνοι] τριγγ M, τρίγωνα Theol.— 14. νε'] Theol., νγ' M.—15. γ'] Theol.,
τρίς M.—16. κα'] κα' γίνονται νε' Theol., om. M.—17. κε'] V, Theol.; βε'
M.—18. γίνονται] Theol., gignunt V, γίνεται M.—19. Πλάτωνα] Tim. 64 e
sqq. —20. τρία σχήματα] Theol., τριῶν σημεῖον M. tria . . . elementa V;
fort. τρία στοιχεῖα.—21. πυραμίς] Theol., πυράμειον M.— 22. δέ] Theol., V;
om. M.

A comparison of the Armenian fragment with the above passage in
Anatolius shows a number of substantive differences. There are eighteen
deviations obtaining between the two texts. With reference to the
Armenian text, there are nine additions (two of which are due to scribal
errors), in lines 5–6, 7, 14, 18–19, 21, 23–24, 26, 27, 29–30; six omissions,
in lines 20, 24, 32, 35 (two), 38; and three substantially different
readings, in lines 27 and 37 (two). Only one of the seven legitimate
additions underlined in the Armenian text is unquestionably warranted,
i.e. line 26, where in the corresponding Greek line (40.12) the eighth
division is omitted and, consequently, the number of the factors is
reduced to seven (which, when added up, fail to yield the sum of the
decad).[25] Of the six additions underlined in the Greek text, all but one
are warranted (40.10): the alphabetic number seven, which pertains to
the problem just mentioned. Also pertaining to the same problem is the
variant reading of "eight" in the Armenian text (line 27), versus "seven"
in the Greek (40.13). The remaining two variants are certainly in favor
of the Greek text, as indicated in the notes on line 37 (cf. 40.17–18).

Among other differences is the enumeration of the statements on the
decad and its sum. Whereas the last enumerated statement in the
Philonic passage is the "fifth" (line 21; cf. 40.9), the comparable passage
in Anatolius goes on to enumerate the "sixth" (40.13; cf. line 34; the original source probably had ordinal numbers before every statement). Notwithstanding the inherent problems of the Armenian text, it retains a
better reading of the quotation from Plato's *Timaeus* (35B): it has the
exact equivalent of *apheile* in separate words (lines 10–11; cf. 40.2–3).
But the same lines in both texts, and in others as well, omit *to prōton*—
leaving no doubt about their derivation from a secondary source.[26] In
the closing lines of the fragment and in a context of allusions to *Tim.*
53C-57D, the Armenian text omits Plato's name, which the Greek text
maintains (line 35; cf. 40.16).

In light of these departures, the Armenian fragment cannot be a
translation of the passage in Anatolius, nor can the latter be dependent on
the Greek of the former; rather, they seem to depend on a common,

[25] The Greek reads: "the 7 factors of which are generated in the following manner: by 2
= 18, by 3 = 12, by 4 = 9, by 6 = 6, by 9 = 4, by 12 = 3, by 18 = 12, the 7 [factors]
make the number 55."
[26] Cf. Runia, *Philo of Alexandria and the Timaeus of Plato*, 169–70.

independently transmitted arithmological source. On a smaller scale, both
texts may be described as witnesses to two separately evolved textual
traditions. That Philo and Anatolius *et alii* utilized common arithmological sources can be demonstrated also through Anatolius' remaining
statements on the decad and his treatment of the other numbers as well.
There are parallels in Philo for everything on the decad in Anatolius: in
the lines preceding our passage, Anatolius speaks of the decad as *peras*
(39.5; cf. Congr 90); *kamptēr* (39.6; cf. Op 47; Plant 125); *horos* (39.7; cf.
Op 47; Dec 27); and *pantelēs* (39.13; cf. Spec Leg 1.178).[27]

The prominence of Plato's *Timaeus* throughout the fragment is
equally noteworthy: the Platonic quotation with reference to the construction of the soul in the opening lines, and the allusion to the Platonic
theory of the primary elements and the shapes of their derivation in the
closing lines. This theme in the writings of Philo happens to be the subject of a recent study by Runia (*Philo of Alexandria and the Timaeus of
Plato*), who observes: "Philo's references to Plato's elemental theory
occur only in arithmological contexts."[28] Revival of interest in Plato's
Timaeus and Neopythagorean speculations on numbers seem to have
had a profound influence on Philo's thought, as may be concluded from
a similar observation made by Moehring with reference to the number
seven in the writings of Philo. After listing the purely arithmological
statements on the number, Moehring remarks on the list: "Philo almost
certainly took it over from some Neopythagorean work."[29] Furthermore,
there is hardly anything on the number seven in Anatolius (35.5–38.5)
that could not be found in Philo. Certain passages appear even in the
same sequence in both writers; e.g., both cite consecutive passages from
Solon and Hippocrates—obviously from a secondary source (Op 104–
105; Anatolius 37.5–38.5).

This part of the discussion may be concluded by stating that we here
possess a Philonic fragment with contents that are not original with
Philo, as is the case with all of his arithmological statements apart from

[27] Cf. *panteleia* with reference to the decad in Op 47; Abr 244; Vita Mos 2.79; and Dec
20. On Philo's treatment of the decad, see Staehle, *Die Zahlenmystik bei Philon*, 53–58;
M. Alexandre, *PM*, 16.242–44.

[28] For publisher and date of publication, see above, n. 15; the quotation is from p. 255.
The author is to be commended for the thoroughness of his work.

[29] H. Moehring, "Arithmology as an Exegetical Tool in the Writings of Philo of Alexandria," *SBL Seminar Papers* (1978) 1.191–227, especially 202–4. For more on the question
of arithmological sources in Philo, see F. E. Robbins, "Posidonius and the sources of
Pythagorean Arithmology," *Classical Philology* 15 (1920) 309–22; Idem, "The Tradition
of Greek arithmology," ibid. 16 (1921) 92–123; Idem, "Arithmetic in Philo Judaeus," ibid.
26 (1931) 345–61; also Staehle, *Die Zahlenmystik bei Philon von Alexandreia*, 11–18.
Staehle objects to Robbins' efforts to locate Philo's arithmological sources in the early
commentaries on the *Timaeus* and insists that they must be sought in early arithmological
works.

biblical application. The word "Philonic" does not necessarily mean original with Philo or thought up by him; it includes his utilization of sources. There are no good reasons why the "authorship" should be denied to Philo.

IV. Ascription of the Fragment to Philo's *De Numeris*

Assigning the fragment to a lost part of the Philonic corpus must be done cautiously. Runia, with whom I had shared a preliminary translation of the fragment, suggests that it may belong to a missing part of the *Quaestiones*.[30] Although the compositional characteristics of the latter are absent in the fragment, one finds similar, lengthy arithmological passages in the *Quaestiones*.[31] However, when we consider the reconstructed scriptural coverage of the original six books of the *Quaestiones et solutiones in Genesin*,[32] we cannot find a verse with reference to the number ten that is not accounted for in the Armenian translation.[33] The same holds true for the *Quaestiones et solutiones in Exodum*—notwithstanding its many missing parts. When we take into consideration the scriptural coverage of the original six books,[34] we do not find a passage there with reference to the number ten that is not accounted for in the Armenian translation.[35] There are three references to the number ten in those parts of Exodus that extend beyond the reconstructed coverage of the original *Quaestiones*: 34:28, the ten commandments; 37:1 (MT 36:8), the ten curtains; and 37:10 (MT 38:12), the ten pillars and their ten sockets. All three references have earlier occurrences in the book of Exodus. The ten commandments in Ex 20:2–17 are not part of the Babylonian *parashiyyot* and hence do not belong to the *Quaestiones*[36] (the absence of the word "ten" in the chapter would have posited no hindrance to Philo). The ten curtains are mentioned earlier in Ex 26:1, on which Philo remarks:

> Many a time has much been said about the number ten in other places, which for those who wish to prolong the discussion it would be easy to transfer here. But brevity of speech is liked by us, and

---

[30] *Philo of Alexandria and the Timaeus of Plato*, 170.

[31] E.g., Quaes Gen 1.83, 91; 3.56; etc.

[32] James R. Royse, "The Original Structure of Philo's *Quaestiones*," *SP* 4 (1976–77) 52.

[33] See the treatment of Gen 24:10 and 22 in Quaes Gen 4.92 and 110. Philo does not treat the words "ten days" of vs. 55 in Quaes Gen 4.131; he also omits the words "ten years" of Gen 16:3 in Quaes Gen 3.121; and Gen 18:32 with its reference to ten righteous people is not used in the *Quaestiones*.

[34] Royse, "The Original Structure of Philo's *Quaestiones*," 61–62.

[35] See Philo's brief remarks on Ex 26:1 in Quaes Ex 2.84. He does not treat Ex 26:16; 27:12.

[36] Royse, "The Original Structure of Philo's *Quaestiones*," 61.

sometimes a reminder of what has been said is as effective and sufficient (Quaes Ex 2.84).

And the ten pillars with their sockets are likewise mentioned earlier, in
Ex 27:12, on which he does not comment.

Possible dependence on the contents of this fragment may be discerned in Quaes Gen 1.83: "The ten [digits] added one by one—1, 2, 3, 4,
5, 6, 7, 8, 9, 10 . . . make 55" (cf. lines 1, 12, 21). In the same passage
Philo makes similar use of double, triangular, tetragonal, pentagonal,
hexagonal, and heptagonal numbers. The first two of these: 1, 3, 6, 10,
etc., and 1, 4, 9, 16, etc., have parallels in lines 31–34.[37] Besides looking
for such progressions of numbers in the *Quaestiones*, we ought to consider also the relationship of this fragment to Philo's theory of the primary bodies, such as propounded in Quaes Gen 3.49.[38] Note his remarks
on the numbers 6 and 36 (cf. line 21, the hexad as "the most productive
number," as in Op 13) and his perception of the geometrical forms of
the elements not simply as triangles and squares but as pyramids and
cubes (cf. lines 34–40; note his play on the resemblance between
puramis and *pur*).

Philo's extensive use of arithmology in the *Quaestiones* and, to a
lesser extent, in the other commentaries has been observed repeatedly by
those who have studied the arithmological tradition in his works.[39] This
comprehensive use of numbers is due in part to his earlier compilation of
an arithmological handbook, the lost *Peri arithmōn* (*De numeris*), in
preparation for his exegetical study of the Pentateuch. Philo refers to it
specifically in Quaes Gen 4.110, 151; Quaes Ex 2.87; and Vita Mos
2.115.[40] The extensive and systematic use of numbers in the extant works
of Philo was enough for Staehle to try to reconstruct this treatise in
broad outlines.[41] It is only logical to ascribe our fragment to this lost and
earliest work of Philo—after having described the present locus of the
fragment in the Philonic corpus and having eliminated the possibility of
its belonging to the *Quaestiones* or being a translation of some extant
arithmological work in Greek literature.

---

[37] Similar use of numbers may be observed in Vita Mos 2.79; Dec 20–21, and elsewhere;
see also the passages cited by Runia, *Philo of Alexandria and the Timaeus of Plato*, 169.

[38] For a discussion see ibid., 252–55. See also his discussion of the composition of the
cosmic soul, in Op 48 and 91, pp. 167–70.

[39] See above, n. 29; also Marcus, *PLCL* Suppl. 1.x.

[40] Marcus in the *PLCL* Supplements fails, like Aucher before him, to recognize the
direct references to the *Peri arithmōn* at the end of Quaes Gen 4.151 and in Quaes Ex
2.87. Cf. the allusions made to it in Quaes Gen 3.49 and Spec Leg 2.200. The proposed
discussion in Op 52 points to sections 93–100 and not to another treatise.

[41] *Die Zahlenmystik bei Philon von Alexandreia*, 1–18. Staehle is correct in his understanding that the *De numeris* was a *catena* of extracts from earlier writers and served as a
source-book for Philo's own use.

THE BEGINNING OF THE SELEUCID ERA
AND THE CHRONOLOGY OF THE DIADOCHOI*

BEN ZION WACHOLDER

Hebrew Union College–Jewish Institute of Religion

Several ancient authorities date the assassination of Alexander IV, the posthumous son of Alexander the Great and Roxane, in 305 or 304 B.C. But scholarly consensus, citing other Greek testimony, now places the time of the murder of the young Macedonian king in 311 or 310 B.C.[1] The evidence assembled in this paper from contemporary Egyptian papyri and Akkadian cuneiform tablets corroborates the late Greek tradition which

---

* In addition to the standard abbreviations, the following have been used in this article:

ABC	*Assyrian and Babylonian Chronicles* by A. K. Grayson
AJPh	*American Journal of Philology*
ClPh	*Classical Philology*
CT	Cuneiform Texts from Babylonian Tablets in the British Museum
FGrH	*Die Fragmente der griechischen Historiker* by Felix Jacoby
REA	*Revue des études anciennes*
TCS	Texts from Cuneiform Sources
UVB	*Vorläufige Berichte über die . . . Ausgrabungen in Uruk-Warka*
VAT	Tafelsignaturen der Vorderasiatischen Abteilung der Berlin Museen

[1] B. Niese, *Geschichte der griechischen und makedonischen Staaten* (Gotha, 1893) I, 304, esp. n. 2; Eduard Meyer, *Forschungen zur alten Geschichte* (Halle, 1899) II, 457–59, cited below more fully in n. 80; W. Tarn in *Cambridge Ancient History* VI (1927) 493; F. Lübker, *Reallexikon* (Leipzig and Berlin, 1914) 44b; G. T. Griffith, in *OCD* (1961) 34b; H. Bengtson, *Griechische Geschichte*[3] (Munich, 1965) 365; E. J. Bickerman, *Chronology of the Ancient World* (Ithaca, N.Y., 1968) 159, who alone among the authorities, lists Alexander IV's death as having occurred in 312 B.C. Alan E. Samuel, *Ptolemaic Chronology* (Münchener Beiträge zur Papyrusforschung, 43, Munich, 1962) 3, sums up the current view succinctly: "Even after the death of Alexander IV, [Ptolemy I] Soter did not immediately assume the royal title. According to Diodorus [19.105], the murder of Alexander . . . occurred in 311/10 during the archonship of Simonides. However, another date, 310/9 is provided by the Parian Chronicle, which places the event in the archonship of Hieromnemon, who held office immediately after Simonides (note cites K. Beloch, *Griechische Geschichte* IV.1, p. 138). Whichever is correct, we know that a fiction was maintained for some years after 310 that Alexander IV was alive, since documents continued to be dated according to his reign."

asserts that the Argead dynasty was not wiped out until 305/304 B.C. My study argues that the testimony cited by modern savants in support of an earlier dating rests upon a misreading of a passage in Diodorus and upon a lacuna in an inscription which has been filled on the basis of this misreading. If this timing of Alexander IV's death is correct, the question arises whether there existed a causal relationship between it and the coronation of the new Macedonian kings. An analysis of the accounts preserved in Diodorus and Plutarch shows no such link, but the writings of Appian, Justin, and the Heidelberg Epitome certainly hint of such a causal relationship. The contemporary testimony gleaned from the Akkadian tablets and Egyptian papyri tends to support the latter view, at least as far as some of the Diadochoi are concerned. Ptolemy, who had instituted the reckoning of a Macedonian regnal era by Alexander IV, began his own era only after the death of the former king in 304 B.C. Seleucus showed even greater loyalty to the Argead dynasty. The Seleucid era, which after 300 B.C. was reckoned either from the autumn of 312 or the spring of 311 B.C., did not in fact begin, as is putatively assumed, at that point in time. It commenced, according to Akkadian tablets, with year 1 of Seleucus' kingship, which was also reckoned as year 7 of his (second) satrapal rule, on Nisanu 1 of 305 and ran to Addaru 29 of 304. This does not mean that the other satraps, such as Lysimachus and Cassander, necessarily showed the same loyalty to the reigning Macedonian monarch as did Ptolemy and Seleucus. But what Greek historians say or do not say about such loyalty makes interesting reading.

I. Egyptian Evidence

Egypt offers no contemporary evidence as to the date of Alexander the Great's death. But a tradition, preserved in Pseudo-Callisthenes Codex A, dates his death on Pharmuthi 4 (June 13 or 14) of 323 B.C. This diverges by two days from the cuneiform tablet's timing of Aiaru 29, or June 10/11.[2] The difference may be due to the translation from the Babylonian day, which began at dusk, to the Egyptian day, commencing at sunrise. Alexander's death was celebrated in Egypt the 30th of Daisios, or June 11–12. The Pseudo-Callisthenes date, however, had referred not to the day of Alexander the Great's death, but to the official assumption of kingship by his successor, Philip Arrhidaeus.[3] A demotic papyrus (Bibliothèque Nationale, 219) dated in the month of Hathyr of the eighth regnal year of Philip Arrhidaeus (January 9/10–February 7/8 of

---

[2] See below n. 22.

[3] The date of his kingship assumed special significance as the beginning of *aera Philippi*. See F. K. Ginzel, *Handbuch der mathematischen und technischen Chronologie* (Leipzig, 1906) I, 143–47.

316), is the latest document available using this king's era.[4] A new regnal reckoning was introduced in Egypt shortly thereafter; papyrus Loeb 27 is dated on Mechir 2 of year 1 of Pharaoh Alexander the son of Alexander (April 10/11 of 316). In other words, sometime between January 9 and April 10 of 316 official couriers informed the scribes that the old king had died and that a new Macedonian monarch was now reigning in Egypt.[5] So far the chronology is straightforward, except that Skeat, after noting that a Babylonian tablet apparently still dates by Philip Arrhidaeus' era on August 13 of 316, adds: "But no reliable parallels can be drawn between Egyptian and Babylonian datings."[6] This is one of the few imprecise statements in an excellent study.

Papyrus Elephantine 1 offers a synchronistic dating that is puzzling: "year 7 of Pharaoh Alexander, the son of Alexander, which is year 14 of Ptolemy the satrap."[7] Since this is the only known document which appends Ptolemy's satrapal era to the regnal era of Alexander IV, the question is whether this represents a formula commonly used in Egypt or whether this synchronism is an exception. Elephantine papyri 2, 3, and 4, dated in the Ptolemaic fortieth and forty-first years, indicate that this synchronism was not an exception.[8] The Greek scribes, in contrast to the natives who ignored satrapal rule altogether, probably appended Ptolemy's satrapal year to that of the king of Macedonia.[9] But this dual dating apparently reflected a Ptolemaic custom only; no such practice is attested in Babylonia perhaps because Seleucus showed a more steadfast loyalty to the Argead dynasty than his fellow generals.

Two papyri come from Alexander IV's last month in office or shortly after his death. They contain the date of Hathyr year 13 of Pharaoh Alexander the son of Alexander (Louvre 2427; 2440), which corresponds to January 6/7–February 4/5 of 304. Two other papyri in the British Museum (numbers 13 and 14) contain the identical timing.[10] The datings

---

[4] The Egyptian evidence is presented here in an abbreviated form from Theodore C. Skeat, *The Reigns of the Ptolemies* (Münchener Beiträge zur Papyrusforschung, 39, Munich, 1954) 27–32; Samuel, *Ptolemaic Chronology* (n. 1) 3–30, presents more detailed documentation.

[5] Skeat, *Reigns*, 27–28; Samuel, *Ptolemaic Chronology*, 3.

[6] Skeat, ibid. 28. For the Akkadian evidence, see below n. 51.

[7] O. Rubensohn, *Elephantine-Papyri* (Berlin, 1907) 19; Skeat, ibid. 28–29; Samuel, *Ptolemaic Chronology*, 3.

[8] Rubensohn, *Elephantine-Papyri*, 22; Skeat, ibid. 30–31; Samuel, ibid. 11–12.

[9] The conservatism of the scribes of Thebes can be shown from the following: (1) They refused to modify the formula of dating in the face of the Macedonian insistence to compute the regnal year from the date of the ruler's accession; (2) they upheld the view that there can be only one Pharaoh, refusing to append Ptolemy's satrapal era to that of the Macedonian king; and (3) even after Ptolemy became king in 305/304 they, in contrast to the Greek scribes, refused to reckon his kingship from the time of his satrapal rule.

[10] S. R. K. Glanville, *Catalogue of Demotic Papyri in the British Museum* (Oxford, 1939) I, 53.

in these documents by the Macedonian king have aroused heated debate
not in the matter of the time of Alexander IV's death, but as to the date
of the assumption of the diadem by Ptolemy Soter, son of Lagus.[11] The
Astronomical Canon and Porphyry, as shown below, place Ptolemy's first
regnal year in 305/304.[12] But the precise date of the event can only be
determined by contemporary evidence.

Samuel presents a detailed analysis of the literary and papyrological
evidence from which he concludes that Ptolemy Soter's coronation took
place on Thoth 1 or November 7/8 of 305.[13] Diodorus and Plutarch,
according to Samuel, dated the crowning in 306, soon after that of
Antigonus and Demetrius;[14] the Parian Chronicle, the Astronomical
Canon, and Porphyry, in 305. The remark in Diodorus that Ptolemy's
coronation was an act of defiance in the face of his defeat at Cyprus,
Samuel says, refers in fact to Egypt's successful repulsion of Demetrius'
invasion force.[15] This victory, which took place in December of 306,
motivated the satrap to assume kingship in 305 on the traditional Egyptian new year's day, Thoth 1, a day also chosen for similar symbolic
reasons by Augustus in 30 B.C. What to do with the four papyri which
still dated by the era of the preceding king—Alexander IV—in January–
February of 304 presents a problem Samuel never solves. It is inconceivable that the news of Ptolemy's coronation in Alexandria had not
reached Thebes' scribes two months after the event on Thoth 1 of 305
although the distance was only 500 miles or ten days travel time away.
Therefore, Ptolemy's coronation occurred at the time or soon after the
dating of January 6/7–February 4/5 of 304 by the era of Alexander IV,
as Skeat argues.[16]

It follows that Alexander IV remained the recognized Macedonian
king of Egypt at least until January 6/7–February 4/5 of 304. The scholars who have dealt with this papyrological material (Volkmann, Skeat,
Samuel) accept the opinion that the last king of the Argead dynasty died
in 311 or 310.[17] But the datings in the papyri present irrefutable evidence that the news of the assassination of Alexander IV reached Thebes

---

[11] See the literature cited by R. Volkmann, R. E. 23, 2 (1959) 1621f.; Samuel, *Ptolemaic
Chronology*, 10.

[12] See below, nn. 76–78.

[13] Samuel, *Ptolemaic Chronology*, 3–11.

[14] Diod. 20.53.3; Plut. *Demetr.* 17.1. There is no assurance, however, as Samuel grants,
that Diodorus and Plutarch had intended to date Ptolemy's coronation, except that it
occurred after that of Antigonus.

[15] Samuel, *Ptolemaic Chronology*, 6–11. For a similar view see Volkmann (n. 11)
1622.

[16] Skeat, *Reigns of the Ptolemies*, 29–30; cf. Volkmann (n. 11) 1621f.

[17] Skeat, ibid. 28; Volkmann (n. 11) 1621; Samuel, above n. 1.

sometime after the beginning of 304 B.C.[18] Unfortunately, no contemporary testimony exists as to the actual date of the coronation of Ptolemy I, except that it took place after the death of the son of Alexander the Great and Roxane.

II. Babylonian Evidence

The chronographic picture that emerges from an analysis of the Akkadian tablets suggests that the new Macedonian rulers intervened more readily with the Babylonian mode of dating than they did in Egypt. The scribes of Egypt regarded Alexander and his successors as just another new dynasty of Pharaohs, requiring hardly a change in the ancient Egyptian calendar or mode of regnal reckoning. The cuneiform scribes, however, introduced a Macedonian mode of regnal reckoning that for a short period modified traditional Akkadian practices and whose precise form still eludes students of ancient chronography.[19] A word also needs to be said about the chronographic authoritativeness of the cuneiform tablets. Some tablets, like the Egyptian papyri, are contemporary documents: diaries, business transactions, religious notes, or colophons. Others are historical reconstructions: chronicles, king lists, and astronomical charts. For the evaluation of current practice during a period such as that of the Diadochoi, the contemporary evidence is often crucial since only it mirrors the chaotic conditions of the time. But it should be added that Akkadian historical reconstructions are as a rule of high quality, comparing favorably with similar Greek material. Especially valuable are the astronomical lists as they are verifiable by modern physics.[20]

---

[18] The demotic scribes of Thebes were difficult to control (see above n. 9). It is inconceivable that men who had refused to use the era of a living satrap would have consented to reckon by a deceased king, a practice unprecedented in Egypt's tradition.

[19] In contrast to the papyrological material, there exists at present no adequate treatment of the chronographic aspects of the Akkadian material for the period of the Diadochoi. I thank Mr. C. B. F. Walker, Assistant Keeper of the Western Asiatic Antiquities, the British Museum, for his bibliographic assistance. I am also grateful to my colleague David Weisberg for his help in the reading of Akkadian texts. See E. Cavaignac, "La chronologie des Séleucides d'après les documents cunéiformes," RA 28 (1931) 73–79; "Appendice à la chronologie cunéiforme des Séleucides," RA 34 (1937) 140–43. The basic works are: A. J. Sachs and D. J. Wiseman, "A Babylonian King List of the Hellenistic Period," Iraq 16 (1954) 202–12; reprinted in J. B. Pritchard's Ancient Near Eastern Texts Relating to the Old Testament[3] (Princeton, 1969) 566–67; R. A. Parker and W. Dubberstein, Babylonian Chronology: 626 B.C.–A.D. 75 (Providence, 1956). See now A. K. Grayson, "Königslisten und Chroniken. B. Akkadisch" in Reallexikon der Assyriologie und Vorderasiatischen Archaeologie (Berlin and New York, 1980) 97–100.

[20] It is unfortunate that polemic has sometimes marred the evaluation of the cuneiform evidence relating to classical studies. Cf. A. T. Olmstead, "Cuneiform Texts and Hellenistic Chronology," ClPh 32 (1937) 1–14, who questioned the reliability of the Akkadian

Since time immemorial, postdating, i.e. crediting the fraction of the year of a new ruler (called *reš šarruti*) to the deceased king, was an inflexible rule of Akkadian chronography. The reckoning by the new king began only on Nisanu 1 following his *de facto* assumption of power. It has often been said, erroneously, that Alexander introduced the Macedonian form of regnal dating into Babylonia.[21] But what these innovations were and whether they persisted during the period of his successors requires clarification.

Alexander became king of Macedonia in the summer of 336; he conquered Egypt in November-December of 332, and won Akkad in the battle of Arbela, which took place on October 1 of 331. An astronomical cuneiform tablet dates Alexander's death on Aiaru 29 (June 10/11) of 323, which harmonizes with the Royal Diaries' dating of the evening of Daisios 28.[22] It follows that Alexander's actual reign lasted in Macedonia twelve years and about ten months; in Egypt, eight years and about seven months; in Babylonia, seven years, seven months and eleven days. By Macedonian and Greek reckoning no distinction was drawn between the actual and the official regnal years. Egyptian custom, however, followed the principle of antedating. Beginning with November 10, the year 324 is credited to Alexander's successor, the imbecile half-brother, Philip Arrhidaeus. By Babylonian traditional reckoning, Alexander's reign as king of Akkad should have commenced on Nisanu 1 (April 2/3) of 330 and ended on April 10/11 of 323, for a reign of eight years.

But Alexander the Great cared or knew little about the sensibilities of the Akkadian scribes. In Egypt evidently the priests computed his kingship from the time of his conquest of the land. In Babylonia, however, Alexander ordered the scribes to date from his assumption of Macedonian kingship. The question confronting us is: does this mean that year 1 of Alexander began, as with Egyptian antedating, in the new year (April 5/6) of 336; or at accession time, as was the Macedonian custom, in the summer of 336? The earliest Akkadian contemporary dating by Alexander was written on Shabatu 6 (February 7/8) of year 6; the last, in addition to the one mentioned above, was dated in year 13.[23]

traditions (cf. below, n. 22); Sachs and Wiseman, ibid. 205, n. 1; H. Bengtson, *Historia* 4 (1955) 113f.; H. W. Ritter, *Diadem und Königsherrschaft* (Munich, 1965) 104, n. 7.

21 Parker and Dubberstein, 19.

22 This date is now certain. See A. J. Sachs, *Late Babylonian Astronomical and Related Texts* (Providence, 1955) xiii, cited in Alan E. Samuel, *Greek and Roman Chronology* (Munich, 1972) 141. See also J. Oelsner, "Ein Beitrag zu keilschriftlichen Königstitulaturen in hellenistischer Zeit," ZA 54 (1964) 262–74; cf. ZA 61 (1971) 159–70.

23 Oluf Krückmann, *Babylonische Rechts- und Verwaltungs-Urkunden* (Weimar, 1931) 10, citing CT 4, 39c, gives the earliest date by Alexander the Great; E. Unger, *Babylon, die heilige Stadt* (Berlin und Leipzig, 1931) 319 (note), who does not cite the above record. Unger does offer, however, one of year 13 of Alexander, citing VAT 6453. Year 13

The available material offers no conclusive testimony as to the exact form of regnal dating employed by Babylon's scribes during Alexander's time. As will be shown below, a unique combination of antedating and postdating, not recorded elsewhere, was used in the regnal era of Philip Arrhidaeus.

Philip Arrhidaeus

After the death of Alexander in Babylon on June 10/11 of 323, the generals chose Arrhidaeus, the half-brother of Alexander, now called Philip Arrhidaeus, as the king of Macedonia. Since this choice was a controversial one and since it was not arrived at before civil war was threatened, some time must have elapsed before the new Macedonian monarch was officially announced. The exact date of the official proclamation is not known.[24] A cuneiform tablet from Babylon, dated in year 1 of Philip, unhappily lacks the day and month.[25] What is the Julian date of this tablet? By the old system of postdating, it was written in 322/321; by Egypt's antedating, between the time of Philip's assumption of kingship, say in the summer of 323, and Nisanu 1 of 322; by the Macedonian custom from the summer of 323 to the summer of 322. This uncertainty applies, however, only to year 1; subsequently, Philip Arrhidaeus' kingship must have been recognized as of June 12 of 323.

The question remains, however, whether the Akkadian scribes reckoned year 2 of Arrhidaeus as beginning on Nisanu 1 (April 3/4) or on Panemos 1 (June 11/12) of 322. An astronomical date of the solar eclipse in year 2 of Philip, dated on Ululu 28 (September 25 of 322),[26] shows conclusively that the ancient custom of postdating was either no longer in existence or that it underwent a radical change. By the tradition of postdating prevailing in Babylonia this solar eclipse would have occurred in year 1 of Philip, not 2 as stated in the tablet. Our tablet is not helpful, however, in answering the question of whether the second year of Philip commenced on the traditional new year's day or on Panemos 1, the anniversary of Philip's official accession. This question of Philip's regnal dating, it should be remembered, refers only to contemporary reckoning. The chronology of the Akkadian astronomical tables and king lists is

---

by Alexander must refer to Alexander the Great, as Alexander IV has no regnal year 13 in current Akkadian reckoning. It follows that Olmstead's remark (*ClPh* 32 [1937] 4) that we have no records dated contemporaneously by Alexander the Great is erroneous. Parker and Dubberstein's statement on the chronology of Alexander lacks their usual precision. Cf. also the works cited above in n. 20.

[24] See Beloch, *Griech. Gesch.* IV. 2, 104 f.

[25] The dating in the Astronomical Canon is no proof one way or the other as Philip eventually was regarded as Alexander's successor without an interregnum.

[26] VAT 13103, in Berlin, as cited by Unger, *Babylon*, 319 (note), Urkunde 16.

clear: year 1 of Philip commenced on Nisanu 1 of 323.[27] If the style used in Akkadian historical chronography reflected contemporary usage, the above-mentioned tablet, dated in year 1 of Philip, could have been inscribed only between the time of the proclamation of Philip as Alexander's successor (late summer of 323) and the last day of Addaru in 322.

Fortunately, two tablets clear up the problem. But before discussing this evidence it is necessary to establish the time of Philip's death. Diodorus and the Heidelberg Epitome give him a reign of six years and four months,[28] which, counting from Daisios 30 (June 1/2) of 323 must have ended on or about the last day of Ululu (October 1/2) of 317. However, the usually reliable Astronomical Canon credits Philip with a reign of seven years, clearly implying that his rule ended not earlier than November 10 of 317 but not later than November 9 of 316. A fragment of Porphyry likewise credits Philip with seven years, but another fragment of Porphyry gives Philip eight years.[29] Modern scholarship accepts Diodorus' attribution of six years and four months to Philip's reign, but generally dates Alexander IV's assumption of kingship by the Astronomical Canon, which indicates that Philip died after November 19 of 317, hence acknowledging a difference of about a month between the two sources.[30]

For the timing of the death of Philip Arrhidaeus the contemporary testimony should be decisive. A demotic papyrus in the Bibliothèque Nationale (number 219) is dated in Hathyr of the eighth year of Philip. It follows that as of January 9–February 7 of 316 Philip Arrhidaeus was still recognized as the king of Egypt. Papyrus Loeb 27, written two months later, dates by the new regnal era Mechir 2 of year 1 of "Pharaoh Alexander the son of Alexander" (April 10) of 316.[31] Papyrological evidence supports the Canon's chronology that Philip was still alive on November 10 of 317, while Diodorus dates his death about October of the previous year.

From year 8 of Philip two cuneiform tablets have been published

---

[27] It is customary to cite the Saros cycles, published by J. N. Strassmaier, ZA 7 (1892) 197–204, which credit Philip with Nisanu 1 of 323, and which are cited by Meyer, *Forschungen*, II, 457, and Beloch, *Griech. Gesch.* IV.2, 105, as proof that the Babylonian scribes antedated during Philip's reign. This is no proof, however, since the astronomical tablets are learned reconstructions which sometimes may diverge from the current style of dating.

[28] Diod. 19.11.5; *FGrH* 155 F 2, 2. Cf. Justin, 14.5.10. See also Beloch, *Griech. Gesch.* IV.2, 104.

[29] Eus. *Chron.* (Arm.) 74, 27 and *FGrH* 260 F 2 give Philip 7 years; Eus. *Chron.* 109, 19; *FGrH* 260 F 3, have 8 years, which Jacoby emends to 7. But since the Babylonian sources, as shown below, do give Philip 8 years, the emendation remains doubtful.

[30] Skeat, *Reigns of the Ptolemies*, 27.

[31] Ibid., 27.

dated Nisanu 23 and Abu 20.[32] What are their Julian equivalents? By traditional Babylonian reckoning, year 8 of Philip began on the new year of Nisanu 1 (316); according to the Macedonian mode, it began on the day of accession, in the case of Philip on Panemos (Simanu) 1. If the former, the tablet of Abu 20 was written later than the one of Nisanu 23. But if the latter, it would follow that Philip was still the recognized king of Babylon about May 5 of 315. This is out of the question, because it would run counter to Egyptian and Greek evidence. Thus the tablet dated on Nisanu 23 of year 8 antedates the one of Abu 20 and we conclude both tablets were written in the same Julian year, i.e. 316. If so, the position taken by scholars that the Babylonian scribes had adopted the Macedonian system of regnal dating[33] is erroneous. Even during the period of Macedonian domination, the numbering of the regnal years changed on Nisanu 1, regardless of the accession date. It follows that Philip's second year commenced not on Daisios 30 of 322 but on Nisanu 1 (April 14/15) of 323. It further follows that the tablet dated on Abu 20 in the eighth year of Philip makes no claim that Philip was necessarily alive at the time, but only that he had been king on new year's day or on March 27/28 of 316 (dating the tablet of Nisanu 23 of April 19/20 and that of Abu 20 as of August 12/13, 316). Combining the papyrological testimony that Philip died between January 9 and April 10 of 316 with that of the cuneiform tablets which suggest that he was still the recognized king of Akkad on March 27/28 of the same year, we could get a theoretical day of death between March 29 and April 10. This is, however, unlikely, as Philip was murdered in Macedonia and four to six weeks must be added before the information became available either in Alexandria or in Babylon. February 316 appears to be the likely date of the murder of Philip and the accession of Alexander IV, the posthumous son of Alexander the Great and Roxane. Such a timing harmonizes with (1) the Astronomical Canon and (2) the demotic papyri, but differs with cuneiform tablets which assume that Philip reigned on March 27/28 of 316. What apparently happened was that the information on the actual day of the king's death came to Akkad, because of the civil war among the Macedonian Generals, after Abu 20 (August 12/13) of 316.

From what has been said so far, it follows that the Babylonian tablets relating to the period of the Diadochoi may contain three chronological systems:

---

[32] A colophon to a religious text: S. Langdon, RA 12 (1915) 84; Krückmann, *Babylonische Rechts- und Verwaltungs-Urkunden*, 20, citing Cont. 249, an economic text from Uruk; Unger, *Babylon*, 317 (note), Urkunden 19–20.

[33] Cf. Meyer, *Forschungen*, II.457; Beloch, *Griech. Gesch.*, IV.2, 104f; Olmstead, *ClPh* 32 (1937) 4 n. 15; Bengtson, *Die Strategie in der hellenistischen Zeit* (Munich, 1937) I, 114.

1. From the time of accession, the scribes immediately began to date according to the first year of the new king.
2. On Nisanu 1 following the king's accession, commenced his second regnal year; the same for third, fourth, etc.
3. In historical documents, such as chronicles and astronomical tables, however, customs differed. Some scribes credited each ruler with *both* his year of accession and the year of his death, but in totaling up, deducted one year per ruler. Other scribes, such as those responsible for the Uruk king list, standardized the tables of the period of the Diadochoi with Akkadian practice.

TABLE I

REGNAL ERAS OF ALEXANDER THE GREAT
AND PHILIP ARRHIDAEUS IN AKKAD

ALEXANDER THE GREAT

year 5	331/330	(until October 1, 331, year 5 of Darius III)
		(in current dating only after October 1, 331)
year 6	330/329	(later counted also as year 1 of Alexander)
year 7	329/328	(later counted as year 2)
year 8	328/327	(later counted as year 3)
year 9	327/326	(later counted as year 4)
year 10	326/325	(later counted as year 5)
year 11	325/324	(later counted as year 6)
year 12	324/323	(later counted as year 7)
year 13	323/322	(in current dating until his death on June 10/11 or shortly thereafter)
		(in current dating, in summer or fall of 323, year 1 of Philip Arrhidaeus)
		(later counted as year 1 of Philip Arrhidaeus)

PHILIP ARRHIDAEUS

year 1	323/322	(until June 10/11, or shortly thereafter, also year 13 of Alexander)
		(in current dating, in the summer or fall of 323)
		(later year 1)
year 2	322/321	
year 3	321/320	
year 4	320/319	
year 5	319/318	
year 6	318/317	
year 7	317/316	(later also year 1 of Antigonus)
		(later also year 1 of Alexander IV)

year   8   316/315   (about the middle of 316 current dating changes
                                from year 8 of Philip to year 2 of Antigonus)
                                (later also year 2 of Antigonus)
                                (later also year 1 or 2 of Alexander IV)

Antigonus Monophthalmus

It has been conjectured that Philip Arrhidaeus was still recognized as
king of Akkad on Abu 20 (August 12/13) 316, although he had been
murdered about February of that year, and that the delay in the reporting of the official news was probably caused by the civil war among the
Macedonian generals. A Babylonian chronicle published by Sidney Smith
in 1924[34] adds new details to the wealth of information found in Diodorus, Plutarch and Justin. Especially valuable is the perspective of the
chronicle. The classical writers seem to follow Hieronymus of Cardia
whereas the Akkadian accounts surely reflect the official Seleucid
version.[35] Here, however, we are only concerned with the chronology of
the period, and for this the fragments of the chronicle contribute in
large measure. Antigonus' first attack on Akkad, according to the chronicle, occurred in the fifth year of Philip (319/318), but he did not con-
quer Babylon until Arahsamnu of year 8 (October 21–November 18/19
of 316).[36]

We can presume that it was about this time that Antigonus initiated
his own era. Instead of reckoning by the era of the king of Macedonia,
Alexander IV, he must have ordered the scribes to reckon by himself,
not as king but as *rab uqu* or *strategos*. But since Philip had died in
Shabatu or Addaru of his seventh year, the remainder of that year was
fictively credited to Antigonus. By principle one, listed above, 317/316
thus became year 1 of Antigonus' generalship, and 316/315 became year
2, although current dating by Antigonus started only at the earliest in
November of 316. On Nisanu 1 (April 15/16) of 315 commenced his
third year. Cassander and his allies, on the other hand, counted according to the reign of Alexander IV as of about February of 316.

The following contemporary tablets dated by Antigonus have
appeared in print:

---

[34] Sidney Smith, *Babylonian Historical Texts* (London, 1924) 124–49; "The Chronology
of Philip Arrhidaeus, Antigonus and Alexander IV," *RA* 22 (1925) 179–97. See now A. K.
Grayson, *Assyrian and Babylonian Chronicles* (TCS V) (Locust Valley, N.Y., 1975) 25–26
and especially 115–19 where a fresh translation and commentary to the chronicle are
provided.

[35] The classical accounts on the period of the Diadochoi (Plutarch *Demetr.*; Diod. 19–20)
are said to go back to Hieronymus of Cardia. Cf. Jacoby's commentary on *FGrH* 155; see
also below n. 97.

[36] Chronicle, obverse lines 6–16, pp. 140, 142f. (Smith); obverse lines 7ff. (Grayson). For
the sake of convenience I retain Smith's line enumeration.

A. A contract written in Babylon from Tashritu of year 5.[37]
B. A similar document for year 6.[38]

TABLE II[39]

THE REGNAL YEARS OF ANTIGONUS IN AKKAD

year 1	317/316	(currently year 7 of Philip Arrhidaeus)
		(later also counted as year 1 of Alexander IV)
year 2	316/315	(currently dated as year 8 of Philip, for a part of the year)
		(currently dated by Antigonus only from about November of 316)
		(later also counted as year 1 of Alexander IV)
year 3	315/314	(later also counted as year 2 of Alexander IV)
year 4	314/313	(later also counted as year 3 of Alexander IV)
year 5	313/312	(later also counted as year 4 of Alexander IV)
year 6	312/311	(later also counted as year 5 of Alexander IV)

Alexander IV

One of the first acts of Seleucus upon his reentry into the satrapy of Babylonia in the spring or summer of 312[40] was apparently to abolish

---

[37] T. G. Pinches, *Guide to the Nimroud Central Saloon* (London, 1886) 123, No. 109.

[38] Pinches, in *Proceedings of the Society of Biblical Archaeology* 6 (1884) 104: "Several small tablets . . . the latest date being in his (Antigonus') 6th."

[39] F. X. Kugler, *Von Moses bis Paulus* (Munster, 1922) 307–9; P. J. Schaumberger, *Analecta Orientalia* 6 (1933) 3–12; *Orientalia*, n.s. 2 (1933) 103f., has published an astronomical tablet containing observations of Jupiter which notes that on Nisanu 10 of Antigonus' year 14, i.e., 10 SE, Jupiter appeared in Taurus. Did then Antigonus, as implied in his note written in 90 SE, recapture Babylon, holding it on May 1/2 of 302? Why does this tablet make the 14th, instead of the 16th year of Antigonus whose equivalent of 10 SE is astronomically secure, as year 1 of Antigonus equal to 317/316?

[40] Diod. 19. 73–76 indicates spring; Marmor Parium B 16. But summer 312 may be right after all, despite the erroneous proofs adduced in support of this view by Hans Hauben, "On the Chronology of the Years 313–311 B.C.," *AJPh* 94 (1973) 256–67. To begin with, Hauben attempts to deduce a date for the murder of "King Pumijaton of Kition" from the use of an alleged era of Kition mentioned in a Phoenician inscription (cf. H. Donner–W. Röllig *KAI* No. 40 lines 1–2 and Hauben 261–63). It is obvious, however, that there never existed an independent era of Kition and that the era in this inscription can only refer to SE, which in Phoenicia began on Tishri 1 of 312 and in Babylon on Nisanu 1 of 311. But whenever it began, (Iyyar) 7 57 SE equals May 18/19 of 255 B.C. (Parker and Dubberstein, 38).

This inscription, however, presents an interesting synchronism of Ptolemaic and Seleucid chronography, wherein the former era, perhaps to assuage Egyptian sensitivity, is called "the era of the Kition," and not as Hauben has it, "the year of the men of Kition" (261). Secondly, Hauben misquotes the Babylonian chronicle: "that Seleucus fought for 'the palace' in year 6 of Alexander IV and that he again tried to take it in the month of Abu," identified in n. 36 as 311. The text, however, line 2 reverse, reads (according to

the public reckoning by Antigonus. Of all the Diadochoi, only Antigonus had instituted an era after himself, showing contempt for the principle of a united Macedonian kingdom and disloyalty to the dynasty of the Argeadae. Antigonus, it is true, never had referred to himself as king while in Babylonia; only as *rab uqu*, "the general," but reckoning by a satrap was regarded as *lèse-majesté*, even if preceded by the royal era. Ptolemy, the satrap of Egypt since 323, did allow the mention of his rule. Seleucus, however, never did.[41] Thus Antigonus showed the least respect to the idea of a united Macedonian kingdom; Seleucus, the most; Ptolemy somewhere in the middle. Interestingly, Seleucus was the only one of the Diadochoi who kept his Persian wife, remaining faithful to Alexander's legacy. The alliance of the Diadochoi against Antigonus was founded on the principle of a united empire under an Argead king. In the peace treaty of 311/310, Antigonus recognized Alexander IV as his sovereign (Diod. 19.105.1), which presumably meant that he would henceforth restore the standard regnal reckoning. But no Akkadian evidence exists that would verify whether Antigonus in fact did so, since Babylonia from whence the evidence comes had fallen to Seleucus in the summer of 312.

Seleucus' reintroduction of Alexander IV's regnal era in 312/311 B.C. needs special emphasis. It contradicts scholarly opinion about the origins of the Seleucid reckoning. Much speculation exists concerning its early development. The opinion prevalent in the nineteenth century that Seleucid reckoning commemorated either Ptolemy's victory in the battle of Gaza in the spring of 312 or the death of Alexander IV in 311 has been abandoned. Instead, current handbooks such as Bickerman's *Ancient Chronology*, Samuel's *Greek and Roman Chronology*, and Seibart in *Encyclopedia Britannica* (1974) repeat the view, first popularized by Eduard Meyer, that Seleucus initiated the era bearing his name soon after his reconquest of Babylon in the summer of 312 B.C.[42] But it has

S. Smith): "in the 6th year of Antigonus," which, according to the Saros tablet, cited in Parker and Dubberstein (20), by Hauben's reasoning, should have been Abu 312 (June 9/10–August 7/8), and hence contrary to Hauben, confirming the hypothesis that the Battle of Gaza was fought in the spring rather than in the summer of 312. But Hauben's principal point may be valid. Line 6 reverse (Smith): "In the month of Abu, Seleucus, to capture the palace," may be referring not to the 6th regnal year of Antigonus (312 B.C. line 2), but to the following year (311); unfortunately, the part of the tablet which contained it is now lost. But see now Grayson, *ABC*, 117, who corrects the reading of Smith in line 2 reverse to MU. VII. KÁM; hence, "in the seventh year, Antig[onus . . .]".

[41] The Greek scribes of Alexandria appended the satrapal era to that of Alexander IV, while the demotic scribes of Thebes did not. It might be argued, therefore, that since the Seleucid evidence comes exclusively from Akkadian sources, it is conceivable that Seleucus' Greek scribes did in fact use the satrapal era prior to the time it was used by the cuneiform writers. This is not a valid argument because the Akkadian scribes display the chronographic tendencies of the Greeks of Alexandria, not those of the demotic scribes.

[42] On the origin and early formulation of SE, see L. Ideler, *Handbuch der mathematischen und technischen Chronologie* (Berlin, 1825) I, 446–55; Kubitschek, "Aera," *R.E.* 8

never been explained why the Seleucid era starts in many cities such as Antioch not in August but in October. Neither have scholars accounted for the fact that in Babylonia and in other cities, Seleucid reckoning starts on Nisanu 1 of 311 B.C.[43] But the fact that Seleucus had reintroduced the regnal era of Alexander IV in 312 or 311 and that dating by Seleucus himself commenced only seven or eight years later invalidates the standard opinions on the origin and beginning of the Seleucid era found in the textbooks.

Interestingly, Egyptian and Akkadian scribes diverged only slightly in the formulas they employed in the reckoning by Alexander IV. In the papyri he is called "Pharaoh Alexander son of Alexander"; in the cuneiform tablets, "Alexander, the son of Alexander, the king." Some Akkadian scribes, however, used the formula: *A-lik-sa-an-dar da-du*, the "beloved son (of Alexander)."[44] The following economic texts, contemporaneously dated, have come to my attention:

A.	Simanu 4	year 6[45]
B.	Nisanu 1	year 6[46]
C.	Abu 12	year 7[47]
D.	? 21	year 9[48]
E.	"a number of"	year 10[49]
F.	Shabatu 9	year 10[50]
G.	? 25	year 11(?)
H.	Addaru ?	year 11[51]

What is the Julian key to the "regnal" years of Alexander IV?

(1894) 632–34; E. Meyer, *Forschungen* II, 457–58; 467 (see below, n. 80); F. M. Abel, "L'ère des Séleucides," *RB* 47 (1938) 198–213; E. Bickerman, *Berytus* 8 (1944) 73–81; *Chronology of the Ancient World*, 71; A. Samuel, *Greek and Roman Chronology*, 245; J. Seibert, in *Encyclopedia Britannica* (1974) 16:503a; B.Z. Wacholder, in *Encyclopedia Hebraica* 26 (1974) 233–36.

[43] It is taken for granted, without proof, that in its original form SE commenced on Dios 1 of 312 and that the Babylonian version which is reckoned from Nisanu 1 of 311 reflects a modification. See the works cited in the previous note.

[44] P. dem. Louvre 2427; Samuel, *Ptolemaic Chronology*, 7; S. Smith, *Babylonian Historical Texts*, 130; *RA* 22 (1925); see Oelsner (n. 22), who disputes the view that *da-du* was used as a royal title.

[45] British Museum 40463; Unger, *Babylon*, 320 (note), Urkunde 24.

[46] M. Rutten, *Contracts de l'époque séleucide conservés au Musée du Louvre* (Paris, 1935) 13.

[47] Unger, *Babylon* 320 (note), Urkunde 25a.

[48] *Révue archéologique* 6 (1849) 514; Unger, *Babylon* 320 (note), Urkunde 26.

[49] Pinches, *Proceedings of SBA* VI (1884) 104; Unger, *Babylon* 320 (note), Urkunde 27.

[50] Smith, *RA* 22 (1925), 190.

[51] For G., see Strassmaier, *ZA* 3 (1888) 148; Unger, *Babylon* 320 (note), Urkunde 28. Cf. Krückmann, 21, n. 3, who attributes this date to 10 SE. For H., see D. A. Kennedy, *CT* 49, 25; 2: ITI.ŠE MU 11 KÁM. I am grateful to Professor David Weisberg for this reference.

Schnabel said that year 1 of Alexander IV equaled 323/322; Sidney Smith: 322/321; Otto, Olmstead, Bengtson, Sachs and Wiseman: 317/316; Parker and Dubberstein: 316/315.[52] A review of the evidence shows the following:

1. The Astronomical Canon combined with the Egyptian papyri, cited above,[53] fit best into a scheme that dates the murder of Philip Arrhidaeus and the accession of Alexander IV in February of 316; by the Babylonian system of regnal dating, the first regnal year of Alexander IV was computed as of Nisanu 1 (March 27/28) of 316.[54] In contrast with Antigonus, Seleucus reintroduced postdating in 311/310, evidently looking for sympathy from among the Akkadian scribes.[55]

2. The Babylonian chronicle, as translated by Sidney Smith, makes sense only if year 1 of Alexander equaled 316/315. As line 2 reverse reads: "In the sixth year of Antigonus . . . ," lines 3–5 reverse go on to describe the initial attack by Seleucus on Babylon in the summer and fall of 312; lines 6–12 reverse record the final capture of Babylon's palace in the month of Ab of the next year as well as the alliance of friendship in Arahsamnu, concluding with the mention of the "war with the Gutium." All this could only refer to events of 311/310.[56] If so, line 13, which follows, "in the seventh year of Alexander the king, the son of Alexander," refers to 310/309. Thus year 1 equaled 316/315. Antigonus' occupation of Akkad in 316–312 may account for the fact that there exist no cuneiform tablets dated by Alexander IV for that period.

3. Line 5 obverse of the king list published by Sachs and Wiseman records: "Alexander the son of Alex[ander] . . . year 6." This could only refer to year 6 of the Seleucid Era (306/305), given the context of the tablet, and to the last year of Alexander IV's reign.[57]

4. Tablets G and H listed above credit Alexander IV with at least eleven regnal years in Akkad, in contrast to Egypt where he is credited

---

52 P. Schnabel, *Berossos und die babylonische Literatur* (Leipzig and Berlin, 1923) 7; W. Tarn, *JHS* 44 (1924) 287f.; S. Smith *Babylonian Historical Texts*, 128; *RA* 22 (1925) 179–97; Walter Otto in *Sitzungsberichte der Bayerischen Akademie der Wissenschaften* (Munich, 1925); Olmstead, *ClPh* 32 (1937) 4; Bengtson, *Strategie* I, 114, n. 1; 127, n. 1; Bickerman, *Berytus* 8 (1944) 75, n. 11, who has year 1 of Alexander both as 317/316 and 316/315; Parker and Dubberstein, 20; cf. Ritter, *Diadem*, 104 (105), n. 7.

53 See nn. 10–16.

54 See works cited in nn. 4–6.

55 It is possible, if not probable, that lines 2–4, reverse, of the Chronicle (Smith, 141; 143) refer to Seleucus' revision of the regnal dating and the introduction of the Babylonian calendar as an institution embracing the entire empire: " . . . said thus. In the 6th year Antigonus . . . Seleucus, the generals and chief priests in the month . . . Seleucus the *šatammu* priest of Emeslam . . . " (Smith's translation). See now Grayson's revision of Smith's reading and the accompanying commentary in *ABC*, 117.

56 See above n. 40. For older interpretations, see works cited in nn. 19–20.

57 Sachs and Wiseman, *Iraq* 16 (1954) 205 and n. 1. Cf. A. Aymard, *REA* 57 (1955) 108–12.

with twelve years and some months. If we assume that year 11 was his last year,[58] which the king list dates in 306/305, then year 1 of Alexander IV equaled 316/315.[59]

5. An astronomical tablet, first published by Kugler and Schaumberger, containing notations on the visibility of Jupiter, offers conclusive evidence as to the dates of (a) Alexander IV's last regnal year in Akkad; (b) year 1 of Seleucus' kingship; and (c) the introduction of the Seleucid era. The chronological notes are not contemporaneous, but are astronomically confirmed as referring to year 305/304: "Year 1 of Seleucus, which is year 7."[60] In the light of the king list's repetition: "Year 7 which is (his) first year (that) Seleucus (ruled as) king," and which goes on to attribute twenty-five years of kingship to Seleucus and gives month VI of 31 SE as the time of his death, this could only mean that according to this Akkadian chronicler Seleucus counted his first regnal year in what subsequently became 7 SE. By the principle of postdating, reintroduced into Akkad in 312/311 or 311/310, this means that in the chronicler's view Seleucus was crowned, either prior to, or on the new year, i.e., Nisanu 1 (March 25/26) of 305.[61] It follows that, as first assumed by Schnabel, there was never a contemporary Seleucid era prior to 305/304. And if 305/304 was the first year that Seleucus introduced a double dating after himself (year 1 of King Seleucus which is his seventh year as a satrap), 306/305 was computed as the last year of Alexander IV, who according to Akkadian chronology, had eleven regnal years, the first five

[58] According to Krückmann (n. 23) year 11 of Alexander IV is a misreading of the tablet. If so, this paragraph should be bracketed. But year 11 of Alexander IV, according to the Babylonian regnal dating, must be assumed anyway by the papyrological evidence cited above (nn. 7f.). See now J. Oelsner, ZA 61 (1971) 163, n. 9; see also Document H, cited above, n. 51.

[59] Sachs and Wiseman, Iraq 16 (1954) 205. The following chronology comes from an Uruk tablet first published by J. van Dijk in UVB 18 (1962) 53–60, a translation of which was provided by A. L. Oppenheim in J. B. Pritchard, ANET³ (1969) 566. The appended Julian dates are mine.

    5 years: Darius (III) 335/334–331/330
    7 years: Alexander (the Great) 330/329–324/323
    6 years: Philip (Arrhidaeus) 323/322–318/317
    6 years: Antigonus (Monophthalmus) 317/316–312/311
    31 years: Seleucus (I) 311/310–281/280

It should be noted that there seems to be a basic difference between the Uruk list, where Alexander IV's reign is divided between Antigonus and the Seleucid era, and the lists coming from Babylon where the memory of the last Argead ruler was kept alive.

[60] Kugler, Von Moses bis Paulus, 309; Schaumberger, Analecta Orientalia 6 (1933) 7, obverse line 4, mistranslated on p. 8; cf. Sachs and Wiseman, Iraq 16 (1954) 205, n. 1.

[61] Chronicle Concerning the Diadochoi, reverse, lines 42 f. (Smith's translation, p. 144). "In the first year of . . . (43) . . . . the king to the Babylonians . . . " probably also alludes to Seleucus' coronation in 305/304. It follows that it refers to events that were dated, now missing, in year 11 of Alexander IV. Note that Grayson restores "A[lexander]", ABC, p. 119.

of which had been usurped by a rebellious general.[62]

TABLE III

REGNAL YEARS OF ALEXANDER IV

year 1	316/315	(contemporaneously dated as year 8 of Philip) (contemporaneously dated as year 2 of Antigonus)
year 2	315/314	(contemporaneously dated as year 3 of Antigonus)
year 3	314/313	(contemporaneously dated as year 4 of Antigonus)
year 4	313/312	(contemporaneously dated as year 5 of Antigonus)
year 5	312/311	(in part contemporaneously dated as year 6 of Antigonus)
year 6	311/310	(after 305–304 counted as year 1 SE)
year 7	310/309	(after 305/304 counted as year 2 SE)
year 8	309/308	(after 305/304 counted as year 3 SE)
year 9	308/307	(after 305/304 counted as year 4 SE)
year 10	307/306	(after 305/304 counted as year 5 SE)
year 11	306/305	(after 305/304 counted as year 6 SE)

It should be emphasized, however, that the evidence gleaned so far attests to the absence of Seleucid dating prior to 7 SE or 305/304. But nothing so far cited indicates when Seleucid dating was actually introduced. This could only be shown by contemporary regnal reckoning. The first such reckoning is attested, according to Krückmann, for Nisanu 3 year 8 (April 16/17 of 304). This gives us current testimony, by the principle of postdating, that Seleucus was *in fact* king during a small part of the year 305/304.[63]

By fusing the Egyptian and Babylonian testimony, we can arrive at the proximate timing of the coronations of both Ptolemy and Seleucus. In Thebes Pharaoh was still believed alive in the month of Hathyr, corresponding to January 6/7 until February 4/5 of 304, while cuneiform tablets date the crowning of Seleucus on April 13/14 of 304, which corresponds to Nisanu 1 of year 8. Both Ptolemy and Seleucus must have assumed their diadems sometime between the period of January 6/7–February 4/5 and April 13/14 of 304. The timing of King Alexander IV's assassination or at least its announcement in Alexandria and Babylon seems to fall within this range of two or three months.

---

[62] P. Schnabel, cited in F. Altheim, *Weltgeschichte Asiens im griechischen Zeitalter* (Halle, 1947) I, 280.

[63] *CT* 4, 29d; Krückmann, 21.

This sequence of events raises interesting questions about the flow of communication among Macedonia, Egypt, and Babylonia.[64] If to the chronological sequence we add the claim asserted plausibly in the Greek tradition that Ptolemy's coronation inspired that of Seleucus,[65] it follows that there was a remarkably speedy interaction between the Akkadian and the Egyptian satraps, whose emissaries kept in touch with the events in Macedonia.

The following chronology suggests itself: Alexander IV's assassination occurred about December of 305 or January of 304. Three or four weeks later the news reached Alexandria and, after ten more days, Thebes. Ptolemy's coronation probably occurred in February of 304, the announcement thereof reaching Babylon at the beginning of March. Toward the end of March, certainly prior to April 12/13, Seleucus decided to emulate his fellow satrap. The formal coronation became part of the festivities of Akitu, the traditional New Year procession on Nisanu 1 of SE 8 or April 13/14 of 304.

There is a basic difference between the regnal numberings of Ptolemy and Seleucus. Unlike Ptolemy, Seleucus incorporated his second satrapy into his regnal era. The formula "Year 1 of Seleucus' kingship which is year 7 of his satrapal rule" has no parallel in Egyptian dating. Perhaps, as suggested above, Egyptian scribes were simply less amenable to royal interference than their Babylonian counterparts. In part however, it would seem, the differing mode of antedating used in Egypt and that of postdating practiced in Akkad also influenced Seleucus' divergence. Though crowned about February of 304, because of antedating Ptolemy was regarded as king of Egypt since Thoth 1 or November 7 of 305.[66] Because of postdating, however, Seleucus' regnal era was to start only on Nisanu 1 (April 13/14) of 304. Anxious to outrank his colleague and mentor, he ordered that the entire year of 305/304 be reckoned as year 1 of his kingship and year 7 of his satrapy. He also ordained that beginning with Nisanu 1 of 304 the distinction between regnal and satrapal era be ignored and that the next year be listed as year 8 SE. Henceforth SE was computed as if it had started on Nisanu 1 (April 3/4) of 311. This chronographic subterfuge gave more regnal years to Seleucus than to any other new Macdonian king, including Antigonus, who evidently became king in the summer of 306.

The available evidence suggests that in its original form SE was computed as if it had begun in the spring of 311 B.C. What accounts for the reckoning of SE from the autumn of 312, which became standard Greek tradition, remains problematic. There is no evidence that the

[64] Cf. Samuel, *Ptolemaic Chronology*, 7–8.
[65] Plutarch, *Demetr.* 17, 1.
[66] See Volkmann, in *R.E.* 23, 2 (1959) 1621f.

autumnal SE was ever used prior to the foundation of Antioch in 300 B.C.[67]

III. Greek Traditions

The account in Diodorus is the basic source used to time the death of Alexander IV. Diodorus says that Alexander's popularity in Macedonia prompted Cassander to order the secret execution of the young king and his mother (Diod. 19.105.2). Diodorus lists the assassination among the items that presumably occurred during the archonship of Simonides (Diod. 19.105.1), roughly from June 311 to July 310.

An analysis of the passage suggests, however, that it need not and probably does not mean to date the murder during 311/310. The account begins with the provisions of the peace treaty between Antigonus and the allied Cassander, Ptolemy, and Lysimachus. Cassander was to remain the general of Macedonia until Alexander IV reached the age of maturity. Lysimachus would retain Thrace; Ptolemy, Egypt and the adjacent area; and Antigonus would remain supreme in Asia. Diodorus notes, however, that each of the signatories, in violation of the covenant, attempted to gain power for himself. As an example of a flagrant breach, Diodorus recounts the murder of Alexander IV. With the Macedonian dynasty extinct, hopes of kingship rose among the major and minor governors.

From a chronological point of view, Diod. 19.105.1–4 contains three sequential items:

---

[67] The following explanations for the difference between the form of the eras of autumn 312 and spring 311 have come to my attention: the autumn SE celebrates Seleucus' victory over Antigonus; spring SE recalls the murder of Alexander IV (Kubitschek, *R.E.*, I [1894] 634); the Macedonian new year, unlike that of Babylonia, began on Dios 1 (Ginzel, *Handbuch*, I, 137); and a divergent reckoning of the death of Philip Arrhidaeus and the succession of Alexander IV (Bickerman, *Berytus* 8 [1944] 75, n. 11; *Chronology of the Ancient World*, 71 [cited also by Samuel, *Greek and Roman Chronology*, 245]). All three explanations are based on a mistaken chronology. Alexander IV was not murdered in 311; Philip Arrhidaeus did not die in the autumn of 317 (see above, nn. 4–5 and 32); and there is no evidence that the Macedonian new year fell on Dios 1, or that they had a new year at all prior to their adoption of the Babylonian calendar. Circumstantial evidence seems to suggest that the autumnal beginning of SE reflects a modification of the older form of Seleucid regnal dating whose SE commenced in the spring of 311 B.C. This modification probably began in 300 B.C. with the foundation of Antioch. The change to an autumnal new year came from Syrian or Phoenician influence whose new year traditionally began in the fall (cf. the Gezer Calendar and Exod. 23:16). See Strabo (15.2, 4–5) on the foundation of Antioch, and cf. also Downey, *Ancient Antioch* (Princeton, 1963) 31f. The Syrians were among the earliest settlers of Antioch; under Phoenician influence, the Eleusinian mysteries were celebrated there in the fall. After Antioch became the capital of the Seleucid empire, Dios 1 of 312 B.C. became more widespread than the original spring SE.

1. The peace treaty.[68]
2. The violations of the treaty's provisions, including the king's murder.
3. The ambitions of kingship among the Macedonian generals.

The putative view has all of these events occurring in 311/310. In fact, however, only the treaty is dated; Diodorus places it during the archonship of Simonides.

As to the timing of the other items in Diodorus' account, there is no reason to insist that the violations began during the same year as the treaty; and even if they did, it surely does not mean that the breaches of the treaty ceased at the end of the year.

Other considerations also suggest that Diodorus' account of the assassination of Alexander IV is a digression into events which would occur some time after the peace treaty. After recording Cassander's share of Alexander the Great's Empire (Europe), Diodorus adds: "until Alexander the son of Roxane will come of age." This might mean, and has been so interpreted by some scholars, that Alexander IV's expected rule was to be limited to Cassander's satrapy.[69] Such a construction of the codicil prompts the question: why would Cassander have agreed to a provision that he alone among the satraps would yield his portion to the young king? Moreover, as we have seen above, in both Egypt and Babylonia Alexander IV's sovereignty over the empire conquered by his father

---

[68] Diod. 19.105:

105: Ἐπ' ἄρχοντος δ' Ἀθήνησι Σιμωνίδου Ῥωμαῖοι μὲν ὑπάτους κατέστησαν Μάρκον Οὐαλλέριον καὶ Πόπλιον Δέκιον. ἐπὶ δὲ τούτων οἱ περὶ Κάσανδρον καὶ Πτολεμαῖον καὶ Λυσίμαχον διαλύσεις ἐποιήσαντο πρὸς Ἀντίγονον καὶ συνθήκας ἔγραψαν. ἐν δὲ ταύταις ἦν Κάσανδρον μὲν εἶναι στρατηγὸν τῆς Εὐρώπης μέχρι ἂν Ἀλέξανδρος ὁ ἐκ Ῥωξάνης εἰς ἡλικίαν ἔλθη, καὶ Λυσίμαχον μὲν τῆς Θράκης κυριεύειν, Πτολεμαῖον δὲ τῆς Αἰγύπτου καὶ τῶν συνοριζουσῶν ταύτῃ πόλεων κατά τε τὴν Λιβύην καὶ τὴν Ἀραβίαν, Ἀντίγονον δὲ ἀφηγεῖσθαι τῆς Ἀσίας πάσης, τοὺς δὲ Ἕλληνας αὐτονόμους εἶναι. οὐ μὴν ἐνέμεινάν γε ταῖς ὁμολογίαις ταύταις, ἀλλ' ἕκαστος αὐτῶν προφάσεις εὐλόγους ποριζόμενος πλεονεκτεῖν ἐπειρᾶτο. Κάσανδρος δὲ ὁρῶν Ἀλέξανδρον τὸν ἐκ Ῥωξάνης αὐξόμενον καὶ κατὰ τὴν Μακεδονίαν λόγους ὑπό τινων διαδιδομένους ὅτι καθήκει προάγειν ἐκ τῆς φυλακῆς τὸν παῖδα καὶ τὴν πατρῴαν βασιλείαν παραδοῦναι, φοβηθεὶς ὑπὲρ ἑαυτοῦ προσέταξε Γλαυκίᾳ τῷ προεστηκότι τῆς τοῦ παιδὸς φυλακῆς τὴν μὲν Ῥωξάνην καὶ τὸν βασιλέα κατασφάξαι καὶ κρύψαι τὰ σώματα, τὸ δὲ γεγονὸς μηδενὶ τῶν ἄλλων ἀπαγγεῖλαι. ποιήσαντος δ' αὐτοῦ τὸ προσταχθὲν οἱ περὶ Κάσανδρον καὶ Λυσίμαχον καὶ Πτολεμαῖον, ἔτι δ' Ἀντίγονον ἀπηλλάγησαν τῶν ἀπὸ τοῦ βασιλέως προσδοκωμένων φόβων· οὐκέτι γὰρ ὄντος οὐδενὸς τοῦ διαδεξομένου τὴν ἀρχὴν τὸ λοιπὸν ἕκαστος τῶν κρατούντων ἐθνῶν ἢ πόλεων βασιλικὰς εἶχεν ἐλπίδας καὶ τὴν ὑφ' ἑαυτὸν τεταγμένην χώραν εἶχεν ὡσανεί τινα βασιλείαν δορίκτητον.

[69] See for example, Bengtson, Griech. Gesch.[3] (1965) 365.

remained unchallenged even after the treaty of 311.[70] All this suggests that the phrase "until Alexander the son of Roxane will come of age" referred to the portions of the other Diadochoi as well as that of Cassander.[71] But if so, why did Diodorus insert the codicil only in reference to Cassander's satrapy?

One answer could conceivably be that the record of Cassander's share in the empire appeared first in the compact. Another possible explanation is that the recognition of Alexander IV as the heir of his father's empire was a central provision of the pact of 311, especially as far as Antigonus was concerned. But Diodorus attached the codicil to Cassander in order to point out the latter's motivation for the regicide. But if the recognition of Alexander IV as the king of a united Macedonian empire was a central provision of the peace treaty, and a concession extracted from Antigonus at that, it seems quite improbable that the king's murder occurred immediately after the signing of the peace treaty. Moreover, in recounting the story of Cassander's murder of Heracles the son of Alexander the Great and Barsine, dated in 309/308, Diodorus presumes that his half-brother, Alexander IV, was still alive about two years after the peace treaty.[72] In brief, it is not necessary to assume that Diod. 19.105.1–4 dates the murder of Alexander IV in 311/310.

The only ancient source that might be cited in support of the putative dating of Alexander IV's assassination is item B 18 of the chronicle known as Marmor Parium, a generally reliable authority, which was inscribed in 264/263 B.C.[73] Referring to events that occurred during the archonship of Hieronymus (310/309 B.C.), lines 21–22 of column B, as restored by A. Wilhelm, read: "When Ale[x]a[nder the son of Alexander] dies; and the other son (of Alexander) from the daughter of Artabazus, Heracles." The second part of this sentence obviously refers to the murder of the fourteen-year-old (Justin, 15.2.3; but seventeen years old, Diod. 20.20.1) Heracles, slain by Polyperchon in 310 B.C. Wilhelm lends his considerable authority to the view that the first part of B 18 recorded the murder of Alexander IV.

Despite the fact that this restoration of line B 18 has received the approval of scholars such as Felix Jacoby and Karl Beloch,[74] it ought to be reconsidered. To begin with, the cogency of the insertion of Alexander IV

---

[70] Cf. above n. 41.

[71] Cf. the Heidelberg Epitome, *FrGH* 155 F 1.

[72] Diod. 20.20.1.

[73] *FGrH* 239. B 18:

ἀφ᾽ οὗ ᾽Αλε[ξ]α[νδρος ὁ ᾽Αλεξάνδρου] τελευτᾶι καὶ ἕτερος ἐκ τῆς ᾽Αρταβάζου θυγατρὸς ῾Ηρακλῆς.

[74] Beloch, *Griech. Gesch.* IV. 2, 104. Jacoby, in *FGrH* 239, 19, p. 1004, makes no allusion in his commentary to this emendation.

into the lacunae rested upon the assumption that Diod. 19.105 dates the king's death at about the same time. Secondly, Wilhelm's restoration does not resolve the conflict between Diodorus, who allegedly recorded the king's death during the archonship of Simonides, and the Parian chronicle which placed it a year later. Moreover, traditional exegesis of Marmor Parium B 18 and Diod. 19.105 ignores Diodorus' account of the arrival of Heracles in Epirus and his ensuing murder. Not only does Diodorus never link the assassinations of Alexander the Great's two sons, but on the contrary, he suggests that Heracles was murdered in order to save Alexander IV. Polyperchon felt aggrieved that the treaty which had reaffirmed Alexander IV as king of Macedonia and which divided the empire among the other Diadochoi (Diod. 19.105) excluded him altogether. He therefore brought the seventeen-year-old Heracles and his mother from Pergamon (Diod. 20.20.1), an action clearly viewed by Cassander as threatening. Alexander IV, then about thirteen years of age, remained a minor, while Polyperchon's candidate, Heracles, had reached the age of regnal maturity at seventeen. Cassander therefore promised all he could to Polyperchon as a price for murdering Heracles (Diod. 20.28). In other words, the assassination of Heracles and Barsine, according to Diodorus, occurred ostensibly to protect the diadem of Alexander IV since Diod. 20.20 and 28 clearly presume his being very much alive when his half-brother was murdered in 309/308. Wilhelm's reading: "Ale[x]a[andros tou Alexandrou]" creates so many historical questions that it ought to be rejected.[75] In brief, there is no conflict between Diod. 19.105 and B 18 as to the date of Alexander IV's death since neither meant to place it either in 311/310 or 310/309.

In fact, Marmor Parium B 23, in recording the accession of Ptolemy I to the crown in 305/304, seems indirectly to affirm the validity of the chronology of the Diadochoi recorded in the Astronomical Canon and Porphyry. The chronology of Alexander the Great and the Diadochoi as preserved in the Astronomical Canon found in Claudius Ptolemy's *Almagest* and reconstructed by Ginzel[76] is as follows:

---

[75] What to put in its place in the lacuna of M.P. B 18 remains a problem. Certainly the reading of Ἀλέ[ξ]α[νδρ . . . cannot be challenged. But whether the name appeared in the nominative or genitive remains doubtful. If the former, the Parian chronicler may have referred to the many officials by that name (Polyperchon's son, for example). If the latter, B 18 may be recording the death of the cronies of Alexander the Great.

[76] Ginzel, *Handbuch* I, 189.

Name of the King	Years of Rule	Era of Nabu-nasir	Era of Philip	Period of rule by the Egyptian movable year (given here in Julian dates)
Alexander Macedonian	8	424		from Nov. 14, 332 to Nov. 11, 324
Philip Arrhidaeus	7	431	7	from Nov. 12, 324 to Nov. 9, 317
Alexander (II) IV	12	443	19	from Nov. 10, 317 to Nov. 6, 305
Ptolemy Lagos	20	463	39	from Nov. 7, 305 to Nov. 1, 285

This Astronomical Canon, which lists the name of the rulers from year 1 of Nabu-nasir (February 27 of 747 B.C.) to year 23 of Antoninus Pius (August 20 of A.D. 160), dates the murder of Alexander IV on or later than November 7 of 305 but before November 6 of 304. This is so because by the Canon's style of reckoning, called antedating, the fraction of the year of the dead ruler is always credited to the new king and, for chronological purposes, the entire year is counted as part of the new reign. In Egypt the new year began with Thoth 1. Thus year 324/323 is given to Philip, although Alexander died on June 11 of 323; Ptolemy Soter, according to this table, became king some time between November 7 of 305 and November 6 of 304, the year during which Alexander IV was presumed to have been assassinated. As shown above, the murder appears to have occurred on the basis of contemporary documents about January of 304.

Porphyry of Tyre or Batanea (in Palestine), a third century philosopher and chronographer, wrote a chronicle of the ancient world which employed the Olympic Era (beginning with the summer of 776 B.C.). Porphyry's chronicle is lost, but Eusebius quotes him: "After Alexander the Macedonian, who died in Olympiad 114 year 2 (323/322), leaving no heirs, Arrhidaeus, now called Philip, who was the brother of Alexander, not of the same mother, but the son of Philinna of Larissa and Philip, became king. He reigned seven years (322/321–317/316); and was slain in Macedonia by Polyperchon, the son of Antipater."[77] In another fragment, however, Porphyry credits Philip with a reign of eight

---

[77] Eusebius, *Chronik* (Armenian, ed. by J. Karst, Leipzig, 1911) 4; *FGrH* 260 F 2. Eusebius' own chronology suppresses Alexander IV's reign altogether, making Cassander the successor of Philip Arrhidaeus. This suggests that the Christian historian preserves a tradition on the mode of Cassander's regnal dating which seems strikingly similar to the regnal chronology of Seleucus and Ptolemy (in the Greek tradition). In other words, Cassander included the years of his satrapal rule in the computation of his regnal era.

years, but likewise dates his death in Olympiad 115 year 4 (317/316).
Although fragments of Porphyry fail to give specific dates of Alexander
IV's reign, enough remains of Porphyry's work to show that he credited
him with a reign of twelve years, from 316/315 to 306/305. Ptolemy
Soter, who according to Porphyry followed Alexander IV, ruled as satrap
of Egypt seventeen years (322/321–305/304), as king twenty-one years
(304/303–285/284), plus two years during the reign of Ptolemy II Phila-
delphus, for a total rule of forty years.[78]

Although Porphyry has the same chronology as the Astronomical
Canon, assigning to Alexander IV a reign of twelve years, Porphyry's
source must have come from an independent authority. For not only
does Porphyry use a different calendar year, but he also has a divergent
convention of regnal dating. The Canon, as we have seen, uses the mode
called antedating; Porphyry employs postdating, a system followed in
Babylonia, crediting the deceased ruler with the fraction of his uncom-
pleted year and beginning the new ruler's reign with Nisanu of the next
year. This means that, according to Porphyry, Alexander IV died in
305/304, exactly as is implied in the Astronomical Canon. Both the datings of the Astronomical Canon and of Porphyry harmonize perfectly
with the testimony of the papyrological and cuneiform documents which
time the extinction of Alexander the Great's progeny and the ensuing
coronation of Ptolemy and Seleucus during the early months of 304.

In view of the uncontradicted testimony of the ancients dating the
death of Alexander IV circa January of 304, the question arises as to the
unanimous opinion of modern scholarship that he had died six or seven
years earlier, but because of fictional dating the reckoning by his regnal
era continued until 306/305.[79] The phrase "fictional dating," first proposed by Eduard Meyer, is puzzling.[80] Diod. 19.105.2, it is true, does say
that Cassander did not announce publicly the impending assassination,
but Diodorus does not suggest that knowledge of the murder of the wife
and son of Alexander the Great could have been kept secret for five or
six years. There is in fact no ancient source which even hints at what

---

[78] Eusebius, ibid., 109; FGrH F 3 (pp. 1203f.).

[79] See n. 1.

[80] Eduard Meyer (Forschungen zur alten Geschichte, II, 457–59) dated the death of
Philip Arrhidaeus circa November or the beginning of winter of 317 (p. 457); a date also
accepted by K. Beloch (Griech. Gesch. IV, 2, 105). As to Alexander IV's death, it is perhaps worth quoting Meyer's own words: "In Aegypten hat man während der thatsächlich
königslosen Zeit nach Philippos Ermordung sich, wie der ptolemäische Kanon lehrt und
eine bekannte aegyptische Inschrift bestätigt (n. 1 cites papyrus: see above nn. 5–6), damit
beholfen, dass man (vom. 10. Nov. 317 an) nach Jahren des jungen um 311 von Kassander
ermordeten Alexander II. zählte, bis dann vom 7. Nov. 305 ab nach Königsjahren des
Ptolemaeos gerechnet wurde" (458f.). But Meyer modifies the apparent certainty of this
sentence by concluding with a remark about the indefiniteness of the evidence, including
doubt concerning the published cuneiform texts.

modern scholars call fictional reckoning by a dead king. The phrase "fictional reckoning" is ambiguous. It might mean, on the one hand, that the people believed the king of Macedonia was still alive, and, on the other, that the public was aware that they were counting time by a dead monarch. Either possibility is conceivable, sometimes even likely for a short period, but I know of no precedent for regnal era by a deceased prince for six or seven years. Incidentally, Berenice's attempt to keep secret the death of her husband, Antiochus II Theos, in 246/245 B.C., failed.[81]

In fairness to Eduard Meyer, it should be said that with the evidence available at the end of the last century, the assumption of a fictional reckoning is perhaps reasonable. For on the basis of the Greek evidence, combined with the then-published papyrological and cuneiform texts, Meyer became aware of the difficulty of defending an early dating of Alexander IV's death. But Meyer seems to have been troubled by the origin of the era named after Seleucus. Evidently a convinced monarchist himself, Meyer seems to have reasoned, rightly it turns out, that a mere satrap such as Seleucus would not have installed an era after himself as long as Macedonia had a recognized king. Meyer suggested that Alexander IV died "um 311,"[82] not in 310/309, as found in the restored reading of the Parian Chronicle. With the king of Macedonia out of the way, at least historiographically, Seleucus could have legitimately begun the dating of his own reign which, according to Meyer, commemorated his reconquest of Babylon in the summer of 312.

IV. Extinction of Argeadae and the Hellenistic Kings

So far it has been argued that there is nothing in the Greek tradition which necessarily differs with the testimony that dates the death of Alexander IV in 304. This does not mean, however, that the accounts of Diodorus and Plutarch which relate to this period quite harmonize with the papyri and cuneiform tablets. For the papyri and the tablets imply that Ptolemy Soter and Seleucus Nicator assumed their diadems only after the last progeny of the Argead kings had expired. The Heidelberg Epitome states this bluntly in regard to the coronation of Cassander.[83] No matter what other factors impelled the birth of the new monarchies, the role of legality and appearance was not altogether ignored. But classical writings, evidently going back to the work of Hieronymus of Cardia, a contemporary author who served under Antigonus,[84] present different

[81] Cf. E. Will, *Histoire politique du monde hellénistique* (Nancy, 1966) 223–26.
[82] See above n. 80.
[83] Heidelberg Epitome, *FGrH* 155 F1; see below n. 98.
[84] On Hieronymus of Cardia, see Jacoby, *FGrH* 154; T. S. Brown, *AHR*, 53 (1947) 684–96.

accounts as to the origin of the new Macedonian kingdoms. Thus we know of the coronation only of Antigonus, not the other Diadochoi. The diadems of the others, if mentioned at all, are merely appended to the description of Antigonus' assumption of kingship.[85]

Plutarch's lengthy account of Antigonus deals with ethos and personality, but hardly alludes to the political aspects of the founding of a new Macedonian dynasty. Plutarch's interest is in anecdote and drama, ascribing the assumption of kingship to a courier's flattery followed by a spontaneous royal salute of the army.[86] Plutarch times the coronation of both Antigonus and Demetrius soon after the battle of Cyprus, which took place in the spring of 306. Plutarch's account does not date the crownings of the other Diadochoi.[87] Only in regard to Ptolemy does Plutarch clearly connect the coronation with the Egyptian defeat at Salamis. But Plutarch's failure to allude to the progeny of Alexander the Great in connection with the foundation of the Macedonian dynasties suggests that he presumed that the Argeadae had become extinct.[88] The account of the birth of the new Macedonian monarchies in Diod. 20.53 lacks Plutarch's dramatic presentation, but otherwise presents a similar sequence of events.[89]

The documents emanating from Egypt and Babylonia neither assert nor contradict the classical accounts of the timing of the coronations of Antigonus and Demetrius. But they do show that the Greek tradition which makes the crowning of Ptolemy an outgrowth of the battle of Cyprus is erroneous. Cyprus might have been the event that ultimately led to the Diadochoi's coronations. But legality, or the appearance of legality, was not altogether absent among the generals. The Diadochoi, other than Antigonus and Demetrius, did not emulate the Antigonid action until the progeny of Alexander the Great had been utterly wiped out.

But a number of Greek sources, whose reputation for authoritativeness is judged lower than the traditions found in Plutarch's *Life of Demetrius* and Diod. 20.53, harmonize with the Egyptian and Akkadian

---

[85] For recent accounts of the coronations, see Ritter, *Diadem und Königsherrschaft*; O. Müller, *Antigonos Monophthalmos und "Das Jahr der Könige."* *Saarbrücker Beiträge zur Altertumskunde* 11 (Bonn, 1973); G. M. Cohen, "The Diadochoi and the New Monarchies," *Athenaeum* 52 (1974) 177–79.

[86] Plut., *Demetr.* 16.3–17.1.

[87] Ibid., *Demetr.* 17.1–2. Cf. now Samuel, *Ptolemaic Chronology*, 6f.; above, n. 14.

[88] On the other hand, Plutarch was writing a life of Demetrius and his father; silence about the fate of Alexander IV, whose death is not recorded in Plutarch's extant vitae, does not reveal whether the young king was alive at the time of Antigonus' coronation.

[89] Diod. 20.53,2, says that Antigonus and Demetrius were crowned on account of the victory at Salamis; Ptolemy, because, or despite, of his defeat; the other generals, because it became fashionable. Unlike Plutarch, who remarks that Cassander had never accepted kingship (*Demetr.* 17.1), Diodorus specifically lists Cassander's assumption of the diadem.

documents. Even Diodorus may have preserved a view that differs with his own account of the beginnings of the new Macedonian kingship. After describing Cassander's murder of King Alexander and Roxane, Diod. 19.105.3 asserts that the elimination of the Argead dynasty brought relief to the Diadochoi, including Antigonus.[90] This might mean that the Diadochoi had been crowned prior to the assassination of Alexander IV (say, summer of 306) but lacked a feeling of security as long as the progeny of Alexander the Great was living. This construction, however, seems unlikely in view of Diodorus' criticism of the satrapal coronations in the next sentence: "For henceforth (i.e. Alexander IV's murder), there being no longer anyone to inherit the realm, each of those who had rule over nations or cities entertained hopes of royal power and held the territory that had been placed under his authority as if it were a kingdon won by the spear."[91] This statement seems to suggest that the hope for kingship followed, rather than preceded, Alexander IV's death. Our interpretation of Diodorus' enigmatic words becomes plausible on the basis of Diod. 19.52.4. After describing Cassander's murder of Olympias, the mother of Alexander the Great, in 316 B.C., Diodorus anticipates the regicide, mentioned in 19.105: "But Cassander had decided to destroy Alexander's son and the son's mother Roxane, in order that there be no successor to the kingdom."[92]

Whatever the meaning of the obscurity in Diod. 19.105.3–4 and 19.52.4, there is no doubt that Appian does mention, almost as an afterthought, the link between the death of Alexander IV and the origin of the new Macedonian dynasties. In Syr. 54, Appian mentions first Ptolemy's tremendous victory at Gaza (311 B.C.), and then records the defeat of Ptolemy near Cyprus, a battle led by Antigonus' son Demetrius. "On account of this feat, the army began to call them, Antigonus and Demetrius, kings." But Appian adds: "Arrhidaeus the son of Philip, Olympias, and the sons of Alexander being dead."[93] Like Plutarch and Diod. 20.53, Appian credits Ptolemy's royal title to the initiative of the army. In other words, although it would be unseemly for a satrap to crown himself, it is acceptable to do so if the army demands it. But he also notes that the old Macedonian dynasty had become extinct, thus legitimizing the new kings on a basis other than that of the feat of arms.

---

[90] See n. 68.

[91] See n. 68.

[92] Put positively, Diod. 19.52.4 suggests that Cassander eliminated Alexander IV in order to become the successor to the kingdom.

[93] Appian, Syr. 54:

> ἐφ' ὅτῳ λαμπροτάτῳ γενομένῳ ὁ στρατὸς ἀνεῖπεν
> ἄμφω βασιλέας, Ἀντίγονόν τε καὶ Δημήτριον, ἤδη καὶ τῶν
> βασιλέων τεθνεώτων, Ἀριδαίου τε τοῦ Φιλίππου καὶ Ὀλυμπιάδος
> καὶ τῶν υἱῶν Ἀλεξάνδρου.

In contrast to this confusing passage, which merely alludes to the extinction of Macedonian royalty as a subsidiary reason, *Syr.* 52 remarks briefly: "Not long afterwards (Perdiccas' apportionment of Alexander's empire on the authority of Philip Arrhidaeus) the kings (i.e. the true Macedonian kings) died and the satraps became kings."[94] In this passage at least, if not in *Syr.* 54, Appian assumes a causal link between the extinction of the Argead rulers and the new Macedonian monarchies.

Pompeius Trogus and even more so the Heidelberg Epitome present the same view more clearly. Justin deals with this matter in two passages. In 15.2, he describes first Cassander's order to murder Heracles, the son of Alexander and Barsine, and subsequently the command to murder Alexander and his mother Roxane with equal treachery, adding that these murders were quite otiose, since he could have attained Macedonian kingship without regicide.[95] This passage claims a causal link between Cassander's order to slay Alexander IV and his hope to become king of Macedonia. In 15.2.13, however, the matter is presented in a somewhat different form. He briefly repeats the account of the Diadochoi's coronations making the victory of Demetrius at Salamis the event which inspired them. But then he adds surprisingly: "But they all abstained from wearing royal insignia as long as any of the sons of their king (Alexander the Great) survived."[96] This remark represents the clearest statement in a classical source which affirms that Alexander IV was alive in 306/305.

The two references in Justin linking the assassination of Alexander IV with the desire of the Diadochoi for kingship may indicate the existence of a source other than that of Hieronymus of Cardia, as preserved in Diodorus and Plutarch. The Heidelberg Epitome also seems free of

---

[94] Appian, *Syr*, 52:

'Αλέξανδρος μὲν δὴ βασιλεὺς ἦν ἐπὶ Πέρσαις Σύρων, ὁ καὶ πάντων βασιλεὺς ὅσων εἶδεν· 'Αλεξάνδρου δ' ἀποθανόντος ἐπὶ παισὶ τῷ μὲν βραχεῖ πάνυ τῷ δὲ ἔτι κυϊσκομένῳ, οἱ μὲν Μακεδόνες, πόθῳ τοῦ Φιλιππείου γένους, εἵλοντο σφῶν βασιλεύειν 'Αριδαῖον τὸν ἀδελφὸν 'Αλεξάνδρου, καίπερ οὐκ ἔμφρονα νομιζόμενον εἶναι, μετονομάσαντες δὴ Φίλιππον ἀντὶ 'Αριδαίου, τρεφομένων ἔτι τῶν παίδων 'Αλεξάνδρου (ἐφύλαξαν γὰρ δὴ καὶ τὴν κύουσαν), οἱ φίλοι δ' ἐς σατραπείας ἐνείμαντο τὰ ἔθνη, Περδίκκου διανέμοντος αὐτοῖς ὑπὸ τῷ βασιλεῖ Φιλίππῳ. καὶ οὐ πολὺ ὕστερον τῶν βασιλέων ἀποθανόντων βασιλεῖς ἐγένοντο οἱ σατράπαι.

[95] Justin 15.2.3–4: "Deinde, ne Hercules, Alexandri filius, qui annos XIV excesserat, favore paterni nominis in regnum Macedoniae vocaretur, occidi eum tacite cum matre Barsine iubet corporaque eorum terra obrui, ne caedes sepultura proderetur, et quasi parum facinoris in ipso primum rege, mox in matre eius Olympiade ac filio admisisset, alterum quoque filium cum matre Roxane pari fraude interfecit, scilicet quasi regnum Macedoniae, quod adfectabat, aliter consequi quam scelere non posset."

[96] Justin, 15.2.13: "Huius honoris ornamentis tam diu omnes abstinuerunt, quam diu filii regis sui superesse potuerunt."

Antigonid bias, reflecting perhaps a source similar to that used by Pompeius Trogus (Justin).[97] It flatly asserts that Cassander, "who wished to be the successor of the entire kingdom," ordered the murder of Alexander IV. In the ensuing disorder, the anonymous author continues, the satraps became kings.[98]

TABLE IV

THE CHRONOLOGY OF THE DIADOCHOI

Death of Alexander the Great	June 10/11 of 323
Succession of Philip Arrhidaeus	June 11/12 of 323
Death of Philip Arrhidaeus	circa February of 316
Antigonus Monophthalmus begins his own era	March (?) of 316
Seleucus reintroduces regnal era of Alexander IV	Summer of 312
Coronation of Antigonus and Demetrius	Summer of 306
Death of Alexander IV	December of 305 or January of 304
Coronation of Ptolemy	January–March of 304
Coronation of Seleucus	March–April 304
Proclamation of Seleucid era reckoning	March–April of 304
Retroactive dating of SE to 311/310 reckoning	April 13/14 of 304
Retroactive dating of SE to 312/311	300 B.C

[97] On the dependence of Plutarch's *Demetrius* and of Books 19 and 20 of Diodorus on Hieronymus, see Jacoby's commentary, *FGrH* 154 pp. 544f.; for the relationship between Hieronymus and the Heidelberg Epitome, see *FGrH* 155 F 1, p. 549.

[98] Heidelberg Epitome, *FGrH* 155 F 1:

(6) εἶτα ὁ Κάσανδρος μισθωσάμενός τινας τῶν βασιλικῶν διακόνων ἐδολοφόνησε τήν τε Ὀλυμπιάδα καὶ Ῥωξάνην καὶ τὸν υἱὸν αὐτῆς τὸν Ἀλέξανδρον τὸν υἱὸν Ἀλεξάνδρου, ὃς ἔμελλεν εἶναι διάδοχος τῆς ὅλης βασιλείας. ἐγένετο δὲ ταῦτα ἐν Μακεδονίαι [[τῆς Ὀλυμπιάδος τῆς μητρὸς Ἀλεξάνδρου]]. (7) ἐντεῦθεν σύγχυσις ἐγένετο τῶν σατραπειῶν, καὶ ἐπεβούλευον ἄλλοι ἄλλοις καὶ προσετίθουν ταῖς ἑαυτῶν καὶ μείζονας περιεβάλλοντο δυνάμεις οἱ πανουργότεροι καὶ ἐφόνευον τοὺς ἀσθενεστέρους.

POSTSCRIPT—The recent work by Ludwig Schober, *Untersuchungen zur Geschichte Babyloniens und der Oberen Satrapien von 323–303 v. Chr.* (Frankfurt am Main, 1981), came to my attention too late to be employed in this study. I would like to thank John Reeves for his assistance in the preparation of this essay for publication.

SAMUEL SANDMEL'S CORRESPONDENCE
WITH VALENTIN NIKIPROWETZKY

Perhaps nothing better reflects Samuel Sandmel's humanity, insight and courage than his correspondence with his close friend, Valentin Nikiprowetzky, during the last months of his life. Among Sandmel's multitude of friends and colleagues, he enjoyed a special relationship with Nikiprowetzky, then Professor of Hebrew and Jewish Studies at the University of Paris III, La Sorbonne Nouvelle.* The two were bound together by many ties: their special devotion to the study of Philo of Alexandria, their common family backgrounds in the Ukraine, and a shared openness of vision as to the role of Judaism in history and its relationships with Christianity. They both were marked by great human warmth. Mrs. Frances Sandmel and Professor Nikiprowetzky have graciously made the following correspondence available, as a tribute and a record. Professor Nikiprowetzky's letters have been translated from the French with his approval by Earle Hilgert.

Nikiprowetzky to Sandmel, Paris, July 9, 1979.

Mon cher Samuel,
    Ma lettre va sans doute vous rejoindre à votre lieu de vacances. Les tâches particulièrement accaparantes de cette fin d'année universitaire m'ont empêché de vous écrire plus tôt et de vous féliciter, comme il convenait de le faire, pour la sortie en librairie de *Philo of Alexandria: An Introduction*. Cet excellent ouvrage, qui atteint parfaitement le but visé, attirera certainement de nouveaux lecteurs à Philon. J'ai été *extrêmement touché* par la dédicace que vous m'en avez faite. Je considère que c'est un grand honneur que vous m'avez fait et je vous en remercie du fond du coeur. L'édition du livre est admirable et je suis sûr qu'il fera une excellente carrière.

[My dear Samuel,
    Doubtless my letter will find you at your summer place. Particularly demanding duties at the end of this academic year have kept me from writing you sooner and congratulating you, as is fitting, on the publication of *Philo of Alexandria: An Introduction*. This excellent work,

---

* Valentin Nikiprowetzky died December 19, 1983.

which meets perfectly its intended goal, will surely attract new readers to Philo. I was *extremely touched* by your dedication of it to me. I consider it a great honor you have done me and I thank you from the bottom of my heart. The way in which the book is printed is admirable, and I am sure it will have much success. . . .]

Sandmel to Nikiprowetzky, Waterville, Maine, July 23, 1979.

Dear Valentin:

I am happy to have your letter of July 9. I am pleased at your response to my dedicating the book to you. You cannot know what pleasure it gave me to do so.

The difference between Chicago and Hebrew Union College can be summarized in two ways. On the negative side, one cannot expect at Chicago to find the richness of Jewish background that one finds in Cincinnati, and all that means is that that is all the more reason for someone like me to be at Chicago to try to supply it. On the other hand, the breadth of possibilities at Chicago is wondrously attractive. I have been invited to serve on a committee called Ancient Mediterranean Studies, been made a guest member of The Renaissance Society, and find increasing relationships with academicians in areas remote from my own whom I find exceedingly attractive. I hope you will be pleased to note that all incoming Divinity School students take an Introduction to the New Testament, which is offered in three segments over three terms. I have been asked to teach two of the three terms. That a Jew should teach these courses at a Protestant Divinity School is one of the wondrous gratifications of our being here.

It was a very busy school year. I have had a number of lecture obligations and through circumstances that I find difficult to control, I find myself a bit busier than I should have liked to be. One modest gratification was an honorary degree from a Roman Catholic college in Chicago. It was a very fruitful year, but I hope that next year will be considerably more restful. Towards the end of the year, I felt quite fatigued and so the doctors have been putting me through various tests, and meantime on the one hand, the fatigue has lasted and on the other hand, the doctors have found nothing negative in any of the x-rays and other devices which they have. . . .

I am dictating this from our summer place in Maine. We are, however, returning to Cincinnati, . . . so that the doctors can look a bit into what this fatigue is for which the tests so far gave no explanation. Meantime, I continue to do a little writing and a good bit of reading.

Sandmel to Nikiprowetzky, Cincinnati, August 10, 1979.

My dear Valentin,

Two weeks ago came your welcome letter telling me that you and your wife met David and Betsy, and a week ago your article on the Therapeutae arrived, along with a letter including some comments on the Paul manuscript, for the continued reading of which I am most grateful.

Your kind letter also expressed concern for the undue and therefore troubling fatigue I had mentioned. I am sorry to have to tell you that much of our time in Maine was spent undergoing medical examination. While the doctors kept finding nothing but negative results, there was strong suspicion that because of my condition (extreme fatigue, weight loss) there was something the tests were not revealing. Accordingly, at the time when you and your wife were with David and Betsy, the doctor in Maine advised us to return to Cincinnati, as an exploratory operation might solve what had been without solution. The surgery disclosed a malignancy in the wall of the stomach which, because of its location, had defied detection before. There is no connection between this and the illness of two years ago. . . .

Valentin, you and I have had a most unique relationship. I wonder if anyone else has read as much of your writing as I have. I know that no one, even my wife, has read as much of my writing as you have. How gratifying it was to dedicate the little Philo book to you!

You will understand why I dictate this note to you now, to try to say several things. If, on the one hand, I have been discouraged by this recent development, I have not lost any courage. There is a manuscript I am now working on which is quite different from anything else I have written. In due course, I look forward to the privilege of sending it on to you to read.

It is a sort of autobiography, an odyssey setting forth from my childhood in the close family life of Ukranian immigrants, across always deepening seas of scholarly and religious inquiry into the life (still questing) of complex considerations you and I so rewardingly share. Or, to put it another way, it is a personal examination of the career of one who has tried to be both a scientific scholar of Christian origins, and a loyal Jew, in a world of scholarship that had scarcely existed before and which has opened up before me.

Perhaps the interest in the manuscript will not be widespread, but nevertheless it seems to me that the implications to Jews and Christians, in a context of scholarship which is always honest, might have more than passing interest. Whether this is so or not, I want to write it, and Frances wants me to write it, and that is how I will spend whatever may be the period of convalescence.

There are many things to touch on: the first time I entered a church, the first glance into the New Testament, the endless experiences, whether in colleges or in the military, which had their own relationships and revelations. Somehow this seems now all worth talking about. How else can we Jews understand where we are in this world?

What joy scholars like you have brought me! What joy I have in this particular correspondence!

You always send me regards from your wife. It is a pleasure to let my wife record this letter, and to extend to you our most profound affection.

Nikiprowetzky to Sandmels, Paris, September 2, 1979.

Chers amis,

J'ai trouvé, à mon retour à Paris, votre lettre du 10 août 1979. Je l'ai lue avec des sentiments mélangés de joie, de détresse et d'admiration.

J'y ai lu en effet la nouvelle que, depuis votre dernière lettre de Juillet, je redoutais de lire et à quoi je n'avais cessé de penser durant tout mon séjour dans les Alpes Maritimes.

Mais le calme serein et le courage avec lesquels vous faites face à cette nouvelle épreuve sont communicatifs et m'ont moi-même réconforté.

J'ai terminé la lecture de votre lettre avec moins de chagrin que je ne l'avais commencée, et je peux dire avec vous, "If, on the one hand, I have been discouraged by this recent development, I have not lost any courage."

Je mets tout mon espoir dans cette chimiothérapie que vous avez commencée. Je suis tout à fait de l'avis de Mrs. Sandmel relativement à l'autobiographie à laquelle vous songez. Vos immenses mérites non seulement scientifiques, main encore proprement littéraires, tels qu'ils éclatent dans *Alone Atop the Mountain* et peut-être plus encore dans *Paul, a Novel*, en feront certainement une oeuvre classique dans la mémoire du peuple juif et d'un intérêt universel. Elle conservera à jamais le reflet d'un homme admirable dans lequel il m'a semblé trouver ce que les Juifs et l'Amerique peuvent offrir de meilleur: un esprit pénétrant, une ouverture de coeur affinée par des épreuves millénaires à quoi s'ajoutent une spontanéité, une générosité, une fraicheur de sentiments, un format humain que je n'ai rencontrés qu'aux Etats-Unis et qui malgré les critiques qui lui sont faites m'ont conduit à aimer ce pays et ses habitants.

Votre amitié est donc pour moi un rare privilège et la manière dont vous l'exprimez dans votre dernière lettre m'a rempli de joie. . . .

Avec nos voeux les plus ardents pour le complet rétablissement de Samuel et pour la poursuite de ses grands et beaux travaux, nous vous prions d'agréer, bien chers amis, l'expression de nos sentiments les plus cordiaux et les plus fidèles. Nous restons suspendus à vos nouvelles. . . .

[Dear Friends,

On returning to Paris I found your letter of August 10. I read it with mixed emotions of joy, distress and admiration. There I read the news that, ever since your last letter of July, I feared reading and about which I have thought continually during my stay in the Maritime Alps. But the serene calm and the courage with which you are facing this new trial are contagious and have been a comfort to me as well.

I finished reading your letter with less sorrow than I began, and I can say with you, "If, on the one hand I have been discouraged by this recent development, I have not lost any courage."

I put all my hope in the chemotherapy that you have begun. I am entirely in agreement with Mrs. Sandmel in regard to the autobiography you are contemplating. Your immense gifts, not only scientific, but also specifically literary, so evident in *Alone Atop the Mountain* and perhaps even more in *Paul, a Novel*, will certainly make it a classic in the memory of the Jewish people and of universal interest. It will preserve permanently the reflection of an admirable man in whom I sense to have found what the Jews and the U.S. best offer: a penetrating mind, an openness of heart refined by millenia of trial, to which is added a spontaneity, a generosity and a freshness of feeling, a human format that I have found only in the United States and which, in spite of criticisms leveled against it, has led me to love the country and its people . . . .

Your friendship is a rare privilege for me, and the way in which you express it in your last letter filled me with joy. . . .

With our most ardent best wishes for Samuel's complete recovery and the further pursuit of his great and splendid undertakings, we ask you to accept, our dear friends, the expression of our most cordial and faithful sentiments. We will eagerly anticipate further news of you. . . .]

Frances Sandmel to Nikiprowetzkys, Cincinnati, October 6, 1979.

Dear Friends,

I know with what anxiety and emotion you have been awaiting some word about *our* beloved Samuel. I must apologize for my delay, forced upon me by day by day concerns, in answering your letter, which gave my husband so much personal joy and scholarly satisfaction. The affection of a valued friend, the reasoned admiration of a colleague, what better, more heartening tonic could be administered?

If only such spiritual sustenance could invigorate the body as well! It grieves me to grieve you by telling you that Sam is seriously ill. After his courageous letter to you from the hospital in August (actually a credo, expressed to you, with whom he can communicate fondly and openly), he was at home for a month, receiving treatment at the Clinic, enjoying his garden, writing his autobiography, and presumably recovering, or at least recuperating. He celebrated Rosh Hashona and the next day, his 68th birthday, joyfully, though in a very weak condition. Shortly afterwards, he developed a fever and showed signs of disorientation. He re-entered the hospital Erev Yom Kippur, and has been under intense observation ever since. Every conceivable kind of test is being taken, and while some possible additional problems have been ruled out, the answers are not yet clear. I am impressed by the thoroughness and the quality of the care he is receiving. When I expressed appreciation of this to one of the young doctors who is assisting, he said, surprisingly, "He deserves it!"

Dear friends, I am writing you this disquieting news to soften, if possible, what I fear will be the eventual blow. We have been told the prognosis is not good. Sam is often uncomfortable but not in great pain, and the disorientation seems to shield him from worry. When his mind is clear, for several hours a day, he reads, converses, permits me to interview him and take notes for his autobiography. It is strange that in his more clouded times, he does not speak of work; you will be touched to know that the only mention he has made of it is a repeated out of context request for a copy of his *Philo of Alexandria*. . . .

I have just told Sam that I am responding to your letter and he asked me to re-read your words of friendship and good wishes. I have just done so, twice, and again, he is deeply gratified by the sense of communion.

I extend my gratitude for your devotion, and my affectionate good wishes for the New Year.

Nikiprowetzky to Frances Sandmel, Paris, November 18, 1979.

Chère amie,

Il m'est difficile de vous dire avec quelle douleur j'ai appri . . . la triste nouvelle de la fin de notre cher Samuel.

Malgré votre lettre, hélas fort claire, d'octobre, je ne pouvais ni croire ni me résigner à une issue fatale si proche. Cette mort que je ressens comme une injustice est la première pensée qui me visite chaque matin et je ne parviens pas à me consoler de la disparition d'un homme qui, lorsque je l'avais vu à Chatenay Malabry en 1978, m'avait paru en pleine santé et plein d'énergie.

Sa derniére lettre de Chicago me le montrait au terme d'une année universitaire brillante et remplie d'activités multiples. Il est mort comme un héros antique, dans la pensée du travail et d'un nouveau livre, de cette autobiographie qu'hélas il n'a pu écrire.

Bien sûr, au delà de sa disparition, il reste bien vivant parmi nous. Sa voix nous parle toujours dans les beaux livres qu'il nous a laissés et qui honorent le judaïsme et l'humanité. La leçon qu'il nous a donnée demeure, mais je n'arrive pas à m'habituer à l'idée que je ne recevrai plus de lui ces lettres amicales et stimulantes, ces livres si riches et si beaux, dont l'un attend encore un éditeur.

Chère amie, ma femme et moi nous ressentons de tout coeur la douleur qui est la vôtre et celle des enfants et de tous les proches de ce grand homme, de cet homme admirable que nous pleurons et dont l'absence sera toujours pour nous une poignante douleur. Nous vous embrassons très affectuesement.

[Dear Friend,

It is difficult for me to say with what pain I learned . . . the sad news of the end of our dear Samuel.

In spite of your letter—alas, so clear—of October, I could neither bring myself to believe nor resign myself to a fatal outcome so quickly. This death, which seems so unjust, is the first thought that comes to me each morning, and I have not succeeded in consoling myself for the demise of a man who, when I saw him at Chatenay Malabry in 1978 [at the annual meeting of the Society of New Testament Studies], appeared to be in the best of health and full of energy.

His last letter from Chicago showed him at the conclusion of a brilliant academic year filled with many activities. He died like an ancient hero, thinking of his work and a new book, the autobiography that, alas, he was unable to write.

Indeed, quite beyond the fact of his absence, he remains very alive among us. His voice continues to speak to us in the wonderful books he has left us, which are an honor to Judaism and to humanity. The lesson he gave us remains, but I cannot get used to the idea that I will never again receive his friendly and stimulating letters, his rich and wonderful books, of which one yet awaits publication.

Dear friend, my wife and I sense with full hearts the pain that is yours and your children's and of all who were close to this great man, this admirable man whom we mourn and whose absence will always bring us poignant sadness. We embrace you with much affection.]

Nikiprowetzky to Frances Sandmel, Paris, January 14, 1981.

Chère Madame et Chère amie,

J'ai beaucoup pensé à Sam, à vous au début du mois de novembre 1980, en ces jours qui marquaient le premier anniversaire de la disparition de notre cher Sam. Le douleur et l'émotion provoquées par les nouvelles alarmantes qui se succédaient depuis l'été 1979 jusqu'à votre lettre, puis l'annonce solennelle par le bulletin de l'"Hebrew Union College" de la mort de Samuel, sont vivantes en mon coeur comme au premier jour. Votre dernière lettre éveille donc en moi un écho multiple et douloureux. A cause de sa personnalité hors du commun, Sam est à la fois plus présent que les autres défunts et plus cruellement absent par le regret qu'il nous inspire d'être désormais incapable de la rencontrer en personne, alors que nous avons l'impression d'entendre à chaque instant ses propos si pleins d'élévation et de sereine sagesse. Je sais d'après une lettre qui m'a été écrite en français au nom d'Alfred Gottschalk que le deuil à Hebrew Union College est le même. La dédicace du Vol. L de HUCA le montre éloquemment aussi.

Il nous reste les livres de Sam, son oeuvre où bien des générations continueront à puiser l'amour de tout ce qui lui a été à lui-même cher. . . .

[Dear Madam and Friend,

I thought much of Sam and of you at the beginning of November 1980, during the days that marked the first anniversary of the disappearance of our dear Sam. The pain and emotion aroused by the alarming news which kept coming from the summer of 1979 onward until your letter, then the solemn announcement by the bulletin from HUC of Samuel's death, are as alive with me as they were the first day. So your last letter awakes in me many and painful echoes. Because of his extraordinary personality, Sam is at the same time more keenly present than others who have died, yet more cruelly absent because of the regret that he inspires in us for being no longer capable of meeting him in person, although we have the sense of hearing his remarks constantly, so filled with high-mindedness and serene wisdom. I know through a letter written me in French from Alfred Gottschalk that the mourning at Hebrew Union College is the same. The dedication of *HUCA*, Vol. 50, eloquently demonstrates this, as well.

Sam's books remain to us, his work, from which many generations will continue to imbibe the love of all that was dear to him.]

THE WRITINGS OF SAMUEL SANDMEL:
A BIBLIOGRAPHY

compiled by
FREDERICK E. GREENSPAHN
University of Denver

Samuel Sandmel's writings are found in esoteric foreign journals and Sunday newspaper supplements. He wrote short stories and popular books on subjects ranging from ancient thinkers' treatment of isolated biblical phrases to interfaith relations in the modern world.

The entries in the following list of his published writings are arranged by date of publication. Within this chronological sequence are first books and pamphlets, then articles, and finally reviews, each in alphabetical order. Volumes edited by Sandmel are indicated with an asterisk, and works in which his contributions are included among those of others (symposia, interviews, etc.) designated by a small circle. In general, each item is listed only once, according to the date of its first publication, although reprints, translations, and foreign language editions have been noted wherever such information was available. Revised and augmented editions are listed separately by their date of publication.

The wealth and diversity of Sandmel's writings as well as the fact that some of his works are still in press suggest that not everything he published has come to our attention. The compiler accepts responsibility for any errors or omissions and would welcome information about additional writings.

Special gratitude is due those whose assistance made the list's current breadth possible, including Duncan Brockway, Michael Cook, Kendig Brubaker Kelly, Fred Denny, Pierce Ellis, Richard Freund, Michael Greenwald, Earle Hilgert, Doris Katz, Marcia Posner, Randy Ringer, Bernard Rabenstein, David Sandmel, Frances Sandmel, Ida Selavan, Anita Wenner, and especially Miriam November, whose resources provided the skeleton for this list and whose kind support and initiative led to the discovery of additional information.

The American Jewish Archives at the Hebrew Union College–Jewish Institute of Religion in Cincinnati maintains a collection of Samuel Sandmel papers, which includes manuscripts and correspondence from 1928 to 1980. Other relevant materials can be found in their Nearprint File.

1949

1 Review of *Philo: Foundations of Religious Philosophy in Judaism, Christianity and Islam* by Harry Austryn Wolfson, *Classical Philology* 44 (1949) 49–52.

1951

2 "Abraham's Knowledge of the Existence of God," *Harvard Theological Review* 44 (1961) 137–39.

3 "Judaism, Jesus, and Paul: Some Problems of Method in Scholarly Research," *Vanderbilt Studies in the Humanities* 1 (1951) 220–50 (reprinted in no. 150 below, pp. 120–46 and 342–44).

4 Review of *The Gentleman and the Jew* by Maurice Samuel in *The Pastor* 14:10 (June, 1951) 42.

1953

5 "The Clew to Survival," *Central Conference of American Rabbis Yearbook* 63 (1953) 199–208.

6 Review of *The Servant Messiah: A Study of the Public Ministry of Jesus* by T.W. Manson, *Jewish Social Studies* 17 (1953) 331–32.

1954

7 "Philo's Environment and Philo's Exegesis," *Journal of Bible and Religion* 22 (1954) 248–53.

8 "Philo's Place in Judaism, A Study of the Conception of Abraham in Jewish Literature" (part 1), *Hebrew Union College Annual* 25 (1954) 209–37 (included also in no. 13 below).

9 Review of *The Church and the Jewish People*, ed. Göte Hedenquist, *Religion in Life* 24 (1954–55) 158–59.

10 Review of *The Third and Fourth Books of the Maccabees*, ed. and trans. Moses Hadas, *Journal of the American Oriental Society* 74 (1954) 97–98.

1955

11 "Philo and His Pupils: An Imaginary Dialogue," *Judaism* 4 (1955) 47–57 (reprinted in no. 150 below, pp. 265–78).

12 "Philo's Place in Judaism, A Study of the Conception of Abraham in Jewish Literature" (part 2), *Hebrew Union College Annual* 26 (1955) 151–332 (included also in no. 13 below).

1956

13 *Philo's Place in Judaism: A Study of Conceptions of Abraham in Jewish Literature*. Cincinnati: Hebrew Union College Press, 1956 (incorporating nos. 8 and 12 above; see also no. 144 below).

14   "Myths, Genealogies, and Jewish Myths and the Writing of Gospels," *Hebrew Union College Annual* 27 (1956) 201–11 (reprinted in no. 150 below, pp. 158–65 and 345–48).

1957

15   *A Jewish Understanding of the New Testament*. Cincinnati: Hebrew Union College Press, 1957 (chap. 10 reprinted in *Jewish Expressions on Jesus: An Anthology*, ed. Trude Weiss-Rosmarin. New York: Ktav, 1977. Pp. 99–115; see also no. 170 below).

16   Review of *The Apocrypha, Bridge of the Testaments: A Reader's Guide to the Apocryphal Books of the Old Testament* by Robert C. Denton, *Studies in Bibliography and Booklore* 3 (1957–58) 32–33.

17   Review of *The Bridge: A Yearbook of Judeo-Christian Studies*, vol. 1, ed. John M. Oesterreicher, *Journal of Bible and Religion* 25 (1957) 342–43.

18   Review of *The Bridge: A Yearbook of Judeo-Christian Studies*, vols. 1–2, ed. John M. Oesterreicher, *Studies in Bibliography and Booklore* 3 (1957–58) 83–84.

19   Review of *Maccabees, Zealots, and Josephus: An Inquiry into Jewish Nationalism in the Greco-Roman Period* by William R. Farmer, *Studies in Bibliography and Booklore* 3 (1957–58) 37–39.

20   Review of *The New Testament and Rabbinic Judaism* by David Daube, *Journal of Biblical Literature* 76 (1957) 64–65.

21   Review of *Second Thoughts on the Dead Sea Scrolls* by Frederick F. Bruce, *Studies in Bibliography and Booklore* 3 (1957–58) 32.

1958

22   *The Genius of Paul, A Study in History*. New York: Farrar, Straus, and Cudahy, 1958 (see no. 130 below).

23   "Isaac Mayer Wise's 'Jesus Himself,'" in *Essays in American Jewish History*. Cincinnati: American Jewish Archives, 1958. Pp. 325–58 (reprinted in no. 150 below, pp. 232–57).

24   Review of *The Early Church: Studies in Early Christian History and Theology* by Oscar Cullman, *Jewish Social Studies* 20 (1958) 188–90.

25   Review of *Hillel the Elder: The Emergence of Classical Judaism* by Nahum N. Glatzer, *Studies in Bibliography and Booklore* 3 (1957–58) 176.

26   Review of *Primitive Christianity in Its Contemporary Setting* by Rudolf Bultmann, *Jewish Social Studies* 20 (1958) 107–8.

27   Review of *The Relevance of Apocalyptic: A Study of Jewish and Christian Apocalypses from Daniel to the Revelation* by H. H. Rowley, *Jewish Social Studies* 20 (1958) 103–4.

1959

28   "Biblical Theology—A Dissent," *CCAR Journal* no. 24 (January, 1959) 15–20.

29   "The Colleagues of Mr. Chips," *Prairie Schooner* 33 (1959) 296–317 (reprinted in *The Best American Short Stories, 1961*, ed. Martha Foley and David Burnett [Boston: Houghton Mifflin Co., 1961] 314–39, and in *Motive* 23 [January, 1963] 28–36.)

1960

30   *Judaism and Christianity*. Washington, D.C.: Bnai Brith Youth Organization, 1960 (translated into Norwegian as *Jødedom og Kristendom*. Oslo: Skandinavisk Jødisk Ungdomsforbund, 1967. See also no. 171 below).

31   "Filón y sus Discipulos," *Davar* 85 (1960) 3–19.

32   "Rabbis and Recruitment of Rabbinical Students," *CCAR Journal* 8:1 (April, 1960) 45–47, 52.

33   Review of *The Later Herods* by Stewart Perowne, *Jewish Bookland* in *JWB Circle* 15:4 (September, 1960) 4.

1961

34   "Dedication Week at the Cincinnati Campus," *CCAR Journal* 9 (April, 1961) 4–5.

35   "The Evasions of Modern Theology," *The American Scholar* 30:3 (Summer, 1961) 1–14 (reprinted in no. 150 below, 28–41).

36   "Genesis 4:26b," *Hebrew Union College Annual* 32 (1961) 19–29 (reprinted in no. 150 below, pp. 305–15 and 353–54).

37   "Greeks, Jews, and Christians," *Graduate Comment* (Wayne State University, Graduate Division of Instruction and Research) 4:4 (February, 1961) 4–7.

38   "The Haggada Within Scripture," *Journal of Biblical Literature* 80 (1961) 105–22 (reprinted in no. 114 below, pp. 94–118, and in no. 150 below, pp. 316–34).

39   "Torah—Law or Revelation," *Jewish Heritage* 4 (Summer, 1961) 21–23.

40   Review of *Ethics and the Gospel* by T. W. Manson, *Journal of Biblical Literature* 80 (1961) 390.

41   Review of *The Powers That Be: Earthly Powers and Demonic Rulers in Romans 13:1–7* by Clinton Morrison, *Journal of Biblical Literature* 80 (1961) 89–90.

42   "Ahikar" in *The Interpreter's Dictionary of the Bible*, ed. Arthur Buttrick. Nashville: Abingdon Press, 1962. 1.68.

43   "Annas" in *The Interpreter's Dictionary of the Bible*, ed. Arthur Buttrick. Nashville: Abingdon Press, 1962. 1.138.

44   "Archelaus" in *The Interpreter's Dictionary of the Bible*, ed. Arthur Buttrick. Nashville: Abingdon Press, 1962. 1.207–8.

45   "Aristobulus" in *The Interpreter's Dictionary of the Bible*, ed. Arthur Buttrick. Nashville: Abingdon Press, 1962. 1.221–22.

46   "Bernice" in *The Interpreter's Dictionary of the Bible*, ed. Arthur Buttrick. Nashville: Abingdon Press, 1962. 1.386.

47   "Caiphas" in *The Interpreter's Dictionary of the Bible*, ed. Arthur Buttrick. Nashville: Abingdon Press, 1962. 1.481–82.

48   "Christianity and Judaism—A Jewish Reply," *Jewish Heritage* 5 (Winter, 1962–63) 10–14.

49   "Drusilla" in *The Interpreter's Dictionary of the Bible*, ed. Arthur Buttrick. Nashville: Abingdon Press, 1962. 1.872–73.

50   "Ethnarch" in *The Interpreter's Dictionary of the Bible*, ed. Arthur Buttrick. Nashville: Abingdon Press, 1962. 2.178–79.

51   "Felix, Antoninus" in *The Interpreter's Dictionary of the Bible*, ed. Arthur Buttrick. Nashville: Abingdon Press, 1962. 2.264.

52   "Festus, Porcius" in *The Interpreter's Dictionary of the Bible*, ed. Arthur Buttrick. Nashville: Abingdon Press, 1962. 2.265–66.

53   "Herod" in *The Interpreter's Dictionary of the Bible*, ed. Arthur Buttrick. Nashville: Abingdon Press, 1962. 2.585–94.

54   "Herodians" in *The Interpreter's Dictionary of the Bible*, ed. Arthur Buttrick. Nashville: Abingdon Press, 1962. 2.594–95.

55   "Herodias" in *The Interpreter's Dictionary of the Bible*, ed. Arthur Buttrick. Nashville: Abingdon Press, 1962. 2.595.

56   "Jairus" in *The Interpreter's Dictionary of the Bible*, ed. Arthur Buttrick. Nashville: Abingdon Press, 1962. 2.789.

57   "John" in *The Interpreter's Dictionary of the Bible*, ed. Arthur Buttrick. Nashville: Abingdon Press, 1962. 2.930.

58   "Lysanias" in *The Interpreter's Dictionary of the Bible*, ed. Arthur Buttrick. Nashville: Abingdon Press, 1962. 3.193.

59   "Parallelomania" (1961 Society of Biblical Literature Presidential Address), *Journal of Biblical Literature* 81 (1962) 1–13 (reprinted in no. 150 below, pp. 291–304 and 352–53).

60   "Pilate" in *The Interpreter's Dictionary of the Bible*, ed. Arthur Buttrick. Nashville: Abingdon Press, 1962. 3.811–13.

61   "Quirinius" in *The Interpreter's Dictionary of the Bible*, ed. Arthur Buttrick. Nashville: Abingdon Press, 1962. 3.975–77.

62   "Tetrarch" in *The Interpreter's Dictionary of the Bible*, ed. Arthur Buttrick. Nashville: Abingdon Press, 1962. 4.579.

63   Review of *On the Trial of Jesus* by Paul Winter, *Journal of the American Oriental Society* 82 (1962) 386–87.

1963

64　*The Hebrew Scriptures, An Introduction to Their Literature and Religious Ideas.* New York: Alfred A. Knopf, 1963 (see also no. 221 below).

65　"Gamaliel" in *Dictionary of the Bible*, ed. James Hastings, rev. Frederick C. Grant and H. H. Rowley. 2d ed., Edinburgh: T. & T. Clark; New York: Charles Scribner's Sons, 1963. P. 315.

66　"Hasideans" in *Dictionary of the Bible*, ed. James Hastings, rev. Frederick C. Grant and H. H. Rowley. 2d ed., Edinburgh: T. & T. Clark; New York: Charles Scribner's Sons, 1963. P. 366.

67　"Judaismo y Cristianismo," *Davar* 96 (January-March, 1963) 62–75.

68　"Mass Crime and the Judeo-Christian Tradition," *The Minnesota Review* 3 (Winter, 1962–63) 220–27 (reprinted in no. 150 below, pp. 42–52).

69　"New Testament Study in Relation to the Jewish Tradition," *Jewish Teacher* 31 (April, 1963) 23.

70　"Phylacteries, Frontlets" in *Dictionary of the Bible*, ed. James Hastings, rev. Frederick C. Grant and H. H. Rowley. 2d ed., Edinburgh: T. & T. Clark; New York: Charles Scribner's Sons, 1963. Pp. 770–71.

71　"Prolegomena to a Commentary on Mark," *Journal of Bible and Religion* 31 (1963) 294–300 (reprinted in *New Testament Issues*, ed. R. Batey [London: SCM, 1970] pp. 45–56, and in no. 150 below, pp. 147–57 and 344).

72　"Sanhedrin" in *Dictionary of the Bible*, ed. James Hastings, rev. Frederick C. Grant and H. H. Rowley. 2d ed., Edinburgh: T. & T. Clark; New York: Charles Scribner's Sons, 1963. Pp. 886–87.

73　"Son of Man" in *In The Time of Harvest, Essays in Honor of Abba Hillel Silver on the Occasion of His 70th Birthday*, ed. Daniel Jeremy Silver. New York: Macmillan Co., 1963. Pp. 355–67 (reprinted as "'Son of Man' in Mark" in no. 150 below, pp. 166–77 and 349).

74　Review of *The Bible and the Ancient Near East: Essays in Honor of William Foxwell Albright*, ed. G. Ernest Wright, *Jewish Social Studies* 25 (1963) 205–6.

75　Review of *The Death of Jesus* by Joel Carmichael, *Jewish Bookland* in *JWB Circle* 18:4 (September, 1963) 2–3.

1964

76　"A Jewish View of Ecumenism" in *The Ecumenical Movement: A Dialogue.* New York: National Conference of Christians and Jews, 1964. Pp. 38–47.

77 "Persecution is Irreligious" in *ADL Bulletin* (September, 1964) 5–6 (reprinted in *The Star and the Cross: Essays on Jewish-Christian Relations*, ed. Katherine T. Hargrove, R.S.C.J. Milwaukee: Bruce Publishing Co., 1966. Pp. 82–86).

78 Review of *The Conscience of Israel: Pre-Exilic Prophets and Prophecy* by Bruce Vawter, C.M., *Jewish Social Studies* 26 (1964) 179–80.

79 Review of *Hebrew Origins* by Theophile James Meek, *Jewish Social Studies* 26 (1964) 256.

80 Review of *Moses and the Original Torah* by Abba Hillel Silver, *Jewish Social Studies* 26 (1964) 179.

81 Review of *Religion in the Old Testament: The History of a Spiritual Triumph* by Robert H. Pfeiffer, *Jewish Social Studies* 26 (1964) 109–10.

1965

82 *We Jews and Jesus.* New York: Oxford University Press, 1965 (see also no. 159 below).

83 "Gentile" in *Encyclopedia Britannica*. Chicago: William Benton, 1965. 10.111.

84 "The Judeo-Christian Tradition: Theology versus History," *News Digest of the International Association for Liberal Christianity and Religious Freedom* 56 (September, 1965) 21–25.

85 "Montefiore, Claude Joseph Goldsmid" in *Encyclopedia Britannica*. Chicago: William Benton, 1965. 15.781.

86 "Reflections on the Problem of Theology for Jews," *Journal of Bible and Religion* 33 (1965) 101–12 (reprinted in no. 150 below, pp. 53–69 and 341).

87 "Some Jewish Reflections About Jesus," *American Lutheran* 48:7 (July, 1965) 6–10 and 25 (also printed as a separate pamphlet by the Anti-Defamation League).

88 Translation of Psalm 33 in *The Source* by James A. Michener. New York: Random House, 1965. P. 269 (translations of Psalm 6 and Proverbs 31 on pp. 270 and 418–19 taken from no. 64 above).

89 Review of *Isaac M. Wise: His Life, Work, and Thought* by James G. Heller, *New York Times Book Review* (June 27, 1965) 12–14.

90 Review of *Neutestamentliche Zeitgeschichte: Die biblische Welt* by Bo Reicke, *Journal of Biblical Literature* 84 (1965) 466–67.

1966

91 "Bultmann on Judaism" in *The Theology of Rudolf Bultmann*, ed. Charles W. Kegley. New York: Harper & Row, 1966. Pp. 211–20 (reprinted in no. 150 below, pp. 223–31 and 350).

92   Communication (regarding students at the Hebrew Union College), *CCAR Journal* 13 (April, 1966) 94–95.

93   "Jesus in World History" (Report of an address with summary of questions and answers), *News Digest of the International Association for Liberal Christianity and Religious Freedom* 60 (Spring, 1967) 22–25 (full text on deposit at I.A.R.F. Secretariat, The Hague; revised version in no. 150 below, pp. 178–94).

94   "Jewish and Catholic Biblical Scholarship" in *Torah and Gospel, Jewish and Catholic Theology in Dialogue,* ed. Philip Scharper. New York: Sheed & Ward, 1966. Pp. 63–79 (reprinted in no. 150 below, pp. 94–107).

95   "On Canon," *Catholic Biblical Quarterly* 28 (1966) 203–7 (reprinted in no. 114 below, pp. 243–47, and no. 150 below, pp. 335–39).

96   Review of *The Church and the Jewish People* by Augustin Cardinal Bea and *The Passover Plot, New Light on the History of Jesus* by Hugh J. Schonfeld, *The Saturday Review* 49:49 (December 3, 1966) 42–43.

97   Review of *The Oxford Annotated Apocrypha*, ed. Bruce M. Metzger, *CCAR Journal* 13 (June, 1966) 75.

98   Review of *Religion*, ed. Paul Ramsey, *Jewish Social Studies* 28 (1966) 179–80.

99   Review of *The Setting of the Sermon on the Mount* by W. A. Davies, *Theology Today* 23 (1966–67) 290–94.

1967

100   *Herod, Profile of a Tyrant*. Philadelphia: Lippincott, 1967 (published in German as *Herodes, Bildnis eines Tyrannen*, trans. Ulrich Bracher. Stuttgart: Kohlhammer, 1968).

101   *We Jews and You Christians, An Inquiry into Attitudes*. Philadelphia: Lippincott, 1967.

102   "Antiquarianism and Contemporaneity: The Relevance of Studies in Religion," *Journal of the American Academy of Religion* 35 (1967) 372–78 (reprinted in no. 150 below, pp. 20–27).

103   Communication (regarding Jakob Petuchowski), *CCAR Journal* 14 (October, 1967) 71.

104   "Introduction" to *Josephus, The Man and the Historian* by H.S.J. Thackeray. New York: Ktav, 1967 (reprint of 1929 edition). Pp. v–xvi.

105   "The Jewish Scholar and Early Christianity" in *The Seventy-Fifth Anniversary Volume of the Jewish Quarterly Review*, ed. Abraham A. Neuman and Solomon Zeitlin. Philadelphia: Jewish Quarterly Review, 1967. Pp. 473–81 (reprinted in no. 150 below, pp. 13–19).

106 "Judaism," *The Methodist Woman* 27:11 (July-August, 1967) 4–7.

107 "The Parting of the Ways," *Phoenix Bijbel Pockets, Het Evangelie in Jeruzalem en Antiochie* 25 (1967) 137ff. (reprinted in no. 150 below, pp. 258–64).

108 "The Pastoral Epistles," *Salt* 4:4 (Winter, 1967) 1–5.

109 "Understanding & Misunderstanding: Prepossession versus Malice," *Dialog* 6 (1967) 284–89 (reprinted in no. 150 below, pp. 108–19).

110 Review of *A Historical Introduction to the New Testament* by Robert M. Grant, *Jewish Social Studies* 29 (1967) 64–65.

111 Review of *The Problem of the Hexateuch and Other Essays* by Gerhard von Rad, *Religion in Life* 36 (1967) 467–70.

112 Review of *Überlieferung und Geschichte des Exodus* (BZAW 91) by Georg Fohrer, *Jewish Social Studies* 29 (1967) 112–13.

113 Review of *The Untold Story of Qumran* by John C. Trever, *Religious Education* 62 (1967) 78 and 216–17.

1968

114 **Old Testament Issues*. New York: Harper & Row, 1968 (includes nos. 38 and 95 above).

115 "An Appreciation" (of Erwin Goodenough) in *Religions in Antiquity, Essays in Memory of Erwin Ramsdell Goodenough*, ed. Jacob Neusner. Leiden: E.J. Brill, 1968. Pp. 3–17.

116 "The Confrontation of Greek and Jewish Ethics: Philo, De Decalogo," *CCAR Journal* 15 (January, 1968) 54–63, 96 (reprinted in *Judaism and Ethics*, ed. Daniel Jeremy Silver. New York: Ktav, 1970, pp. 161–70, and in no. 150 below, pp. 279–90 and 352).

117 "The Higher Illiteracy," *Antioch Review* 28 (Spring, 1967) 91–107.

118 "Zu Englischen Bibelübersetzungen," *Kairos* 10 (1968) 289–90.

119 Review of *The Book of God and Man, A Study of Job* by Robert Gordis, *CCAR Journal* 15 (April, 1968) 87–89.

120 Review of *Psalms I, 1–50*, translation and notes by Mitchell Dahood, *CCAR Journal* 15 (April, 1968) 89–90.

121 Review of *The Rise and Fall of the Judaean State, A Political and Religious History of the Second Commonwealth*, vol. 2, by Solomon Zeitlin, *Journal of Biblical Literature* 87 (1968) 98–100.

122 Review of *Studies in Sin and Atonement in the Rabbinic Literature of the First Century* by Adolph Büchler, *Journal of the American Academy of Religion* 36 (1968) 393–94.

123 Review of *The Theme of Jewish Persecution of Christians in the Gospel According to St. Matthew* by Douglas R. A. Hare, *Journal of Ecumenical Studies* 5 (1968) 769–70.

1969

124   *The First Christian Century in Judaism and Christianity: Certainties and Uncertainties.* New York: Oxford University Press, 1969.

125   "The New Movement," *Common Ground* 23:2 (Summer, 1969) 6–15 (reprinted as "Christianity and Judaism: The Historic Differences" in *Jewish Affairs* 24:8 [August, 1969] 43–51, and condensed under the title "Religious Vocabulary Differences in Christianity and Judaism" in *Jewish Digest* 15 [January, 1970] 11–18).

126   "The Rabbi and His Community," *Living Judaism* 3 (1969) 93–95 (a condensed version of the material published in no. 164 below).

127   "Teaching the Bible," *Religious Education* 64 (1969) 176–79.

128   Review of *Old Testament Life and Literature* by Gerald A. Larue, *Religious Education* 64 (1969) 68–70.

129   Review of *Yahweh and the Gods of Canaan* by William Foxwell Albright, *Religous Education* 64 (1969) 250.

1970

130   *The Genius of Paul, A Study in History.* New York: Schocken, 1970 (new edition of no. 22 above, with a new introduction).

131   °"The Amsterdam Colloquium: Europe and Israel," *European Judaism* 4:2 (Summer, 1970) 3–14, and 5:1 (Winter, 1970–71) 32–47.

132   "Jewish and Christian Marriage: Some Observations," *Heythrop Journal* 11 (1970) 237–50.

133   "The Leo Baeck College," *CCAR Journal* 17 (June, 1970) 65–70.

134   "The Present State of Theology Among Jews," *American Benedictine Review* 21 (1970) 326–34.

135   "Scholar or Apologist?" in *The Teaching of Judaica in American Universities, The Proceedings of a Colloquium,* ed. Leon A. Jick. New York: Association for Jewish Studies and Ktav, 1970. Pp. 101–111.

136   Review of *The Bible Reader, An Interfaith Interpretation,* ed. Walter Abbott et al., *Journal of Ecumenical Studies* 7 (1970) 824–26.

137   Review of *The Jerome Biblical Commentary,* ed. Raymond E. Brown, S.S., Joseph A. Fitzmyer, S.J., and Roland E. Murphy, O. Carm., *Heythrop Journal* 11 (1970) 173–75.

138   Review of *Les Oeuvres de Philon d'Alexandrie,* ed. Roger Arnaldez, Jean Pouilloux, and Claude Mondésert (vols. 4, 15, 20, 22, and 31), *Erasmus* 22 (1970) 680–83.

139   Review of *The "Suffering Servant" of Isaiah: According to the Jewish Interpreters*, trans. Samuel R. Driver and Adolph Neubauer, *Jewish Bookland* in *JWB Circle* 25:5 (October, 1970) 5.

1971

140   **Hebrew Union College Annual* 42 (1971).

141   *Philo's Place in Judaism: A Study of Conceptions of Abraham in Jewish Literature.* New York: Ktav, 1971 (augmented edition of no. 13 above, with a new introduction).

142   *The Several Israels and an Essay: Religion and Modern Man.* The James A. Gray Lectures, 1968. New York: Ktav, 1971.

143   "Apostle" in *Encyclopedia Judaica.* Jerusalem: Keter Publishing, 1972. 3.215–17.

144   "Aramaic: The 'Cousin' Jews Adopted," *Keeping Posted* 17 (December, 1971) 6–7.

145   "The Trial of Jesus: Reservations," *Judaism* 20:1 (1971) 69–74.

146   Review of *The Book of Amos, A Commentary* by Erling Hammershaimb, *Ezra Studies* by Charles C. Torrey, *Pseudo-Ezekiel and the Original Prophecy* by Charles C. Torrey, *The Song of Songs and Coheleth* by Christian D. Ginsburg, *Rabbinic Literature and Gospel Teaching* by C. G. Montefiore, and *The Dead Sea Isaiah Scroll* by Joseph R. Rosenbloom, *Jewish Bookland* in *JWB Circle* 26:5 (October, 1971) 5.

147   Review of *Jesus and Israel* by Jules Isaac and *The Star of Redemption* by Franz Rosenweig, *Saturday Review* 54:15 (April 10, 1971) 21–22.

1972

148   *The Enjoyment of Scripture.* New York: Oxford University Press, 1972.

149   **Hebrew Union College Annual* 43 (1972).

150   *Two Living Traditions, Essays on Religion and the Bible.* Detroit: Wayne State University Press, 1972 (includes nos. 3, 11, 14, 23, 35, 36, 38, 59, 68, 71, 73, 86, 91, 94, 95, 102, 105, 107, 109, and 116 above, as well as "Jesus in World History" [pp. 178–94; a revision of no. 93 above], "The Husk and the Kernel" [pp. 87–93], "The Jewish Community and the Outside: The Christian Community" [pp. 70–86], "Modern and Ancient Problems in Communication: Rabbinic Judaism, Hellenistic Judaism, and Early Christianity" [pp. 212–22], and "Paul Reconsidered" [pp. 195–211 and 349–50]).

151   "The Ancient Mind and Ours" in *Understanding the Sacred Text, Essays in Honor of Morton S. Enslin on the Hebrew Bible and Christian Beginnings*, ed. John Reumann. Valley Forge, PA: Judson Press, 1972. Pp. 27–44.

152 "Man and Society," *The Review* (Indiana University Graduate School of Arts and Sciences) 15:1 (Fall, 1972) 17–24.

153 "The Welch Survey: One Man's Opinion," *Bulletin of the Council on the Study of Religion* 3:2 (April, 1972) 8–12.

154 "Wissenschaft des Judentums und religiöse Reform," *Emuna* 7 (1972) 243–48.

155 Review of *The Jewish Jesus* by Robert Aron, *Religious Education* 67 (1972) 319.

156 Review of *Rome: From Its Foundation to the Present* by Stewart Perowne, *The Review of Books and Religion* 1:8 (Mid-April, 1972) 6.

157 Review of *Les Temps Apostoliques: 1er Siecle* by Jean Dauviller, *Biblica* 53 (1972) 453–57.

1973

158 *Alone Atop the Mountain.* Garden City, NY: Doubleday, 1973.

159 *We Jews and Jesus.* New York: Oxford University Press, 1973 (reprint of no. 82 above with additional preface).

160 "The Bible as Literature," *CCAR Journal* 20:2 (Spring, 1973) 57–71.

161 "The Books That Were Kept Out," *Keeping Posted* 18:5 (February, 1973) 19–23.

162 "The Enjoyment of Scripture, An Esthetic Approach," *Judaism* 22 (Fall, 1973) 455–67.

163 "The Need of Cooperative Study" in *Theological Soundings, Notre Dame Seminary Jubilee Studies, 1923–1973,* ed. Imre Mihalik. New Orleans: Notre Dame Seminary, 1973. Pp. 30–35.

164 "The Rabbi and His Community," *Reform Judaism: Essays in Reform Judaism Dedicated to Rabbi Werner van der Zyl,* ed. Dow Marmur. London: Reform Synagogues of Great Britain, 1973. Pp. 143–53 (published in condensed form as no. 126 above).

165 Review of *American Protestantism and a Jewish State* by Hertzel Fishman, *Choice* 10 (1973) 1219.

166 Review of *The Book of Isaiah, A New Translation,* ed. H.L. Ginsberg illus. by Chaim Gross, *Choice* 10 (1973) 1004.

167 Review of *Herod Antipas* by Harold W. Hoehner, *Catholic Biblical Quarterly* 35 (1973) 91–92.

1974

168　*After the Ghetto: Jews in Western Culture, Art, and Intellect.* Syracuse, NY: Department of Religion, Syracuse University, 1974 (condensed in *The Jewish Digest* 20 [May, 1975] 55–65; republished in *Tradition and Change in Jewish Experience*, ed. A. Leland Jamison. Syracuse, NY: Department of Religion, Syracuse University, 1978. Pp. 198–210.

169　*Biblical Thought*, a correspondence course for the Academy for Jewish Studies Without Walls. New York: American Jewish Committee, 1974.

170　*A Jewish Understanding of the New Testament.* New York: Ktav, 1974 (augmented edition of no. 15 above).

171　*Judaism and Christianity.* Washington, D.C.: Bnai Brith Youth Organizaton, 1974 (revised edition of no. 30 above).

172　"La Biblia como literatura," *Maj'shabot–Pensamientos* 13 (1974) 55–65.

173　Jewish introductions in *Ecumenical Commentaries on the Books of the Bible*, ed. R.A.F. MacKenzie. Chicago: Catholic Press, 1974–75.

174　"NFTY's National Academy, To Enrich Our Life," *CCAR Journal* 21 (Spring, 1974) 26–28.

175　"Virtue and Reward in Philo" in *Essays in Old Testament Ethics: J. Philip Hyatt, in Memoriam*, ed. J. L. Crenshaw and J. T. Willis. New York: Ktav, 1974. Pp. 215–23.

176　"Which Jew is a Good Jew?" in *Christians and Jews* (Concilium 98) ed. Hans Küng and Walter Kaiser. New York: Seabury Press, 1974–75. Pp. 44–49 (translated also for Dutch, French, German, Italian, Portugese, and Spanish editions).

177　Review of *The Divine Warrior in Early Israel* by Patrick D. Miller Jr., *Choice* 11 (1974) 614.

178　Review of *The Gospel and the Land* by W. D. Davies, *Reform Judaism* 3:2 (October, 1974) 6.

179　Review of *Jesus as Others Saw Him* by Joseph Jacobs, *Reprint Bulletin-Book Reviews* 19:2 (Summer, 1974) 11.

180　Review of *Judentum und Hellenismus*, 2d ed., by Martin Hengel, *Journal of Ecumenical Studies* 11 (1974) 701–2.

181　Review of *Proof of the Accuracy of the Bible* by Elihu A. Schatz, *Choice* 11 (1974) 111.

182　Review of *Proof of the Accuracy of the Bible* by Elihu A. Schatz, *The Commentary of Rabbi David Kimhi on Psalms CXX-CL*, ed. and trans. Joshua Baker and Ernest W. Nicholson, *3 Enoch or the Hebrew Book of Enoch*, ed. and trans. Hugo Odeberg, *Peoples of Old Testament Times*, ed. D. J. Wiseman in *Jewish Bookland* in *JWB Circle* 29:5 (October, 1974) 2.

183 Review of *The Song of Songs*, commentary by Robert Graves, *The Book of Jeremiah*, intro. by Bernard Bamberger, *The Book of Psalms, The Books of Esther and Judith*, commentary by George T. Montague, and *The Targum to the Five Megilloth*, ed. Bernard Grossfeld, in *Jewish Bookland* in *JWB Circle* 29:6 (November, 1974) 1.

184 Review of *Die Welt der altorientalischen Bildsymbolik und das AT: am Beispiel der Psalmen* by O. Keel, *Catholic Biblical Quarterly* 36 (1974) 113–15.

1975

185 *A Jewish View of Jesus*. London: Jewish Information Service, 1975.

186 *Leo Baeck on Christianity*. New York: Leo Baeck Institute, 1975.

187 *A Little Book on Religion (For People Who Are Not Religious)*. Chambersburg, PA: Wilson Books, 1975.

188 "Christians, Their Problem of Jesus, and We Jews" in *Justice, Justice Shalt Thou Pursue, Papers Assembled on the Occasion of the 75th Birthday of the Reverend Dr. Julius Mark*, ed. Ronald B. Sobel and Sidney Wallach. New York: Ktav, 1975. Pp. 161–77.

189 "L'Ecriture dans le Judaïsme," *Concilium* 102 ("L'Ecriture Sainte dans la Liturgie," February, 1975) 31–38 (translated also for German, Portugese, and Spanish editions).

190 "Jesus: A Jewish View," *The Living Light* 12 (1975) 130–42 (revised and published separately by National Federation of Temple Youth, UAHC Kutz Camp Institute, 1975).

191 Response to "The Idea of Conscience in Philo of Alexandria" by Richard T. Wallis, *Protocol of the Thirteenth Colloquy of the Center for Hermeneutical Studies in Hellenistic and Modern Culture* (1975) 19.

192 Review of *Faith and Fratricide* by Rosemary Radford Ruether, *Choice* 12 (1975) 703.

193 Review of *The First Book of the Bible, Genesis Interpreted* by Benno Jacob and *The Book of Exodus: A Critical, Theological Commentary* by Brevard S. Childs, *The Review of Books and Religion* 4:4 (Mid-January, 1975) 9.

194 Review of *The History of the Jewish People in the Age of Jesus Christ (175 B.C.–A.D. 135)* by Emil Schürer, vol. 1 . . . rev. by Geza Vermes and Fergus Millar, *The Classical World* 69 (1975–76) 89.

195 Review of *Let My People Live! An Indictment* by Dagobert D. Runes, *Religious Studies Review* 1:1 (September, 1975) 38.

196 Review of *The Palm Tree of Deborah* by Moses Cordovero, *Reprint Bulletin-Book Reviews* 20:2 (Summer, 1975) 8.

1976

197   *The New English Bible with the Apocrypha, Oxford Study Edition. New York: Oxford University Press, 1976.

198   "Isaac Mayer Wise's Pronaos to Holy Writ" in Bicentenniel Festschrift . . . J. R. Marcus, ed. Bertram W. Korn. New York: American Jewish Historical Society and Ktav, 1976. Pp. 517–27.

199   "Israel, Conceptions of" in The Interpreter's Dictionary of the Bible. Supplementary Volume, ed. Keith Crim. Nashville: Abingdon, 1976. Pp. 461–63.

200   "Jews, New Testament Attitudes Toward" in The Interpreter's Dictionary of the Bible. Supplementary Volume, ed. Keith Crim. Nashville: Abingdon, 1976. Pp. 477–79.

201   Review of Aspects of Religious Propaganda in Judaism and Early Christianity, ed. Elisabeth Fiorenza, Religious Studies Review 2:4 (October, 1976) 52.

202   Review of The Crucifixion of the Jews by Franklin Littell, Judaism 25:1 (1976) 123–25.

203   Review of Disputation and Dialogue: Readings in the Jewish Christian Encounter, ed. Frank E. Talmage, Choice 13 (1976) 843.

204   Review of Judaism in America, From Curiosity to Third Faith by Joseph L. Blau, Religion in Life 45 (1976) 386–87.

205   Review of The Roots of Pagan Anti-Semitism in the Ancient World, Supplements to Novum Testamentum, vol. XLI, by J. N. Sevenster, Religious Studies Review 2:1 (January, 1976) 43–44.

206   Review of A Short History of Anti-Semitism by Vamberto Morais, Choice 13 (1976) 1312.

207   Review of Thy Brother's Blood, The Roots of Christian Anti-Semitism by Malcolm Hay, Choice 13 (1976) 384–85.

208   Review of The Word and the Book by Robert Gordis, Reprint Bulletin-Book Reviews 21:3–4 (1976) 10.

1977

209   *Tomorrow's American. New York: Oxford University Press, 1977.

210   When a Jew and Christian Marry. Philadelphia: Fortress Press, 1977 (chapter 1 reprinted in The Chaplain 34:1 [1977] 30–42).

211   "Hellenism and Judaism" in Great Confrontations in Jewish History, ed. Stanley M. Wagner and Allen D. Breck. Denver: University of Denver, Department of History, 1977. Pp. 21–38.

212   "The People Israel," CCAR Journal 24:2 (Spring, 1977) 47–51.

213   "The Political Jesus? Thesis or Truth," Encounter 48:4 (April, 1977) 83–84.

214 "The Rationalist Denial of Jewish Tradition in Philo" in *A Rational Faith: Essays in Honor of Levi A. Olan*, ed. Jack Bemporad. New York: Ktav, 1977. Pp. 137–43.

215 Response to "The Hero Pattern and the Life of Jesus" by Alan Dundes in *Protocol of the Twenty-fifth Colloquy of the Center for Hermeneutical Studies in Hellenistic and Modern Culture* (1976) 61.

216 °"Scholar of Common Sense, Samuel Sandmel Interviewed by Kendig Brubaker Cully," *The New Review of Books and Religion* 2:4 (December, 1977) 4.

217 Review of *The New Testament Environment* by Eduard Lohse, *Religious Studies Review* 3 (1977) 60.

218 Review of *Synagogue Life, A Study in Symbolic Interaction* by Samuel C. Heilman, *The New Review of Books and Religion* 1:7 (March, 1977) 18.

219 Review of *The Temple of Solomon, Archaeological Fact and Medieval Tradition in Christian, Islamic, and Jewish Art*, ed. Joseph Gutmann, *Religious Studies Review* 3 (1977) 252.

1978

220 *Anti-Semitism in the New Testament?* Philadelphia: Fortress Press, 1978.

221 *The Hebrew Scriptures: An Introduction to Their Literature and Religious Ideas.* New York: Oxford University Press, 1978 (new edition of no. 64).

222 *Judaism and Christian Beginnings.* New York: Oxford University Press, 1978.

223 "Jewish-Christian Relations in Our Time" in *Jews in a Free Society: Challenges and Opportunities*, ed. Edward A. Goldman. Cincinnati: Hebrew Union College Press, 1978. Pp. 103–14.

224 °"The Meaning of Easter Time," *Family Weekly* (March 26, 1978) 6.

225 "Philo's Knowledge of Hebrew: The Present State of the Problem," *Studia Philonica* 5 (1978) 107–12.

226 "Why I am Not a Unitarian–Universalist," *Kairos, An Independent Quarterly of Liberal Religion* 9–10 (1977–78) 3 and 19 (adapted from part 2 of a curriculum entitled "Our Experiencing, Believing, and Celebrating" to be published by the Unitarian Universalist Association).

227 Review of *Anti-Judaism in Christian Theology* by Charlotte Klein, *Choice* 15 (1978) 892–93.

228 Review of *Evangelicals and Jews in Conversation on Scripture, Theology, and History* by Marc H. Tanenbaum, Marvin R. Wilson, and A. James Rudin, *Choice* 15 (1978) 1070.

229   Review of *Exploring the Talmud* by Haim Z. Dimitrovsky, *Religious Education* 73 (1978) 728.

230   Review of *God and History in the Old Testament* by Denis Baly, *Religious Education* 73 (1978) 380–81.

231   Review of *On Being a Christian* by Hans Küng, *Religious Studies Review* 4 (1978) 99–101.

232   Review of *Paul and Palestinian Judaism, A Comparison of Patterns of Religion* by E. P. Sanders, *Religious Studies Review* 4 (1978) 158–60.

233   Review of *Reading Through Romans* by C.K. Barrett, *Reprint Bulletin-Book Reviews* 23:2 (1978) 8.

1979

234   *Philo of Alexandria: An Introduction.* New York: Oxford University Press, 1979.

235   "Apocalypse and Philo" in *Essays on the Occasion of the Seventieth Anniversary of the Dropsie University (1909–1979)*, ed. Abraham I. Katsh and Leon Nemoy. Philadelphia: The Dropsie University, 1979. Pp. 383–87.

236   Foreword to *Israelis, Jews, and Jesus* by Pinchas Lapide. Garden City, NY: Doubleday, 1979. Pp. v-x.

237   "Palestinian and Hellenistic Judaism and Christianity: The Question of the Comfortable Theory," *Hebrew Union College Annual* 50 (1979) 137–48.

238   Review of *The Early History of Israel* by Roland de Vaux, *The New Review of Books and Religion* 3:7 (March, 1979) 22–23.

1980

239   **The Divine Helmsman, Studies on God's Control of Human Events Presented to Lou H. Silberman*, ed. with James L. Crenshaw. New York: Ktav, 1980.

240   "Some Comments on Providence in Philo" in *The Divine Helmsman, Studies on God's Control of Human Events Presented to Lou H. Silberman*, ed. James L. Crenshaw and Samuel Sandmel. New York: Ktav, 1980. Pp. 79–85.

241   Review of *Elusive Presence, Toward a New Biblical Theology* by S. Terrien, *Religious Education* 75 (1980) 111–12.

1983

242   "Foreword for Jews" in *The Old Testament Pseudepigrapha*, vol. 1, *Apocalyptic Literature and Testaments*, ed. James H. Charlesworth. Garden City, NY: Doubleday, 1983. Pp. xi-xiii.

243   "Philo Judaeus: an Introduction to the Man, His Writings, and His Significance" in *Aufstieg und Niedergang der römischen Welt*, ed. Wolfgang Haase, II. 21:1. Berlin: De Gruyter, 1984. Pp. 3–46.